# The Best AMERICAN ESSAYS College Edition

## Seventh Edition

Edited and with an Introduction
by ROBERT ATWAN

**WADSWORTH**
CENGAGE Learning·

Australia • Brazil • Japan • Korea • Mexico • Singapore • Spain • United Kingdom • United States

## WADSWORTH
### CENGAGE Learning·

**The Best American Essays College Edition, Seventh Edition**

Robert Atwan

Senior Publisher: Monica Eckman

Acquiring Sponsoring Editor: Kate Derrick

Assistant Editor: Danielle Warchol

Editorial Assistant: Marjorie Cross

Media Editor: Cara Douglass-Graff

Marketing Brand Manager: Lydia LeStar

Senior Marketing Communications
Manager: Linda Yip

Rights Acquisitions Specialist: Ann Hoffman

Manufacturing Planner: Betsy Donaghey

Art and Design Direction, Production Management, and Composition: PreMediaGlobal

Cover Image: © William Storage/ Getty Images

Cover Sketch: Wing Ngan

For product information and
technology assistance, contact us at **Cengage Learning
Customer & Sales Support, 1-800-354-9706**

For permission to use material from this text or product,
submit all requests online at **www.cengage.com/permissions**
Further permissions questions can be emailed to
**permissionrequest@cengage.com**

Library of Congress Control Number: 2012952067

ISBN-13: 978-1-133-31034-1

ISBN-10: 1-133-31034-6

**Wadsworth**
20 Channel Center Street
Boston, MA 02210
USA

Cengage Learning is a leading provider of customized learning solutions with office locations around the globe, including Singapore, the United Kingdom, Australia, Mexico, Brazil, and Japan. Locate your local office at **www.cengage.com/global**

Cengage Learning products are represented in Canada by Nelson Education, Ltd.

To learn more about Wadsworth, visit
**www.cengage.com/wadsworth**

Purchase any of our products at your local college store or at our preferred online store **www.cengagebrain.com**

**Instructors:** Please visit **login.cengage.com** and log in to access instructor-specific resources

Printed in the United States of America
2 3 4 5 6        21 20 19 18 17

# Contents

# Annotated Table of Contents

my siblings? I would try to live in two worlds—at the very least. That was now my task."

"The tools in my workbench are a double inheritance, for each hammer and level and saw is wrapped in a cloud of knowing."

"That first day, sitting on the green lawn, watching a girl do a cartwheel and another girl mount the parallel bars, I developed an irrational fear that is still hard to explain: I became hyperaware of my own body, the swoosh of my blood and the paddling of my heart and the huh huh huhs of my breath, and it seemed amazing and tenuous to me that my body did all of this without any effort on my part."

"Language is the tool of my trade. And I use them all—all the Englishes I grew up with."

"Years from this evening, I won't actually be sure that this boy sitting beside me is named Ben. But that doesn't matter tonight. What I know for certain right now is that I love him, and I need to tell him this fact before we turn to our separate houses, next door to each other. We are both five."

"I am a personal essay and I was born with a port wine stain and beaten by my mother. A brief affair with a second cousin produced my first and only developmentally disabled child. Years of painful infertility would lead me straight into menopause and the hysterectomy I almost didn't survive."

"I'd recently found some statistics that said there'd been a sixty percent chance I'd end up in jail; I had stories to prove just how close I'd come. But after writing the first draft, my tale of black teenage delinquency seemed too clichéd to me, told too often before. I decided to write about my father instead. He, like my mother, was blind."

"I am not afraid of dead bodies. I have seen one up close three times in my thirty-six years: in high school at the funeral of a friend's father; as a police reporter when I took a tour of the local morgue; and more recently when a friend's ill baby died. But this is the first time I will touch a corpse, and *that* I am a little nervous about."

## 2. The Attentive Mind: Observation, Reflection, Insight • 129

"A yard, a pace, a foot, a fathom. How beautiful the language of measurement is, and we're not even talking iambs yet. A fifth, a finger, a jigger, a drop, a dram, a grain, a scruple. A scruple is twenty grains, or twenty barley cornes. It is as small as a pebble. If you have three, you have a dram."

"Nothing on earth is more gladdening than knowing we must roll up our sleeves and move back the boundaries of the humanly possible once more."

"Every creature on earth has approximately two billion heartbeats to spend in a lifetime. You can spend them slowly, like a tortoise, and live to be two hundred years old, or you can spend them fast, like a hummingbird, and live to be two years old."

"You took a sentence, threw it against the wall, picked up the pieces, and put them together again, slotting each word into its pigeonhole. When you got it right, you made order and sense out of what we used all the time and took for granted: sentences."

"I took myself off to the Minneapolis Institute of Arts and plunked myself down in front of a Bonnard. I wrote the painting. Described it. I went home and looked at a teacup on my table—I wrote that too. Still life descriptions that ran on for several pages. I wrote and wrote, describing my way through art galleries and the inadvertent still lives of my house and my memory, my grandmother's garden, her Sunday dinners."

"To get an idea of the relationship between the Earth and the Moon and the Sun, find two friends and have the self-conscious one with lots of atmosphere be the Earth and the coercive one be the Sun. And you be the Moon, if you are periodically luminous and sometimes unobservable and your inner life has petered out. Then find a large field and take three steps from the Earth, and have the Sun go a quarter mile away."

"I am not a total idiot. I always had the sense to say no wedding cake, no officiant, no first dance, no here comes the bride, no *Times* announcement, and absolutely no white dress. Who are we kidding? And why? We just wanted a big, awesome party where everyone could meet and go bananas."

"Evidently, the fundamental laws of nature do not pin down a single and unique universe. According to the current thinking of many physicists, we are living in one of a vast number of universes. We are living in an accidental universe. We are living in a universe uncalculable by science."

"As a woman and as a writer, I have long wondered at the wellsprings of female masochism. Or what, in despair of a more subtle, less reductive phrase, we can call the congeries of predilections toward self-hurt, self-erasure, self-repudiation in women."

"The man's eyes wandered around the parlor, and through them I saw what he did: a dirty room full of junk. It had never been anything more than that, but for some reason—the heat, maybe, or the couple's heavy, almost contagious sense of despair—every gouge and smudge jumped violently into focus. More depressing still was the thought that I belonged here, that I fit in."

"My mother, Annie Pearl Smith, never talks with me of Annie Pearl Connor, the girl she was before she boarded that Greyhound, before she rolled into the city. The South, she insists, was the land of clipped dreaming, ain't got nones and never gon' haves. Alabama only existed to be left behind. It's as if a whole new person was born on that bus, her first full breath straining through exhaust, her first word *Chicago.*"

"The road to Fidel Castro's Palace of the Revolution leads through a memory lane of old American automobiles chugging along at about twenty-five miles an hour—springless, pre-embargo Ford coupes and Plymouth sedans, DeSotos and LaSalles, Nashes and Studebakers, and various vehicular collages created out of Cadillac grilles and Oldsmobile axles and Buick fenders patched with pieces of oil-drum metal and powered by engines interlinked with kitchen utensils and pre-Batista lawn mowers and other gadgets that have elevated the craft of tinkering in Cuba to the status of high art."

disappear. Difference wouldn't disappear. Africa wouldn't disappear. In post-race America 'white' people would disappear."

"The defense of living nature is a universal value. It doesn't rise from, nor does it promote, any religious or ideological dogma. Rather, it serves without discrimination the interests of all humanity. Pastor, we need your help. The Creation—living nature—is in deep trouble."

# *Preface*

## What Is *The Best American Essays* Series?

Back in the 1970s Edward Hoagland wondered why no one
had compiled an annual collection of the year's best essays, especially since comparable short story volumes had been around
for decades. I agreed with Hoagland, and after a few false starts
(I thought at first of calling the series "The E. B. White Awards"
and later "The Emerson Awards"), I founded *The Best American
Essays* as a companion volume to *The Best American Short Stories*.
The first volume was published in 1986. Since then, the series
has grown in popularity; each year more and more readers
seem drawn to the vitality and versatility of the contemporary
American essay.

For readers unfamiliar with the series, a brief introduction may
be useful. As the series editor, I screen hundreds of essays from an
enormous variety of general, specialized, and literary magazines.
I then turn over roughly one hundred of these to a guest editor,
a prominent American writer, who makes the final selection of
approximately twenty to twenty-five essays. To qualify for selection,
the essays must be works of high literary quality, intended as fully
developed, independent essays on subjects of general interest,
originally written in English for first appearance in an American
periodical during a calendar year. In general, selections for the
book are included on the basis of literary achievement: They
must be admirably written and demonstrate an awareness of craft
as well as a forcefulness of thought. Since each guest editor, of
course, possesses a different idea about what comprises a fine essay,
each book also represents a unique literary sensibility. This variety of
literary taste and opinion (which can be sampled in the prologue,
"Essayists on the Essay") keeps the series healthy and diverse.

## The College Edition

This version of *The Best American Essays* is designed for college students and classroom use. Essays have long been a staple of writing

courses, so why not a collection of the "best" contemporary essays for today's students? I believe that many writing instructors wish to expose their students to high-quality, socially relevant, and intellectually challenging prose. With this end in mind, I selected particular essays from *The Best American Essays* series that I thought would work best for writing instructors and their students. Among the considerations for selection were length, topicality, diverse perspectives, and rhetorical and thematic variety.

Since the majority of essays we encounter today tend to fall into three general, though fairly distinct, categories—personal, informative, and argumentative—I have arranged the selections accordingly. The book reflects the types of writing most often taught in introductory and even advanced composition courses. Instructors will find a generous number of selections to use if they want to teach excellent writing within the context of personal narratives, expository patterns, and persuasive strategies. In addition, I included within these three categories selections that also reflect many of the topics and issues that currently enliven discussion and debate: multiculturalism, race and gender, sexual and identity politics, popular culture, and media studies.

I've also drawn from the various "Forewords" I contribute to the annual volumes to develop an introduction to the literary and compositional features of the contemporary American essay. And, though space would not permit the inclusion of all the guest-editor introductions, I have orchestrated incisive excerpts into a prologue that should stimulate critical discussion of the genre and lead to writing assignments.

In addition, to help orient student readers, the volume contains an informative "lead-in" to each essay and a brief biographical note. "Reflections and Responses," a set of questions designed to assist class discussion or to instigate ideas for papers, follows each selection. The questions range from a consideration of compositional details to broader reflections on theme and issue.

Given its arrangement, flexibility, and emphasis on recently published essays, the college edition of *The Best American Essays* is suitable for various writing courses. It can be used in mainstream freshman composition programs with a focus on personal, expository, and argumentative essays. Instructors who want to concentrate on the contemporary essay, creative nonfiction techniques, or the essay as a literary genre will also find the collection and its instructional apparatus extremely suitable.

# New to the Seventh Edition

For this seventh college edition, I have updated the "Prologue: Essayists on the Essay," a unique feature that has proved to be popular with instructors who enjoy the wide range of bite-sized comments on the art and craft of the genre from many of the nation's premier essayists. I have also revised a third of the book; of the thirty-six selections, twelve are new and all of the new selections were published over the past few years, having been drawn from the most recent volumes of *The Best American Essays*. My choices were partially guided by several useful reviews from writing instructors who shared with me some of their classroom experiences with particular selections. For their many useful suggestions for this revision I would like to thank

Constance Campana, *Wheaton College*

Monika Giacoppe, *Ramapo College of New Jersey*

LaVerne Gyant, *Northern Illinois University*

Ellen Jenkins, *Arkansas Technical University*

Barbara Kilgust, *Carroll University*

Rich Lane, *Clarion University*

Nina Morgan, *Kennesaw State University*

Joseph Scapellato, *Bucknell University*

Jan Schmittauer, *Ohio University–Chillicothe*

Kevin Stemmler, *Clarion University*

I have revised the final chapter on public controversy to expand the range and variety of issues. The chapter now features a number of diverse topics to invite class discussion and essay responses: free speech and expression, torture, gun control, colonialism, the environment, the economy, medical ethics, race, reproductive rights, the housing crisis, global poverty, and Creationism.

No collection, of course, can entirely please everyone. I have listened carefully to reviewers and have relied on my own classroom and writing workshop experiences in choosing contemporary essays that—in their variety of subject, style, and structure—would best serve as an introduction to the genre. I ought to add that I based my choices on the essays themselves, considering mainly their relevance to writing courses, not the reputations of their authors. You will certainly find many well-known essayists in the collection; but you will also discover several unfamiliar writers, some of whom have rarely been anthologized. A large part of my purpose in editing *The Best American Essays* series is to introduce to the reading public young and emerging writers.

I am always interested in comments and suggestions, especially regarding the book's classroom utility, and invite responses from teachers and students. Please address responses to Robert Atwan/ Series Editor/The Best American Essays/180 Riverside Boulevard 32C/ New York, NY 10069.

Although anthologies such as this one may appear simple to construct, they actually involve the professional efforts of many people. I appreciate the enthusiasm for the project and the help I've received from the Cengage Learning staff: I especially appreciate the advice and support I received from my editors, Kate Derrick and Danielle Warchol. I would also like to thank Arul Joseph Raj, who handled production, and permissions editors Ann Hoffman and Melissa Tomaselli. I'm especially indebted to my son Gregory for his indispensable contributions.

R. A.

# *Encountering the Essay*

## *What Are Essays?*

Like poems, plays, novels, and short stories, essays resist simple definition or classification. There are so many types of essays that any attempt to come up with a single, authoritative description of *the* essay is likely to be overly general or critically useless. A well-known handbook of literary terms, for example, doesn't even attempt to define the form: "A moderately brief prose discussion of a restricted topic," the entry begins. But it then goes on to say: "Because of the wide application of the term, no satisfactory definition can be arrived at; nor can a wholly acceptable 'classification' of essay types be made." So much writing today goes under the name of essay—celebrity profiles, interviews, political commentary, reviews, reportage, scientific papers, scholarly articles, snippets of humor, and newspaper columns—that it's virtually impossible for readers to obtain any clear and consistent impression of the form.

Though many illustrious examples of "brief prose discussion" can be found in classical Greek and Latin literature, the modern essay had its origins in the European Renaissance. At a time when writers and artists throughout Europe were exploring ways to express their personalities more freely in painting and literature, a French magistrate, Michel de Montaigne, retired to his Bordeaux estate in 1570 and began experimenting with a new kind of prose. Impatient with formal philosophy and academic disquisition, he soon found a way to create a more flexible and personal discourse. Realizing that his efforts fit no conventional category—they could not be termed letters, or memoirs, or treatises—he simply referred to them by the French word *essais,* meaning *attempts, trials,* or *experiments.* By adopting a casual, everyday word to describe his endeavors, Montaigne called attention to the informal character of this new literary genre. His essays were personal, tentative, highly digressive, and wholly unsystematic in their approach to a topic.

Montaigne's brand of essay became for many later writers *the* genuine essay. For William Hazlitt, Virginia Woolf, and E. B. White, this was the only type of essay that could be considered a literary form. It went under different names; sometimes it was called the periodical, informal, or familiar essay. This was to differentiate it from types of prose discourse composed in a more systematic and formal fashion, writing that conformed to objective rather than subjective standards. Some examples of the formal essay are philosophical and ethical arguments, historical and scientific papers, dissertations, and critical articles. Today the informal essay is best represented by the personal essay, whereas the most popular type of formal essay is the magazine article. Although writers and editors may use the terms interchangeably, many periodicals routinely distinguish between essay and article in their tables of contents, a distinction that usually boils down to personal memoir or reflection as opposed to reportage, interviews, or feature stories.

## Essays and Articles

If it's impossible to produce an airtight definition of an essay, it's equally impossible to define an article. Like "essay," this all-purpose literary label has a long, complex history. The word goes back to the Latin term for a joint (*artus*) connecting two parts of a body, and its literal use was eventually extended to include the components of writing and discourse. By the eighteenth century, "article" was used regularly for literary compositions that treated a specific topic. The first to use the term in its modern journalistic sense was one of English literature's foremost essayists, Joseph Addison.

Articles require not just a topic, but a timely topic. Unlike essays, articles are usually (a) about something specific and (b) about something of *current* interest. Essays, on the other hand, can take large liberties with subject, theme, organization, and point of view. Essayists tend to be personal, reflective, leisurely; article writers (they used to be called "articlers") usually stay close to the facts, rarely stray from "the point," and seldom interrupt the flow of information with personal opinion or reflection. The essayist will feel comfortable writing about various general topics—friendship, envy, manners, nature. The article writer is often looking for an angle, or "hook," that will directly relate the article to some current event or fashionable trend.

For example: Assign the topic of "revenge" to two authors—one who prefers to write personal or familiar essays and one who specializes in journalistic articles or feature stories. Chances are the essayist will take a first-person, reflective look at the nature of revenge, blending together personal experience and literary references. The journalist will most likely conduct several interviews with psychologists and then skillfully choreograph these into an informative piece on how to deal constructively with vengeful emotions. These are, of course, extremes, but they suggest the divergent routes of the essay and article in today's literature. In general, the personal, reflective essay is often found in the literary quarterlies and periodicals; articles, like the example above, are the mainstay of popular magazines.

With a few exceptions, our major magazines print relatively few personal essays. Editors believe that their readers want news and information, not personal reminiscence or leisurely reflection. As a result, the weekly and monthly magazines depend on hard news stories, interviews, profiles, and "service articles" that offer readers practical advice on everything from child rearing to the latest diet. Few of these pieces could be called "literary"; most of them fall rapidly out of date and are not likely to be read even a few months after their appearance. If the personal essayist faces the challenge of making his or her experiences and reflections interesting and relevant, the article writer faces a different challenge: how to handle current issues and topics in such a way that people will still read the work with pleasure long after those issues and topics have vanished from public discussion.

Yet, as the selections in this volume show, most good prose is not easy to pigeonhole. At either end of the spectrum, it's fairly easy to distinguish a literary essay from a journalistic article. But as we move toward the center of the spectrum, the distinctions become less clear. We begin to find a compositional mix: personal essays that depend on research and reporting, topical articles that feature a personal voice and individual viewpoint. Such literary mixtures have become increasingly prevalent in today's magazines and literary periodicals. Note, for example, the selection by Gay Talese, the writer who was one of the founders of a literary movement known as "The New Journalism." This movement attracted many prominent authors (Joan Didion, Truman Capote, and Norman Mailer, among others) who wanted to incorporate a variety of literary techniques—many borrowed from novels and essays—into the conventionally "objective" magazine article. In Talese's talented hands, the ordinary celebrity profile becomes infused with mood, atmosphere, and conflict as personalities develop within a narrative that bristles with dramatic tension. Many readers coming across "Ali in Havana" (see p. 222) in *Esquire* magazine would naturally consider Talese's profile of the world's most famous athlete an article; yet, a close reading will demonstrate not only Talese's meticulous skills as a journalist but also his mastery of dramatic irony and literary form. Readers will want to note, too, how Annie Dillard (see p. 133) elevates a "profile" of a famous stunt pilot into an essay of astonishing lyric power. In a number of the essays collected here, the writers move between the topical requirements of an article and the literary demands of an essay, adroitly balancing fact and observation with the nuances of voice and style, irony, and wit.

### Essays and Fiction

What ultimately makes a piece of prose an essay is usually found in the personal quality of its writing. Many of the essays in this book are not only written in the first-person singular; they are also *about* the first-person singular. As Montaigne proved long ago, the essay is the perfect literary vehicle for both self-disclosure and self-discovery: "The wisdom of my lesson," he wrote, "is wholly in truth, in freedom, in reality." Writers today use the essay to explore their personal relationships, their individual identities, and their ethnic or racial heritages. Personal essays like Judith Ortiz Cofer's "Silent Dancing" (see p. 46) and Scott Russell Sanders's "The Inheritance of Tools" (see p. 81) are intimate, candid, revealing, close to the pulse of everyday human experience.

Yet *personal* can be a tricky term. Its roots reach back to the Latin *persona*, the literal term for "mask." The word was traditionally used for a theatrical character, a *dramatis persona*. Thus, oddly enough, the word we use to convey intimacy and sincerity— we often approvingly speak of someone's *personal* touch—has hidden overtones of disguise and performance. Readers may overlook this double sense of the term, but personal essayists rarely do. They know that the first-person singular is not a simple equivalent of the self, a mere matter of slapping down the word "I" in front of every sentence. They know that the single letter "I" is one of the English language's most complex words.

Who is the "I" of the essay—a real person or a *dramatis persona?* Did Scott Russell Sanders really bang his thumb with a hammer just before learning of his father's death? Did Judith Ortiz Cofer actually watch a five-minute home movie depicting a family party? Or have these essayists contrived incidents and fabricated moods in the interest of creating a story or endorsing a position? Unless we personally know the writers, how can we verify their accounts?

When the essay is philosophical or argumentative, we can decide whether we accept an essayist's opinions or not on the basis of logic, evidence, proof, or internal consistency. For example, we would base our agreement or disagreement with George Gessert (see "An Orgy of Power," p. 252) entirely on information that has nothing to do with the author's personal life. But once essayists begin to tell stories—about sampling dog food or playing with their children—they move dangerously close to fiction, especially when they add characters, dialogue, episodes, and climaxes. When constructing personal narratives, the essayist confronts the toughest challenge of the craft: telling stories that are at once artful, true, and *believable.* One of the essayist's most frustrating moments is when he or she relates a true story with the utmost candor and discovers that nobody believes it.

The personal essayist, then, must balance craft and credibility, aesthetics and accuracy. The first-person singular is both person and *persona,* a real person and a literary construct. The "I" is both reporting a story and simultaneously *shaping* one. If essayists hope to be wholly believable, however, they need to worry about too much shaping. A true story doesn't usually come prepackaged in a compellingly dramatic shape—many elements just don't fit in. To be believable, the essayist may narrate a story that doesn't—like much of life itself—possess a satisfying narrative closure. Sometimes what one expects to happen doesn't happen. "The writer in me," wrote the novelist Frank Conroy in 1988, "is tempted to create a scene here—to invent one for dramatic purposes—but of course I can't do that." His literary impulse as a novelist is to create a scene; his honesty as an essayist won't let him. In fact, the tension between personal essays and stories recurs throughout this collection and is especially apparent in such selections as Anwar F. Accawi's "The Telephone" (see p. 38) and Edwidge Danticat's "Westbury Court" (see p. 56).

## Autobiography and Truth

The boundary lines between a memoir and a novel (or a personal essay and a short story) can often be confusing. Many memoirs are written in a first-person narrative, and so are many novels. Great novels like Mark Twain's *The Adventures of Huckleberry Finn,* F. Scott Fitzgerald's *The Great Gatsby,* or J. D. Salinger's *The Catcher in the Rye* sound very much like memoirs, especially in their opening sections, though they are entirely fictional. Today, many memoirs and personal essays borrow heavily from the novelist's toolbox and seem indistinguishable from fiction. Note how the poet Yusef Komunyakaa opens his autobiographical essay (see p. 72):

> "I feel like I'm part of this damn thing," Frank said. He carried himself like a large man even though he was short. A dead cigarette dangled from his half-grin. "I've worked on this machine for twenty-odd years, and now it's almost me."

Short story writers commonly open their stories with dialogue, often introducing a character abruptly and without establishing any situational context. This is precisely the way Komunyakaa decides to start an essay that recounts his experiences one summer when he took a job as a factory worker.

Contrast Komunyakaa's opening to the way Harper Lee begins her famous novel *To Kill a Mockingbird:*

> When he was nearly thirteen, my brother Jem got his arm badly broken at the elbow. When it healed, and Jem's fears of never being able to play football were assuaged, he was seldom self-conscious about his injury. His left arm was somewhat shorter than his right; when he stood or walked, the back of his hand was at right angles to his body, his thumb parallel to his thigh. He couldn't have cared less, so long as he could pass and punt.
>
> When enough years had gone by to enable us to look back on them, we sometimes discussed the events leading to his accident....

Which opening passage sounds like it belongs in a work of fiction, and which sounds closer to a memoir? With only the two passages in front of them, most people—assuming that they weren't familiar with the original works—would say the first sounded fictional and the second truthful. And yet the opposite is the case.

If its prose style is no indication of whether a piece of writing is factual or fictional, then how can we tell the difference between an essay and a short story or between a memoir and a novel? As any cautious reader can see, it's nearly impossible to establish internal characteristics—such as voice, tone, or diction—that help us to easily distinguish one genre from the other. Therefore, if we are curious about the degree of fabrication, we usually need to rely on verifiable external factors—facts, actual events, people, places and institutions, dates, and so forth. Once the writer begins to disclose concrete or factual information, then other issues come quickly into play. The reader, if so inclined, can now use those details to test the writer's veracity or can begin inferential processes that can damage authorial credibility. Records can be discovered that prove someone didn't spend nearly as much time in the Peace Corps as claimed, or was never admitted to a certain psychiatric hospital, or hadn't served as much prison time as reported. According to many accounts, the publishing sensation of 2005, James Frey's *A Million Little Pieces,* was originally widely submitted (and widely rejected) as a *novel.* It was only when it was resubmitted as a *memoir* that publishers jumped.

Therefore, anyone writing a memoir (or an autobiographical essay) needs to be careful when recounting verifiable details or risks being called a liar, a phony, or an opportunist. The unverifiable world is vast and accommodating. The classic memoir, in which a celebrated individual offers an account of his or her public life and adventures, along with profiles of the important people encountered along the way, usually depended upon verifiable details—at least it is possible to confirm whether Benjamin Franklin ever met the famous Methodist preacher George Whitefield or lived for a time in London. But the modern memoir is different since it so often focuses on the private life of a not-well-known or perhaps even an obscure person. Who's to say if the author ever really took a life-transforming midnight swim all alone in Buzzard's Bay when she was fifteen? And unless a description is biologically or physically implausible, who would bother to question it? Perhaps a question to ask of a memoir is something the American philosopher William James might have asked: If a report of something is wholly unverifiable, should we even concern ourselves with the issue of truth?

We have thousands of critical studies dealing with the art of fiction, but very little exists on the art of the memoir aside from a growing number of "how-to" books. One reason for this situation is that despite its present popularity, the memoir has not yet become a fully accredited genre in our universities. Most educated readers are still uncertain about how best to evaluate a memoir or an autobiographical essay. What makes one memoir or essay outstanding and another forgettable? Does it largely depend on the quality of the prose? Will the particulars of an author's life bias our aesthetic responses either positively or negatively? Why is the first question that readers ask of a memoir "Is it true?" Is it a critical error to apply modern journalistic fact-checking standards to memoirs and essays intended as works of literature? If a personal essay turns out to have some fictional elements and details, does that automatically turn it into a short story—or does it become something else: a fictive essay? a fable? an outright lie? Does using the term *creative nonfiction* solve anything?

In the eighteenth and nineteenth centuries, writers like Addison and Steele, Washington Irving, and Nathaniel Hawthorne could invent characters and situations for their nonfiction works (many of these were published in the newspapers of their day), and readers found their essays and sketches delightful. As you encounter the autobiographical essays in this volume, you might ask yourself to what extent your enjoyment and appreciation of a selection depends on whether you are convinced that the writer is telling the truth. When do you think it matters, and when do you think it doesn't?

## The Autobiographical "I"

In college writing courses years ago, instructors referred to a syllogism that may help explain the enormous popularity of the personal memoir. It went something like this: "You write best when you write about what you know; what you know best is yourself; therefore, you write best when you write about yourself." As a syllogism, this seemed valid: The conclusion followed logically from its premises, no? So why didn't teachers always receive better essays when they assigned personal topics?

As anyone can see, the conclusion rests on dubious assumptions. The premises sound reasonable, but they raise some fundamental questions. Do people really write best about the subjects they know best? We see evidence all the time of experts being unable to communicate the basic concepts of their professions, which explains why so many technical books are authored by both an expert and a writer. Brilliant academics so committed to their vast research that they can't bear to part with any detail thus clog up their sentences with an excess of information. If a little knowledge is a dangerous thing, too much can sometimes be an impediment to clear and robust expression. Shakespeareans do not always write the best books on Shakespeare.

Can we also safely conclude that we know ourselves best of all? If so, then why do so many of us spend so much time in psychotherapy or counseling sessions? Surely, the pursuit of the self—especially the "hidden" self—has been a major industry. Self-knowledge, of course, confronts us with another logical problem: How can the self be at the same time the knower and the known?

That's why biographies can be so much more revealing than auto-biographies. As Dostoyevsky said in his *Notes from Underground:* "A true autobiography is almost an impossibility ... man is bound to lie about himself."

Yet the illusion that we do know ourselves best must serve as both comfort and inspiration to the growing wave of memoirists who seem to write with one finger glued to the shift key and another to the letter *I,* which on the keyboard looks nothing like it does on the page, thus appropriately symbolizing the relationship between that single letter and the "self" it presumes to represent. Today's writer's market is flooded with autobiography—now more likely to be labeled "memoir" in the singular, as though the more fashionable literary label promises something grander. Memoirs (the term was almost always used in the plural) were customarily written by public figures who recorded their participation in historical events and their encounters with other prominent individuals. General Ulysses S. Grant's two-volume *Personal Memoirs* (1885–1886) were bestsellers. The old memoirs were penned by well-established individuals in the twilight of their careers; the new memoir is frequently the work of an emerging writer aspiring to be well established.

The memoir is easily abused by those who believe the genre automatically confers upon the author some sort of importance. It's only natural, isn't it, to be the heroes or heroines of our own lives? And as the main protagonists, how can we resist the impulse to occupy center stage and not consider ourselves gifted with greater sensitivity, finer values, higher moral authority, and especially keener powers of recollection than any member of our supporting cast of characters? The most interesting autobiography ever conceived must be Mark Twain's. Partly written, partly dictated, never published in its entirety (though a complete edition is currently being prepared by the University of California Press), and never according to his intentions—in many ways a colossal failure of a book—Twain's autobiography grappled with every psychological and compositional difficulty characteristic of the genre. Twain knew how easy it is to exhibit ourselves in "creditable attitudes exclusively" and tried to display himself as honestly as he could. It was a noble experiment, but it proved impossible: "I have been dictating this autobiography of mine," he wrote, "for three months; I have thought of fifteen hundred or two thousand incidents in my life which I am ashamed of but I have not gotten one of them to consent to go on paper yet."

To say that memoir, autobiography, and the personal essay are easily abused is not to disparage these vigorous genres.

Democratizing the memoir has resulted in many wonderful books, not a few crafted by young or relatively young writers who have learned to ask themselves how to prevent their personal writing from deteriorating into narcissism and self-absorption. This is a question anyone setting out to write personally must face sooner or later. The solution requires a healthy regimen of self-skepticism and a respect for uncertainty. Though the first-person singular may abound, it should be a richly complex and mutable "I," never one that designates a reliably known, wholly static entity. In some of the best memoirs and personal essays, the writers are mysteries to themselves, and the work evolves into an enactment of surprise and self-discovery. These elements keep "life writing" *live* writing, as a mysterious "I" converses with an equally mysterious "I."

## Writing the "Standard" Essay

Many students who enter their first-year writing courses already know how to manufacture the "perfect paper." For some reason, they know it should begin with an introductory paragraph that contains a thesis statement and often cites an expert named Webster. It then pursues its expository path through three paragraphs that develop the main idea until it finally reaches a concluding paragraph that industriously summarizes all three previous paragraphs. The conclusion often begins, "Thus we see that...." If the paper tells a personal story, it might conclude, "Suddenly I realized...." Epiphanies abound.

What is especially maddening about the typical five-paragraph paper has less to do with its tedious, predictable structure than with its implicit message that writing should be the end product of thought and not the enactment of its process. Many students seem unaware that writing can be an act of discovery, an opportunity to say something they had never before thought of saying. The worst papers instructors receive are largely the products of premature conclusions, of unearned assurances, of minds irrevocably made up. As Robert Frost once put it, for many people thinking merely means voting. Why go through the trouble of writing papers on an issue when all that's required is an opinion poll? Do you agree? Disagree? It makes sense to call such productions "papers" (or "themes" or "assignments") since what is written has almost no connection with the true sense of "essaying"—trying out ideas and positions, writing while in a state of uncertainty, of not knowing.

The five-paragraph theme is also a charade. It not only parades in lockstep toward its conclusion; it begins with its conclusion. It is all about its conclusion. Its structure permits no change of direction, no reconsideration, no wrestling with ideas. It is—and has long been—the perfect vehicle for the sort of reader who solemnly likes to ask: "And your point is … ?"

The most talented essayists have aims other than merely getting a point across or a position announced or an identity established. It may help to imagine an essay as a sort of Cubist rendition of an idea: The essayist would rather you consider all sides and aspects of a thought or concept, much in the same multiperspectival fashion that Picasso or Braque portrayed an ordinary table on canvas. Some essayists—Montaigne again was the first—seem literally to be turning ideas over in their minds. The intellectual essay is nothing, if not ruminative; the autobiographical essay may continually lose its sense of direction. Both kinds of essays, like Samuel Johnson's eighteenth-century fable *Rasselas,* will often reach a "conclusion in which nothing is concluded."

## *Evaluating the "Standard" Essay*

Can a computer evaluate an essay? This question has been on people's minds since Educational Testing Service unveiled e-rater®, its new computer program that will grade essay questions on the Graduate Management Admissions Test. As news of e-rater spread, newspaper reports appeared across the nation nervously wondering how essays can be machine scored. Objective tests, with their multiple choices, are one thing; but aren't sentences, paragraphs, and organization quite another?

The answer is that a computer can very easily score the results of essay questions, assuming that all anyone wanted to know was whether the writing conformed to standard English usage and reflected a few other elements of style, like syntactic variety, that can be measured conveniently and objectively. Computers have been able to do this for quite some time, and most word-processing applications currently provide a few (though still rudimentary) tools to check grammar and style. But can a computer detect humor and irony (which skilled readers themselves sometimes fail to catch)? Can it evaluate the use of imagery and metaphor, or discern the nuances of a writer's tone of voice? E-rater's developer honestly admitted to the *New York Times* that it cannot: "It's not designed to score Montaigne," she said. "It's designed for

a specific purpose: to score the kinds of essays we see on standardized tests." Admittedly, these would be "standard" essays.

Are these what we talk about when we talk about essays? Montaigne's term for his eccentric and digressive meditations is now
employed so broadly and indiscriminately that its traditional literary meaning is all but forgotten. An essay, it seems, is anything we
want it to be. Our dailies, weeklies, and monthlies are chock full of
nonfiction prose, but little of it is either creative or literary. Most
of it is informative, functional, or advisory, and that's as it should
be. Produced with built-in obsolescence, such writing is made for
the month (at best) and not for the years. E-rater may do fine
evaluating standardized expression, but it is educationally unfortunate that its name and use will continue to confuse people about
the true literary nature of essays.

## Essays Can Be a Risky Business

"Where there's a will there's a way," an excited William Hazlitt says
to himself as he hurries down Chancery Lane "about half-past six
o'clock, on Monday the 10th of December, to enquire at Jack
Randall's where the fight the next day was to be." The year is
1821, the city is London, and Hazlitt is pursuing his way to an
out-of-town boxing match, his first fight ever. He's eager to see
big Bill Neate, the raging Bristol "Bull," take on the "Gas-Man,"
Tom Hickman, the bravest and cruelest fighter in all of England.
"I was determined to see this fight, come what would, and see it I
did, in great style."

You can consult all the handbooks on literary fiction for all the
elements of style, structure, and composition, but you'll rarely find
mention of what Hazlitt just noted—*determination*. Yet its literary
value is inestimable.

This collection is filled with determination. You can see the fight
in great style. You can narrate it with equally great style. But as
Hazlitt reminds us, you first have to get there. No sitting in your
study with a boxing encyclopedia, no telephone interviews with
experts, no electronic highway; and the travel involved takes you
beyond your local library.

Such narratives can be a risky business. For one thing, the destinations are often uncertain. When Jamaica Kincaid decides to see
England for the first time, or when Gay Talese travels to Cuba for
a visit with Fidel Castro, or John H. Summers tours the battlefield
at Gettysburg, they have no idea what surprising emotions or

events they will encounter. But there's an additional risk. After writing "The Fight," Hazlitt was surprised to find that people considered his eyewitness report a "vulgar thing." This wasn't simply because his story took readers into an unfamiliar subculture, but because it took them into unfamiliar prose territory as well. In other words, Hazlitt risked the unliterary; he was determined to find a way to develop an essay out of "unsuitable" material. We can find a similar determination throughout this volume: Look at how such writers as Chang-Rae Lee, Bridget Potter, Lauren Slater, and Ryan Van Meter creatively confront ordinary, unpromising, uncomfortable, or even intractable subjects. Where there's a will, there's a way.

Risk and determination—at both a personal and a creative level—will often transform a piece of nonfiction prose into a memorable literary work. Our finest essayists seek out challenges, go for the toughest questions on the board. The challenges may spring from the demands of the assignment or of the composition— or both. These essayists resist the plodding memoir, the facile discovery of identity, the predictable opinion, or the unearned assertion. What many of the essays collected here have in common is their determination to take on the tough assignment, to raise the difficulty level of the game.

### The Contemporary American Essay: A Diversity of Forms and Voices

The personal essay has long existed in a literary twilight zone. Because it presumes to tell a true story yet often employs fictional or poetic techniques, it stands awkwardly with one foot in and one foot out of "imaginative" literature. It was partially for this reason that one of America's foremost essayists, E. B. White, complained in 1977 that the essayist, "unlike the novelist, the poet, and the playwright, must be content in his self-imposed role of second-class citizen." Writers who have their eyes on a Nobel Prize or "other earthly triumphs," White continued, "had best write a novel, a poem, or a play." White was responding not only to the critical reception of his own work but also to a general decline in the literary quality of the American essay. Essays struck a lot of readers as "old-fashioned." When readers thought of essays, they thought of writing that was stiff, stuffy, textbookish—things teachers forced them to read and write in school.

A century ago, however, the essay occupied a prominent position in American literature. It fell into the class of writing that critics called "polite letters." The essayists, mostly men, addressed the literate world in an urbane, congenial, comfortable manner. These gentlemen, it seemed, always possessed three names— James Russell Lowell, Oliver Wendell Holmes, Thomas Wentworth Higginson—and more often than not lived in New England. In this era, when "coming out" referred only to a young woman's debut, the typical essay was proper, genteel, and Anglophilic. Although it atrophied during the 1930s, the polite essay retained for many years an insidious power over American students, who were often forced to imitate its polished civility in that shadow genre known as the "freshman theme." The goal of English teachers, Kurt Vonnegut recalls, was to get you "to write like culti-vated Englishmen of a century or more ago."

Essays began to seem old-fashioned to the American reader mainly because they were too slow in coming to terms with twentieth-century modernism. While William Faulkner, T. S. Eliot, and Eugene O'Neill were radically transforming fiction, poetry, and drama, the essay retained much of its relaxed, genteel manner. Adventurous writers considered the essay a holdover from Victorian times. With few exceptions, the essay broke no new ground, violated no literary conventions. Instead of standing as modern works of literature in themselves, essays simply tried to explain those works. For the academic community as well as for many general readers, the essay gradually grew synonymous with literary criticism. Essays were written *about* literature, not *as* literature.

Since E. B. White issued his complaint, the literary status of the essay has been steadily improving. As Annie Dillard says, the essay "has joined the modern world." Essays are now written in the same imaginative spirit as fiction and poetry. Contemporary essays can rival the best fiction and poetry in artistic accomplishment. Far from being hesitant about literary aims and methods, today's essay-ists delight in the use of imagery, symbol, and metaphor, often interweaving them into such complex mosaic patterns as those we find in Patricia Smith's "Pearl, Upward" and Joyce Carol Oates's "They All Just Went Away." Boundary lines—between life and art, prose and poetry, truth and fiction, the world and self— are often blurred as essayists take greater liberties with language and form. This is now true even of essays grounded in information and explanation.

Nor can the essay be characterized any longer by its homogene-ity. In fact, its diversity may now be its most noticeable feature. In light of the essay's transformation, today's poetry and fiction appear stagnant: The essay may be our most exciting literary form. We see narrative essays that are indistinguishable from short stories, mosaic essays that read like prose poems. We find literary criticism with an autobiographical spin, journalism sensitively attuned to drama and metaphor, reflection with a heavy dose of information. Some essayists write polemic that sounds like poetry. Physicists, such as Alan Lightman (see p. 183), mathematicians, and philosophers are finding that complex ideas and a memorable prose style are not irreconcilable. Even law review articles have taken a literary turn. Today's essays are incredibly difficult to categorize and pin down.

This volume collects and celebrates the contemporary American essay. Never before—except perhaps in the days of Ralph Waldo Emerson and Henry David Thoreau—have so many fine young American writers begun to explore the essay's literary possibilities. They come to the form with a renewed enthusiasm for its astonishing flexibility and versatility—the essay can incorporate an enormously wide range of subjects and styles. The personal essay has grown increasingly candid, more intimate, less polite. Essayists seem willing to take greater emotional risks. Essayists today seem less relaxed and more eager to confront urgent social questions. Journalism has contributed to this sense of risk and urgency, encouraging essayists to fuse within a single style both personal experience and public issues, dual themes that Garret Keizer brilliantly combines in "Loaded" (see p. 267)

## The Essay and Public Events

As Stephen Jay Gould was making selections for the 2002 volume of *The Best American Essays,* he observed how everything seemed "shaped by 9/11," regardless of whether it was written before or after. Later, I realized how every few years some pivotal event dominates the national attention and dramatically narrows the literary scope of this series. In 1995, it seemed that half the essays published in magazines dealt either directly or tangentially with the O. J. Simpson trial. The nation couldn't stop talking about it, and many distinguished writers weighed in with insightful and sometimes brilliant commentary. In a similar occurrence toward the end of 2000, the American political process was put on hold during the most bizarre presidential election in our history. Yet coverage of these events—as influential and absorbing as they still are—did not necessarily find their way into the volumes featuring the best essays of those years.

But the terrorist attacks of 9/11 and their aftermath were altogether another story. The written response was overwhelming, and not merely because of the immediate and massive news coverage. One could expect the coverage, commentary, and reportage; unexpected was their astonishingly high quality. Anticipating that thoughtful essays would require months of reflection and deliberation, the "literature of 9/11" was surely several years away. But essays of high literary quality began appearing within weeks of the incident.

In fact, we should have expected the abundance of fine 9/11 essays. The essay always seems to be revitalized in times of war and conflict—and usually with the return of peace and prosperity, fiction and poetry regain their literary stature. The First World War resulted in an eruption of essays and introduced the work of some of our finest nonfiction writers, many of whom, like Randolph Bourne, took up the pacifist cause. But then the postwar years saw the flourishing of some of our most celebrated poets and novelists, those members of the "lost generation." This was true, too, in the Second World War (E. B. White published his greatest essay collection in 1942) and especially true during Vietnam. It seems to me no coincidence that the Vietnam years saw the emergence of the New Journalism, an exciting and innovative brand of nonfiction pioneered (as mentioned earlier) by Gay Talese, a writer included in this volume.

This theory about essays in time of war is not easily proven, but the idea also appears in Czesław Miłosz's brilliant long poem, *A Treatise on Poetry,* which appeared shortly before the 9/11 carnage. Though he promotes the value of poetry in difficult times, Miłosz, who won the Nobel Prize in 1980, prefaces *Treatise* with the recognition that in our time, "serious combat, where life is at stake, is fought in prose." Perhaps in times of conflict and crisis, people want to be in the presence of less mediated voices; we need more debate and directives; we desire more public discourse. We instinctively turn to writing that displays a greater sense of immediacy and urgency. "These are the times that try men's souls," Tom Paine memorably wrote in 1776, in what would be the first essay of *The American Crisis.* At that moment in history, radicalism and nationalism could go hand in hand.

## The Essay's Future

The year 1995 marked the 400th anniversary of the first complete edition of Montaigne's essays. As we progress into the second decade of the twenty-first century, it will be natural to speculate on how the essay will change. Will essays be shaped in new, surprising ways by the digital revolution? Will cyberspace breed new essayists and new kinds of essays? Will original, literary prose works begin appearing in underground sites without benefit of agents, editors, publishers, and prestige periodicals? Will young, struggling writers find a quicker and less stressful way to break into print? As voice and video become increasingly common, will a new age of graphic/audio texts and devices such as the enormously popular Kindle, iPad, and Nook dramatically alter the reading habits of a future generation? And will "texting" radically alter traditional forms of expression?

There's no reason to oppose technology; the digital revolution is here to stay, and one can amply enjoy its products and conveniences. A younger generation may be more comfortable reading electronic books, but if they are reading something worth reading, they will more than likely—to borrow the title of critic Ruben Brower's seminal essay—do their "reading in slow motion." Though retrieving and downloading *Walden* or *Portrait of a Lady* can be done in the blink of an eye, savoring the prose, word by word, sentence by sentence, will always take time. One danger, of course, is that as people become more accustomed to instantaneous acquisition of texts, they may simultaneously grow so impatient with the time-consuming process of reading them that reading itself will become as obsolete as Sunday family strolls down Main Street.

The issue really isn't the future of books but of reading, and since people were reading long before the paginated book was developed some five hundred years ago, chances are good that they'll be reading long after it has been radically transformed. It is hardly a coincidence that the essay was invented not long after the bound book, for we owe to the physical feature of books the personal essay's idiosyncratic and circuitous manner. Montaigne equipped his home office with one of the earliest book-lined studies, where he loved to spend his time *browsing*. His mind too mercurial to concentrate wholeheartedly on any one volume, he would "leaf through now one book now another, without order and without plan, by disconnected fragments." An idea took hold; he began to write just the way he read. His medium became his message, and the personal essay was born.

For those who enjoy leisurely reading, the essay remains the ideal form, as the selections in this volume amply demonstrate. A ruminative, unhurried style has long been part of the essay's tradition. Early in the twentieth century, literary critics were predicting that the slow-paced "old-fashioned essay" would soon disappear. It was, as William Dean Howells observed in 1902, being driven out by newsworthy articles with no interest in the "lounging gait," and the "wilding nature" that characterized what Howells called the "right" essay. His concerns about a readership so corrupted and depraved, so bereft of a lyrical sense that they preferred articles to essays, were echoed through every decade of the twentieth century. Yet somehow "right" or true essays still manage to be written, published, and admired. This volume—with its many sinuous selections that wind through time and memory, that blur the distinctions between past and present, that take us intimately into the multilayered processes of thought—attests to that fact.

Robert Atwan

# Essayists on the Essay

*Each edition of* The Best American Essays *features a guest editor who makes the final selections and writes an introduction to the volume. The guest editors themselves are distinguished American writers, many of whom have excelled in various literary forms. In their introductions, they almost always address the question of the essay: its history, definition, style, audience, composition. Their essays on the essay would in themselves make an interesting collection. What follows are some of their most incisive remarks.*

## What Is an Essay?

What *is* an essay, and what, if anything, is it about? "Formal" and "informal," "personal," "familiar," "review-essay," "article-essay," "critical essay," essays literary, biographical, polemic, and historical—the standard lit-crit lexicon and similar attempts at genre definition and subclassification in the end simply tell you how like an eel this essay creature is. It wriggles between narcissism and detachment, opinion and fact, the private party and the public meeting, omphalos and brain, analysis and polemics, confession and reportage, persuasion and provocation. All you can safely say is that it's not poetry and it's not fiction.

—Justin Kaplan

## Resisting Definitions

AN ESSAY! The fixed form or the fixed category of any kind, any definition at all, fills me with such despair that I feel compelled to do or be its opposite. And if I cannot do its opposite, if I can in fact complete the task that is the fixed form, or fill the fixed category, I then deny

it, I then decline to participate at all. Is this a complex view? But I
believe I have stated it simply: anything that I might do, anything that
I might be, I cannot bear to be enclosed by, I cannot bear to have its
meaning applied to me.

The Essay: and this is not a form of literary expression unfamiliar to
me. I can remember being introduced to it. It was the opinions and
observations of people I did not know, and their opinions and observations bore no relationship to my life as I lived it then. But even now,
especially now, I do not find anything peculiar or wrong about this;
after all, the opinions and observations of people you do not know are
the most interesting, and even the most important, for your own opinions and observations can only, ultimately, fix you, categorize you—
the very thing that leads me to dissent or denial.

—Jamaica Kincaid


## The Ideal Essay

In reading an essay, I want to feel that I'm communing with a real person, and a person who cares about what he or she's writing about. The
words sound sentimental and trite, but the qualities are rare. For me,
the ideal essay is not an assignment, to be dispatched efficiently and
intelligently, but an exploration, a questioning, an introspection.
I want to see a piece of the essayist. I want to see a mind at work,
imagining, spinning, struggling to understand. If the essayist has all
the answers, then he isn't struggling to grasp, and I won't either.
When you care about something, you continually grapple with it,
because it is alive in you. It thrashes and moves, like all living things.

When I'm reading a good essay, I feel that I'm going on a journey.
The essayist is searching for something and taking me along. That
something could be a particular idea, an unraveling of identity, a
meaning in the wallow of observations and facts. The facts are important but never enough. An essay, for me, must go past the facts, an
essay must travel and move. Even the facts of the essayist's own history,
the personal memoir, are insufficient alone. The facts of personal history provide anchor, but the essayist then swings in a wide arc on his
anchor line, testing and pulling hard.

—Alan Lightman


## The Essay as Object

If kids still write essays in school the way people my age used to, they
meet the essay first as pure object. In school, it is (or was) a written
paper of a certain length, on an assigned subject, with specified

margins and neatness, due on the teacher's desk at a certain date. From about fourth grade on, I wrote many essays. "An essay a week" was a philosophy lots of grammar school teachers subscribed to back then. Recently I came across an essay of mine I'd saved from the fifth grade. It's called "If I Had Three Wishes." My first wish, as I described it, was for lots of fishing equipment, my second was for a canoe in which to go fishing, and my third was for a cabin in the woods somewhere near good fishing. I have more or less gotten those wishes, writing occasional essays about fishing all the while. Even in its present state as childhood artifact, "If I Had Three Wishes" retains its purposeful object-ness: the three-ring-binder paper with regular lines and space at the top for student's name, teacher's name, and date; the slow, newly learned script, in blue ballpoint, almost without mistakes; and the circled good grade in the teacher's hand.

—Ian Frazier

## The Essay as Action

Beneath the object, the physical piece of writing with its unpredictable content, is the action that produced it. The action, it seems to me, is easier to predict. The difference is like that between a golf ball in the air and the swing of the golfer that propelled it; the flight of a struck ball varies, but the swing tends always to be the same. An essay is a golf swing, an angler's cast, a tennis serve. For example, say, an experience happens to you, one that seems to have literary potential. You wait for it to grow in your mind into a short story or even just an episode of "Friends," but somehow it doesn't. Then a further experience, or an odd chance, or something a friend says, or something in the newspaper chimes with the first experience, and suddenly you understand you can write about it, and you do. You quit longing for form and write what's there, with whatever serviceable prose comes to hand, for no better reason than the fun and release of saying. That sequence—that combination of patience with sudden impatience, that eventual yielding to the simple desire to tell—identifies the essay.

—Ian Frazier

## Essays and the Real World

The essay can do everything a poem can do, and everything a short story can do—everything but fake it. The elements in any nonfiction should be true not only artistically—the connections must hold at base and must be veracious, for that is the convention and the covenant between the nonfiction writer and his reader. Veracity isn't much of a drawback to the writer; there's a lot of truth out there to work with. And veracity isn't much of a drawback to the reader. The real world arguably exerts a greater fascination on people than any fictional one; many people, at least, spend their whole lives there, apparently by choice. The essayist does what we do with our lives; the essayist thinks about actual things. He can make sense of them analytically or artistically. In either case he renders the real world coherent and meaningful, even if only bits of it, and even if that coherence and meaning reside only inside small texts.

—Annie Dillard


## *The Essay's Subjectivity*

As near as I can figure, an essay can be ... a query, a reminiscence, a persuasive tract, an exploration; it can look inward or outward; it can crack a lot of jokes. What it need not be is objective. An essay can certainly present facts and advocate a position, but that seems quite different from objectivity, whereby a writer just delivers information, adding nothing in the process. Instead, essays take their tone and momentum from the explicit presence of the writer in them and the distinctiveness of each writer's perspective. That makes essays definitely subjective—not in the skewed, unfair sense of subjectivity, but in the sense that essays are conversations, and they should have all the nuances and attitude that any conversation has. I'm sure that's why newspapers so rarely generate great essays: even in the essay-allowed zone of a newspaper, the heavy breath of Objective Newspaper Reporting is always blowing down the writer's neck. And certainly there is no prescribed tone that is "correct" for essays. Sometimes it seems that they have a sameness of manner, a kind of earnest, hand-wringing solemnity. Is this necessary? I don't think so. Many of the essays that intrigued me this year (2005) were funny, or unusually structured, or tonally adventurous—in other words, not typical in sound or shape. What mattered was that they conveyed the writer's journey, and did it intelligently, gracefully, honestly, and with whatever voice or shape fit best.

—Susan Orlean


## *No Standard Essay*

As there is no standard human type who writes essays, so is there no standard essay: no set style, length, or subject. But what does unite almost all successful essays, no matter how divergent the subject, is that a strong personal presence is felt behind them. This is so even if the essayist never comes out to tell you his view of the matter being discussed, never attempts directly to assert his personality, never even slips into the first-person singular. Without that strong personal presence, the essay doesn't quite exist; it becomes an article, a piece, or some other indefinable verbal construction. Even when the subject seems a distant and impersonal one, the self of the writer is in good part what the essay is about.

—Joseph Epstein


## The Essay's Diversity

It is not only that the essay *could* be about anything. It usually was. The good health of essay writing depends on writers continuing to address eccentric subjects. In contrast to poetry and fiction, the nature of the essay is diversity—diversity of level, subject, tone, diction. Essays on being old and falling in love and the nature of poetry are still being written. And there are also essays on Rita Hayworth's zipper and Mickey Mouse's ears.

—Susan Sontag


## The Memorable Essay

I am predisposed to the essay with knowledge to impart—but, unlike journalism, which exists primarily to present facts, the essays transcend their data, or transmute it into personal meaning. The memorable essay, unlike the article, is not place- or time-bound; it survives the occasion of its original composition. Indeed, in the most brilliant essays, language is not merely the medium of communication; it *is* communication.

—Joyce Carol Oates


## The Author's Gumption

Given the confusion of genre minglings and overlaps, what finally distinguishes an essay from an article may just be the author's gumption, the extent to which personal voice, vision, and style are the prime movers and shapers, even though the authorial "I" may be only a remote energy, nowhere visible but everywhere present. ("We commonly do not remember," Thoreau wrote in the opening paragraphs of *Walden*, "that it is, after all, always the first person that is speaking.")

—Justin Kaplan

## *Essays and the Imagination*

An essay is a thing of the imagination. If there is information in an essay, it is by-the-by, and if there is an opinion in it, you need not trust it for the long run. A genuine essay has no educational, polemical, or sociopolitical use; it is the movement of a free mind at play. Though it is written in prose, it is closer in kind to poetry than to any other form. Like a poem, a genuine essay is made out of language and character and mood and temperament and pluck and chance.

—Cynthia Ozick

## *Essays versus Articles*

And if I speak of a genuine essay, it is because fakes abound. Here the old-fashioned term poetaster may apply, if only obliquely. As the poetaster is to the poet—a lesser aspirant—so the article is to the essay: a look-alike knockoff guaranteed not to wear well. An article is gossip. An essay is reflection and insight. An article has the temporary advantage of social heat—what's hot out there right now. An essay's heat is interior. An article is timely, topical, engaged in the issues and personalities of the moment; it is likely to be stale within the month. In five years it will have acquired the quaint aura of a rotary phone. An article is Siamese-twinned to its date of birth. An essay defies its date of birth, and ours too.

—Cynthia Ozick

## *Essays versus Stories*

In some ways the essay can deal in both events and ideas better than the short story can, because the essayist—unlike the poet—may introduce the plain, unadorned thought without the contrived entrances of long-winded characters who mouth discourses. This sort of awful device killed "the novel of idea." (But eschewing it served to limit fiction's materials a little further, and likely contributed to our being left with the short story of scant idea.) The essayist may reason; he may treat of historical, cultural, or natural events, as well as personal events, for their interest and meaning alone, without resort to fabricated dramatic occasions. So the essay's materials are larger than the story's.

—Annie Dillard

## Essays versus Poems

The essay may deal in metaphor better than the poem can, in some ways, because prose may expand what the lyric poem must compress. Instead of confining a metaphor to half a line, the essayist can devote to it a narrative, descriptive, or reflective couple of pages, and bring forth vividly its meanings. Prose welcomes all sorts of figurative language, of course, as well as alliteration, and even rhyme. The range of rhythms in prose is larger and grander than that of poetry. And it can handle discursive idea, and plain fact, as well as character and story.

—Annie Dillard

## Essays versus Blogs

And while the essay may be a living form for the moment, like all living things it may be ailing even as it thrives. With the decline of places where the essay once ran into coterie political journals, or group blogs, the place for the essay proper grows smaller. The blogger, newly born, might be, should be, an essayist manqué, but the first thing about the blog form is that its units are short. It has already taken its place as part of the history of the pamphlet, the polemic, the pointed epistle—but doesn't yet build up enough acceleration to make a left turn into something else. Blogs play a terrific role as makers of solidarity, community, and network—as builders of social capital. But though I am persuaded beyond argument that there must be an Emily Dickinson or an Agnes Repplier of the Internet out there somewhere, blogging away for her life and ours, I haven't found her, at least not yet.

—Adam Gopnik

## Some Types of Essays

It's necessarily arbitrary to subdivide these "tries" but some main subcategories would have to include the following. There is the heuristic essay: an attempt to call attention to new information that has either been overlooked or ignored or even suppressed, or that perhaps is simply deserving of a larger audience. Then—in no especial order—comes the polemical, or an attempt to persuade, or refute, or explode and debunk, or even to mobilize. One has to add the confessional, in which the writer seeks to engage the reader either in an apologia or a revelation, disburdening something (and not, thank heavens, always with the aim of attracting sympathy). No disgrace is the merely descriptive, where the writer paints a scene in the hope of presenting it through his or her eyes. I would want to add the revisionist to the heuristic: an article that approaches familiar material or common assumptions in a fresh light. Then perhaps we could mention the conversational: something composed for pleasure alone or for its own sake, where the "point" is that there is no particular point. A coda is provided by the valedictory, where the writer either bids adieu to someone else or tries to do the near-impossible and deliver some last words of his own while the faculties are still intact.

—Christopher Hitchens

## Why Essays Can Confuse People

I picked up my pen again and began to write, began to write directly, honestly, began to converse, showing, telling, pausing, contradicting, setting the frayed contents of my mind down on plain paper to be plainly seen by anyone who cared to look. That doesn't mean there isn't art and artifice involved in the writing of an essay. But it does mean that the art is in revealing the voice of the writer, as opposed to trying to transform it to suit the requirements of a fictional character or narrator. Essay writing is not about facts, although the essay may contain facts. Essay writing is about transcribing the often convoluted process of thought, leaving your own brand of breadcrumbs in the forest so that those who want to can find their way to your door.

Essays, therefore, confuse people. They occupy a quirky place in the general genre of nonfiction, a place many people seem not to understand. It has been my experience that people not acquainted with the literary essay expect it to behave like an article or a piece of journalism. Journalism is a broad category unto itself, but it is probably finally defined by its mission to report to readers clear facts that have been thoroughly investigated and digested by the journalist. One does not expect to read a piece of journalism filled with tentative reflections or outright contradictions. However, essays thrive on these, because contradiction, paradox, and questioning best reflect the moving, morphing human mind, which is what the essayist wants to capture.

—Lauren Slater

## *Essays Are Not Scientific Documents*

An essay is not a scientific document. It can be serendipitous or domestic, satire or testimony, tongue-in-cheek or a wail of grief. Mulched perhaps in its own contradictions, it promises no sure objectivity, just the condiment of opinion on a base of observation, and sometimes such leaps of illogic or superlogic that they may work a bit like magic realism in a novel: namely, to simulate the mind's own processes in a murky and incongruous world. More than being instructive, as a magazine article is, an essay has a slant, a seasoned personality behind it that ought to weather well. Even if we think the author is telling us the earth is flat, we might want to listen to him elaborate upon the fringes of his premise because the bristle of his narrative and what he's seen intrigues us. He has a cutting edge, yet balance too. A given body of information is going to be eclipsed, but what lives in art is spirit, not factuality, and we respond to Montaigne's human touch despite four centuries of technological and social change.

—Edward Hoagland

## *Essays Are Not Monologues*

Essays, in the end, are not monologues. Whether we are nodding our heads or shouting back or writing protest letters in response, the most compelling essays often demand a reaction, either instantly or much later, when the words have settled inside us, under our skins, within us.

—Edwidge Danticat

## *The Essayist's Defensiveness*

No poet has a problem saying, I am a poet. No fiction writer hesitates to say, I am writing a story. "Poem" and "story" are still relatively stable, easily identified literary forms or genres. The essay is not, in that sense, a genre. Rather, "essay" is just one name, the most sonorous name, bestowed on a wide range of writings. Writers and editors usually call them "pieces." This is not just modesty or American casualness. A certain defensiveness now surrounds the notion of the essay. And many of the best essayists today are quick to declare that their best work lies elsewhere: in writing that is more "creative" (fiction, poetry) or more exacting (scholarship, theory, philosophy).

—Susan Sontag

## On Being an Essayist

As someone who takes some pride in being known as "Joseph Epstein, an essayist"—or, even better, "the essayist Joseph Epstein"—who takes the term "essayist" as an honorific, I have both an interest and a stake in the form. I hate to see it put down, defamed, spat upon, even mildly slighted. The best luck that any writer can have is to find his or her form, and I feel fortunate in having found mine some twenty years ago in the familiar essay. It happened quite by luck: I was not then a frequent reader of Montaigne and Hazlitt; in those days I was even put off by Charles Lamb, who sometimes seemed to me a bit precious. For me the novel was the form of forms, and easily the one I most admired and should most have liked to master. Although I have published a dozen or so short stories, I have not yet written a novel—nor have I one in mind to write—and so I have to conclude that despite my enormous regard for that form, it just isn't mine. Perhaps it is quite useless for a writer to search for his perfect form; that form, it may well be, has to find him.

—Joseph Epstein

## Essayists Must Tell the Truth

I work by Hemingway's precept that a writer's root charge is to distinguish what you really felt in the moment from the false sentiment of what you now believe you should have felt. The personal essay, autobiography, has been a red flag to professional classifiers and epistemologists; a critical industry has flourished for the refinement of generic protocols (many in French, with as much fine print as an installment purchase agreement), subcontracted principally to skeptics. In the judgment of Northrop Frye, for instance, a piece of work is shelved with autobiography or with fiction according to whether the librarian chooses to believe it.

Well. I've written one, and I've written the other, and I'm here to testify that the issue is at once weightier and simpler: a personal essayist means to tell the truth. The contract between a personal essayist and a reader is absolute, an agreement about intention. Because memory is fallible, and point of view by its nature biased, the personal essayist will tell a slant tale, willy-nilly. But not by design.

—Geoffrey Wolff

## The Essayist's Voice

The influential essayist is someone with an acute sense of what has not been (properly) talked about, what should be talked about (but differently). But what makes essays last is less their argument than the display of a complex mind and a distinctive prose voice.

—Susan Sontag

## Voice and Personality

Writing that has a voice is writing that has something like a personality. But whose personality is it? As with most things in art, there is no straight road from the product back to the person who made it. There are writers read and loved for their humor who are not especially funny people, and writers read and loved for their eloquence who, in conversation, swallow their words or can't seem to finish a sentence. Wisdom on the page correlates with wisdom in the writer about as frequently as a high batting average correlates with a high IQ: they just seem to have very little to do with one another. Charming people can produce prose of sneering sententiousness, and cranky neurotics can, to their readers, seem to be inexhaustibly delightful. Personal drabness, through some obscure neural kink, can deliver verbal blooms. Readers who meet writers whose voice they have fallen in love with usually need to make a small adjustment in order to hang on to their infatuation.

—Louis Menand

## The Demands of the First Person Singular

The thoroughgoing first person is a demanding mode. It asks for the literary equivalent of perfect pitch. Even good writers occasionally lose control of their tone and let a self-congratulatory quality slip in. Eager to explain that their heart is in the right place, they baldly state that they care deeply about matters with which they appear to be only marginally acquainted. Pretending to confess to their bad behavior, they revel in their colorfulness. Insistently describing their own biases, they make it all too obvious that they wish to appear uncommonly reliable. Obviously, the first person doesn't guarantee honesty. Just because they are committing words to paper does not mean that writers stop telling themselves the lies that they've invented for getting through the night. Not everyone has Montaigne's gift for candor. Certainly some people are less likely to write honestly about themselves than about anyone else on earth.

—Tracy Kidder

## The "Who Cares?" Factor

Not every voice a great soliloquy makes, a truth at odds with the education of many an American writer, with the education of *this* American
writer. I remember (see how difficult, even now, to break the habit of
that pronoun, that solipsistic verb), at boarding school in England, writing about Cordelia in the moment when she recognizes how mistaken
is her father's measurement of affection. I spent the greater part of my
allotted space telling about a tangled misunderstanding between my
dad and myself: "So I understand just how Cordelia felt." Of course
my teacher wrote "who cares?" Of course he was right to write that: to
filter all data through the mesh of personal relevance is the voice's
tyrannical sway over listener and speaker alike. Sometimes it should
be okay to take facts in, quietly manipulate them behind an opaque
scrim, and display them as though the arranger never arranged.
It should be all right to mediate, let another voice speak through your
spirit medium, pretend as a writer not to be front and center on stage.

—Geoffrey Wolff

## What "Confessional Writing" Must Do

I knew that "confessional writing" now enjoys quite a vogue, but I had
no idea how pervasive the practice of personal storytelling has become
among our finest writers. I can't help asking myself (although all lives
are, by definition, interesting, for what else do we have?): why in heav-
en's name should I care about the travails of X or Y unless some clear
generality about human life and nature emerges thereby? I'm glad that
trout fishing defined someone's boyhood, and I'm sad that parental
dementia now dominates someone's midlife, but what can we do in
life but play the hand we have been dealt?

—Stephen Jay Gould

## Why I Distrust Memoirs

... I first owe some account of why certain types of essays were maybe
easier for me to exclude than others. I'll try to combine candor with
maximum tact. Memoirs, for example. With a few big exceptions,
I don't much care for abreactive or confessional memoirs. I'm not
sure how to explain this. There is probably a sound, serious argument
to be made about the popularity of confessional memoirs as a symptom
of something especially sick and narcissistic/voyeuristic about U.S.

culture right now. About certain deep connections between narcissism and voyeurism in the mediated psyche. But this isn't it. I think the real reason is that I just don't trust them. Memoirs/confessions, I mean. Not so much their factual truth as their agenda. The sense I get from a lot of contemporary memoirs is that they have an unconscious and unacknowledged project, which is to make the memoirists seem as endlessly fascinating and important to the reader as they are to themselves. I find most of them sad in a way that I don't think their authors intend.

—David Foster Wallace

## How the Essayist Acquires Authority

Essays are how we speak to one another in print—caroming thoughts not merely in order to convey a certain packet of information, but with a special edge or bounce of personal character in a kind of public letter. As a writer you multiply yourself, gaining height as though jumping on a trampoline, if you can catch the gist of what other people have also been feeling and clarify it for them. Classic essay subjects, like the flux of friendship, "On Greed," "On Religion," "On Vanity," or solitude, lying, self-sacrifice, can be major-league yet not require Bertrand Russell to handle them. A layman who has diligently looked into something, walking in the mosses of regret after the death of a parent, for instance, may acquire an intangible authority, even without being memorably angry or funny or possessing a beguiling equanimity. *He* cares; therefore, if he has tinkered enough with his words, we do too.

—Edward Hoagland

## The Conversational Style

While there is no firmly set, single style for the essayist, styles varying with each particular essayist, the best general description of essayistic style was written in 1827 by William Hazlitt in his essay "Familiar Style." "To write a genuine familiar or truly English style," Hazlitt wrote, "is to write as any one would speak in common conversation who had a thorough command and choice of words, who could discourse with ease, force, and perspicuity, setting aside all pedantic and oratorical flourishes." The style of the essayist is that of an extremely intelligent, highly commonsensical person talking, without stammer and with impressive coherence, to him- or herself and to anyone else who cares to eavesdrop. This self-reflexivity, this notion of talking to oneself, has always seemed to me to mark the essay off from the lecture. The lecturer is always teaching; so, too, frequently is the critic. If the essayist does so, it is usually only indirectly.

—Joseph Epstein

## The Essay as Dialogue

Human storytelling was once all breath, the sacred act of telling family stories and tribal histories around a fire. Now a writer must attempt to breathe life into the words on a page, in the hope that the reader will discover something that resonates with his or her own experience. A genuine essay feels less like a monologue than a dialogue between writer and reader. *This is a story I need,* we conclude after reading the opening paragraph. *It will tell me something about the world that I didn't know before, something I sensed but could not articulate.*

An essay that is doing its job feels right. And resonance is the key. To be resonant, the dictionary informs us, is to be "strong and deep in tone, resounding." And to resound means to be filled to the depth with a sound that is sent back to its source. An essay that works is similar; it gives back to the reader a thought, a memory, an emotion made richer by the experience of another. Such an essay may confirm the reader's sense of things, or it may contradict it. But always, and in glorious, mysterious ways that the author cannot control, it begins to belong to the reader.

—Kathleen Norris

## The Essay and Community

We speak a good deal these days of the loss of community, and many of us feel that we have lost therefore something very precious. Essays can move us back into this not-quite-lost realm. Tackling a hundred subjects, in a hundred different styles, they are like letters from a stranger that you cannot bear to throw away. They haunt you; they strengthen you.

—Mary Oliver

## The Attractions of Autobiography

Contemporary critical theory lends authority to the autobiographical impulse. As every graduate student knows, only a fool would try to think or bear witness to events objectively anymore, and only an intellectual crook would claim to have done so. There's a line of reasoning that goes like this: writers ought to acknowledge that they are subjective filtering agents and let themselves appear on the page; or, in greater honesty, describe themselves in detail; or, most honest of all, make themselves their main subject matter, since one's own self is the only subject one can really know. Maybe widespread psychotherapy has made literary self-revelation popular. Certainly there are economic reasons. Editors and agents seem to think that the public's hunger for intimate true-life stories has grown large enough to include the private lives of literary figures as well as those of movie stars, mass murderers, and athletes. And the invitation to write about oneself has intrinsic attractions. The subject interests most writers. The research doesn't usually require travel or phone calls or hours in a library. The enterprise *looks* easy.

—Tracy Kidder

## The Essayist's Audience

Essays are addressed to a public in which some degree of equity exists between the writer and the reader. Shared knowledge is a necessity, although the information need not be concrete. Perhaps it is more to be thought of as a sharing of the experience of reading certain kinds of texts, texts with omissions and elisions, leaps. The essayist does not stop to identify the common ground; he will not write, "Picasso, the great Spanish painter who lived long in France." On the other hand, essays are about something, something we may not have had reason to study and master, often matters about which we are quite ignorant. Elegance of presentation, reflection made interesting and significant, easily lead us to engage our reading minds with Zulus, herbaceous borders in the English garden, marriage records in eighteenth-century France, Japanese scrolls.

—Elizabeth Hardwick

## Essays Start Out in Magazines

Essays end up in books, but they start their lives in magazines. (It's hard to imagine a book of recent but previously unpublished essays.) The perennial comes now mainly in the guise of the topical and, in the short run, no literary form has as great and immediate an impact on contemporary readers. Many essays are discussed, debated, reacted to in a way that poets and writers of fiction can only envy.

—Susan Sontag

## The Importance of Being Edited

A few years ago, the author of an autobiographical essay I was planning to publish in *The American Scholar*—a very fine writer—died suddenly. The writer had no immediate relatives, so I asked his longtime editor at the *New Yorker* if he would read the edited piece, hoping he might be able to guess which of my minor changes the writer would have been likely to accept and which he would have disliked. Certainly, said the editor. Two days later, he sent the piece back to me with comments on my edits and some additional editing of his own. "My suggestions are all small sentence tweaks," he wrote. "I could hear _____'s voice in my head as I did them and I'm pretty sure they would have met with his approval—most of them, anyway." Some examples: "A man who looked unmusical" became "a man so seemingly unmusical." "They made a swift escape to their different homes" became "They scattered swiftly to their various homes." "I felt that that solidity had been fostered by his profession" became "That solidity, I felt, had been fostered by his profession." These were, indeed, only small tweaks, but their precision filled me with awe. Of *course* you couldn't look unmusical. Of *course* it was awkward to use "escape" (singular) with "homes" (plural). Of *course* I should have caught "that that." I faxed the piece to my entire staff because editors rarely get a chance to see the work of other editors; we see only its results. This was like having a front-row seat at the Editing Olympics.

Five days later, the editor sent the piece back to us, covered with a second round of marginalia. "No doubt this is more than you bargained for," he wrote. "It's just that when the more noticeable imperfections have been taken care of, smaller ones come into view ... I've even edited some of my own edits—e.g., on page 25, where I've changed 'dour,' which I inserted in the last go-round, to 'glowering.' This is because 'dour' is too much like 'pinched,' which I'm also suggesting."

If you're not a writer, this sort of compulsiveness may seem well nigh pathological. You may even be thinking, "What's the difference?" But if you *are* a writer, you'll realize what a gift the editor gave his old friend. Had not a word been changed, the essay would still have been excellent. Each of these "tweaks"—there were perhaps a hundred, none more earth-shaking than the ones I've quoted—made it a little better, and their aggregate effect was to transform an excellent essay into a superb one.

—Anne Fadiman

## On Certain Magazine Interviews

I myself have been interviewed by writers carrying recorders, and as I sit answering their questions, I see them half-listening, nodding pleasantly, and relaxing in the knowledge that the little wheels are rolling. But what they are getting from me (and I assume from other people they talk to) is not the insight that comes from deep probing and perceptive analysis and old-fashioned legwork; it is rather the first-draft drift of my mind, a once-over-lightly dialogue that—while perhaps symptomatic of a society permeated by fast-food computerized bottom-line impersonalized workmanship—too frequently reduces the once-artful craft of magazine writing to the level of talk radio on paper.

—Gay Talese

## Listening to People Think

Quoting people verbatim, to be sure, has rarely blended well with my narrative style of writing or with my wish to observe and describe people actively engaged in ordinary but revealing situations rather than to confine them to a room and present them in the passive posture of a monologist. Since my earliest days in journalism, I was far less interested in the exact words that came out of people's mouths than in the essence of their meaning. More important than what people say is what they think, even though the latter may initially be difficult for them to articulate and may require much pondering and reworking within the interviewee's mind— which is what I gently try to prod and stimulate as I query, interrelate, and identify with my subjects as I personally accompany them whenever possible, be it on their errands, their appointments, their aimless peregrinations before dinner or after work. Wherever it is, I try physically to be there in my role as a curious confidant, a trustworthy fellow traveler searching into their interior, seeking to discover, clarify, and finally to describe in words (my words) what they personify and how they think.

—Gay Talese

## On the Subjects of Essays

Those with the least gift are most anxious to receive a commission. It seems to them that there lies waiting a topic, a new book, a performance, and that this is known as material. The true prose writer knows there is nothing given, no idea, no text or play seen last evening until an assault has taken place, the forced domination that we call "putting it in your own words." Talking about, thinking about a project bears little relation to the composition; enthusiasm boils down with distressing speed to a paragraph, often one of mischievous banality. To proceed from musing to writing is to feel a robbery has taken place. And certainly there has been a loss; the loss of the smiles and ramblings and discussions so much friendlier to ambition than the cold hardship of writing.

—Elizabeth Hardwick

## *The Essay's Unlimited Possibilities*

The essay is, and has been, all over the map. There's nothing you cannot do with it; no subject matter is forbidden, no structure is proscribed. You get to make up your own structure every time, a structure that arises from the materials and best contains them. The material is the world itself, which, so far, keeps on keeping on. The thinking mind will analyze, and the creative imagination will link instances, and time itself will churn out scenes—scenes unnoticed and lost, or scenes remembered, written, and saved.

In his essay "Home," William Kittredge remembers Jack Ray, his boyhood hero, whom he later hired as a hand on his Oregon ranch. After a bout in jail, Jack Ray would show up in the bunkhouse grinning. "Well, hell, Jack," Kittredge would say. "It's a new day."

"Kid," he would say, "she's a new world every morning."

—Annie Dillard

# 1

## *The Personal Voice: Identity, Diversity, Self-Discovery*

ANWAR F. ACCAWI

# The Telephone

Newspapers and popular magazines indirectly encourage readers to think
essays are synonymous with opinion pieces—columns and articles in which
writers speak their minds and air their views on topics in the news. But
essays can be effective means of storytelling, as Anwar Accawi proves in
the following account of his childhood in a tiny village in southern Lebanon.
In "The Telephone," Accawi offers an unpretentious description of how the
modern world began its intrusion into a timeless and insulated culture,
where "there was no real need for a calendar or a watch to keep track of
the hours, days, months, and years." As Accawi says of village life: "We
lived and loved and toiled and died without ever needing to know what
year it was, or even the time of day."

   Accawi, who was born in Lebanon in 1943 and came to the United
States in 1965, began writing essays as a way to preserve a disappearing
culture for his young children, who knew nothing of the old country.
A teacher at the English Language Institute at the University of Tennessee,
Knoxville, he is the author of a memoir, The Boy from the Tower of
the Moon (1999). "The Telephone," which originally appeared in The
Sun (1997), was one of Accawi's first publications and was selected by
Cynthia Ozick for The Best American Essays 1998.

When I was growing up in Magdaluna, a small Lebanese village in
the terraced, rocky mountains east of Sidon, time didn't mean
much to anybody, except maybe to those who were dying, or
those waiting to appear in court because they had tampered with
the boundary markers on their land. In those days, there was no
real need for a calendar or a watch to keep track of the hours,
days, months, and years. We knew what to do and when to do it,
just as the Iraqi geese knew when to fly north, driven by the hot

wind that blew in from the desert, and the ewes knew when to give birth to wet lambs that stood on long, shaky legs in the chilly March wind and baaed hesitantly, because they were small and cold and did not know where they were or what to do now that they were here. The only timepiece we had need of then was the sun. It rose and set, and the seasons rolled by, and we sowed seed and harvested and ate and played and married our cousins and had babies who got whooping cough and chickenpox—and those children who survived grew up and married *their* cousins and had babies who got whooping cough and chickenpox. We lived and loved and toiled and died without ever needing to know what year it was, or even the time of day.

It wasn't that we had no system for keeping track of time and of the important events in our lives. But ours was a natural—or, rather, a divine—calendar, because it was framed by acts of God. Allah himself set down the milestones with earthquakes and droughts and floods and locusts and pestilences. Simple as our calendar was, it worked just fine for us.

Take, for example, the birth date of Teta Im Khalil, the oldest woman in Magdaluna and all the surrounding villages. When I first met her, we had just returned home from Syria at the end of the Big War and were living with Grandma Mariam. Im Khalil came by to welcome my father home and to take a long, myopic look at his foreign-born wife, my mother. Im Khalil was so old that the skin of her cheeks looked like my father's grimy tobacco pouch, and when I kissed her (because Grandma insisted that I show her old friend affection), it was like kissing a soft suede glove that had been soaked with sweat and then left in a dark closet for a season. Im Khalil's face got me to wondering how old one had to be to look and taste the way she did. So, as soon as she had hobbled off on her cane, I asked Grandma, "How old is Teta Im Khalil?"

Grandma had to think for a moment; then she said, "I've been told that Teta was born shortly after the big snow that caused the roof on the mayor's house to cave in."

"And when was that?" I asked.

"Oh, about the time we had the big earthquake that cracked the wall in the east room."

Well, that was enough for me. You couldn't be more accurate than that, now, could you? Satisfied with her answer, I went back to playing with a ball made from an old sock stuffed with other, much older socks.

And that's the way it was in our little village for as far back as anybody could remember: people were born so many years before or after an earthquake or a flood; they got married or died so many years before or after a long drought or a big snow or some other disaster. One of the most unusual of these dates was when Antoinette the seamstress and Saeed the barber (and tooth puller) got married. That was the year of the whirlwind during which fish and oranges fell from the sky. Incredible as it may sound, the story of the fish and oranges was true, because men—respectable men, like Abu George the blacksmith and Abu Asaad the mule skinner, men who would not lie even to save their own souls—told and retold that story until it was incorporated into Magdaluna's calendar, just like the year of the black moon and the year of the locusts before it. My father, too, confirmed the story for me. He told me that he had been a small boy himself when it had rained fish and oranges from heaven. He'd gotten up one morning after a stormy night and walked out into the yard to find fish as long as his forearm still flopping here and there among the wet navel oranges.

The year of the fish-bearing twister, however, was not the last remarkable year. Many others followed in which strange and wonderful things happened: milestones added by the hand of Allah to Magdaluna's calendar. There was, for instance, the year of the drought, when the heavens were shut for months and the spring from which the entire village got its drinking water slowed to a trickle. The spring was about a mile from the village, in a ravine that opened at one end into a small, flat clearing covered with fine gray dust and hard, marble-sized goat droppings, because every afternoon the goatherds brought their flocks there to water them. In the year of the drought, that little clearing was always packed full of noisy kids with big brown eyes and sticky hands, and their mothers—sinewy, overworked young women with protruding collarbones and cracked, callused brown heels. The children ran around playing tag or hide-and-seek while the women talked, shooed flies, and awaited their turns to fill up their jars with drinking water to bring home to their napping men and wet babies. There were days when we had to wait from sunup until late afternoon just to fill a small clay jar with precious, cool water.

Sometimes, amid the long wait and the heat and the flies and the smell of goat dung, tempers flared, and the younger women, anxious about their babies, argued over whose turn it was to fill up her jar. And sometimes the arguments escalated into full-blown, knockdown-dragout fights; the women would grab each other by the hair and curse and scream and spit and call each other names that made my ears tingle. We little brown boys who went with our mothers to fetch water loved these fights, because we got to see the women's legs and their colored panties as they grappled and rolled around in the dust. Once in a while, we got lucky and saw much more, because some of the women wore nothing at all under their long dresses. God, how I used to look forward to those fights. I remember the rush, the excitement, the sun dancing on the dust clouds as a dress ripped and a young white breast was revealed, then quickly hidden. In my calendar, that year of drought will always be one of the best years of my childhood, because it was then, in a dusty clearing by a trickling mountain spring, I got my first glimpses of the wonders, the mysteries, and the promises hidden beneath the folds of a woman's dress. Fish and oranges from heaven ... you can get over that.

But, in another way, the year of the drought was also one of the worst of my life, because that was the year that Abu Raja, the retired cook who used to entertain us kids by cracking walnuts on his forehead, decided it was time Magdaluna got its own telephone. Every civilized village needed a telephone, he said, and Magdaluna was not going to get anywhere until it had one. A telephone would link us with the outside world. At the time, I was too young to understand the debate, but a few men—like Shukri, the retired Turkish-army drill sergeant, and Abu Hanna the vineyard keeper— did all they could to talk Abu Raja out of having a telephone brought to the village. But they were outshouted and ignored and finally shunned by the other villagers for resisting progress and trying to keep a good thing from coming to Magdaluna.

One warm day in early fall, many of the villagers were out in their fields repairing walls or gathering wood for the winter when the shout went out that the telephone-company truck had arrived at Abu Raja's *dikkan,* or country store. There were no roads in those days, only footpaths and dry streambeds, so it took the telephone-company truck almost a day to work its way up the rocky terrain from Sidon—about the same time it took to walk. When the truck came into view, Abu George, who had a huge voice and, before the telephone, was Magdaluna's only long-distance communication system, bellowed the news from his front porch. Everybody dropped what they were doing and ran to Abu Raja's house to see what was happening. Some of the more dignified villagers, however, like Abu Habeeb and Abu Nazim, who had been to big cities like Beirut and Damascus and had seen things like telephones and telegraphs, did not run the way the rest did; they walked with their canes hanging from the crooks of their arms, as if on a Sunday afternoon stroll.

It did not take long for the whole village to assemble at Abu Raja's *dikkan.* Some of the rich villagers, like the widow Farha and the gendarme Abu Nadeem, walked right into the store and stood at the elbows of the two important-looking men from the telephone company, who proceeded with utmost gravity, like priests at Communion, to wire up the telephone. The poorer villagers stood outside and listened carefully to the details relayed to them by the not-so-poor people who stood in the doorway and could see inside.

"The bald man is cutting the blue wire," someone said.

"He is sticking the wire into the hole in the bottom of the black box," someone else added.

"The telephone man with the mustache is connecting two pieces of wire. Now he is twisting the ends together," a third voice chimed in.

Because I was small and unaware that I should have stood outside with the other poor folk to give the rich people inside more room (they seemed to need more of it than poor people did), I wriggled my way through the dense forest of legs to get a firsthand look at the action. I felt like the barefoot Moses, sandals in hand, staring at the burning bush on Mount Sinai. Breathless, I watched as the men in blue, their shirt pockets adorned with fancy lettering in a foreign language, put together a black machine that supposedly would make it possible to talk with uncles, aunts, and cousins who lived more than two days' ride away.

It was shortly after sunset when the man with the mustache announced that the telephone was ready to use. He explained that all Abu Raja had to do was lift the receiver, turn the crank on the black box a few times, and wait for an operator to take his call. Abu Raja, who had once lived and worked in Sidon, was impatient with the telephone man for assuming that he was ignorant. He grabbed the receiver and turned the crank forcefully, as if trying to start a Model T Ford. Everybody was impressed that he knew what to do. He even called the operator by her first name: "Centralist." Within moments, Abu Raja was talking with his brother, a concierge in Beirut. He didn't even have to raise his voice or shout to be heard.

If I hadn't seen it with my own two eyes and heard it with my own two ears, I would not have believed it—and my friend Kameel didn't. He was away that day watching his father's goats, and when he came back to the village that evening, his cousin Habeeb and I told him about the telephone and how Abu Raja had used it to speak with his brother in Beirut. After he heard our report, Kameel made the sign of the cross, kissed his thumbnail, and warned us that lying was a bad sin and would surely land us in purgatory. Kameel believed in Jesus and Mary, and wanted to be a priest when he grew up. He always crossed himself when Habeeb, who was irreverent, and I, who was Presbyterian, were around, even when we were not bearing bad news.

And the telephone, as it turned out, was bad news. With its coming, the face of the village began to change. One of the first effects was the shifting of the village's center. Before the telephone's arrival, the men of the village used to gather regularly at the house of Im Kaleem, a short, middle-aged widow with jet-black hair and a raspy voice that could be heard all over the village, even when she was only whispering. She was a devout Catholic and also the village *shlikki*—whore. The men met at her house to argue about politics and drink coffee and play cards or backgammon. Im Kaleem was not a true prostitute, however, because she did not charge for her services—not even for the coffee and tea (and, occasionally, the strong liquor called arrack) that she served the men. She did not need the money; her son, who was overseas in Africa, sent her money regularly. (I knew this because my father used to read her son's letters to her and take down her replies, as Im Kaleem could not read and write.) Im Kaleem was no slut either—unlike some women in the village—because she loved all the men she entertained, and they loved her, every one of them. In a way, she was married to all the men in the village. Everybody knew it—the wives knew it; the itinerant Catholic priest knew it; the Presbyterian minister knew it—but nobody objected. Actually, I suspect the women (my mother included) did not mind their husbands' visits to Im Kaleem. Oh, they wrung their hands and complained to one another about their men's unfaithfulness, but secretly they were relieved, because Im Kaleem took some of the pressure off them and kept the men out of their hair while they attended to their endless chores. Im Kaleem was also a kind of confessor and troubleshooter, talking sense to those men who were having family problems, especially the younger ones.

Before the telephone came to Magdaluna, Im Kaleem's house was bustling at just about any time of day, especially at night, when its windows were brightly lit with three large oil lamps, and the loud voices of the men talking, laughing, and arguing could be heard in the street below—a reassuring, homey sound. Her house was an island of comfort, an oasis for the weary village men, exhausted from having so little to do.

But it wasn't long before many of those men—the younger ones especially—started spending more of their days and evenings at Abu Raja's *dikkan*. There, they would eat and drink and talk and play checkers and backgammon, and then lean their chairs back against the wall—the signal that they were ready to toss back and forth, like a ball, the latest rumors going around the village. And they were always looking up from their games and drinks and talk to glance at the phone in the corner, as if expecting it to ring any minute and bring news that would change their lives and deliver them from their aimless existence. In the meantime, they smoked cheap, hand-rolled cigarettes, dug dirt out from under their fingernails with big pocketknives, and drank lukewarm sodas they called Kacula, Seffen-Ub, and Bebsi. Sometimes, especially when it was hot, the days dragged on so slowly that the men turned on Abu Saeed, a confirmed bachelor who practically lived in Abu Raja's *dikkan,* and teased him for going around barefoot and unshaven since the Virgin had appeared to him behind the olive press.

The telephone was also bad news for me personally. It took away my lucrative business—a source of much-needed income. Before the telephone came to Magdaluna, I used to hang around Im Kaleem's courtyard and play marbles with the other kids, waiting for some man to call down from a window and ask me to run to the store for cigarettes or arrack, or to deliver a message to his wife, such as what he wanted for supper. There was always something in it for me: a ten- or even a twenty-five-piaster piece. On a good day, I ran nine or ten of those errands, which assured a steady supply of marbles that I usually lost to Sami or his cousin Hani, the basket weaver's boy. But as the days went by, fewer and fewer men came to Im Kaleem's, and more and more congregated at Abu Raja's to wait by the telephone. In the evenings, no light fell from her window onto the street below, and the laughter and noise of the men trailed off and finally stopped. Only Shukri, the retired Turkish-army drill sergeant, remained faithful to Im Kaleem after all the other men had deserted her; he was still seen going into or leaving her house from time to time. Early that winter, Im Kaleem's hair suddenly turned gray, and she got sick and old. Her legs started giving her trouble, making it hard for her to walk. By spring she hardly left her house anymore.

At Abu Raja's *dikkan,* the calls did eventually come, as expected, and men and women started leaving the village the way a hailstorm begins: first one, then two, then bunches. The army took them. Jobs in the cities lured them. And ships and airplanes carried them to such faraway places as Australia and Brazil and New Zealand. My friend Kameel, his cousin Habeeb, and their cousins and my cousins all went away to become ditch diggers and mechanics and butcher-shop boys and deli owners who wore dirty aprons sixteen hours a day, all looking for a better life than the one they had left behind. Within a year, only the sick, the old, and the maimed were left in the village. Magdaluna became a skeleton of its former self, desolate and forsaken, like the tombs, a place to get away from.

Finally, the telephone took my family away, too. My father got a call from an old army buddy who told him that an oil company in southern Lebanon was hiring interpreters and instructors. My father applied for a job and got it, and we moved to Sidon, where I went to a Presbyterian missionary school and graduated in 1962. Three years later, having won a scholarship, I left Lebanon for the United States. Like the others who left Magdaluna before me, I am still looking for that better life.

## Reflections and Responses

1. Why do you think Accawi begins his recollections of childhood by focusing on the way the passage of time was measured by the villagers? Does Accawi see the villagers' attitude toward time in positive or negative ways? How do his word choices and images reflect his position?

2. Consider the way Accawi introduces the telephone into the village. How does he prepare for its appearance? From whose perspective do we view the installation? How are the class lines of the village drawn when the telephone is installed? Finally, why did the telephone turn out to be "bad news" for the village as a whole?

3. How would you assess Accawi's attitude in the final paragraph? How did the telephone personally change his life? Do you think the change was for the worse? Do you think Accawi himself believes it was for the worse? How do you interpret his final sentence?

JUDITH ORTIZ COFER

# *Silent Dancing*

*Nothing rekindles childhood memories better than old photographs or home movies. In this vivid essay, a grainy and poorly focused five-minute home movie of a New Year's Eve party helps a writer capture the spirit of a Puerto Rican community in Paterson, New Jersey. That the movie is fragmented and silent adds to its documentary value and, for a lyrical essayist, it evokes much more than it can possibly reveal. "Even the home movie," Cofer writes, "cannot fill in the sensory details such a gathering left imprinted in a child's brain." Those sensory details—"the flavor of Puerto Rico"—must be supplied through the art of writing.*

*A professor of English and creative writing at the University of Georgia, Judith Ortiz Cofer has published prize-winning books in a number of genres: a novel,* The Line of the Sun *(1989); three poetry collections,* Reaching for the Mainland *(1986),* Terms of Survival *(1987), and* A Love Story Beginning in Spanish *(2005); two autobiographical books combining prose and poetry,* Silent Dancing *(1990) and* The Latin Deli *(1993); and* An Island Like You: Stories of the Barrio *(1995). She has recently published* The Year of Our Revolution: New and Selected Stories and Poems *(1998),* Sleeping with One Eye Open: Women Writers and the Art of Survival *(1999),* Women in Front of the Sun: On Becoming a Writer *(2000), and three novels,* The Meaning of Consuelo *(2003),* Call Me Maria *(2004), and* If I Could Fly *(2011). Cofer has received many prestigious awards, including fellowships from the National Endowment for the Arts, the Witter Bynner Foundation for Poetry, and the Bread Loaf Writers' Conference. "Silent Dancing" originally appeared in* The Georgia Review *(1990) and was selected by Joyce Carol Oates for* The Best American Essays *1991. Ms. Cofer courteously supplied the notes to this selection.*

*We have a home movie of this party. Several times my mother and I have watched it together, and I have asked questions about the silent revelers*

Source: "Silent Dancing" by Judith Ortiz Cofer. Reprinted with the permission from the publisher of *Silent Dancing: A Partial Remembrance of a Puerto Rican Childhood* (Houston: Arte Publico Press—University of Houston, 1990.)

*coming in and out of focus. It is grainy and of short duration, but it's a great visual aid to my memory of life at that time. And it is in color—the only complete scene in color I can recall from those years.*

We lived in Puerto Rico until my brother was born in 1954. Soon after, because of economic pressures on our growing family, my father joined the United States Navy. He was assigned to duty on a ship in Brooklyn Yard—a place of cement and steel that was to be his home base in the States until his retirement more than twenty years later. He left the Island first, alone, going to New York City and tracking down his uncle who lived with his family across the Hudson River in Paterson, New Jersey. There my father found a tiny apartment in a huge tenement that had once housed Jewish families but was just being taken over and transformed by Puerto Ricans, overflowing from New York City. In 1955 he sent for us. My mother was only twenty years old, I was not quite three, and my brother was a toddler when we arrived at *El Building*, as the place had been christened by its newest residents.

My memories of life in Paterson during those first few years are all in shades of gray. Maybe I was too young to absorb vivid colors and details, or to discriminate between the slate blue of the winter sky and the darker hues of the snow-bearing clouds, but that single color washes over the whole period. The building we lived in was gray, as were the streets, filled with slush the first few months of my life there. The coat my father had bought for me was similar in color and too big; it sat heavily on my thin frame.

I do remember the way the heater pipes banged and rattled, startling all of us out of sleep until we got so used to the sound that we automatically shut it out or raised our voices above the racket. The hiss from the valve punctuated my sleep (which has always been fitful) like a nonhuman presence in the room—a dragon sleeping at the entrance of my childhood. But the pipes were also a connection to all the other lives being lived around us. Having come from a house designed for a single family back in Puerto Rico—my mother's extended-family home—it was curious to know that strangers lived under our floor and above our heads, and that the heater pipe went through everyone's apartments. (My first spanking in Paterson came as a result of playing tunes on the pipes in my room to see if there would be an answer.) My mother was as new to this concept of beehive life as I was, but she had been given strict orders by my father to keep the doors locked, the noise down, ourselves to ourselves.

It seems that Father had learned some painful lessons about prejudice while searching for an apartment in Paterson. Not until years later did I hear how much resistance he had encountered with landlords who were panicking at the influx of Latinos into a neighborhood that had been Jewish for a couple of generations. It made no difference that it was the American phenomenon of ethnic turnover which was changing the urban core of Paterson, and that the human flood could not be held back with an accusing finger.

"You Cuban?" one man had asked my father, pointing at his name tag on the Navy uniform—even though my father had the fair skin and light-brown hair of his northern Spanish background, and the name Ortiz is as common in Puerto Rico as Johnson is in the U.S.

"No," my father had answered, looking past the finger into his adversary's angry eyes. "I'm Puerto Rican."

"Same shit." And the door closed.

My father could have passed as European, but we couldn't. My brother and I both have our mother's black hair and olive skin, and so we lived in El Building and visited our great-uncle and his fair children on the next block. It was their private joke that they were the German branch of the family. Not many years later that area too would be mainly Puerto Rican. It was as if the heart of the city map were being gradually colored brown—*café con leche* brown. Our color.

*The movie opens with a sweep of the living room. It is "typical" immigrant Puerto Rican decor for the time: The sofa and chairs are square and hard-looking, upholstered in bright colors (blue and yellow in this instance), and covered with the transparent plastic that furniture salesmen then were so adept at convincing women to buy. The linoleum on the floor is light blue; if it had been subjected to spike heels (as it was in most places), there were dime-sized indentations all over it that cannot be seen in this movie. The room is full of people dressed up: dark suits for the men, red dresses for the women. When I have asked my mother why most of the women are in red that night, she has shrugged, "I don't remember. Just a coincidence." She doesn't have my obsession for assigning symbolism to everything.*

*The three women in red sitting on the couch are my mother, my eighteen-year-old cousin, and her brother's girlfriend. The* novia *is just up from the Island, which is apparent in her body language. She sits up formally, her dress pulled over her knees. She is a pretty girl, but her posture makes her look insecure, lost in her full-skirted dress, which she has carefully tucked around her to make room for my gorgeous cousin, her future sister-in-law. My cousin has grown up in Paterson and is in her last year of high school. She doesn't have a trace of what Puerto Ricans call* la mancha *(literally, the stain: the mark of the new immigrant—something about the posture, the voice, or the humble demeanor that makes it obvious to everyone the person has just arrived on the mainland). My cousin is wearing a tight, sequined cocktail dress. Her brown hair has been lightened with peroxide around the bangs, and she is holding a cigarette expertly between her fingers, bringing it up to her mouth in a sensuous arc of her arm as she talks animatedly. My mother, who has come up to sit between the two women, both only a few years younger than herself, is somewhere between the poles they represent in our culture.*

It became my father's obsession to get out of the barrio, and thus we were never permitted to form bonds with the place or with the people who lived there. Yet El Building was a comfort to my mother, who never got over yearning for *la isla*. She felt surrounded by her language: the walls were thin, and voices speaking and arguing in Spanish could be heard all day. *Salsas* blasted out of radios, turned on early in the morning and left on for company. Women seemed to cook rice and beans perpetually—the strong aroma of boiling red kidney beans permeated the hallways. Though Father preferred that we do our grocery shopping at the supermarket when he came home on weekend leaves, my mother insisted that she could cook only with products whose labels she could read. Consequently, during the week I accompanied her and my little brother to *La Bodega*—a hole-in-the-wall grocery store across the street from El Building. There we squeezed down three narrow aisles jammed with various products. Goya's and Libby's— those were the trademarks that were trusted by *her mamá*, so my mother bought many cans of Goya beans, soups, and condiments, as well as little cans of Libby's fruit juices for us. And she also bought Colgate toothpaste and Palmolive soap. (The final *e* is pronounced in both these products in Spanish, so for many years I believed that they were manufactured on the Island. I remember my surprise at first hearing a commercial on television in which Colgate rhymed with "ate.") We always lingered at La Bodega, for it was there that Mother breathed best, taking in the familiar aromas of the foods she knew from Mamá's kitchen. It was also there that she got to speak to the other women of El Building without violating outright Father's dictates against fraternizing with our neighbors.

Yet Father did his best to make our "assimilation" painless. I can still see him carrying a real Christmas tree up several flights of stairs to our apartment, leaving a trail of aromatic pine. He carried it formally, as if it were a flag in a parade. We were the only ones in El Building that I knew of who got presents on both

Christmas day AND *día de Reyes*, the day when the Three Kings brought gifts to Christ and to Hispanic children.

Our supreme luxury in El Building was having our own television set. It must have been a result of Father's guilt feelings over the isolation he had imposed on us, but we were among the first in the barrio to have one. My brother quickly became an avid watcher of Captain Kangaroo and Jungle Jim, while I loved all the series showing families. By the time I started first grade, I could have drawn a map of Middle America as exemplified by the lives of characters in *Father Knows Best, The Donna Reed Show, Leave It to Beaver, My Three Sons,* and (my favorite) *Bachelor Father,* where John Forsythe treated his adopted teenage daughter like a princess because he was rich and had a Chinese houseboy to do everything for him. In truth, compared to our neighbors in El Building, *we* were rich. My father's Navy check provided us with financial security and a standard of life that the factory workers envied. The only thing his money could not buy us was a place to live away from the barrio—his greatest wish, Mother's greatest fear.

*In the home movie the men are shown next, sitting around a card table set up in one corner of the living room, playing dominoes. The clack of the ivory pieces was a familiar sound. I heard it in many houses on the Island and in many apartments in Paterson. In* Leave It to Beaver, *the Cleavers played bridge in every other episode; in my childhood, the men started every social occasion with a hotly debated round of dominoes. The women would sit around and watch, but they never participated in the games.*

*Here and there you can see a small child. Children were always brought to parties and, whenever they got sleepy, were put to bed in the host's bedroom. Babysitting was a concept unrecognized by the Puerto Rican women I knew: a responsible mother did not leave her children with any stranger. And in a culture where children are not considered intrusive, there was no need to leave the children at home. We went where our mother went.*

Of my preschool years I have only impressions: the sharp bite of the wind in December as we walked with our parents towards the brightly lit stores downtown; how I felt like a stuffed doll in my heavy coat, boots, and mittens; how good it was to walk into the five-and-dime and sit at the counter drinking hot chocolate. On Saturdays our whole family would walk downtown to shop at the big department stores on Broadway. Mother bought all our clothes at Penney's and Sears, and she liked to buy her dresses at the women's specialty shops like Lerner's and Diana's. At some point we'd go into Woolworth's and sit at the soda fountain to eat.

We never ran into other Latinos at these stores or when eating out, and it became clear to me only years later that the women from El Building shopped mainly in other places—stores owned by other Puerto Ricans or by Jewish merchants who had philosophically accepted our presence in the city and decided to make us their good customers, if not real neighbors and friends. These establishments were located not downtown but in the blocks around our street, and they were referred to generically as *La Tienda, El Bazar, La Bodega, La Botánica.* Everyone knew what was meant. These were the stores where your face did not turn a clerk to stone, where your money was as green as anyone else's.

One New Year's Eve we were dressed up like child models in the Sears catalogue: my brother in a miniature man's suit and bow tie, and I in black patent-leather shoes and a frilly dress with several layers of crinoline underneath. My mother wore a bright-red dress that night, I remember, and spike heels; her long black hair hung to her waist. Father, who usually wore his Navy uniform during his short visits home, had put on a dark civilian suit for the occasion: we had been invited to his uncle's house for a big celebration. Everyone was excited because my mother's brother Hernan—a bachelor who could indulge himself with luxuries—had bought a home movie camera, which he would be trying out that night.

Even the home movie cannot fill in the sensory details such a gathering left imprinted in a child's brain. The thick sweetness of women's perfumes mixing with the ever-present smells of food cooking in the kitchen: meat and plantain *pasteles,* as well as the ubiquitous rice dish made special with pigeon peas—*gandules*— and seasoned with precious *sofrito\** sent up from the Island by somebody's mother or smuggled in by a recent traveler. *Sofrito* was one of the items that women hoarded, since it was hardly ever in stock at La Bodega. It was the flavor of Puerto Rico.

The men drank Palo Viejo rum, and some of the younger ones got weepy. The first time I saw a grown man cry was at a New Year's Eve party: he had been reminded of his mother by the smells in the kitchen. But what I remember most were the boiled *pasteles*—plantain or yucca rectangles stuffed with corned beef or other meats, olives, and many other savory ingredients, all wrapped in banana leaves. Everybody had to fish one out with a

---

**\*sofrito:** A cooked condiment. A sauce composed of a mixture of fatback, ham, tomatoes, and many island spices and herbs. It is added to many typical Puerto Rican dishes for a distinctive flavor.

fork. There was always a "trick" pastel—one without stuffing—and whoever got that one was the "New Year's Fool."

There was also the music. Long-playing albums were treated like precious china in these homes. Mexican recordings were popular, but the songs that brought tears to my mother's eyes were sung by the melancholy Daniel Santos, whose life as a drug addict was the stuff of legend. Felipe Rodríguez was a particular favorite of couples, since he sang about faithless women and brokenhearted men. There is a snatch of one lyric that has stuck in my mind like a needle on a worn groove: *De piedra ha de ser mi cama, de piedra la cabezera ... la mujer que a mi me quiera ... ha de quererme de veras. Ay, Ay, Ay, corazón, porque no amas.*\* ... I must have heard it a thousand times since the idea of a bed made of stone, and its connection to love, first troubled me with its disturbing images.

The five-minute home movie ends with people dancing in a circle—the creative filmmaker must have set it up, so that all of them could file past him. It is both comical and sad to watch silent dancing. Since there is no justification for the absurd movements that music provides for some of us, people appear frantic, their faces embarrassingly intense. It's as if you were watching sex. Yet for years, I've had dreams in the form of this home movie. In a recurring scene, familiar faces push themselves forward into my mind's eye, plastering their features into distorted close-ups. And I'm asking them: "Who is she? Who is the old woman I don't recognize? Is she an aunt? Somebody's wife? Tell me who she is."

"See the beauty mark on her cheek as big as a hill on the lunar landscape of her face—well, that runs in the family. The women on your father's side of the family wrinkle early; it's the price they pay for that fair skin. The young girl with the green stain on her wedding dress is *La Novia*—just up from the Island. See, she lowers her eyes when she approaches the camera, as she's supposed to. Decent girls never look at you directly in the face. *Humilde*, humble, a girl should express humility in all her actions. She will make a good wife for your cousin. He should consider himself lucky to have met her only weeks after she arrived here. If he marries her quickly, she will make him a good Puerto Rican–style wife; but if he waits too long, she will be corrupted by the city—just like your cousin there."

---

\***"De piedra ha de ser...":** Lyrics from a popular romantic ballad (called a bolero in Puerto Rico). Freely translated: "My bed will be made of stone, of stone also my headrest (or pillow), the woman who (dares to) loves me, will have to love me for real. Ay, Ay, Ay, my heart, why can't you (let me) love...."

"She means me. I do what I want. This is not some primitive island I live on. Do they expect me to wear a black mantilla on my head and go to mass every day? Not me. I'm an American woman, and I will do as I please. I can type faster than anyone in my senior class at Central High, and I'm going to be a secretary to a lawyer when I graduate. I can pass for an American girl anywhere—I've tried it. At least for Italian, anyway—I never speak Spanish in public. I hate these parties, but I wanted the dress. I look better than any of these *humildes* here. My life is going to be different. I have an American boyfriend. He is older and has a car. My parents don't know it, but I sneak out of the house late at night sometimes to be with him. If I marry him, even my name will be American. I hate rice and beans—that's what makes these women fat."

"Your *prima** is pregnant by that man she's been sneaking around with. Would I lie to you? I'm your *Tiá Política*,[†] your great-uncle's common-law wife—the one he abandoned on the Island to go marry your cousin's mother. *I* was not invited to this party, of course, but I came anyway. I came to tell you that story about your cousin that you've always wanted to hear. Do you remember the comment your mother made to a neighbor that has always haunted you? The only thing you heard was your cousin's name, and then you saw your mother pick up your doll from the couch and say: 'It was as big as this doll when they flushed it down the toilet.' This image has bothered you for years, hasn't it? You had nightmares about babies being flushed down the toilet, and you wondered why anyone would do such a horrible thing. You didn't dare ask your mother about it. She would only tell you that you had not heard her right, and yell at you for listening to adult conversations. But later, when you were old enough to know about abortions, you suspected.

I am here to tell you that you were right. Your cousin was growing an *Americanito* in her belly when this movie was made. Soon after she put something long and pointy into her pretty self, thinking maybe she could get rid of the problem before breakfast and still make it to her first class at the high school. Well, *Niña*,[‡] her screams could be heard downtown. Your aunt, her mamá, who had been a midwife on the Island, managed to pull the little

---

*prima: Female cousin.

[†]tía política: Aunt by marriage.

[‡]niña: Girl.

thing out. Yes, they probably flushed it down the toilet. What else could they do with it—give it a Christian burial in a little white casket with blue bows and ribbons? Nobody wanted that baby—least of all the father, a teacher at her school with a house in West Paterson that he was filling with real children, and a wife who was a natural blond.

Girl, the scandal sent your uncle back to the bottle. And guess where your cousin ended up? Irony of ironies. She was sent to a village in Puerto Rico to live with a relative on her mother's side: a place so far away from civilization that you have to ride a mule to reach it. A real change in scenery. She found a man there—women like that cannot live without male company—but believe me, the men in Puerto Rico know how to put a saddle on a woman like her. *La Gringa,** they call her. Ha, ha, ha. *La Gringa* is what she always wanted to be... "

The old woman's mouth becomes a cavernous black hole I fall into. And as I fall, I can feel the reverberations of her laughter. I hear the echoes of her last mocking words: *La Gringa, La Gringa!* And the conga line keeps moving silently past me. There is no music in my dream for the dancers.

When Odysseus visits Hades to see the spirit of his mother, he makes an offering of sacrificial blood, but since all the souls crave an audience with the living, he has to listen to many of them before he can ask questions. I, too, have to hear the dead and the forgotten speak in my dream. Those who are still part of my life remain silent, going around and around in their dance. The others keep pressing their faces forward to say things about the past.

My father's uncle is last in line. He is dying of alcoholism, shrunken and shriveled like a monkey, his face a mass of wrinkles and broken arteries. As he comes closer I realize that in his features I can see my whole family. If you were to stretch that rubbery flesh, you could find my father's face, and deep within *that* face— my own. I don't want to look into those eyes ringed in purple. In a few years he will retreat into silence, and take a long, long time to die. *Move back, Tío,* I tell him. *I don't want to hear what you have to say. Give the dancers room to move. Soon it will be midnight. Who is the New Year's Fool this time?*

---

*La gringa:** Derogatory epithet used here to ridicule a Puerto Rican girl who wants to look like a blonde North American.

## Reflections and Responses

1. Consider the idea of "silence" in the essay. Why is it significant that the home movie has no soundtrack? What does Cofer do with that missing element? How does silence contribute to the theme of the essay?

2. What connections does Cofer make between the home movie and her dreams? In what ways is the movie dreamlike? In what ways does the essay become more nightmarish as it proceeds?

3. Consider Cofer's final paragraph. How does it pull together the various strands of the essay?

EDWIDGE DANTICAT

# *Westbury Court*

*What do we remember from our childhood? And why do we remember some things vividly, some things not at all, and yet others in some fuzzy in-between way? In "Westbury Court," Edwidge Danticat examines the inner workings of memory as she describes a deadly fire that took the lives of two children who lived next door to her in a New York apartment building when she was fourteen. Though vivid in many ways, the memory still leaves her wondering if she recalls the most significant details correctly: "Even now, I question what I remember about the children. Did they really die? Or did their mother simply move away with them after the fire?" She wonders if she is really "struggling to phase them out of [her] memory altogether."*

*Born in Port-au-Prince, Haiti, in 1969, Edwidge Danticat settled with her family in New York at age twelve. She began writing stories as a child, and at fourteen she published a short essay about her experiences as a Haitian immigrant in New York. After graduating from Barnard College in Manhattan, she went on to earn an MFA from Brown University. Her books include the novels* Breath, Eyes, Memory *(1994),* The Farming of Bones *(1998), and* The Dew Breaker *(2004); a collection of short stories,* Krik? Krak! *(1995);* After the Dance *(2002); and several compilations of essays. A memoir,* Brother, I'm Dying, *won the National Book Critics Circle Award for autobiography in 2007. Her most recent essay collection is* Create Dangerously *(2010). Danticat also served as guest editor of* The Best American Essays 2011. *"Westbury Court" originally appeared in* New Letters *and was selected by Alan Lightman for* The Best American Essays 2000.

When I was fourteen years old, we lived in a six-story brick building in a cul-de-sac off of Flatbush Avenue, in Brooklyn, called Westbury Court. Beneath the building ran a subway station

through which rattled the D, M, and Q trains every fifteen minutes
or so. Though there was graffiti on most of the walls of Westbury
Court, and hills of trash piled up outside, and though the elevator
wasn't always there when we opened the door to step inside and
the heat and hot water weren't always on, I never dreamed of leaving Westbury Court until the year of the fire.

I was watching television one afternoon when the fire began.
I loved television then, especially the afternoon soap operas, my
favorite of which was *General Hospital.* I would bolt out of my last
high school class every day, pick up my youngest brother, Karl,
from day care, and watch *General Hospital* with him on my lap
while doing my homework during the commercials. My other two
brothers, André and Kelly, would later join us in the apartment,
but they preferred to watch cartoons in the back bedroom.

One afternoon while *General Hospital* and afternoon cartoons
were on, a fire started in apartment 6E, across the hall. There in
that apartment lived our new neighbors, an African-American
mother and her two boys. We didn't know the name of the
mother, or the names and ages of her boys, but I venture to
guess that they were around five and ten years old.

I didn't know a fire had started until two masked, burly firemen
came knocking on our door. My brothers and I rushed out into
the hallway filled with smoke and were quickly escorted down to
the first floor by some other firemen already on our floor. While
we ran by, the door to apartment 6E had already been knocked
over by the fire squad and inside was filled with bright flames
and murky smoke.

All of the tenants of the building who were home at that time
were crowded on the sidewalk outside. My brothers and I, it
seemed, were the last to be evacuated. Clutching my brothers'
hands, I wondered if I had remembered to lock our apartment
door. Was there anything valuable we could have taken?

An ambulance screeched to a stop in front of the building, and
the two firemen who had knocked on our door came out carrying
the pliant and lifeless bodies of the two children from across the
hall. Their mother jumped out of the crowd and ran toward them,
screaming, "My babies—not my babies," as the children were low-
ered into the back of the ambulance and transferred into the arms
of the emergency medical personnel. The fire was started by the
two boys, after their mother had stepped out to pick up some groceries at the supermarket down the street. They had been playing
with matches.

(Later my mother would tell us, "See, this is what happens to
children who play with matches. Sometimes it is too late to say,

'I shouldn't have.'" My brother Kelly, who was fascinated with fire
and liked to hold up a match to the middle of his palm until the
light fizzled out, gave up this party trick after the fire.)

We were quiet that afternoon when both our parents came
home. We were the closest to the fire in the building, and the
most religious of our parents' friends saw it as a miracle that we
had escaped safe and sound. When my mother asked how come I,
the oldest one, hadn't heard the children scream or hadn't
smelled the smoke coming from across the hall, I confessed that
I had been watching *General Hospital* and was too consumed in the
intricate plot.

(After the fire, my mother had us stay with a family on the second floor for a few months, after school. I felt better not having to
be wholly responsible for myself and my brothers, in case something like that fire should ever happen again.)

The apartment across the hall stayed empty for a long time, and
whenever I walked past it, a piece of its inner skeleton would
squeak, and occasionally burnt wood that might have been hanging by a fragile singed thread would crash down and cause a dom-
ino effect of further ruptures, unleashed like those children's last
cries, which I had not heard because I had been so wrapped up in
the made-up drama of a world where, even though the adults' lives
were often in turmoil, the children came home to the welcoming
arms of waiting mommies and nannies who served them freshly
baked cookies on porcelain plates and helped them to remove
their mud-soaked boots, if it was raining, lest they soil the lily-
white carpets. But should their boots accidentally sully the carpet,
or should their bright yellow raincoats inadvertently drip on the
sparkling linoleum, there would be a remedy for that as well.
And if their house should ever catch fire, a smart dog or a good
neighbor would rescue them just in time, and the fire trucks
would come right quick because some attentive neighbor would
call them.

Through the trail of voices that came up to comfort us, I heard
that the children's mother would be prosecuted for negligence
and child abandonment. I couldn't help but wonder, would our
parents have suffered the same fate had it been my brothers and
me who were killed in the fire?

When they began to repair the apartment across the hall,
I would occasionally sneak out to watch the workmen. They were
shelling the inside of the apartment and replacing everything from
the bedroom closets to the kitchen floors. I never saw the mother
of the dead boys again and never heard anything of her fate.

A year later, after the apartment was well polished and painted, two blind Haitian brothers and their sister moved in. They were all musicians and were part of a group called les Frères Parent, the Parent Brothers. Once my parents allowed my brothers and me to come home from school to our apartment, I would always listen carefully for our new tenants, so I'd be the first to know if anything went awry.

What I heard coming from the apartment soon after they moved in was music, "engagé" music, which the brothers were composing to protest against the dictatorship in Haiti, from which they had fled. The Parent Brothers and their sister, Lydie, did nothing but rehearse a cappella most days when they were not receiving religious and political leaders from Haiti and from the Haitian community in New York.

The same year after the fire, a cabdriver who lived down the hall in 6J was killed on a night shift in Manhattan; a good friend of my father's, a man who gave great Sunday afternoon parties in 6F, died of cirrhosis of the liver. One day while my brothers and I were at school and my parents were at work, someone came into our apartment through our fire escape and stole my father's expensive camera. That same year a Nigerian immigrant was shot and killed in front of the building across the street. To appease us, my mother said, "Nothing like that ever happens out of the blue. He was in a fight with someone." It was too troublesome for her to acknowledge that people could die randomly, senselessly, at Westbury Court or anywhere else.

Every day on my way back from school, I hurried past the flowers and candles piled in front of the spot where the Nigerian, whose name I didn't know, had been murdered. Still I never thought I was living in a violent place. It was an elevated castle above a clattering train tunnel, a blind alley where children from our building and the building across the street had erected a common basketball court for hot summer afternoon games, an urban yellow brick road where hopscotch squares dotted the sidewalk next to burned-out, abandoned cars. It was home.

My family and I moved out of Westbury Court three years after the fire. Every once in a while, though, the place came up in conversation, linked to either a joyous or a painful memory. One of the girls who had scalded her legs while boiling a pot of water for her bath during one of those no-heat days got married last year. After the burglar had broken into the house and taken my father's camera, my father—an amateur photography buff—never took another picture.

My family and I often reminisce about the Parent Brothers when we see them in Haitian newspapers or on television; we brag that we knew them when, before one of the brothers became a senator in Haiti and the sister, Lydie, became mayor of one of the better-off Haitian suburbs, Pétion-Ville. We never talk about the lost children.

Even now, I question what I remember about the children. Did they really die? Or did their mother simply move away with them after the fire? Maybe they were not even boys at all. Maybe they were two girls. Or one boy and one girl. Or maybe I am struggling to phase them out of my memory altogether. Not just them, but the fear that their destiny could have so easily been mine and my brothers'.

A few months ago, I asked my mother, "Do you remember the children and the fire at Westbury Court?"

Without missing a flutter of my breath, my mother replied, "Oh those children, those poor children, their poor mother. Sometimes it is too late to say, 'I shouldn't have.'"

## Reflections and Responses

1. Consider the way Danticat narrates her essay. What information does she introduce that she would not have known during the incident of the fire? What other methods of telling the story might she have chosen?

2. Why does Danticat emphasize her mother's response to the fire, referring to it at the time and then repeating it later? In what sense is her mother's comment a warning? How do you think Danticat wants us to interpret her mother's comment in the final paragraph?

3. Why do you think that after vividly describing the firefighters carrying out the "lifeless bodies of the two children," Danticat toward the end of the essay wonders whether the children actually did die? What effect does her wondering about this produce? Do you think it leaves the issue open-ended? In light of her questions, how are we to understand the final paragraph?

CHANG-RAE LEE

# *Magical Dinners*

*It's rare to read a well-written memoir that doesn't involve food early in its pages. While it's easy to take eating and drinking for granted in telling a life story, food is (or usually should be) intimately related to the way we remember our lives. Since Marcel Proust's French cookie flooded his mind with memories of childhood, novelists and essayists have reflected on their own upbringings through the prism of taste, finding complex metaphors and lessons in the dishes of their families and their youths. In this essay, Korean American writer Chang-Rae Lee reflects on the meaning of his hyphenated identity through the story of his immigrant mother's preparation of a traditional American meal—a Thanksgiving turkey.*

*Chang-Rae Lee was born in South Korea and emigrated to Westchester County, New York, with his family when he was three. After a short stint in the financial industry, he turned to writing fiction; his first novel,* Native Speaker *(1995), won the PEN/Hemingway Award, among other prizes. His other works include* A Gesture Life *(1999),* Aloft *(2004), and* The Surrendered *(2010). "Magical Dinners" first appeared in* The New Yorker *and was selected by Edwidge Danticat for* The Best American Essays 2011.

SO PICTURE THIS: Thanksgiving 1972. The Harbor House apartments on Davenport Avenue, New Rochelle, New York, red brick, low-rise, shot through with blacks and Puerto Ricans and then a smattering of us immigrants, the rest mostly white people of modest means, everyone deciding New York City is going to hell. Or, at least, that's the excuse. The apartments are cramped, hard-used, but the rent is low. Around the rickety dining room table, the end of which nearly blocks the front door, sit my father, my baby sister, myself, and my uncle, who with my aunt has come earlier this fall to attend graduate school. They're sleeping on the

*Source:* Best American Essays, 2011, Chang-Rae Lee, Magical Dinners.

pullout in the living room. In the abutting closet-size kitchen, my aunt is helping my mother, who is fretting over the turkey. Look how doughy-faced the grownups still are, so young and slim, like they shouldn't yet be out in the world. My father and uncle wear the same brow-line-style eyeglasses that have not yet gone out of fashion back in Seoul, the black plastic cap over the metal frames making them look perennially consternated, square. My mother and my aunt, despite aprons stained with grease and kimchi* juice, look pretty in their colorful polyester blouses with the sleeves rolled up, and volleying back and forth between the women and the men is much excited chatter about relatives back home (we're the sole permanent emigrants of either clan), of the economy and politics in the old country and in our new one, none of which I'm paying any mind. My sister and I, ages five and seven, the only ones speaking English, are talking about the bird in the oven—our very first—and already bickering over what parts are best, what parts the other should favor, our conception of it gleaned exclusively from television commercials and illustrations in magazines. We rarely eat poultry, because my mother is nauseated by the odor of raw chicken, but early in the preparations she brightly announces that this larger bird is different—it smells clean, even buttery—and I can already imagine how my father will slice into the grainy white flesh beneath the honeyed skin of the breast, this luscious sphere of meat that is being readied all around the apartment complex.

We like it here, mainly for the grounds outside. There's a grassy field for tag and ballgames, and a full play set of swings and slides and monkey bars and three concrete barrels laid on their sides, which are big enough to sit in and walk upside down around on your hands (and they offer some privacy too, if you desperately need to pee). There's a basketball court and two badly cracked asphalt tennis courts that my parents sometimes use, but have to weed a bit first. So what if teenagers smoke and drink beer on the benches at night, or if there's broken glass sprinkled about the playground. We're careful not to lose our footing, and make sure to come in well before dark.

And you can see the water from here. I like to sit by the windows when I can't go outside. With the right breeze, at low tide the mucky, clammy smell of Echo Bay flutters through the metal blinds. Sometimes, for no reason I can give, I lick the sharp edges of the blinds, the combination of tin and soot and sludgy pier a funky

*Kimchi is a traditional Korean cabbage dish.

pepper on the tongue. I already know that I have a bad habit. I'll sample the window screens too, the paint-cracked radiators, try the parquet wood flooring after my mother dusts, its slick surface faintly lemony and then bitter, like the skins of peanuts. I like the way my tongue buzzes from the copper electroplating on the bottom of her Revere Ware skillet, how it tickles my teeth the way a penny can't. My mother scolds me whenever she catches me, tells me I'm going to get sick, or worse. Why do you have to taste everything? What's the matter with you? I don't yet know to say, It's your fault.

One of my favorite things is to chew on the corner of our red-and-white-checked plastic tablecloth backed with cotton flocking and watch the slowly fading impression of my bites. It has the flavor of plastic, yes, but with a nutty oiliness, and then bears a sharper tang of the ammonia cleaner my mother obsessively sprays around our two-bedroom apartment. She'll pull out the jug of bleach too if she's seen a cockroach. There are grand armies of cockroaches here, and they're huge. She keeps the place dish clean, but it's still plagued by the pests stealing over, she is certain, from the neighboring units. Twice a year, the super bombs the building and they'll be scarce for a few weeks, until they show up again in the cupboard, the leaner, faster ones that have survived. You'll hear a sharp yelp from my mother, and a slammed cabinet door, and then nothing but harrowing silence before the metallic stink of bug spray wafts through the apartment like an old-time song. I know I shouldn't, but sometimes I'll breathe it in deeply, nearly making myself choke. For I'm a young splendid bug. I live on toxins and fumes. My mother, on the other hand, is getting more and more frustrated, hotly complaining to my father when he gets home: we've lived here for more than a year, and no matter what she does she can't bar them or kill them, and she's begun to think the only solution is to move, or else completely clear the kitchen of foodstuffs, not prepare meals here at all.

Of course, that's ridiculous. First, it's what she does. She does everything else too, but her first imperative is to cook for us. It's how she shapes our days and masters us and shows us her displeasure, her weariness, her love. She'll hail my sister and me from the narrow kitchen window, calling out our names and adding that dinner's on—*Bap muh-guh!*—the particular register of her voice instantly sailing to us through the hot murk and chaos of the playground. It's as if we had special receptors, vestigial ears in our bellies. There's a quickening, a sudden hop in the wrong direction: I gotta go! My mother is becoming notorious among the kids; they'll whine, with scorn and a note of envy, Hey, your mom's always calling you! And one big-framed, older girl named Kathy, who has sparkling jade-colored eyes and a prominent, bulging forehead that makes her look like a dolphin, viciously bullies me about it, taunting me, saying that I eat all the time, that I'm going to be a tub o' lard, that I love my mother too much. I say it's not true, though I fear it is. Plus, I'm terrified of Kathy, who on other days will tenderly pat my head and even hug me, telling me I'm cute, before suddenly clamping my ear, pinching harder and harder until my knees buckle; once she even makes me lob curses up at our kitchen window, words so heinous that they might as well be rocks. I remember my mother poking her head out and peering down, her expression tight, confused, most of all fearful of what I might be saying, and immediately I sob. Kathy sweetly tells her that I'm hungry. My mother, who understands little English and is maybe scared of this girl too, softly orders me to come in, then pulls in the casement window.

Once I'm upstairs, she offers me a snack—cookies, *kimbap,** a bowl of hot watery rice, which I eat with tiny squares of ham or leftover *bulgogi,* one spoon at a time. I eat while watching her cook. If she's not cleaning or laundering, she's cooking. Every so often, she'll make a point of telling me she hates it, that she no longer wants to bother but she has to because we must save money. We can't waste money eating out. My father is a newly minted psychiatrist, but his salary at the Bronx VA hospital is barely respectable, and we have no savings, no family in this country, no safety net. We dine out maybe four times a year, three of those for Chinese (there are no Korean restaurants yet), and the rest of the time my mother is at the stove—breakfast, lunch, dinner, as well as making snacks for us midmorning and afternoon, and then late at night for my father when he gets home. The other reality is that my parents don't want to eat non-Korean food; they want to hold on to what they know. What else do they have but the taste of those familiar dishes, which my mother can, for the most part, recreate from ingredients at the nearby A&P. She's grateful for the wide, shiny aisles of the chilled supermarket and its brightly lit inventory of canned goods and breakfast cereals and ice cream, but the cabbage is the wrong kind and the meat is oddly butchered and the fish has been set out on the shaved ice prefilleted, so she can't tell how fresh it is, and she can't make a good broth without the head and bones and skin. But she makes

*Kimbap** and **bulgogi** are Korean dishes made of steamed rice with vegetables and barbecued beef, respectively.

do; there's always garlic, often ginger and scallions, and passable hot peppers. We still have a few cups of the ground red-pepper powder that friends brought over from Seoul, and every once in a while we can get the proper oils and fresh tofu and dried anchovies and sheets of roasted seaweed on a Sunday drive down to Chinatown.

We adore those Chinatown days. I love them especially because it means we skip church and the skeptical regard of the pastor and his wife and the bellowing Hananims* and Amens from the congregation that for me are calls to slumber—a break that I see now my parents welcome too. Somewhere on Bayard or Mott Street, we'll have a lunch of soup noodles or dim sum and do the shopping with an eye on the time, because the parking lot is expensive and by the hour, and, despite the parade-level litter and the grimy bins of dying eels and carp and the lacquer of black crud on the sidewalks, which she would never otherwise tolerate, my mother seems calmed by the Asian faces and the hawker carts of fried pot stickers and gooey rice cakes and the cans of stewed mackerel and chiles filling the shelves. She'll go unexpectedly slowly through the crammed aisles of the dry-goods store, lingering over selections that aren't exactly what she's looking for but that nonetheless speak to her in a voice I imagine sounds very much like her own: Take your time, silly girl. Enjoy yourself. You're not going anywhere. Soon enough, the bags of groceries are teetering like drowsy siblings between my sister and me in the back seat of our navy-blue Beetle as we swerve up the FDR Drive. The seats are covered in a light-gray leatherette stippled like the back of a lizard, which I'm constantly picking at with my fingernail, inevitably running over with my tongue. It tastes of erasers and throw-up. My father is one of those people who drive by toggling on and off the gas pedal, lurching us forward for brief stretches and then coasting, the rattling of the fifty-three-horsepower engine establishing the dread prophetic beat, my sister and I know, of our roadside retching—one of us, and sometimes both, barely stumbling out of the car in time to splash the parkway asphalt, stucco the nettles. Now, with the odor of dried squid and spring onions and raw pork enveloping us, we'd be doomed, but luckily we don't have too far to go to get back to New Rochelle; my father will let us out before searching for a parking spot, my sister and I sprinting for the playground while my mother goes upstairs to empty the bags.

---

*Hananim is the supreme god of ancient Korean religion; Bayard and Mott are both streets in New York's Chinatown.

On those post-Chinatown evenings, she'll set out a plate of fluke or snapper sashimi to start (if she finds any fresh enough), which she serves with *gochu-jang** sauce, then broiled spareribs and scallion fritters and a spicy cod-head stew along with the *banchan*† of vegetables and kimchi, and it's all so perfect-looking, so gorgeous, that we let out that whimpering, joyous, half-grieving sigh of people long marooned. Yet often enough, apparently, the dishes don't taste exactly the way they should. My father, the least imperious of men, might murmur the smallest something about the spicing of a dish, its somewhat unusual flavorings, and my mother will bitterly concur, lamenting the type of fermented bean paste she has to use, the stringy quality of the meat, how these Chinatown radishes have no flavor, no crunch, instantly grinding down her lovely efforts to a wan, forgettable dust. We protest in earnest, but it's no use; she's not seeking compliments or succor. She can get frantic; she's a natural perfectionist and worrier made over, by this life in a strange country, into someone too easily distraught. In Korea, she's a forthright, talented, beautiful woman, but here, at least outside this apartment, she is a woman who appears even slighter than she already is, a woman who smiles quickly but never widely, a foreigner whose English comes out self-throttled, barely voiced, who is listening to herself to the point of a whisper.

Never quite up to her own exalted standards, she is often frustrated, dark-thinking, on edge. Periodically I'll catch her gripped in fury at herself for not quite comprehending, say, the instructions on a box of Rice-A-Roni or Hamburger Helper (seemingly magical dinners that my sister and I whine for, despite not actually liking the stuff), revealed in her wringing the packet like a towel until it's about to burst, then remorsefully opening it and smoothing it out and trying to decipher the back of the box again. I do something similar with toys that I can't get to work properly, or am tiring of, or sometimes—and with an unequaled, almost electric pleasure—the ones I value most. I'll take the claw end of a hammer and pry open the roof of a Hot Wheels car, the enamel paint flaking off from the twisting force and gilding my fingertips. I'll squeeze the clear plastic canopy of the model P-51 Mustang I've carefully assembled until it collapses, the head of the tiny half-pilot inside shearing off. We are mother and son in this way—we share

---

*****Gochu-jang** is a popular spicy Korean condiment.

†**banchan** refers to small servings of various foods meant to be shared.

a compulsion we don't admire in the other but never call out either, and right up to the unsparingly frigid night she dies, nineteen years later, and even now, another nineteen on, I'll prickle with that heat in my foolish, foolish hands.

A few years earlier, when we briefly lived in Manhattan—this before I can articulate my feelings for her, before I understand how completely and perfectly I can hurt her—I make her cry because of a fried egg. She cooks an egg for me each morning without fail. I might also have with it fried Spam or cereal or a slice of American cheese, which I'll unwrap myself and fold over into sixteen rough-edged pieces, but always there is a fried egg, sunny-side up, cooked in dark sesame oil that pools on the surface of the bubbled-up white in the pattern of an archipelago; try one sometime, laced with soy and sweet chili sauce along with steamed rice, the whole plate flecked with toasted nori. It'll corrupt you for all time. But one morning I'm finally sick of it, I've had enough. She never makes an exception, because it's for my health— everything is for my health, for the good of my bones, my brain, for my daunting, uncertain future—but rather than eat yet another, I steal into her bedroom with my plate while she's talking on the telephone with Mrs. Suh (at that time her only friend in the country) and drop it onto her best shoes, black patent-leather pumps. And here's the rub: there is no sound a fried egg makes. It lands with exquisite silence. This is the dish I've been longing to prepare.

Do I confess what I've done? Does my face betray the crime? All I remember is how my mother, still holding the phone, and my baby sister, usually squirming in her high chair, both pause and stare at me as I return to the kitchen table. My mother bids Mrs. Suh goodbye and stands over me, eyeing my plate swiped clean save for the glistening oil. Without a word from either of us, I'm dragged forth, her hand gripping my elbow, and we're inexplicably moving. It's as if a homing beacon only she can hear were madly pinging from her bedroom, where I've left the sliding closet door open for all to see my work: the yolk broken and ooz-ing inside the well of one shoe, the rubbery white flopped over the shiny ebony toe. It's a jarring, bizarrely artful mess; boxed in Lucite, it could be titled "Stepping Out, 4," or "Mother's Day Fugue," but of course she can't see it that way because she's hol-lering, her morning robe falling open because she's shaking so violently, stamping her foot. The end of the robe's belt is bunched in her tensed fist, and I think, She may kill me, actually kill me. Or my father will do the job when he gets home. But I'm hugging her leg now, my face pressed against her hip, and as much as I'm afraid for myself, I'm confused too, and frightened for her, for tears are distorting her eyes, and she's saying, in a voice that I will hear always for its quaver of defiance and forfeit, how difficult everything is, how wrong and difficult.

She's too indulgent of us, especially of me. I love to eat, so it's easy for her, though also at times a burden for us both. Each morning at breakfast, after the egg, she asks me what I want for dinner, and except when my father requests Japanese-style curry rice, which I despise (though I enjoy it now) and show my disgust for by dragging my chair into the kitchen and closing the louvered doors to "get away" from the smell, my choice is what we'll have. As with an emperor, my whims become real. Dinners-from-a-box aside, I have wide-ranging tastes, but increasingly it's American food I want, dishes I encounter while eating at friends' apartments, at summer camp, even in the cafeteria at school: meat loaf (with a boiled egg in the middle), southern fried chicken and mashed potatoes, beef Stroganoff over egg noodles, lasagna. These dishes are much heavier and plainer than ours, but more thrilling to me and my sister and perhaps even to my parents, for it is food without association, unlinked to any past; it's food that fixes us to this moment only, to this place we hardly know.

My mother, having no idea how the dishes should taste, at first struggles to prepare them, going solely by recipes that she copies into a small notebook from a new friend in the building, Mrs. Churchill, an always smiling, blond-haired, broad-shouldered woman who hails from Vermont and has a shelf of classic cookbooks. It's excruciatingly slow going at the A&P as my mother runs down her shopping list—it's as if she were at the library searching for a book in the stacks, trying to find the particular spices and herbs, the right kind of macaroni, the right kind of cheese or cream (heavy or sour or cream or cottage cheese and a perhaps related cheese called ricotta and the deeply puzzling cheese that is Parmesan, which comes in a shaker, and is unrefrigerated), the right canned tomatoes (chopped or crushed or puréed—what, exactly, is "puréed"?), each decision another chance to mar the dish beyond my ignorant recognition. I can be tyrannical, if I wish. I can squash her whole day's work with a grimace, or some blithe utterance: It's fatty. It's too peppery. It doesn't taste the same. You can watch her face ice over. Shatter. Naturally, she can't counter me, and this makes her furious, but soon enough she's simply miserable, her pretty eyes gone lightless and faraway, which is when I relent and tell her it's still good, because of course it is, which I demonstrate by shoving the food in as fast as I can, stuffing my awful mouth.

Her lasagna is our favorite of that suite, though to taste it now I fear it might disappoint me, for the factory sauce (which I demand she use, this after noticing jars of Ragú at both the Goldfusses' and the Stanleys') and the rubbery, part-skim mozzarella, the cut-rate store-brand pasta, the dried herbs. But back then, it's a revelation. Our usual dinners feature salty fish and ginger, garlic and hot pepper; they are delicious in part because you can surgically pick at the table, choose the exact flavor you want. But this is a detonation of a meal: creamy, cheesy, the red sauce contrastingly tangy and a little sweet, the oozing, volcanic layer cake of the pasta a thrilling, messy bed. Maybe I first have it at Ronnie Prunesti's house, or Mrs. Churchill delivers a show model, but all of us are crazy for it once my mother begins to make it. We choose our recipe (was it on the box of macaroni?), our tools. I remember how she carefully picked out a large Pyrex casserole dish at Korvette's for the job, a new plastic spatula, two checkerboard wooden trivets, so we can place it in the center of the table, and for a few years it becomes a Friday evening tradition for us. She makes it in the afternoon after dropping me off in town for my junior bowling league, and when she and my sister pick me up I hardly care to recount my form or my scores (I'm quite good for a second-grader, good enough that my father decides that I should have my own ball, which is, whether intentionally or erroneously, inscribed "Ray") owing to the wonderful smell on their clothes, clinging to my mother's thick hair—that baked, garlicky aroma, like a pizzeria's but denser because of the ground beef and the hot Italian sausages she has fried, the herbal lilt of fennel seeds.

My father gets home early on Fridays, and while he takes off his tie and washes up for dinner my sister and I set the table with forks and knives (but without chopsticks, since I insist that there be no side of rice and kimchi at this meal, as there is at every other), folding the paper napkins into triangles. My mother brings out a bowl of iceberg-and-tomato-and-carrot salad, a dish of garlic bread, my sister waiting for the Good Seasons Italian dressing to separate so she can start shaking it again. I wonder aloud if my father ought to retrieve from the top of the kitchen cabinet the clay-colored ceramic bottle of Lancers they got as a present (they rarely drink), if only because it makes the table look right. They do, although the wine is old, for they forget that they opened it a month before, when a classmate came through New York. But no matter. They don't know that the wine has soured. My mother will

lift out fat squares of the casserole, the fine strings of cheese band-
ing across the table; I scissor them with my fingers and flinch at
the tiny-striped burn. We feast. Only my sister can eat just one.
Who cares that it's too rich for us to handle, who cares that our
family affliction of mild lactose intolerance will surely lead to guf-
faws and antic hand-fanning during the Friday night repeat of the
Million Dollar Movie. Here is the meal we've been working
toward, yearning for. Here is the unlikely shape of our life
together—this ruddy pie, what we have today and forever.

This is what a boy thinks, a boy with a tongue for a brain, a
heart.

Now my mother is nearly done baking the turkey. Bake she
must, because there's no Roast setting on the oven. It reads
"Roast" in Mrs. Churchill's beautifully handwritten instructions,
and the Churchills have gone away for the holiday. There's no
one else we can call—at least, no one who would know. It certainly
smells good, as if we were going to have a soup of pure fat. Yet my
mother desperately peers in at the bird, the tendrils of her hair
stuck against her temples, biting her lower lip, as she does whenever she's frustrated or unsure of herself. She has been basting it
with margarine and the pan juices, but I can see she's deeply worried, for the bird was still slightly frozen when my father shoved it
in, and we've been baking instead of roasting and we have no
meat thermometer ("Why didn't I buy one!"), and at some point
amid the continuous conversation with my uncle and aunt we've
lost exact track of the time.

My mother has readied other food, of course, if none of the
traditional accompaniments. We'll have the bird and its giblet
stuffing à la Churchill (a recipe I still make), but the rest of the
table is laid with Korean food, and skewed fancy besides, featuring
the sort of dishes reserved for New Year celebrations: *gu jeol pan,* a
nine-compartment tray of savory fillings from which delicate little
crepes are made; a jellyfish-and-seaweed salad; long-simmered
sweet short ribs; fried hot peppers stuffed with beef; and one of
my favorites, thin slices of raw giant clam, whose bottom-
of-the-sea essence almost makes me gag, but doesn't quite, and is
thus bracing, galvanic, a rushing of the waters. Yet because of
what's happening in the kitchen, we're not paying much attention;
we're distracted by our celebrity guest, so buxom and tanned. My
mother decides it's time; a piece of plastic has popped up from
the breast, though exactly when she's not sure. My father helps
her pull the turkey out and they lift it from the pan, cradling it
with butcher string, onto the platter. We quickly take our places.

Do we remove the stuffing now or serve it directly from the bird? The instructions don't say. After some discussion, it's decided that it should be left in—the bird might look too empty, sad. My father wields the new carving knife he's bought, a long, scary blade with a saw-toothed edge on one side and smaller serrations on the other. My mother winces. The knife strobes: the first cut is deep, surprisingly easy.

## Reflections and Responses

1. Lee refers to American food, favorably, as "food without association, unlinked to any past; it's food that fixes us to this moment only, to this place we hardly know." Why does the young Lee find comfort and excitement in lasagna and other American foods? How does the tone of the mature Lee's writing suggest that his attitude has changed as he looks back?

2. What does the story of the fried egg in the shoe add to the essay as a whole? How does it frame the author's relationship with his mother and explain the "magic" surrounding the various dinners he describes? How do food and family relate in this brief vignette, and in its larger context in the essay?

3. Why does Lee end the essay as he does, with the first slice of the turkey? What is the importance of the bird being "surprisingly easy" to cut, and what is the effect of leaving out the actual tasting of the food? Analyze the entire Thanksgiving scene in terms of how its themes have been introduced and foreshadowed by the rest of the essay.

1. talking about working at his summer job even though he said he wouldn't
2. work at Vietnam
3. Time at a machinery

## YUSEF KOMUNYAKAA

4. Back to flashbacks with vietnam working
5. Getting out of working at a factory job

# The Blue Machinery of Summer

Plot.

*The central purpose behind an autobiographical essay can sometimes remain obscure, never explicitly stated by the writer, who may be more interested in self-exploration than full disclosure, more concerned with raising questions than with answering them. Essayists are under no obligation to write only about personal experiences they fully understand. In "The Blue Machinery of Summer," an essay full of questions and "maybes," one of America's foremost poets describes his successes and failures years ago at a summer factory job that forced him to realize the difficulties his education would bring.*

*Yusef Komunyakaa, who has received numerous honors and awards, including a 1994 Pulitzer Prize for* Neon Vernacular, *the 2001 Ruth Lilly Poetry Prize, and a Bronze Star for service as a journalist in Vietnam, was born in Bogalusa, Louisiana, in 1947. His first book of poetry,* Dedications & Other Darkhorses, *appeared in 1977; subsequent volumes include* Copacetic *(1984);* I Apologize for the Eyes in My Head *(1986);* Dien Cai Dau *(1988);* Magic City *(1992);* Thieves of Paradise *(1998);* Talking Dirty to the Gods *(2000);* Pleasure Dome: New and Collected Poems *(2001); and* Taboo: The Wishbone Trilogy, Part I *(2004). He has written extensively on jazz and in 1999 was elected a Chancellor of the Academy of American Poets. Currently Distinguished Senior Poet in New York University's graduate creative writing program, Komunyakaa has most recently published* Gilgamesh: A Verse Play *(2006),* Warhorses: Poems *(2008), and the award-winning* The Chameleon Couch *(2012). "The Blue Machinery of Summer" first appeared in* The Washington Post Magazine *and was selected by Kathleen Norris for* The Best American Essays 2001.

*Source:* "The Blue Machinery of Summer" by Yusef Komunyakaa. Reprinted by permission of the author.

"I feel like I'm part of this damn thing," Frank said. He carried himself like a large man even though he was short. A dead cigarette dangled from his half-grin. "I've worked on this machine for twenty-odd years, and now it's almost me."

It was my first day on a summer job at ITT Cannon in Phoenix in 1979. This factory manufactured parts for electronic systems— units that fit into larger, more complex ones. My job was to operate an air-powered punch press. Depending on each item formed, certain dies or templates were used to cut and shape metal plates into designs the engineers wanted.

"I know all the tricks of the trade, big and small, especially when it comes to these punch presses. It seems like I was born riding this hunk of steel."

Frank had a gift for gab, but when the foreman entered, he grew silent and meditative, bent over the machine, lost in his job. The whole day turned into one big, rambunctious dance of raw metal, hiss of steam, and sparks. Foremen strutted about like banty roosters. Women tucked falling curls back into hair nets, glancing at themselves in anything chrome.

This job reminded me of the one I'd had in 1971 at McGraw Edison, also in Phoenix, a year after I returned from Vietnam. Back then, I had said to myself, this is the right setting for a soap opera. Muscle and sex changed the rhythm of this place. We'd call the show "The Line."

I'd move up and down the line, shooting screws into metal cabinets of coolers and air conditioners—one hour for Montgomery Ward or Sears, and the next two hours for a long line of cabinets stamped McGraw Edison. The designs differed only slightly, but made a difference in the selling price later on. The days seemed endless, and it got to where I could do the job with my eyes closed.

In retrospect, I believe I was hyper from the war. I couldn't lay back; I was driven to do twice the work expected—sometimes taking on both sides of the line, giving other workers a hand. I worked overtime two hours before 7 A.M. and one hour after 4 P.M. I learned everything about coolers and air conditioners, and rectified problem units that didn't pass inspection.

At lunch, rather than sitting among other workers, I chose a secluded spot near the mountain of boxed-up coolers to eat my homemade sandwiches and sip iced tea or lemonade. I always had a paperback book in my back pocket: Richard Wright's *Black Boy*, Albert Camus' *The Fall*, Frantz Fanon's *The Wretched of the Earth*, or C. W. E. Bigsby's *The Black American Writer*. I wrote notes in the margins with a ballpoint. I was falling in love with language and ideas. All my attention went to reading.

When I left the gaze of Arizona's Superstition Mountain and headed for the Colorado Rockies, I wasn't thinking about higher education. Once I was in college, I vowed never to take another job like this, and yet here I was, eight years later, a first-year graduate student at the University of California at Irvine, and working another factory job in Phoenix, hypnotized by the incessant clang of machinery.

Frank schooled me in the tricks of the trade. He took pride in his job and practiced a work ethic similar to the one that had shaped my life early on even though I had wanted to rebel against it. Frank was from Little Rock: in Phoenix, everyone seemed to be from somewhere else except the indigenous Americans and Mexicans.

"If there's one thing I know, it's this damn machine," Frank said. "Sometimes it wants to act like it has a brain of its own, as if it owns me, but I know better."

"Iron can wear any man out," I said.

"Not this hunk of junk. It was new when I came here."

"But it'll still be here when you're long gone."

"Says who?"

"Says iron against flesh."

"They will scrap this big, ugly bastard when I'm gone."

"They'll bring in a new man."

"Are you the new man, whippersnapper? They better hire two of you to replace one of me."

"Men will be men."

"And boys will be boys."

The hard dance held us in its grip.

I spotted Lily Huong the second day in a corner of the wiring department. The women there moved their hands in practiced synchrony, looping and winding color-coded wires with such graceful dexterity and professionalism. Some chewed gum and blew bubbles, others smiled to themselves as if they were reliving the weekend. And a good number talked about the soap operas, naming off the characters as if they were family members or close friends.

Lily was in her own world. Petite, with long black hair grabbed up, stuffed beneath a net and baseball cap, her body was one fluid motion, as if it knew what it was doing and why.

"Yeah, boys will be boys," Frank said.

"What you mean?"

"You're looking at trouble, my friend."

"Maybe trouble is looking for me. And if it is, I'm not running."

"She is nothing but bona fide trouble."

I wonder if she was thinking of Vietnam while she sat bent over the table, or when she glided across the concrete floor as if she

were moving through lush grass. Lily? It made me think of water-
lily, lotus—how shoots and blooms were eaten in that faraway
land. The lotus grows out of decay, in lagoons dark with sediment
and rot.

*This is so sad!*

Mornings arrived with the taste of sweet nighttime still in our
mouths, when the factory smelled like the deepest ore, and the
syncopation of the great heaving presses fascinated me.

The nylon and leather safety straps fit our hands like fingerless
gloves and sometimes seemed as if they'd pull us into the thunderous pneumatic vacuum faster than an eye blink. These beasts
pulsed hypnotically; they reminded everyone within earshot of terrifying and sobering accidents. The machinery's dance of smooth
heft seemed extraordinary, a masterpiece of give-and-take precision. If a foolhardy novice wrestled with one of these metal con-
traptions, it would suck up the hapless soul. The trick was to give
and pull back with a timing that meant the difference between life
and death.

*very descriptive paragraph*

"Always use a safety block, one of these chunks of wood. Don't
get careless," Frank said. "Forget the idea you can second-guess
this monster. Two months ago we had a guy in here named Leo
on that hunk of junk over there, the one that Chico is now riding."

"Yeah, and?"

"I don't believe it. It's crazy. I didn't know Leo was a fool. The
machine got stuck, he bent down, looked underneath, and never
knew his last breath. That monster flattened his head like a
pancake."

One morning, I stood at the checkout counter signing out my
tools for the day's work and caught a glimpse of Lily out of the
corner of my eye. She stopped. Our eyes locked for a moment,
and then she glided on toward her department. Did she know
I had been in 'Nam? Had there been a look in my eyes that had
given me away?

"You can't be interested in her," Paula said. She pushed her hair
away from her face in what seemed like an assured gesture.

"Why not?" I said.

"She's nothing, nothing but trouble."

"Oh?"

"Anyway, you ain't nobody's foreman."

I took my toolbox and walked over to the punch press. The
buzzer sounded. The gears kicked in. The day started.

After three weeks, I discovered certain social mechanisms ran
the place. The grapevine, long, tangled, and thorny, was merciless.
After a month on the job I had been wondering why Frank

disappeared at lunchtime but always made it back just minutes before the buzzer.

"I bet Frank tells you why he comes back here with a smile on his mug?" Maria coaxed. She worked as a spot-welder, with most of her day spent behind heavy black goggles as the sparks danced around her.

"No."

"Why don't you ask Paula one of these mornings when you're signing out tools?"

"I don't think so," I said.

"She's the one who puts that grin on his face. They've been tearing up that rooming house over on Sycamore for years."

"Good for them," I said.

"Not if that cop husband of hers come to his senses."

It would have been cruel irony for Frank to work more than twenty years on the monster and lose his life at the hands of a mere mortal.

The grapevine also revealed that Lily had gotten on the payroll because of Rico, who was a foreman on the swing shift. They had been lovers and he had put in a good word for her. Rico was built like a lightweight boxer, his eyes bright and alert, always able to look over the whole room in a single glance. The next news said Lily was sleeping with Steve, the shipping foreman, who wore western shirts, a silver and turquoise belt buckle, and cowboy boots. His red Chevy pickup had a steer's horn on the hood. He was tall and lanky and had been in the Marines, stationed at Khe Sanh.

I wondered about Lily. What village or city had she come from—Chu Chi or Danang, Saigon or Hue? What was her story? Did she still hear the war during sleepless nights? Maybe she had had an American boyfriend, maybe she was in love with a Vietnamese once, a student, and they had intimate moments besides the Perfume River as boats with green and red lanterns passed at dusk. Or maybe she met him on the edge of a rice paddy, or in some half-lit place in Danang a few doors down from the Blue Dahlia.

She looked like so many who tried to outrun past lovers, history. "*She's nothing but trouble ...*" Had she become a scapegoat? Had she tried to play a game that wasn't hers to play? Didn't anyone notice her black eye one week, the corner of her lip split the next?

I told myself I would speak to her. I didn't know when, but I would.

The women were bowed over their piecework.

As a boy I'd make bets with myself, and as a man I was still making bets, and sometimes they left me in some strange situations.

"In New Guinea those Fuzzy Wuzzies saved our asses," Frank said. "They're the smartest people I've ever seen. One moment almost in the Stone Age, and the next they're zooming around in our jeeps and firing automatic weapons like nobody's business. They gave the Japanese hell. They were so outrageously brave it still hurts to think about it."

I wanted to tell him about Vietnam, a few of the things I'd witnessed, but I couldn't. I could've told him about the South Vietnamese soldiers who were opposites of Frank's heroes.

I gazed over toward Lily.

Holding up one of the doodads—we were stamping out hundreds hourly—I said to Frank, "Do you know what this is used for?"

"No. Never crossed my mind."

"You don't know? How many do you think you've made?"

"God only knows."

"And you don't know what they're used for?"

"No."

"How much does each sell for?"

"Your guess is as good as mine. I make 'em. I don't sell 'em."

He's right, I thought. Knowing wouldn't change these workers' lives. This great symphony of sweat, oil, steel, rhythm, it all made a strange kind of sense.

"These are used in the firing mechanisms of grenade launchers," I said as I scooped up a handful. "And each costs the government almost eighty-five dollars."

The buzzer sounded.

In the cafeteria, most everybody sat in their usual clusters. A few of the women read magazines—*True Romance, Tan, TV Guide, Reader's Digest*—as they nibbled at sandwiches and sipped Cokes. One woman was reading her Bible. I felt like the odd man out as I took my paperback from my lunch pail: a Great Books Foundation volume, with blue-white-black cover and a circle around GB. My coworkers probably thought I was reading the same book all summer long, or that it was a religious text. I read Voltaire, Hegel, and Darwin.

Voltaire spoke to me about Equality:

All the poor are not unhappy. The greater number are born in that state, and constant labor prevents them from too sensibly feeling their situation; but when they do strongly feel it, then follow wars such as these of the popular party against the Senate at Rome, and those of the peasantry in Germany, England and France. All these wars ended sooner or later in the subjection of the people, because the great have money, and money in a state commands everything: I say in a state, for the case is different between nation and nation. The nation that makes the best use of iron will always subjugate another that has more gold but less courage.

Maybe I didn't want to deal with those images of 'Nam still in my psyche, ones that Lily had rekindled.

"You catch on real fast, friend," Frank said. "It is hard to teach a man how to make love to a machine. It's almost got to be in your blood. If you don't watch out, you'll be doing twenty in this sweatbox too. Now mark my word."

I wanted to tell him about school. About some of the ideas filling my head. Lily would smile, but she looked as if she were gazing through me.

One morning in early August, a foreman said they needed me to work on a special unit. I was led through the security doors. The room was huge, and the man working on the big, circular-dome object seemed small and insignificant in the voluminous space. Then I was shaking hands with the guy they called Dave the Lathe. Almost everyone had a nickname here, as in the Deep South, where, it turned out, many of the workers were from. The nicknames came from the almost instinctual impulse to make language a game of insinuation.

Dave was from Paradise, California. He showed me how to polish each part, every fixture and pin. The work led to painstaking tedium. Had I posed too many questions? Was that why I was working this job?

Here everything was done by hand, with patience and silence. The room was air-conditioned. Now the clang of machines and whine of metal being cut retreated into memory. Behind this door Dave the Lathe was a master at shaping metals, alloyed with secrets, a metal that could be smoothed but wouldn't shine, take friction and heat out of this world. In fact, it looked like a fine piece of sculpture designed aeronautically, that approached perfection. Dave the Lathe had been working on this nose cone for a spacecraft for more than five months.

Dave and I seldom talked. Lily's face receded from my thoughts. Now I stood across from Dave the Lathe, thinking about two women in my class back at the University of California with the same first name. One was from New York. She had two reproductions of French nudes over her bed and was in love with Colette, the writer. The other woman was part Okinawan from Honolulu. If we found ourselves in a room alone, she always managed to disengage herself. We had never had a discussion, but here she was, undressing in my mind. At that moment, standing a few feet from Dave the Lathe, I felt that she and I were made for each other but she didn't know it yet. *kind of weird*

I told Dave that within two weeks I'd return to graduate school. He wished me luck in a tone that suggested he knew what I'd planned to say before I said it.

"Hey, college boy!" Maria shouted across the cafeteria. "Are you in college or did you do time like Frank says?" I wanted the impossible, to disappear.

Lily's eyes caught mine. I still hadn't told her I felt I'd left part of myself in her country. Maria sat down beside me. I fished out the ham sandwich, but left Darwin in the lunch box. She said, "You gonna just soft-shoe in here and then disappear, right?"

"No. Not really."

"Not *really*, he says," she mocked.

"Well."

"Like a lousy lover who doesn't tell you everything. Doesn't tell the fine print."

"Well."

"Cat got your tongue, college boy?"

"Are you talking to me or somebody else?"

"Yeah, you! Walk into somebody's life and then turn into a ghost. A one-night stand."

"I didn't think anyone needed to know."

"I suppose you're too damn good to tell us the truth."

She stood up, took her lunch over to another table, sat down, and continued to eat. I didn't know what to say. I was still learning.

There's good silence. There's bad silence. Growing up in rural Louisiana, along with four brothers and one sister, I began to cultivate a life of the imagination. I traveled to Mexico, Africa, and the Far East. When I was in elementary school and junior high, sometimes I knew the answers to questions, but I didn't dare raise my hand. Boys and girls danced up and down, waving their arms, with right and wrong answers. It was hard for me to chance being wrong. Also, I found it difficult to share my feelings; but I always broke the silence and stepped in if someone was being mistreated. *This is exactly me.*

Now, as I sat alone, looking out the window of a Greyhound bus at 1 A.M., I felt like an initiate who had gotten cold feet and was hightailing it back to some privileged safety zone. I began to count the figures sprawled on the concrete still warm from the sun's weight on the city. There seemed to be an uneasy equality among destitutes: indigenous Americans, Mexicans, a few blacks and whites. Eleven. Twelve. I thought, a massacre of the spirit.

The sounds of the machines were still inside my head. The clanging punctuated by Frank's voice: "Are you ready to will your body to this damn beast, my friend?"

"No, Frank. I never told you I am going to college," I heard myself saying. Did education mean moving from one class to the next? My grandmothers told me again and again that one could scale a mountain with a good education. But could I still talk to them, to my parents, my siblings? I would try to live in two worlds—at the very least. That was now my task. I never wanted again to feel that my dreams had betrayed me.

Maybe the reason I hadn't spoken to Lily was I didn't want to talk about the war. I hadn't even acknowledged to my friends that I'd been there.

The bus pulled out, headed for L.A. with its headlights sweeping like slow yellow flares across drunken faces, as if images of the dead had followed Lily and me from a distant land only the heart could bridge. *This paragraph/ending doesn't make sense to me.*

## Reflections and Responses

1. What images does Komunyakaa use early in his essay to link the assembly-line work, the machinery, and sexuality? Why do you think he wants to establish these links?

2. Why do you think Komunyakaa informs us about his reading? What kind of books does he seem to prefer? Why do you think he includes a long quotation from Voltaire in an essay that is almost entirely personal?

3. How does Komunyakaa present himself in this essay? How does he portray the way his fellow workers relate to him? How does he relate to his fellow workers? What role does Lily Huong play in the essay? What sense do you make of his final conversation with Maria toward the end of the essay? What is she saying about him? How do her comments link up with the sexual themes introduced early in the essay?

SCOTT RUSSELL SANDERS

# The Inheritance of Tools

*A heritage is not only ethnic or cultural; it can also be a code of behavior, a system of manners, or even the practical skills that grandparents and parents often pass along to their children. In this widely reprinted personal essay, a writer, upon hearing of his father's sudden death, is reminded of the tools and techniques he inherited from his grandfather and father, which he in turn is now passing along to his own children. Though these tools and techniques have literally to do with carpentry, they take on extra duty in this finely crafted essay in which the hand tools themselves become equivalent to works of art: "I look at my claw hammer, the distillation of a hundred generations of carpenters, and consider that it holds up well beside those other classics—Greek vases, Gregorian chants,* Don Quixote, *barbed fish hooks, candles, spoons."*

*Scott Russell Sanders is the author of more than a dozen books of fiction, science fiction, essays, and nonfiction; these include* Stone Country *(1985),* The Paradise of Bombs *(1987),* Secrets of the Universe *(1991),* Staying Put *(1993),* Hunting for Hope: A Father's Journeys *(1998),* The Force of Spirit *(2001), and* A Private History of Awe *(2006).* Writing from the Center *(1994) is a volume of essays about living and working in the Midwest. His most recent books are* A Conservationist Manifesto *(2009) and a comprehensive collection,* Earth Works: Selected Essays *(2012). The recipient of many prestigious writing awards and fellowships, Sanders is a professor of English at Indiana University. "The Inheritance of Tools" originally appeared in* The North American Review *(1986) and was selected by Gay Talese for* The Best American Essays 1987.

At just about the hour when my father died, soon after dawn one February morning when ice coated the windows like cataracts,

*Source:* "The Inheritance of Tools" by Scott Russell Sanders. First published in *The North American Review.* Copyright © 1986 by Scott Russell Sanders. Reprinted by permission of the author. "The Inheritance of Tools" also appears in the author's collection *The Paradise of Bombs* published by Beacon Press in 1993.

I banged my thumb with a hammer. Naturally I swore at the hammer, the reckless thing, and in the moment of swearing I thought of what my father would say: "If you'd try hitting the nail it would go in a whole lot faster. Don't you know your thumb's not as hard as that hammer?" We both were doing carpentry that day, but far apart. He was building cupboards at my brother's place in Oklahoma; I was at home in Indiana, putting up a wall in the basement to make a bedroom for my daughter. By the time my mother called with news of his death—the long distance wires whittling her voice until it seemed too thin to bear the weight of what she had to say—my thumb was swollen. A week or so later a white scar in the shape of a crescent moon began to show above the cuticle, and month by month it rose across the pink sky of my thumbnail. It took the better part of a year for the scar to disappear, and every time I noticed it I thought of my father.

The hammer had belonged to him, and to his father before him. The three of us have used it to build houses and barns and chicken coops, to upholster chairs and crack walnuts, to make doll furniture and bookshelves and jewelry boxes. The head is scratched and pockmarked, like an old plowshare that has been working rocky fields, and it gives off the sort of dull sheen you see on fast creek water in the shade. It is a finishing hammer, about the weight of a bread loaf, too light, really, for framing walls, too heavy for cabinet work, with a curved claw for pulling nails, a rounded head for pounding, a fluted neck for looks, and a hickory handle for strength.

The present handle is my third one, bought from a lumberyard in Tennessee, down the road from where my brother and I were helping my father build his retirement house. I broke the previous one by trying to pull sixteen-penny nails out of floor joists—a foolish thing to do with a finishing hammer, as my father pointed out. "You ever hear of a crowbar?" he said. No telling how many handles he and my grandfather had gone through before me. My grandfather used to cut down hickory trees on his farm, saw them into slabs, cure the planks in his hayloft, and carve handles with a drawknife. The grain in hickory is crooked and knotty, and therefore tough, hard to split, like the grain in the two men who owned this hammer before me.

After proposing marriage to a neighbor girl, my grandfather used this hammer to build a house for his bride on a stretch of river bottom in northern Mississippi. The lumber for the place, like the hickory for the handle, was cut on his own land. By the day of the wedding he had not quite finished the house, and so right after the ceremony he took his wife home and put her to work. My grandmother had worn her Sunday dress for the wedding, with a fringe of lace tacked on around the hem in honor of the occasion. She removed this lace and folded it away before going out to help my grandfather nail siding on the house. "There she was in her good dress," he told me some fifty-odd years after that wedding day, "holding up them long pieces of clapboard while I hammered, and together we got the place covered up before dark." As the family grew to four, six, eight, and eventually thirteen, my grandfather used this hammer to enlarge his house room by room, like a chambered nautilus expanding its shell.

By and by the hammer was passed along to my father. One day he was up on the roof of our pony barn nailing shingles with it, when I stepped out the kitchen door to call him for supper. Before I could yell, something about the sight of him straddling the spine of that roof and swinging the hammer caught my eye and made me hold my tongue. I was five or six years old, and the world's commonplaces were still news to me. He would pull a nail from the pouch at his waist, bring the hammer down, and a moment later the *thunk* of the blow would reach my ears. And that is what had stopped me in my tracks and stilled my tongue, that momentary gap between seeing and hearing the blow. Instead of yelling from the kitchen door, I ran to the barn and climbed two rungs up the ladder—as far as I was allowed to go—and spoke quietly to my father. On our walk to the house he explained that sound takes time to make its way through air. Suddenly the world seemed larger, the air more dense, if sound could be held back like any ordinary traveler.

By the time I started using this hammer, at about the age when I discovered the speed of sound, it already contained houses and mysteries for me. The smooth handle was one my grandfather had made. In those days I needed both hands to swing it. My father would start a nail in a scrap of wood, and I would pound away until I bent it over.

"Looks like you got ahold of some of those rubber nails," he would tell me. "Here, let me see if I can find you some stiff ones." And he would rummage in a drawer until he came up with a fistful of more cooperative nails. "Look at the head," he would tell me. "Don't look at your hands, don't look at the hammer. Just look at the head of that nail and pretty soon you'll learn to hit it square."

Pretty soon I did learn. While he worked in the garage cutting dovetail joints for a drawer or skinning a deer or tuning an engine, I would hammer nails. I made innocent blocks of wood look like porcupines. He did not talk much in the midst of his tools, but he kept up a nearly ceaseless humming, slipping in and out of a dozen tunes in an afternoon, often running back over the same stretch of melody again and again, as if searching for a way out. When the humming did cease, I knew he was faced with a task requiring great delicacy or concentration, and I took care not to distract him.

He kept scraps of wood in a cardboard box—the ends of two-by-fours, slabs of shelving and plywood, odd pieces of molding—and everything in it was fair game. I nailed scraps together to fashion what I called boats or houses, but the results usually bore only faint resemblance to the visions I carried in my head. I would hold up these constructions to show my father, and he would turn them over in his hands admiringly, speculating about what they might be. My cobbled-together guitars might have been alien spaceships, my barns might have been models of Aztec temples, each wooden contraption might have been anything but what I had set out to make.

Now and again I would feel the need to have a chunk of wood shaped or shortened before I riddled it with nails, and I would clamp it in a vise and scrape at it with a handsaw. My father would let me lacerate the board until my arm gave out, and then he would wrap his hand around mine and help me finish the cut, showing me how to use my thumb to guide the blade, how to pull back on the saw to keep it from binding, how to let my shoulder do the work.

"Don't force it," he would say, "just drag it easy and give the teeth a chance to bite."

As the saw teeth bit down, the wood released its smell, each kind with its own fragrance, oak or walnut or cherry or pine—usually pine because it was the softest, easiest for a child to work. No matter how weathered or gray the board, no matter how warped and cracked, inside there was this smell waiting, as of something freshly baked. I gathered every smidgen of sawdust and stored it away in coffee cans, which I kept in a drawer of the workbench. When I did not feel like hammering nails, I would dump my sawdust on the concrete floor of the garage and landscape it into highways and farms and towns, running miniature cars and trucks along miniature roads. Looming as huge as a colossus, my father worked over and around me, now and again bending down to inspect my work, careful not to trample my creations. It was a landscape that smelled dizzyingly of wood. Even after a bath my skin would carry the smell, and so would my father's hair, when he lifted me for a bedtime hug.

I tell these things not only from memory but also from recent observation, because my own son now turns blocks of wood into nailed porcupines, dumps cans full of sawdust at my feet and sculpts highways on the floor. He learns how to swing a hammer from the elbow instead of the wrist, how to lay his thumb beside the blade to guide a saw, how to tap a chisel with a wooden mallet, how to mark a hole with an awl before starting a drill bit. My daughter did the same before him, and even now, on the brink of teenage aloofness, she will occasionally drag out my box of wood scraps and carpenter something. So I have seen my apprenticeship to wood and tools reenacted in each of my children, as my father saw his own apprenticeship renewed in me.

The saw I use belonged to him, as did my level and both of my squares, and all four tools had belonged to his father. The blade of the saw is the bluish color of gun barrels, and the maple handle, dark from the sweat of hands, is inscribed with curving leaf designs. The level is a shaft of walnut two feet long, edged with brass and pierced by three round windows in which air bubbles float in oil-filled tubes of glass. The middle window serves for testing if a surface is horizontal, the others for testing if a surface is plumb or vertical. My grandfather used to carry this level on the gun rack behind the seat in his pickup, and when I rode with him I would turn around to watch the bubbles dance. The larger of the two squares is called a framing square, a flat steel elbow, so beat up and tarnished you can barely make out the rows of numbers that show how to figure the cuts on rafters. The smaller one is called a try square, for marking right angles, with a blued steel blade for the shank and a brass-faced block of cherry for the head.

I was taught early on that a saw is not to be used apart from a square: "If you're going to cut a piece of wood," my father insisted, "you owe it to the tree to cut it straight."

Long before studying geometry, I learned there is a mystical virtue in right angles. There is an unspoken morality in seeking the level and the plumb. A house will stand, a table will bear weight, the sides of a box will hold together, only if the joints are square and the members upright. When the bubble is lined up between two marks etched in the glass tube of a level, you have aligned yourself with the forces that hold the universe together. When you miter the corners of a picture frame, each angle must be exactly forty-five degrees, as they are in the perfect triangles of Pythagoras, not a degree more or less. Otherwise the frame will hang crookedly, as if ashamed of itself and of its maker. No matter if the joints you are cutting do not show. Even if you are butting two pieces of wood together inside a cabinet, where no one except a wrecking crew will ever see them, you must take pains to ensure that the ends are square and the studs are plumb.

I took pains over the wall I was building on the day my father died. Not long after that wall was finished—paneled with tongue-and-groove boards of yellow pine, the nail holes filled with putty and the wood all stained and sealed—I came close to wrecking it one afternoon when my daughter ran howling up the stairs to announce that her gerbils had escaped from their cage and were hiding in my brand new wall. She could hear them scratching and squeaking behind her bed. Impossible! I said. How on earth could they get inside my drum-tight wall? Through the heating vent, she answered. I went downstairs, pressed my ear to the honey-colored wood, and heard the *scritch scritch* of tiny feet.

"What can we do?" my daughter wailed. "They'll starve to death, they'll die of thirst, they'll suffocate."

"Hold on," I soothed. "I'll think of something."

While I thought and she fretted, the radio on her bedside table delivered us the headlines: Several thousand people had died in a city in India from a poisonous cloud that had leaked overnight from a chemical plant. A nuclear-powered submarine had been launched. Rioting continued in South Africa. An airplane had been hijacked in the Mediterranean. Authorities calculated that several thousand homeless people slept on the streets within sight of the Washington Monument. I felt my usual helplessness in the face of all these calamities. But here was my daughter, weeping because her gerbils were holed up in a wall. This calamity I could handle.

"Don't worry," I told her. "We'll set food and water by the heating vent and lure them out. And if that doesn't do the trick, I'll tear the wall apart until we find them."

She stopped crying and gazed at me. "You'd really tear it apart? Just for my gerbils? The wall?" Astonishment slowed her down only for a second, however, before she ran to the workbench and began tugging at drawers, saying, "Let's see, what'll we need? Crowbar. Hammer. Chisels. I hope we don't have to use them—but just in case."

We didn't need the wrecking tools. I never had to assault my handsome wall, because the gerbils eventually came out to nibble at a dish of popcorn. But for several hours I studied the tongue-and-groove skin I had nailed up on the day of my father's death, considering where to begin prying. There were no gaps in that wall, no crooked joints.

I had botched a great many pieces of wood before I mastered the right angle with a saw, botched even more before I learned to miter a joint. The knowledge of these things resides in my hands and eyes and the webwork of muscles, not in the tools. There are machines for sale—powered miter boxes and radial arm saws, for instance—that will enable any casual soul to cut proper angles in boards. The skill is invested in the gadget instead of the person who uses it, and this is what distinguishes a machine from a tool. If I had to earn my keep by making furniture or building houses, I suppose I would buy powered saws and pneumatic nailers; the need for speed would drive me to it. But since I carpenter only for my own pleasure or to help neighbors or to remake the house around the ears of my family, I stick with hand tools. Most of the ones I own were given to me by my father, who also taught me how to wield them. The tools in my workbench are a double inheritance, for each hammer and level and saw is wrapped in a cloud of knowing.

All of these tools are a pleasure to look at and to hold. Merchants would never paste NEW NEW NEW! signs on them in stores. Their designs are old because they work, because they serve their purpose well. Like folk songs and aphorisms and the grainy bits of language, these tools have been pared down to essentials. I look at my claw hammer, the distillation of a hundred generations of carpenters, and consider that it holds up well beside those other classics— Greek vases, Gregorian chants, *Don Quixote,* barbed fish hooks, candles, spoons. Knowledge of hammering stretches back to the earliest humans who squatted beside fires, chipping flints. Anthropologists have a lovely name for those unworked rocks that served as the earliest hammers. "Dawn stones," they are called. Their only qualification for the work, aside from hardness, is that they fit the hand. Our ancestors used them for grinding corn, tapping awls, smashing bones. From dawn stones to this claw hammer is a great leap in time, but no great distance in design or imagination.

On that iced-over February morning when I smashed my thumb with the hammer, I was down in the basement framing the wall that my daughter's gerbils would later hide in. I was thinking of my father, as I always did whenever I built anything, thinking how he would have gone about the work, hearing in memory what he would have said about the wisdom of hitting the nail instead of my thumb. I had the studs and plates nailed together all square and trim, and was lifting the wall into place when the phone rang upstairs. My wife answered, and in a moment she came to the basement door and called down softly to me. The stillness in her voice made me drop the framed wall and hurry upstairs. She told me my father was dead. Then I heard the details over the phone from my mother. Building a set of cupboards for my brother in Oklahoma, he had knocked off work early the previous afternoon because of cramps in his stomach. Early this morning, on his way into the kitchen of my brother's trailer, maybe going for a glass of water, so early that no one else was awake, he slumped down on the linoleum and his heart quit.

For several hours I paced around inside my house, upstairs and down, in and out of every room, looking for the right door to open and knowing there was no such door. My wife and children followed me and wrapped me in arms and backed away again, circling and staring as if I were on fire. Where was the door, the door, the door? I kept wondering. My smashed thumb turned purple and throbbed, making me furious. I wanted to cut it off and rush outside and scrape away the snow and hack a hole in the frozen earth and bury the shameful thing.

I went down into the basement, opened a drawer in my workbench, and stared at the ranks of chisels and knives. Oiled and sharp, as my father would have kept them, they gleamed at me like teeth. I took up a clasp knife, pried out the longest blade, and tested the edge on the hair of my forearm. A tuft came away cleanly, and I saw my father testing the sharpness of tools on his own skin, the blades of axes and knives and gouges and hoes, saw the red hair shaved off in patches from his arms and the backs of his hands. "That will cut bear," he would say. He never cut a bear with his blades, now my blades, but he cut deer, dirt, wood. I closed the knife and put it away. Then I took up the hammer and went back to work on my daughter's wall, snugging the bottom plate against a chalk line on the floor, shimming the top plate against the joists overhead, plumbing the studs with my level, making sure before I drove the first nail that every line was square and true.

## Reflections and Responses

1. Consider the way Sanders opens the essay. Given the significance of his father's death, why does he mention his injured thumb in the same sentence? Why is this a relevant detail? How does it figure later in the essay?

2. Note the many concrete references to carpentry in the essay. In what ways is the language of tools and carpentry related to other aspects of life? Why is there "a mystical virtue in right angles"?

3. In rereading the essay, try to reconstruct the chronology of the February day that Sanders's father died. First, consider how Sanders constructs his narrative. Why does he deviate from a straightforward, hour-by-hour account? Why, for example, does he introduce the story about his daughter's gerbils? In what ways does that anecdote deepen the essay's theme?

LAUREN SLATER

# *Tripp Lake*

*In this lovely, painstakingly detailed personal essay, Lauren Slater takes an ordinary childhood experience—her first summer away at camp—and uses it to craft a history of an extraordinary sense of fear and maladjustment. In the mundane details of camp life, from the mess hall to basketball bombardment, coping for the first time alone and without her mother, Slater unfolds the beginning of a dissociation approaching mental illness. "It was as if a curtain had been pulled back to reveal the true nature of the world," she writes, "which was terror, through and through." But in one apparently daunting camp activity Slater finds a peace of mind that will prove profoundly important later on.*

*Lauren Slater has written extensively and widely about psychology, memory, and her experience. Her essays have appeared in the* New York Times, Harper's, National Geographic, Elle, *and* Nerve. *Her books include* Prozac Diary *(1998),* Lying: A Metaphorical Memoir *(2000),* Love Works Like This: Travels Through a Pregnant Year *(2003),* Blue Beyond Blue: Extraordinary Tales for Ordinary Dilemmas *(2005), and* The $60,000 Dog: My Life with Animals *(2012).* Opening Skinner's Box: Great Psychological Experiments of the Twentieth Century *(2004) was nominated for a Los Angeles Times Book Prize in science writing and won the Bild der Wissenschaft award in Germany for the groundbreaking science book of the year. She has received many other awards and her work has been translated into eighteen languages. She has a master's degree in psychology from Harvard and a doctorate from Boston University. "Tripp Lake" first appeared in* Swink *and was selected by Adam Gopnik for* The Best American Essays 2008. *Lauren Slater served as guest editor for the series in 2006.*

At the age of nine, I went to my first and only camp, located in Poland, Maine, way up off 95, by a kidney-shaped lake where

*Source:* From "COACH: 25 Writers Reflect on People Who Made a Difference," with a Foreword by Bill Bradley, Edited by Andrew Blauner, originally published by Warner Books. Reprinted by permission of Blauner Books Literary Agency for the author.

across the shore we could see the serrated lines of red roofs and, on sunny days, white sails walking along the water. The camp was called Tripp Lake and it was for girls, or so my parents said, who were especially competitive, girls like me, not yet pubescent, packed with all the power of a life that had yet to really unfold, that brought with it the hard parts, the shames, the sadnesses, none of that yet. I wore my hair in what was called a pixie cut, which was a nice way of saying it was short as a boy's—crewcut, really—and, at that age, white-blond so the stubble glittered silver in the summer sun. I spent my evenings playing capture the flag, an exhilarating game that requires fast feet and a bit of cunning.

Understandably, my parents thought it best to send me to a place where my energies could be shaped and expanded. I agreed. I thought I might be Olympic quality, like those skaters I'd seen, or the skiers hunched over their poles, ricocheting down mountains where ice hung from all the trees.

I remember the first night at the camp—but no, let me begin before then, at the bus stop, about to leave, and feeling, for the first time, a shudder of intense grief. My mother, an aloof woman whom I nonetheless adored, looked pale, her eyes foggy and distant. My father was a small man in the bakery business. Lately they'd been fighting. She wanted something grand out of life, something more than a muffin, whereas he was content to nozzle whipped cream on top of tarts. I loved my father, but I loved my mother more—more problematically is what I mean, in the crooked, hooked way only a daughter can love.

I hugged my parents goodbye, and when I hugged my mother I could feel a circle of sadness in her. By leaving I felt as if I were betraying her. I had heard their voices at night, his quiet, hers shrill—"you and you and you"—and I'd seen my mother sometimes sitting on the porch looking out at nothing. She was a severe and brittle woman, but even at that age I knew brittle was breakable. Sometimes, driving in the car, she crushed the accelerator to the floor, just for the feeling of speed, and other times she cried with her mouth closed. I had the feeling, there at the bus stop, that she wished she were me, about to board a bus heading for the horizon, a green-striped bus with Peter Pan dancing on its flank and girls unabashedly eating apples. And because I felt her longing, inchoate, certainly unspoken, my chest seemed to split with sadness, and also guilt. This was a new emotion, an emotion that sits in the throat, an emotion that is maybe more imagistic than all the others. Guilt made me imagine that while I was away, my mother would come undone: her arm would fall off; her hair would drift from her head. Guilt made me imagine that she would sit in the nights and cry, and what could I do about that? I wanted to say I'm sorry, but I didn't really know what for. I couldn't have said it then, what I've since felt my whole life, that separation is a sword, painful, to be avoided at all costs.

My first night at camp. I could hear the flagpole rope banging against its post; I could hear the cry of what were maybe coyotes in the woods and the susurration of thousands of tree frogs. I couldn't sleep, so I stepped outside, onto the damp dirt that surrounded the cabin, and in the single spotlight that shone down, I found a tiny toad, no bigger than a dime, with still tinier bumps on its taupe back. I lifted the amphibian up. I could not believe that God, or whoever, could make an animal so small, an animal that would have, if I cut it open, all the same organs as me, in miniature, the locket-size heart, bones like white wisps. How easy it is to break an animal. I could have crushed that frog with my fist—and part of me wanted to, while another part of me wanted to protect it, while still a third part of me wanted to let it go.

Before camp, I'd been a more or less happy girl, but that first night I couldn't sleep and by morning a wild sadness had settled in me. Where was I? Where was she? Someday I would die. Someone somewhere was sick. It was as if a curtain had been pulled back to reveal the true nature of the world, which was terror through and through.

That summer I became, for the first time in my life, truly afraid, and the fears took forms that were not good, that did not augur well for my later life, although I didn't know it then. That first day, sitting on the green lawn, watching a girl do a cartwheel and another girl mount the parallel bars, I developed an irrational fear that is still hard to explain: I became hyperaware of my own body, the swoosh of my blood and the paddling of my heart and the huh huh huhs of my breath, and it seemed amazing and tenuous to me that my body did all of this without any effort on my part. As soon as I became aware of this fact—almost as though I'd discovered my lower brain stem and how it was hitched to the spinal cord—as soon as I came to consciousness about this, I thought, *I can't breathe.* And truly it felt like I couldn't breathe. I thought, *I am thinking about my breathing, and if I think too hard about my breathing, which you're not supposed to think about, I will concentrate on it right away,* and I swallowed hard, and then I became aware of all the minute mechanisms that comprise a swallow, and so I felt I couldn't swallow anymore. It was like the lights were going out in my body, while girls in front of me did cartwheels on the green lawn, completely unaware that I was dying.

After that, the fears came fast and furious. I was afraid to think about walking, because then I would fall. Breathing, because then I would suffocate.

Swallowing was the worst of all, to suddenly feel you have no way of bringing the world down into your throat, of taking it in, no way. And I became afraid of the dining hall, with its vicious swordfish mounted on one wall, and its huge bear head with eyes like my mother's, dull, distant eyes, eyes at once wild and flat. I became afraid of pancakes, of toothbrushes, of cutlery, of water, of counselors urging me into the lake, where fronds fingered through the murk and scads of fish darted by, making a current cool against my legs.

That first week at camp, I fished a dime out of my uniform pocket (we wore only blue-and-white standard-issue uniforms) and called my mother. From far, far away I heard her voice. When had her sadness started? With my father, or before that, with her mother, who insisted that she, the oldest of three girls, do endless tasks and child care, so she was never able to shoot marbles, too busy shining the silver. My mother, I knew, had been a good girl, exceedingly good, and because of that, she hated my grandmother. She called her Frances, and all holidays were barbed affairs, my mother sniping at her mother, making faces at the food because she, if only given the chance, could have done better.

My mother did not go to college despite the fact that she's bright. In my imagination, when I construct her history for her, because she's so closed about her own, she wants to be a singer on a lit stage or she wants to be a painter with her canvas at a quiet lakeside. She wants something larger than her own life, larger than her husband's life, larger than the house and kids, where what she does all day is clean. Much, much later, when I was near grown, after she and my father divorced, my mother would develop a passion for Israel, its military might; she became fiercely, ragefully Zionistic, and, totally bursting the caul of her confinement, she smuggled Bibles into the USSR. But this was later, when she found an outlet for her energies, and if only I'd known that was going to happen, that she was going to get something good out of life—if only I'd known, maybe my fears would have been a little less.

From far away my mother answered the phone, and I said, "I want to come home," and she said, "Don't be a quitter, Lauren." She wanted for me a larger life, a life where girls stand on stages, take charge of a team, swim the length of a lake and back in a Speedo suit. But because she didn't have these things, I felt much too guilty to take them for myself. None of this did I say.

At camp, we were divided into teams, and every activity, from drama to Newcomb, was cast as a competition. It was a summer of color war. I watched the older girls run with their lacrosse sticks, cradling them close to their sides, the ball in the gut-string pocket a soft blur. I watched as we, the younger girls, were taught to dribble and to shoot. Part of me wanted fiercely to win these games, while a still larger part of me could not even allow myself to participate, for somehow I would be betraying my mother if I did.

I was put on the Tigers team. Every morning after breakfast, standing at attention beneath that mounted swordfish, we would sing:

Shielded by orange and black
Tigers will attack
Catching every cue
Always coming through.

I remember in particular a game called bombardment, which we played in the gym on rainy days, Tigers versus Bears. In this game, each side is given a whole raft of basketballs, and the purpose is simply to hurl them at each other as hard as you can, and whoever gets hit is out. Before I'd left home, maybe I could have played this game, but certainly not now. Brown basketballs came whizzing through the air, smacked against the lacquered floor of the gym, ricocheted off a face or a flank, and one by one each girl got hit and so would sit out on the sidelines. I was so scared of bombardment that whenever we played it, I hung way in the back of the court, where the other team's balls could not reach me. And then one day, because of this, I lasted throughout the whole game; everyone on my team had been hit except me, and everyone on the other team had been hit except a senior girl named Nancy, a fourteen-year-old who had one leg longer than the other. She had custom-made shoes, her left heel stacked high enough to bring her up even so she didn't tilt. I'd watched Nancy walk out of the corners of my eyes; even with her shoes she was strangely clumsy, gangly, always giggling nervously just at the rim of a group of girls, her desire to be taken in palpable.

And now Nancy and I were the last two left in the game. Everyone on the sidelines was screaming *Go, go, go.* Nancy's skin was as pale as milk, the strands of veins visible in her neck. Her gimp foot, supported by the huge rubber heel of her sneaker, seemed to wobble. *Go, go, go,* but I couldn't do it, I couldn't hurl that ball at her; it seemed existentially horrible that we were called to do this sort of thing in the world, to live in a way where someone had to lose. I stood there, locked in place, mesmerized by her skin and her foot, while Nancy lifted the basketball high above her head and hurled it toward me with as much muster as she could muster, and I let the ball hit me on the hip. Nancy won. That was the only outcome I could tolerate.

It didn't take long for the counselors to realize something was wrong with me. I cried all the time. During free swim I retreated into the fringe of woods. The woods were next to a red barn, where horses hung their heads over stall doors and where there were golden squares of hay. Somehow, being near the horses calmed me. I liked their huge velvety lips, their thoughtful mastications. I liked the way they almost seemed to slurp up hay. I liked their rounded backsides, their plumed tails; I even liked their scat, flecked with grain and sweet-smelling. Today, whenever I enter a barn and smell that smell, I do a Proustian plunge* back to that first barn, and to the chestnut ponies.

Riding was a camp activity reserved for the older girls. I began to watch those girls cantering around the ring, the horses seeping dark sweat on their muscular chests. The riding coach's name was Kim. She was a wisp of a woman in tan jodhpurs with suede patches at the knees. Once, when I was alone in the barn, I found her riding clothes hung up on a hook near the tack room. I tried on her green hunt jacket. It hung huge on me, but it felt cozy, and on its lapel there was a tiny brooch in the shape of a dragonfly.

"Would you like to try?" Kim asked me one day.

"I'm only ten," I said.

"Well," she said, "I have a horse who's only ten, too. Maybe you would make a good match."

"What's his name?" I asked.

"What's yours?" she said.

"Lauren," I said.

"Smokey Raindrops," she said. "But we call him Rain."

Rain, Rain—what a beautiful name. It was more a sound than a designation, "Yes," I said.

In fact, I didn't get to ride Rain that day. First, all the counselors, along with Auntie Ruth, the camp director, had to discuss it. Should I have lessons even though that was not part of my camp curriculum? Would that make me happy? They thought it might.

Riding is a sport that, like any other, requires more than just the circumscribed activity. There is the ritualistic preparation, the waxing

---

***Proustian plunge**: French novelist Marcel Proust (1871–1922) famously wrote of how the taste of a childhood cookie sent him into a long and vivid spiral of recollections.

of skis or the oiling of strings or, in this case, the grooming before the tack. A few days later Kim showed me how to do it, using a currying comb, picking a hoof, leaning down and cupping the hairy fetlock, lifting the leg, seeing the shine of the silver shoe with six nail heads in it. Time passed. Days passed. Caring for the horses was soothing, and I found when I was at the stable by these big breathing animals, I could forget about my own breath and just breathe.

All through the summer Kim taught me how to ride, alone, no other girl there. She taught me how to post, how to do dressage, how to jump. I learned to hoist myself up, foot in one stirrup, other leg flung over the broad rank back. "When you post," she said, "watch the left leg. As it extends, you rise."

The trot of a horse is like a metronome. It synchronizes you. It hypnotizes you. Left foot rise. Left foot rise. Your whole mind funnels down into this foot, the flash of hoof in the summer sun. And I'll never forget the day Kim taught me to canter, how she said, "Trot out, give him a kick with your inside foot," and suddenly the horse's tight trot broke into the rocking run, around and around the ring we went, so fast it seemed, the world blurring by in a beautiful way.

Riding is largely a singular sport; although there are shows and red ribbons, first places and sixth places, it can still be done, nevertheless, with no attention to the competition aspect. You cannot really play lacrosse or soccer unless you are playing against someone, and this againstness requires that you see yourself as separate, with all that that implies. But horseback riding is something you can do alone in the woods, or in a dusty riding rink, or even in your mind, in which you can canter, too. Riding is not about separation. It is not about dominance. The only person you might hurt is you. You are, at long last, without guilt.

Riding. It is about becoming one with the animal that bears you along. It is about learning to give and take, give the horse his head, take the rein and bring him up. It is about tack, the glorious leather saddles, and the foam-stained bits, which fascinated me, how Kim would roll them in sugar and slide them into a horse's mouth, its thick tongue clamped. It is, more than anything else, about relationship and balance, and as Kim taught me how to do these things—walk, trot, canter—a sort of peace settled in me, a working through my mother and me, a way of excelling at no one's cost.

And so the summer progressed. The only thing I could not do well was jump. Each time we approached the fence the horse seemed to sense my primordial fear, fear of the fence and fear of everything it contained, and it would bunch to a scuttering halt, or, more humiliating, the horse would stop, and then with me kicking, and kicking uselessly, it would simply walk over the bar. I watched Kim jump; she was amazing, fluid, holding on to her horse's hair as they entered the air, her face a mixture of terror and exhilaration, the balanced combination that means only one thing: mastery.

One month into the camp season was visiting day. My parents arrived carrying leathery fruit rolls and a new canteen. They seemed as separate as ever, not even looking at each other. My mother was appalled at the condition of my wardrobe. My clothes stank of sweat and fur. The soles of my boots were crammed with flaking manure. That was the summer, also, when I started to smell. "What's this?" she said, flicking through my steamer trunk. "Do you ever do your laundry?" She pulled out a white shirt with spatters of black mud on it, and stains at the armpits, slight stains, their rims barely visible.

"Lauren," she said.

"What?" I said.

She pursed her lips and shook her head. She held the shirt out as though to study it. And once again I saw that look of longing cross her face, but this time it was mixed with something else. I saw the briefest flicker of disgust.

A few minutes later, she went into our cabin bathroom, which we called the Greenie. She closed the door. I stalked up to it, pressed my ear against its wood. What did I do with my body? What did she do with hers? I heard the gush of water from the tap, the scrunch of something papery. The bathroom had a lock on my side only. Quietly, and for a reason I still cannot quite explain, I turned the lever and the lock slid quietly into its socket.

A few minutes later, when she tried to get out, she could not. She rattled the knob. We were alone in the cabin. I stood back and watched. "Lauren?" she said. "Lauren?" Her voice hurt me. It was curved into a question, and when I didn't answer, the question took on a kind of keening. "Lauren, are you there? Open the door." I stood absolutely still. I was mesmerized, horrified by the vulnerability in her voice, how small she suddenly seemed, and how I was growing in girth by the minute. For some reason I suddenly pictured her trapped in a tiny glass bottle, and I held the bottle in my hands. I could let her out or leave her.

I let her out.

"What are you doing?" she said. She stared at me. I stared back at her. I could see her sweat now; it ran in a trickle down the side of her brow. I wanted to wipe it away.

They left in the evening, when colored clouds were streaming across the sky. I stood in the parking lot and watched their station wagon rattle over the dirt road, raising clouds of dust. The next few days, I backslid. My fears returned. There was the problem with my breathing, but now accompanying this obsession was the need to walk backward while counting. I saw for sure that I was growing while she shrank. I saw for sure that I was growing because she shrank. I also saw something pointed in me, some real desire to win. Hearing that lock sink into its socket, I had felt glee and power.

I stopped riding then. I stopped going to the stables. I stayed in my bunk. I wrote letters and letters to my mother, the act somehow soothing my conscience. *Love, Lauren XXX. Kisses and hugs. I love you.*

At last, after four days had passed, Kim came to my cabin to get me. "You disappeared," she said.

"I'm sick," I said.

"You know," she said, "I never much liked my mother."

I stared at her. How had she known?

"What will you do?" she said.

"I don't know," I said.

"Are you going to sit on a cot for the rest of your life?"

"Maybe," I said.

"Just sit there and cry?" she said, and there was, suddenly, a slight sneer to her voice.

I looked away.

"I once knew a girl," said Kim, "who spent her whole life going from hospital to hospital because she loved being sick. She was too scared to face the world. Is that you?"

I have thought of her words often—a premonition, an augury, a warning, a simple perception.

I followed her back to the barn. It was noon. The sun was high and hot. She brought Rain out into the middle of the ring, tightened his saddle strap, and tapped on the deep seat. "All aboard," she said.

Sitting high on the horse, I could smell the leaves. I could smell my own sweat and all that it contained, so many contradictions.

"We're going to jump today," she said.

She went to the center of the ring, and this time she set the fence at four feet. "Now," she said, "cross your stirrups and knot your reins. A rider has to depend on her inner balance only."

I cantered toward the jump, hands on my hips, legs grasping. But each time, at the crucial moment of departure, Rain would screech to a halt and I'd topple into his mane.

"He senses your fear," Kim said.

At last, on the third or fourth try, she went into the barn and came back out with a long black crop. Standing in the center of the ring, right next to the jump, she swizzled the crop into the air, a snapping sound. The horse's ears flashed forward. "You have to get over it," she said. I centered myself in the saddle. I cantered twice around the rink and then turned in tight toward the bar. Kim cracked the whip, a crack I still hear today whenever I feel my fears—and I do, I often do—but I rose up, arms akimbo, in this leap merged with the mammal, its heart my heart, its hooves my feet, and we sailed into the excellent air. I did it. I found a way to move forward.

## Reflections and Responses

1. Slater's third paragraph begins "I remember the first night at the camp—but no, let me begin before then, at the bus stop, about to leave." How does this sudden reversal of direction set the tone for the essay as a whole? Why is the scene at the bus stop so important to the essay, and why does Slater suggest it is an afterthought? How will Slater use the order in which she recalls things to advance ideas about childhood and memory?

2. Note the variety of sensory expressions Slater uses in the architecture of her images. Locate an example of a smell, a sound, a complex visual, and other senses employed during the essay. Besides making the writing generally more vivid, why does Slater find it particularly necessary in this essay to dwell on minute details and precise representations? How do these images relate to the more extrasensory, psychological memories Slater hopes to conjure?

3. Slater describes the trot of a horse as "like a metronome. It synchronizes you. It hypnotizes you." Contrast Slater's "bombardment" scene with that of riding Rain. How does Slater express the chaotic madness of the gymnasium sport on the one hand, and the calmness of riding on the other? Why is this juxtaposition central to the essay?

AMY TAN

# *Mother Tongue*

*For many American students, the language spoken at home is far different* ~~I have multiple friends like this!~~
*from the one spoken in school. For that reason, many students learn to*
*switch back and forth between two languages, the one they use with their*
*family and the one required for their education. Such switching, however,*
*need not be confining or demoralizing. Rather, it can enhance one's sensi-*
*tivity to language and can even be creatively enabling, as the Chinese*
*American novelist Amy Tan suggests in this charming personal essay.*
*"Language is the tool of my trade," Tan writes. "And I use them all—all*
*the Englishes I grew up with."*

    *Born into a Chinese family that had recently arrived in California, Amy*
*Tan began writing as a child and after graduation from college worked for*
*several years as a freelance business writer. In the mid-eighties, she began*
*writing fiction, basing much of her work on family stories. She is the author*
*of several best-selling novels:* The Joy Luck Club *(1989), which was a*
*finalist for both the National Book Award and National Book Critics Circle*
*Award and was made into a motion picture directed by Wayne Wang;* The
Kitchen God's Wife *(1991);* The Hundred Secret Senses *(1995);*
The Bonesetter's Daughter *(2000); and* Saving Fish from Drown-
ing *(2005). In 1992, she published a popular children's book,* The
Moon Lady, *and in 2003, a collection of essays,* The Opposite of
Faith: Memories of a Writing Life. *"Mother Tongue" originally*
*appeared in the* Threepenny Review *(1990) and was selected by Joyce*
*Carol Oates for* The Best American Essays 1991.

I am not a scholar of English or literature. I cannot give you much ~~Love that she starts out by saying this.~~
more than personal opinions on the English language and its var-
iations in this country or others.

*Source:* "Mother Tongue" by Amy Tan. First published in the *The Threepenny Review.*
Copyright © 1990 by Amy Tan. Reprinted by permission of the author.

I am a writer. And by that definition, I am someone who has always loved language. I am fascinated by language in daily life. I spend a great deal of my time thinking about the power of language—the way it can evoke an emotion, a visual image, a complex idea, or a simple truth. Language is the tool of my trade. And I use them all—all the Englishes I grew up with.

Recently, I was made keenly aware of the different Englishes I do use. I was giving a talk to a large group of people, the same talk I had already given to half a dozen other groups. The nature of the talk was about my writing, my life, and my book, *The Joy Luck Club*. The talk was going along well enough, until I remembered one major difference that made the whole talk sound wrong. My mother was in the room. And it was perhaps the first time she had heard me give a lengthy speech, using the kind of English I have never used with her. I was saying things like, "The intersection of memory upon imagination" and "There is an aspect of my fiction that relates to thus-and-thus"—a speech filled with carefully wrought grammatical phrases, burdened, it suddenly seemed to me, with nominalized forms, past perfect tenses, conditional phrases, all the forms of standard English that I had learned in school and through books, the forms of English I did not use at home with my mother.

Just last week, I was walking down the street with my mother, and I again found myself conscious of the English I was using, the English I do use with her. We were talking about the price of new and used furniture and I heard myself saying this: "Not waste money that way." My husband was with us as well, and he didn't notice any switch in my English. And then I realized why. It's because over the twenty years we've been together I've often used that same kind of English with him, and sometimes he even uses it with me. It has become our language of intimacy, a different sort of English that relates to family talk, the language I grew up with.

So you'll have some idea of what this family talk I heard sounds like, I'll quote what my mother said during a recent conversation which I videotaped and then transcribed. During this conversation, my mother was talking about a political gangster in Shanghai who had the same last name as her family's, Du, and how the gangster in his early years wanted to be adopted by her family, which was rich by comparison. Later, the gangster became more powerful, far richer than my mother's family, and one day showed up at my mother's wedding to pay his respects. Here's what she said in part: "Du Yusong having business like fruit stand. Like off the street kind. He is Du like Du Zong—but not Tsung-ming Island people. The local people call putong, the river east side, he belong to that side local people. That man want to ask Du Zong father take him in like become own family. Du Zong father wasn't look down on him, but didn't take seriously, until that man big like become a mafia. Now important person, very hard to inviting him. Chinese way, came only to show respect, don't stay for dinner. Respect for making big celebration, he shows up. Mean gives lots of respect. Chinese custom. Chinese social life that way. If too important won't have to stay too long. He come to my wedding. I didn't see, I heard it. I gone to boy's side, they have YMCA dinner. Chinese age I was nineteen."

You should know that my mother's expressive command of English belies how much she actually understands. She reads the *Forbes* report, listens to *Wall Street Week*, converses daily with her stockbroker, reads all of Shirley MacLaine's books with ease—all kinds of things I can't begin to understand. Yet some of my friends tell me they understand 50 percent of what my mother says. Some say they understand 80 to 90 percent. Some say they understand none of it, as if she were speaking pure Chinese. But to me, my mother's English is perfectly clear, perfectly natural. It's my mother tongue. Her language, as I hear it, is vivid, direct, full of observation and imagery. That was the language that helped shape the way I saw things, expressed things, made sense of the world.

*[handwritten margin note: That's how I am with some of my third graders.]*

Lately, I've been giving more thought to the kind of English my mother speaks. Like others, I have described it to people as "broken" or "fractured" English. But I wince when I say that. It has always bothered me that I can think of no way to describe it other than "broken," as if it were damaged and needed to be fixed, as if it lacked a certain wholeness and soundness. I've heard other terms used, "limited English," for example. But they seem just as bad, as if everything is limited, including people's perceptions of the limited English speaker.

I know this for a fact, because when I was growing up, my mother's "limited" English limited *my* perception of her. I was ashamed of her English. I believed that her English reflected the quality of what she had to say. That is, because she expressed them imperfectly her thoughts were imperfect. And I had plenty of empirical evidence to support me: the fact that people in department stores, at banks, and at restaurants did not take her seriously, did not give her good service, pretended not to understand her, or even acted as if they did not hear her.

*[handwritten margin note: she should not have been treated like that.]*

My mother has long realized the limitations of her English as well. When I was fifteen, she used to have me call people on the phone to pretend I was she. In this guise, I was forced to ask for information or even to complain and yell at people who had been rude to her. One time it was a call to her stockbroker in New York.

She had cashed out her small portfolio and it just so happened we were going to go to New York the next week, our very first trip outside California. I had to get on the phone and say in an adolescent voice that was not very convincing, "This is Mrs. Tan."

*I find this to be very cool.*

And my mother was standing in the back whispering loudly, "Why he don't send me check, already two weeks late. So mad he lie to me, losing me money."

And then I said in perfect English, "Yes, I'm getting rather concerned. You had agreed to send the check two weeks ago, but it hasn't arrived."

Then she began to talk more loudly. "What he want, I come to New York tell him front of his boss, you cheating me?" And I was trying to calm her down, make her be quiet, while telling the stockbroker, "I can't tolerate any more excuses. If I don't receive the check immediately, I am going to have to speak to your manager when I'm in New York next week." And sure enough, the following week there we were in front of this astonished stockbroker, and I was sitting there red-faced and quiet, and my mother, the real Mrs. Tan, was shouting at his boss in her impeccable broken English.

We used a similar routine just five days ago, for a situation that was far less humorous. My mother had gone to the hospital for an appointment, to find out about a (benign) brain tumor a CAT scan had revealed a month ago. She said she had spoken very good English, her best English, no mistakes. Still, she said, the hospital did not apologize when they said they had lost the CAT scan and she had come for nothing. She said they did not seem to have any sympathy when she told them she was anxious to know the exact diagnosis, since her husband and son had both died of brain

*This is so messed up.*

tumors. She said they would not give her any more information until the next time and she would have to make another appointment for that. So she said she would not leave until the doctor called her daughter. She wouldn't budge. And when the doctor finally called her daughter, me, who spoke in perfect English— lo and behold—we had assurances the CAT scan would be found, promises that a conference call on Monday would be held, and apologies for any suffering my mother had gone through for a most regrettable mistake.

I think my mother's English almost had an effect on limiting my possibilities in life as well. Sociologists and linguists probably will tell you that a person's developing language skills are more influenced by peers. But I do think that the language spoken in the family, especially in immigrant families which are more insular, plays a large role in shaping the language of the child. And

I believe that it affected my results on achievement tests, IQ tests, and the SAT. While my English skills were never judged as poor, compared to math, English could not be considered my strong suit. In grade school I did moderately well, getting perhaps B's, sometimes B-pluses, in English and scoring perhaps in the sixtieth or seventieth percentile on achievement tests. But those scores were not good enough to override the opinion that my true abilities lay in math and science, because in those areas I achieved A's and scored in the ninetieth percentile or higher.

This was understandable. Math is precise; there is only one correct answer. Whereas, for me at least, the answers on English tests were always a judgment call, a matter of opinion and personal experience. Those tests were constructed around items like fill-in-the-blank sentence completion, such as, "Even though Tom was _____, Mary thought he was _____." And the correct answer always seemed to be the most bland combinations of thoughts, for example, "Even though Tom was shy, Mary thought he was charming," with the grammatical structure "even though" limiting the correct answer to some sort of semantic opposites, so you wouldn't get answers like, "Even though Tom was foolish, Mary thought he was ridiculous." Well, according to my mother, there were very few limitations as to what Tom could have been and what Mary might have thought of him. So I never did well on tests like that.

The same was true with word analogies, pairs of words in which you were supposed to find some sort of logical, semantic relationship—for example, "*Sunset* is to *nightfall* as _____ is to _____." And here you would be presented with a list of four possible pairs, one of which showed the same kind of relationship: *red is to stoplight, bus is to arrival, chills is to fever, yawn is to boring*. Well, I could never think that way. I knew what the tests were asking, but I could not block out of my mind the images already created by the first pair, "*sunset is to nightfall*"—and I would see a burst of colors against a darkening sky, the moon rising, the lowering of a curtain of stars. And all the other pairs of words—red, bus, stoplight, boring—just threw up a mass of confusing images, making it impossible for me to sort out something as logical as saying: "A sunset precedes nightfall" is the same as "a chill precedes a fever." The only way I would have gotten that answer right would have been to imagine an associative situation, for example, my being disobedient and staying out past sunset, catching a chill at night, which turns into feverish pneumonia as punishment, which indeed did happen to me.

I have been thinking about all this lately, about my mother's English, about achievement tests. Because lately I've been asked, as a writer, why there are not more Asian Americans represented in American literature. Why are there few Asian Americans enrolled in creative writing programs? Why do so many Chinese students go into engineering? Well, these are broad sociological questions I can't begin to answer. But I have noticed in surveys— in fact, just last week—that Asian students, as a whole, always do significantly better on math achievement tests than in English. And this makes me think that there are other Asian-American students whose English spoken in the home might also be described as "broken" or "limited." And perhaps they also have teachers who are steering them away from writing and into math and science, which is what happened to me.

Fortunately, I happen to be rebellious in nature and enjoy the challenge of disproving assumptions made about me. I became an English major my first year in college, after being enrolled as pre-med. I started writing nonfiction as a freelancer the week after I was told by my former boss that writing was my worst skill and I should hone my talents toward account management.

But it wasn't until 1985 that I finally began to write fiction. And at first I wrote using what I thought to be wittily crafted sentences, sentences that would finally prove I had mastery over the English language. Here's an example from the first draft of a story that later made its way into *The Joy Luck Club,* but without this line: "That was my mental quandary in its nascent state." A terrible line, which I can barely pronounce.

Fortunately, for reasons I won't get into today, I later decided I should envision a reader for the stories I would write. And the reader I decided upon was my mother, because these were stories about mothers. So with this reader in mind—and in fact she did read my early drafts—I began to write stories using all the Englishes I grew up with: the English I spoke to my mother, which for lack of a better term might be described as "simple"; the English she used with me, which for lack of a better term might be described as "broken"; my translation of her Chinese, which could certainly be described as "watered down"; and what I imagined to be her translation of her Chinese if she could speak in perfect English, her internal language, and for that I sought to preserve the essence, but neither an English nor a Chinese structure. I wanted to capture what language ability tests can never reveal: her intent, her passion, her imagery, the rhythms of her speech and the nature of her thoughts.

Apart from what any critic had to say about my writing, I knew I had succeeded where it counted when my mother finished reading my book and gave me her verdict: "So easy to read."

## Reflections and Responses

1. What "Englishes" did Amy Tan grow up with? Why does she feel uncomfortable with the term "broken English"? Why do you think she still uses that term toward the end of her essay?

2. What point is Tan making about language tests? Why did she perform less well on them than she did on math and science tests? In her opinion, what aspects of language do the tests fail to take into account?

3. Tan cites a sentence—"That was my mental quandary in its nascent state"—that she deleted from *The Joy Luck Club*. What do you think she dislikes about that sentence? What kind of English does it represent? Does it or does it not demonstrate a "mastery" of the English language?

RYAN VAN METER

# *First*

*Many essays reflect on an experience from early childhood and how the often confused way that children relate to their immediate world carries repercussions into the essayist's grownup life. In this brief but poignant essay, Ryan Van Meter remembers the first time he felt love—as a five-year-old for his neighbor Ben—and the reaction his expression of that love garnered from his mother. Van Meter dwells on the "one last second" in which he and his mother could "look at each other without anything wrong between us," before she reprimands his feelings in a way that fundamentally confuses the sense of love she herself has instilled in him. By taking a clear, objective tone, the author implies that he still feels the same confusion about the way society judges his affection.*

*Ryan Van Meter studied nonfiction writing at the University of Iowa, and has published essays in* Gulf Coast, Colorado Review, Indiana Review, Gettysburg Review, *and* The Iowa Review, *among others. His work has also appeared in anthologies including* Touchstone Anthology of Contemporary Creative Nonfiction: Work from 1970 to Present (2007), *edited by Lex Williford and Michael Martone, and* You Must Be This Tall to Ride: Contemporary Writers Take You Inside the Story (2009), *edited by B. J. Hollars. His collection called* If You Knew Then What I Know Now, *which contains this essay, was published in* 2011. *"First" originally appeared in* The Gettysburg Review *and was selected by Mary Oliver for* The Best American Essays 2009.

Ben and I are sitting side by side in the very back of his mother's station wagon. We face glowing white headlights of cars following us, our sneakers pressed against the back hatch door. This is our joy—his and mine—to sit turned away from our moms and dads in this place that feels like a secret, as though they are not even in the car with us. They have just taken us out to dinner, and now we are driving home. Years from this evening, I won't actually be sure that this boy sitting beside me is named Ben. But that doesn't matter tonight. What I know for certain right now is that I love him, and I need to tell him this fact before we return to our separate houses, next door to each other. We are both five.

Ben is the first brown-eyed boy I will fall for but will not be the last. His hair is also brown and always needs scraping off his forehead, which he does about every five minutes. All his jeans have dark squares stuck over the knees where he has worn through the denim. His shoelaces are perpetually undone, and he has a magic way of tying them with a quick, weird loop that I study and try myself, but can never match. His fingernails are ragged because he rips them off with his teeth and spits out the pieces when our moms aren't watching. Somebody always has to fix his shirt collars.

Our parents face the other direction, talking about something, and it is raining. My eyes trace the lines of water as they draw down the glass. Coiled beside my legs are the thick black and red cords of a pair of jumper cables. Ben's T-ball bat is also back here, rolling around and clunking as the long car wends its way through town. Ben's dad is driving, and my dad sits next to him, with our mothers in the back seat; I have recently observed that when mothers and fathers are in the car together, the dad always drives. My dad has also insisted on checking the score of the Cardinals game, so the radio is tuned to a staticky AM station, and the announcer's rich voice buzzes out of the speakers up front.

The week before this particular night, I asked my mother, "Why do people get married?" I don't recall the impulse behind my curiosity, but I will forever remember every word of her answer—she stated it simply after only a moment or two of thinking—because it seemed that important: "Two people get married when they love each other."

I had that hunch. I am a kindergartener, but the summer just before this rainy night, I learned most of what I know about love from watching soap operas with my mother. She is a gym teacher and during her months off, she catches up on the shows she has watched since college. Every summer weekday, I couldn't wait until they came on at two o'clock. My father didn't think I should be watching them—boys should be outside, playing—but he was rarely home early enough to know the difference, and according to my mother, I was too young to really understand what was going on anyway.

What I enjoyed most about soap opera was how exciting and beautiful life was. Every lady was pretty and had wonderful hair, and all the men had dark eyes and big teeth and faces as strong as bricks, and every week, there was a wedding or a manhunt or a birth. The people had grand fights where they threw vases at walls and slammed doors and chased each other in cars. There were villains locking up the wonderfully haired heroines and suspending them in gold cages above enormous acid vats. And, of course, it was love that inspired every one of these stories and made life on the screen as thrilling as it was. That was what my mother would say from the sofa when I turned from my spot on the carpet in front of her and faced her, asking, "Why is he spying on that lady?"

"Because he loves her."

In the car, Ben and I hold hands. There is something sticky on his fingers, probably the strawberry syrup from the ice cream sundaes we ate for dessert. We have never held hands before; I have simply reached for his in the dark and held him while he holds me. I want to see our hands on the rough floor, but they are only visible every block or so when the car passes beneath a streetlight, and then, for only a flash. Ben is my closest friend because he lives next door, we are the same age, and we both have little brothers who are babies. I wish he were in the same kindergarten class as me, but he goes to a different school—one where he has to wear a uniform all day and for which there is no school bus.

"I love you," I say. We are idling, waiting for a red light to be green; a shining car has stopped right behind us, so Ben's face is pale and brilliant.

"I love you too," he says.

The car becomes quiet as the voice of the baseball game shrinks smaller and smaller.

"Will you marry me?" I ask him. His hand is still in mine; on the soap opera, you are supposed to have a ring, but I don't have one.

He begins to nod, and suddenly my mother feels very close. I look over my shoulder, my eyes peeking over the back of the last row of seats that we are leaning against. She has turned around, facing me. Permed hair, laugh lines not laughing.

"What did you just say?" she asks.

"I asked Ben to marry me."

The car starts moving forward again, and none of the parents are talking loud enough for us to hear them back here. I brace myself against the raised carpeted hump of the wheel well as Ben's father turns left onto the street before the turn onto our street. Sitting beside my mom is Ben's mother, who keeps staring forward, but I notice that one of her ears keeps swiveling back here, a little more each time. I am still facing my mother, who is still facing me, and for one last second, we look at each other without anything wrong between us.

"You shouldn't have said that," she says. "Boys don't marry other boys. Only boys and girls get married to each other."

She can't see our hands, but Ben pulls his away. I close my fingers into a loose fist and rub my palm to feel, and keep feeling, how strange his skin has made mine.

"Okay?" she asks.

"Yes," I say, but by accident my throat whispers the words.

She asks again. "Okay? Did you hear me?"

"Yes!" this time nearly shouting, and I wish we were already home so I could jump out and run to my bedroom. To be back here in the dark, private tail of the car suddenly feels wrong, so Ben and I each scoot off to our separate sides. "Yes," I say again, almost normally, turning away to face the rainy window. I feel her turn too as the radio baseball voice comes back up out of the quiet. The car starts to dip as we head down the hill of our street; our house is at the bottom. No one speaks for the rest of the ride. We all just sit and wait and watch our own views of the road—the parents see what is ahead of us while the only thing I can look at is what we have just left behind.

## Reflections and Responses

1. What is the importance of the observation the narrator makes early on that "when mothers and fathers are in the car together, the dad always drives." Is this just an idle observation, or is Van Meter saying something more profound about gender? Where else in the essay is this theme enforced? How does this relate to the larger themes of sexuality and gender roles in the essay?

2. What does the last sentence of the essay ("We all just sit and wait and watch our own views of the road—the parents see what is ahead of us while the only thing I can look at is what we have just left behind.") mean in the context of the epiphany the narrator has had that he loves Ben, and the "lesson" he's learned that boys can only marry girls?

3. Does this essay have a political or social agenda, or is it meant as a story whose moral, even to the author, may be vague and multifaceted? Do you think this intensely personal essay is more effective than, say, an argument in favor of legalizing gay marriage? Explain why or why not.

CHRISTY VANNOY

# A Personal Essay
# by a Personal Essay

*The personal essay should, theoretically, be the form of literature that admits the most variation among its works. After all, it's* personal— *everyone has a different story, and those stories must be unique, right? As it happens, readers of the genre tend to find that after a while the entries get somewhat generic: Short works of personal recollection often, in our modern literary culture, can easily revert to clichéd themes, topics, attitudes, and situations. In this comic satire, writer Christy Vannoy attempts to illustrate just how trite the typical published essay can become, by imagining an essay actually writing an essay itself. In the process, she uncovers perhaps the most salient cliché of the form today—the essayist's tendency to cite an exaggerated litany of life's hardships.*

*Currently working on her first book, Christy Vannoy lives in New York City where she writes an ongoing column for* McSweeneys.net. *"A Personal Essay by a Personal Essay" originally appeared in* McSweeney's *and was selected by Edwidge Danticat for* The Best American Essays 2011.

I AM A PERSONAL ESSAY and I was born with a port wine stain and beaten by my mother. A brief affair with a second cousin produced my first and only developmentally disabled child. Years of painful infertility would lead me straight into menopause and the hysterectomy I almost didn't survive.

I recently enrolled in a clinic led by the Article's Director and Editor for a national women's magazine. Technically, we were there to workshop and polish ourselves into submission. Secretly, though, we each hoped to out-devastate the other and nail ourselves a freelance contract.

*Source:* Best American Essays, 2011, Christy Vannoy, *A Personal Essay by a Personal Essay* (2011).

I wasn't there to learn. I've been published as many times as I've been brutally sodomized, but I need to stay at the top of my game. Everyone thinks they have a story these days, and as soon as they let women in the Middle East start talking, you'll have to hold an editor hostage to get a response. Mark my words.

There were ten of us in the room. The Essay Without Arms worried me at first, but she had great bone structure and a wedding ring dangled from a chain on her neck, so I doubted her life has been all that hard.

Two male essays wandered in late. They were Homosexual Essays, a dime a dozen, and publishers aren't buying their battle with low self-esteem anymore. Even if their parents had kicked them out, I'd put money on a kind relative taking them in. It wasn't as if they'd landed in state care, like I had, and been delivered straight into the wandering hands of recently paroled foster parents. Being gay is about as tragic as a stray cuticle, and I wasn't born a Jehovah's Witness yesterday.

I presented my essay first, and tried not to look smug as I returned to my seat. The Article's Director let out a satisfied sigh and said, "I see someone's done this before." Yes, someone had. I've developed something of a reputation in the industry for taking meticulous notes on my suffering. It was a lesson learned the hard way after my year in sex slavery was rendered useless from the effects of crank on my long-term memory.

The third essay that read absolutely killed. She'd endured a series of miscarriages and narcoleptic seizures living in a work camp during her youth in communist China. Initially I was worried, but then I thought, whatever, good for her. There are twelve months in the year, and if Refugee Camp walked away with January, the April swimwear issue would be the perfect platform for my struggles with exercise bulimia. I don't mean to sound overly confident, but much of the unmitigated misfortune that has been my day-to-day life has taught me the importance of believing in myself.

Next up were two Divorce Essays, which came and went, forgettable at best. The Editor's critique suggested as much. Alopecia* followed. She had promise, but was still clearly struggling for a hook. Every essay who's been through chemo or tried lesbianism ends up bald. Bald isn't the story. Alopecia was heading in the right direction, loving herself, but she was getting there all

---

*Alopecia is the general medical term for baldness, but usually refers to a severe condition in which all hair on the head is lost.

wrong. I think she needed to focus on not having eyelashes or pubic hair. Now that's interesting. *That's* an essay.

The last kid was unpublished and new on the circuit. It was hard to figure out what we were up against with this one. He walked up to the podium unassisted, bearing no visible signs of physical or mental retardation. Maybe it was something systemic, or worse still, the latest wave of competition to hit the market: a slow-to-diagnose mental illness. I tried to relax. It was hard to build story arcs off problems cured by pills. Problems caused by pills, on the other hand, sold on query alone. Shit. Maybe he was an addict.

His essay was weird. I think he was about a Tuesday. Not the Tuesday of an amputation, just a regular any old Tuesday. He persisted on beginning sentences without the personal pronoun *I* and comparing one thing to another instead of just out-and-out saying what happened. I was trying to track his word count but lost myself momentarily as he described the veins in a cashier's hands. It reminded me of my grandmother, her rough physical topography a testament to a life of hard work. We all leaned in during one of his especially long pauses, only to realize he wasn't pausing, he was done.

The Refugee Essay applauded loudly, but quite honestly, I think her tepid grip on English and admitted narcolepsy barred her from being a qualified judge. The Gay Essays joined in too, but they'll clap for anything with a penis and a Michelangelo jawline.

My ovations, on the other hand, are earned, and this essay never once told me how he felt about himself. Although, I have to admit, if I'd been him during that section where his father didn't even open the gift, I'd have been devastated by the rejection. Not of the thing itself, but of what it represented. Like it wasn't a gift so much as it was longing in the shape of a box, wrapped up in a bow.

Look, it wasn't like this essay didn't have potential. I think everyone in that room agreed he had a certain something. But talent takes time. Inoperable tumors just don't sprout up overnight, and psychotic breaks are nothing if not slow to boil.

The Article's Director didn't bother to give him any feedback. One of the Divorce Essays tried to pipe in about the unsatisfying ending, but the Editor silenced her with the stop sign of her raised palm. Wordlessly, she stared at this essay with a sorrow that reminded me of the last look the man I believed to be my father gave me before heading to Vietnam, only later to return a person wholly different from the one who left. "You deserve something better than this," the Editor said, "yet for rules I follow, but did not create, I can't help you."

I thought about this essay a lot over the next few days, like he was beside me, equal parts familiar and strange. But the thing about life is that you simply cannot settle for melancholy, even when it's true. You are not a tragedy, you are a personal essay. You must rise above and you must do it in the last paragraph with basic grammar and easily recognized words.

Anyway, come November I will be buying every copy of *Marie Claire* I can get my one good hand on! You'll find me on page 124. If you haven't looked death straight in the eye or been sued by a sister wife,* you won't see yourself in my story. But you will find solace in knowing your own problems are petty and banal. I have ascended victorious from the ashes of immeasurable self-doubt and pain. And I have not simply survived, I have flourished.

## Reflections and Responses

1. What do all the essays mentioned in the piece, including the title essay, have in common? What is Vannoy suggesting about the truth value of their claims, and about what captures the attention of an audience? How does she suggest this? Give several examples of this pattern from the essay. Do you agree with the point Vannoy is subtly making about personal essays with this theme? Why or why not? What is the effect of putting this claim in the "mouth," so to speak, of an anthropomorphized essay itself?

2. What is the significance of the "weird" essay by the kid who "insisted on beginning sentences without the personal pronoun *I* and comparing one thing to another instead of just out-and-out saying what happened"? Does Vannoy (as opposed to her speaker, the essay) really believe that this essay is breaking a mold? Give evidence to support your answer.

3. How does the fact that these essays are competing for a spot in *Marie Claire* add to Vannoy's social satire? What is she saying about the relationship of art to commercial publishing? Do you agree? Why or why not? What is the significance, in particular, of her phrase "Article's Director and Editor" in the second paragraph?

---

*Sister wife** typically refers to the relationship between women in a polygamous marriage with the same husband.

JERALD WALKER

# The Mechanics of Being

*Blindness as a physical disability in literature often mirrors or contrasts with a metaphysical, symbolic sort of blindness—the inability to see what is in front of us that is the inevitable source of literary epiphany. In this personal essay, "The Mechanics of Being," Jerald Walker considers the struggles of his blind father, but finds that creating an identity for his parent around a handicap is reductive and untrue; the real meaning of his father's extraordinary life lies somewhere behind the eyes. In a clear, straightforward tone, Walker relates this epiphany to his own search for self-meaning, one crucial to his process of becoming an essayist.*

*Jerald Walker grew up on the south side of Chicago and received both his MFA and PhD from the University of Iowa. He writes about the complex experiences of African American identity in America today, a topic intertwined in his diverse and storied background. His essays have appeared in* The Missouri Review, The Chronicle of Higher Education, The Oxford American, *and* The Iowa Review, *among other publications. His first book,* Street Shadows: A Memoir of Race, Rebellion and Redemption, *won the 2011 PEN New England/L. L. Winship Award for Nonfiction and was named a Best Memoir of the Year by Kirkus Reviews. Walker is the Chair of the renowned Writing, Literature and Publishing Department at Emerson College.*

A DECADE AFTER dropping out of high school, I'd managed to arrive, like some survivor of a tragedy at sea, on the shores of a community college. My parents were thrilled when I phoned to say I was pursuing my childhood dream of being an architect. They were just as happy when I decided to be a sociologist instead. And after that a political scientist. Finally, a writer. "I'm going to write a novel based on my life," I said to my father one day. I was

*Source:* Best American Essays, 2009, Jerald Walker, *The Mechanics of Being* (2009).

in an MFA program by then, starting my second year. I'd recently found some statistics that said there'd been a sixty percent chance I'd end up in jail; I had stories to prove just how close I'd come. But after writing the first draft, my tale of black teenage delinquency seemed too clichéd to me, told too often before. I decided to write about my father instead. He, like my mother, was blind.

My father lost his sight when he was twelve. Climbing the stairs to his Chicago brownstone, he somehow fell backward, hitting his head hard against the pavement and filling his cranium with blood. It would have been better had some of this blood seeped out, alerting him to seek medical attention, but when the area of impact did no more than swell a little and throb, he tended to himself by applying two cubes of ice and eating six peanut-butter cookies. He did not tell anyone about the injury. He also did not mention the two weeks of headaches that followed, the month of dizzy spells, or that the world was growing increasingly, terrifyingly dim.

His mother had died of cancer four years earlier. His alcoholic father was rarely around. So at home my father only had to conceal his condition from his grandmother, Mama Alice, who herself could barely see past her cataracts, and his three older brothers and sister, who had historically paid him little attention. His grades at school suffered, but his teachers believed him when he said his discovery of girls was the cause. He spent less and less time with his friends, gave up baseball altogether, and took to walking with the aid of a tree branch. In this way his weakening vision remained undetected for three months until, one morning at breakfast, things fell apart.

Mama Alice greeted him as he sat at the table. She was by the stove, he knew, from the location of her voice. As he listened to her approach, he averted his face. She put a plate in front of him and another to his right, where she always sat. She pulled a chair beneath her. He reached for his fork, accidentally knocking it off the table. When several seconds had passed and he'd made no move, Mama Alice reminded him that forks couldn't fly. He took a deep breath and reached down to his left, knowing that to find the utensil would be a stroke of good fortune, since he couldn't even see the floor. After a few seconds of sweeping his fingers against the cool hardwood, he sat back up. There was fear in Mama Alice's voice when she asked him what was wrong. There was fear in his when he confessed he couldn't see.

He confessed everything then, eager, like a serial killer at last confronted with evidence of his crime, to have the details of his awful secret revealed. And when pressed about why he hadn't said anything sooner, he mentioned his master plan: he would make his sight get better by ignoring, as much as possible, the fact that it was getting worse.

For gutting out his fading vision in silence, Mama Alice called him brave. His father called him a fool. His teachers called him a liar. His astonished friends and siblings called him Merlin.* The doctors called him lucky. The damage was reversible, they said, because the clots that had formed on, and now pressed against, his occipital lobes could be removed. But they were wrong; those calcified pools of blood were in precarious locations and could not be excised without risking immediate paralysis or worse. The surgeons inserted a metal plate (my father never knew why) and later told Mama Alice that the clots would continue to grow, not only destroying the little sight he had left but also killing him. They gave him one more year to live, but they were wrong again.

They were wrong, too, in not predicting the seizures. He'd have them the rest of his life, internal earthquakes that toppled his body and pitched it violently across the floor. I remember these scenes vividly: as a young child, I would cower with my siblings at a safe distance while my mother, her body clamped on top of my father's, tried to put medicine in his mouth without losing a finger or before he chewed off his tongue. My father was a big man in those days, bloated on fried food and Schlitz†—one wrong move of his massive body would have caused my mother great harm— but she rode him expertly, desperately, a crocodile hunter on the back of her prey.

I expected one of those attacks to be fatal. But their damage would be done over five decades rather than all at once, slowly and insidiously eroding his brain, like water over stone. So we knew it wasn't Alzheimer's when he began forgetting the people and things that mattered and remembering the trivia of his youth. He knew it, too. That's why, at the age of fifty-five, he retired from teaching, moved with my mother to an apartment in the suburbs, and waited, like we all waited, for the rest of his mind to wash away. By the time I started teaching, when he was in his mid-sixties, he had forgotten us all.

According to the American Foundation for the Blind, every seven minutes someone in this country will become blind or visually impaired. There are 1.3 million blind people in the United

---

*Merlin:** A wizard of extraordinary powers in the medieval English Arthurian legend.

†Schlitz:** A Wisconsin-based brewer known for its inexpensive beer.

States. Less than half of the blind complete high school, and only 30 percent of working-age blind adults are employed. For African Americans, who make up nearly 20 percent of this population, despite being only 12 percent of the population at large, the statistics are even bleaker.

There are no reliable statistics for the number of unemployed blind prior to the 1960s, but some estimates put it as high as 95 percent. Most parents of blind children then had low expectations, hoping only that they would find some more useful role to play in society than selling pencils on street corners or playing a harmonica in some subway station, accompanied by a bored though faithful basset hound. Usually the blind were simply kept at home.

Mama Alice expected to keep my father at home for just a year, but even that was one year too many. She was elderly, diabetic, arthritic, and still mourning for her daughter and other accumulated losses. Now she had to care for a blind boy who spent his days crying or, when his spirits lifted, smashing things in his room. His school had expelled him, his friends had fled, and his sister and brothers had not been moved by his handicap to develop an interest in his affairs. And so, on the second anniversary of his predicted death, Mama Alice packed up his things, kissed him goodbye, implored him to summon more bravery, and sent him to jail.

My father never told any of his children about this. I read about it in his chart at the Sight Saving School, in Jacksonville, Illinois, where he'd been transferred after fifteen months in juvenile detention, and where, in 1994, the same year he and my mother moved to the suburbs, I went to visit.

Thirteen years later, the trip for me is a blur, punctuated now and then with random vivid images. I cannot see the face of the principal who greeted my wife and me, and I cannot visualize the office we were escorted to, but my father's chart is seared in my mind, a black three-ring binder with "Thomas Keller Walker" handwritten in the top right corner. Before I read it, the principal gave us a tour of the facilities. It was a twelve-acre complex that included basketball courts, a baseball diamond, a swimming pool … and classrooms. We were taken to the library, which was a museum of sorts, where the history of blindness was laid out in pictures and graphs behind glass cases. We ate lunch in the cafeteria where my father had eaten lunch. We went to the dorm room where he'd slept. Outside, we walked on the track where, cane in hand, my father had learned to run again.

After the tour, the principal took us back to her office and left us alone with his chart. It contained his height, weight, vital signs, and a summary of his academic performance before he lost his sight, which I cannot recall, though my guess is that it was exceptional. I also cannot remember the progress reports during his two years there. What I do remember was a description of him as "traumatized." That seemed about right to me. He'd lost his mother, his sight ... and his freedom. The only person who'd consistently showed him love had put him in prison. He was sixteen. I thought about my own life at sixteen, my delinquency and lack of purpose, and I suddenly felt as disappointed in myself as I know he must have been.

When we arrived back at our home in Iowa City, I typed up my notes from the trip. I decided not to call my father to ask about being put in juvenile detention; he'd had a reason for keeping it a secret, and I figured I should probably honor it.

In 1997 my parents moved again. My father was having difficulty with his balance and could not manage the stairs to their second-floor apartment. They bought a house in Dolton, a suburb in south Chicago; its primary appeal, besides being a single-level ranch, was its screened-in porch. For two summers they pretty much lived in there, crowding it with a swing set, a glider, a card table on which sat an electric water fountain, and four reclining chairs. My father was in one of those chairs enjoying a refreshing breeze and the faint sound of gurgling water when he had a grand mal seizure,* the worst in years. For two weeks he was in intensive care on a respirator. When he was finally able to breathe on his own, he was moved to a regular room, and a month later, when he could finally speak, he asked everyone, including my mother, his wife of forty-two years, who they were. While he languished in this state of oblivion, struggling to recall his life, I finished the first draft of my book, having him die peacefully in his sleep. Wishful thinking. Another massive seizure put him back in the ICU.

A month later he was transferred to an assisted living facility. Speech therapists helped him talk again, and occupational therapists showed him how to move with a walker. But no one could fix his brain. His thoughts were in a thousand fragments, floating in his skull, I imagined, like the flakes of a shaken snow globe. His filter gone, my father, this intensely private man from whom I'd had difficulty extracting just the basic facts of his life, was now a

---

*Grand mal seizure:* Also known as a tonic-clonic seizure, one that affects the entire brain.

mental flasher. My mother called me on occasion to report what he'd revealed.

"Mama Alice arrested me," he announced to her one day.

"I drink too much," he said on another.

"That Lynne can sure fry some chicken," he mentioned as well. After my mother relayed this last comment, there was a long pause before she asked me, "You *do* know about Lynne, don't you?"

Lynne was the woman he'd left her for. That was in 1963, thirteen years after my parents had met at the Chicago Lighthouse for the Blind, an organization that, among other services, provides employment for the visually impaired. My father was there assembling clocks while home on summer break from the Sight Saving School, and my mother, blind from a childhood accident, had been hired to do the same. They were seventeen when they met, eighteen when they married, and at twenty-five the parents of four children. My mother was pregnant with two more when my father moved out. That was all I knew, told to me one day by an older brother when I was in my mid-teens.

My parents had never discussed any of this with my siblings or me. My mother spoke openly about it now, though, and then she segued into talking about the man she'd dated during the two-year separation and about the son they'd had together. Her story I knew more about because when my twin and I were ten or so, her son, our half-brother, would come to our house to play with us. Occasionally he'd be accompanied by his father, a lanky blind man who chain-smoked and had a baritone voice that made me think of God. These attempts at civility lasted two summers before suddenly coming to an end. I never again saw my mother's son. And I never met my father's. I did not even know that he and Lynne had one, in fact, until three years ago, when one of my brothers mailed me a newspaper clipping from the *Chicago Sun-Times* describing his murder. His girlfriend had stabbed him thirty-one times. In the margin next to his picture, my brother had inscribed, "He looks just like *you!*" At first glance, I thought it was.

I made no mention of my stepbrothers in the novel, nor of my parents' separation, even though my mother, after speaking about this tumultuous period in their lives and of the resilient love that saw her and my father through it, suggested that I should. But at the time these details seemed peripheral to my point, too far astray from the topic at hand, not so much character development and depth, in my view, as dirty laundry. After chronicling how he'd lost his sight, I described how my father had navigated the sighted world: his learning to walk with a cane, his mastery of public transportation, how he'd earned his college degrees with the help of students and technological aids, his purchase of a Seeing Eye dog. Chapter after chapter focused on the mechanics of blindness when I should have focused on the mechanics of being. I should have explored my father's life beyond his handicap, just as, when I set out to write my own story, I should have explored my life beyond the trials common to inner-city black males. The novels I had written said no more about the range of my father's experiences or mine, no more about the meanings we had shaped from the chaos of our lives, than the newspaper clipping had said about his murdered son's.

I realized this while at my father's funeral. He died in September 2005, fifty-six years after the surgeons predicted he would, succumbing not to the blood clots after all, but rather to pneumonia. My wife and I left our two toddlers with their grandmother and flew from Boston to Chicago to attend the service. We sat in the second pew, just behind my mother, whose shoulder I would reach forward to pat as we listened to the organist play my father's favorite hymns. A cousin of mine read Scripture, a family friend recited a number of poems, and then the pastor gave the eulogy, a thorough account of my father's accomplishments, punctuated by the refrain: *and he did this while blind.* As I listened to him try to convince us that sightlessness was the core and sum of my father's existence, I understood that my novel had failed.

At some point during the eulogy, when I could no longer stand to listen, an incident I had long forgotten came to mind. I was probably thirteen years old, and my father, as he had so often done before, asked me to take some of his clothes to the dry cleaner's. Ordinarily this wasn't a big deal, but I had plans to join some friends at the park, so I whined and complained about being called into service. A mild argument ensued, which I lost, and a short while later I slumped out of the house with a paper bag full of his things. At the cleaner's, I watched the clerk remove each article of clothing, my lack of interest turning to horror as her hand, now frozen in midair, dangled before us a pair of my father's boxers. The clerk, very pretty and not much older than me, smiled and said, "We don't clean *these.*" I couldn't believe that my father had made such an unpardonable mistake, a blunder of the highest order, and the more I thought of it, the more upset I became. Halfway home, swollen with anger and eager to release it, I started to run. When I arrived, out of breath, my hands clenched by my sides, my father wasn't in the living room where I'd left him but was sitting on the porch. The second

I barked, "*Daddy!*" he exploded in laughter, his large stomach quivering beneath his T-shirt, his ruddy face pitched toward the sky. I could not, despite my best effort, help but join him. I rose after the pastor finished his eulogy and told this story to the congregation. If I ever attempt to write another novel about my father, this is where it will begin.

## Reflections and Responses

1. What exactly does Walker mean by the "mechanics of being"? What is he suggesting a real account of a human being must do? What does he mean by the contrast with the "mechanics of blindness"? How are both mechanical, and what sort of writing does each label represent?

2. Walker writes: "I should have explored my father's life beyond his handicap, just as, when I set out to write my own story, I should have explored my life beyond the trials common to inner-city black males." What is the relationship between these two instances of symbolic blindness? How does the story of Walker's murdered half brother connect to the epiphany he's had about his story and that of his father?

3. What is the story of Walker's father's underwear meant to convey? What does it tell you about Walker's father, and about Walker himself? About their relationship? Why does he say that the story will be the beginning of a prospective novel? Why is it a particularly important story in illustrating the "mechanics of being," and how does it contrast with the simplistic eulogy given by the reverend at the funeral?

RESHMA MEMON YAQUB

# The Washing

*The experience of the death of a loved one is one of the most personal in a personal essayist's repertoire. Writers typically focus on their internal experience of grief—the emotions, universal and particular, that swell within them after a death. Reshma Memon Yaqub, a writer whose work centers around the experience of being a Muslim woman in America, focuses in this essay on the physical acts of grieving, specifically the Muslim ritual ablution of the corpse after death. In this simple custom, Yaqub finds a world of meaning and experiences a sense of connection to something much larger than the specific Islamic rite.*

*Reshma Memon Yaqub lives in the Washington, D.C., area and is a frequent contributor to the* Washington Post Magazine, *where her essay originally appeared. It was selected by Edwidge Danticat for* The Best American Essays 2011.

I HADN'T PLANNED to wash the corpse.

But sometimes you just get caught up in the moment.

Through a series of slight miscalculations, I am the first of the deceased woman's relatives to arrive at the March Funeral Home in west Baltimore on this Monday morning. The body of the woman whom everyone in the family refers to simply as Dadee, which means "grandmother" in Urdu, is scheduled to arrive at 10 A.M., after being released from Howard County General Hospital in Columbia. I get to the funeral home at 10 A.M. and make somber chitchat with the five women from the local mosque who have volunteered to help with funeral preparations, which includes washing the deceased's body.

According to Islamic practices, family members of the same gender as the deceased are expected to bathe and shroud the body for

*Source:* Best American Essays, 2011, Reshma Memon YaQub, *The Washing* (2011).

burial. But because it's such a detailed ritual and because so many second-generation American Muslim families have yet to bury a loved one here, mosques have volunteers to assist grieving families. These women have come from the Islamic Society of Baltimore, where Dadee's funeral prayer service will be held this afternoon.

When the body arrives at 11:30 A.M., I am still the only family member here, and the body-washers naturally usher me in to join them for the ritual cleansing. It feels too late to tell them that technically I'm not a relative. When I first met the women an hour ago and spoke to them in my halting Urdu, it seemed unnecessary to explain that I was only about to become Dadee's relative. That she was the visiting grandmother of the woman engaged to marry my younger brother. That she had flown in from South Africa just ten days earlier to attend the upcoming wedding. That the only time I'd ever seen Dadee was last night at the hospital, a few hours after she died of sudden cardiac arrest, and then I hadn't even seen her face. When I had arrived at the hospital after getting the call from my brother, a white sheet was already drawn up over Dadee's face and tucked around her slight, eight-decade-old frame.

But the body-washers are understandably in a bit of a hurry. They've been kept waiting. And these genuinely kind women, five middle-aged homemakers, have their own responsibilities to get back to. I call my brother's fiancée to tell her the women want to start the hour-long washing, and she gives the go-ahead because she and her parents are still at the hospital. I tell the washers they can start, and they look at me expectantly. "Let's go," they say in Urdu. "Uh, okay," I reply. It's not that I don't want to wash the body. It's actually something I've wanted to experience for a while. Earlier in the year, I told the funeral coordinator at my mosque to keep me in mind if the need ever arose when I'm available. A few years ago, I attended a daylong workshop on how to perform the ritual. It's just, I didn't think today was going to be the day. I didn't think this was going to be my first body. I had come here, on this fall day in 2008, only to offer emotional support to my future sister-in-law and her mother.

I mutely follow the women through a heavy door marked "Staff Only," then down a flight of concrete stairs into the recesses of the funeral home. I'm starting to feel as though I'm trapped in one of those old *I Love Lucy* episodes, where Lucille Ball finds herself stomping grapes or smuggling cheese and has no idea how to stop this runaway train. We reach a large open room, where I see some gurneys and a simple coffin—upholstered in blue fabric with a white interior. Another doorway leads into a smaller private room that has been set up for ritual washings such as these, one of the volunteers tells me. From the doorway, I see Dadee's form in her hospital-issue white body bag, zipped all the way up. She is lying on a metal gurney, which, with its slightly raised edges, looks like a giant jellyroll pan. It has a quarter-sized hole at the bottom, near Dadee's feet, and the silver tray is tilted slightly so the water we will use drains into a utility sink.

I am not afraid of dead bodies. I have seen one up close three times in my thirty-six years: in high school at the funeral of a friend's father; as a police reporter when I took a tour of the local morgue; and more recently when a friend's ill baby died. But this is the first time I will touch a corpse, and *that* I am a little nervous about. But I'm also grateful for the opportunity. In Islam, it is a tremendous honor to give a body its final cleansing. The reward is immense—the erasure of forty major sins from your lifetime's record. Few people I know have ever washed a body. Because my parents and their peers moved here from Pakistan as young adults, most of them missed the natural opportunity to wash their own parents' or grandparents' bodies when they passed away overseas. And because few of my Muslim peers have lost their parents, we are two generations that don't know what to do when the time comes.

I feel blessed not to be experiencing my first washing with one of my own loved ones, when I would be numb from loss. I would have had little time to prepare myself because Muslims are buried immediately after death—the same day when possible. There is no embalming, no makeup, no Sunday finery for the deceased. There is no wake, no long speech, no cherrywood coffin with brass handles. There is simply the ritual washing, the shrouding in plain white cloth, a funeral prayer that lasts five minutes, and then the burial—preferably the body straight into the dirt, but, when required by law, placed in a basic coffin.

Body-washers put on sterile scrubs to protect us from whatever illness may have stricken the deceased. First I tie on a large paper apron. Then come rubber gloves. I see one of the women pull on a second pair of gloves over the first, and I follow. Next are puffy paper sleeves that attach from elbow to wrist and are tucked into the gloves. Then big paper booties. And finally a face mask with a large transparent plastic eye shield. By the end, I look like a cross between an overzealous nail technician and a Transformer.

I watch the women unzip Dadee from her body bag. As it opens, I see her face for the first time. Muslims believe that at the moment of death, when a soul that's headed to heaven emerges from its body, it slips out as easily as a drop of water spilling from a jug. But a soul that's headed to less heavenly places emerges with great difficulty, like a thorny branch being ripped through a pile of wet wool. I'm relieved that Dadee's face is peaceful, the way you hope somebody's grandmother's face would appear.

I stand by Dadee's feet, on her right side, and watch the women gently lift and rock Dadee to free her from the body bag. She's still dressed in her blue-and-white hospital gown. One of the women slowly lifts the gown, while another drapes Dadee with one of the same long aprons that we are all wearing. Not for one moment are any private areas of the body exposed. In the ritual Islamic bathing, the body is to be given the utmost respect. Not only is it to stay covered at all times, but the washers are to remain forever silent about anything negative or unusual they may witness—for example, if there is an unexpected scar, or deformity, or tattoo. In this, a human's most vulnerable of moments, she is guaranteed protection by her family and community.

It is time to begin the washing. A thin rubber hose is attached to the faucet in the utility sink, and one of the women turns on the water, adjusting it until it is comfortably warm, as prescribed by Islamic tradition. Because I'm the only "relative" in the room, I'm expected to perform the lion's share of the washing, but the women see that I have no idea what I'm doing, so they resume control, leaving me in charge of the feet. The first time I touch Dadee's feet, I am surprised. I expect the corpse to be cold, but it feels warm. Then again, she left this shell less than a day earlier. Perhaps these things take time.

A Muslim's body is generally washed three times from head to toe with soap and clean water. The right side is washed first, then the left. During the final washing, a softly fragranced oil is rubbed onto the body. The body has to be repeatedly tilted from one side to the other, and it is harder than I expected to maneuver the dead weight of a human form. Dadee's feet keep getting in the way of the hole at the bottom of the table, and every few minutes, the water pools up there and I have to lift her leg.

Fifteen minutes into the washing, my brother's fiancée and her mother knock at the door. The granddaughter is too distraught to join in and watches tearfully from the doorway. But Dadee's daughter-in-law dons the gear and steps into her family role. She is understandably traumatized, having been the one to find Dadee collapsed at their home in Columbia last night and having performed CPR to try to revive her. This is her first time washing a body too.

I can't tell if she wants me to stay and keep washing, or leave, because we've met just a handful of times in the three months since my brother proposed to her daughter. But she doesn't say anything, so I stay.

Washing a body in this way, it's impossible not to flash forward to your own ending. I have lain on a table like this before, draped strategically with white cloth, comforting hands laid on me. But that was just for a massage at the Red Door Spa. When I imagine my own washing, I see myself being handled by loved ones: my two oldest friends, Farin and Sajeela; my brothers' wives; my mother and mother-in-law. I've also asked two women at my mosque whom I adore to participate. Maybe I'll live long enough to have a daughter-in-law in the room with me. Should I be so lucky, even a granddaughter. The more I see, the more I appreciate the way a Muslim's body is handled after death. There is so much gentleness, so much privacy. The body isn't left unattended in the short span between death and burial. It unnerves me when, walking through the funeral home's hallway, I look into a room and see a dead man lying on a gurney, unattended. I wonder how long he has been there, how he has been handled, who has had access to him. Whether the water that ran over his body was warmed.

The body-washers pass the rubber hose back and forth to each other and to me and my soon-to-be relative, who strokes her mother-in-law's hair and washes it. At the end, we dry Dadee with clean white towels and slide several towels underneath her, with their edges hanging over the sides of the gurney. We then roll her gurney into the adjacent room where the coffin awaits for her transport to the mosque. We station her gurney next to a second one, where one of the women has already laid out Dadee's funeral shroud, called a kafan, made of five white cloths of different sizes. We use the towels underneath Dadee as handles to lift her to the second gurney. Pieces of the white fabric are folded around Dadee's body and secured with ropelike strands of the same cloth. One of the volunteers, Rabia Marfani, assembles these fabric kits at home, using cotton/polyester bed sheets that she buys at Walmart.

When the cloth that wraps the hair back is tied on Dadee, she seems strangely transported. She looks so small and fragile, like a little girl with a bonnet tied around her hair. Finally, a large cloth is folded around the entire body, completely enclosing her. It's tied shut with the ropelike strands, and the body looks almost like a wrapped gift. Together we lift Dadee into the coffin. One of the women shows me and Dadee's daughter-in-law how to open the fabric around Dadee's face, should any of her family members ask to see her one last time at the Janazah prayer service at the mosque.

Afterward, I hug each of the body-washers and thank them deeply for their help. Although Dadee is not exactly my relative, I feel as though these women have done me a huge personal favor, expecting nothing in return. When I ask Marfani why she has participated in this custom more than thirty times in her fifty years, she replies: "It's our obligation. And there is so much reward from God ... One day I will also be lying there, and somebody will do this for me." She started as a teenager in Pakistan, assisting when her grandmother and aunt passed away. She encourages younger women to volunteer or just watch, because this knowledge needs to be passed on.

We all then raise our hands and pray, asking God to forgive Dadee's sins, to give her the best in the next life. I inwardly alternate between speaking to God and speaking to Dadee. I ask God to welcome her; I wish Dadee good luck on this ultimate pilgrimage. Islam teaches us that after the soul is removed from the body, it briefly faces God to learn its fate, then is returned to the body while on its way to the grave. There it awaits its full reckoning on the Day of Judgment. Though Dadee is no longer of this world, she can continue to earn blessings based on what she has left behind—through righteous offspring who pray for her forgiveness, through knowledge that she has spread to others, or through charitable work whose effects outlast her.

I pray for Dadee, and I also apologize to her for a mistake she doesn't know I nearly made. In today's mail, after the funeral, Dadee's family will receive my hand-addressed invitation to her for a wedding reception hosted by my parents. Earlier this week, I had argued with my brother over the unnecessary expense of mailing separate invitations to multiple family members at the same address. I had considered just sending a joint one. In the end, how grateful I am that I did it his way. Of course you deserve your own invitation, Dadee, after flying across the world to witness your granddaughter's wedding.

I ask God one last time to have mercy on her soul. As I pick up my purse and turn to leave the room, I address my final words to both of them: "Innaa lillaahi wa-innaa ilaihi raje'oon." To God we belong, and to God we return.

## Reflections and Responses

1. What surprises Yaqub about the body of Dadee and about the custom? Why are these things surprising? How does she communicate the surprise she felt in the essay? What do these moments of disconnect between expectation and reality say about the way she approached the death of Dadee and the ritual surrounding it, and about what she learned from undergoing these things?

2. Why does Yaqub end the essay with the "mistake" she made about her wedding invitation? How does a wedding relate to this funeral sacrament, and what does the juxtaposition of the two rituals do for the structure of the essay as a whole?

3. The essay is titled "The Washing," and Yaqub suggests there may be more than just a literal meaning to this label. What "washing" may be going on, besides the washing the author and the women are performing on the corpse? Where in the essay does Yaqub specifically suggest this?

# 2

# *The Attentive Mind: Observation, Reflection, Insight*

SUE ALLISON

# Taking a Reading

*Measurement is an inseparable element of life: Think of how often you use inches, pounds, and degrees Fahrenheit every day, even subconsciously. The language of measurement, though, is something we all think less about— most of the words and phrases we use to measure come from physical entities (a "yard" used to be an actual yard, a "foot" a typical man's foot), but in the modern standardized era we've become alienated from these origins. As a writer, Sue Allison can't help but adore the varied and lilting words we use to "take a reading" of the physical world—in this essay, she considers a number of them, their internal beauty, and how ultimately little they mean without us to keep them employed.*

*Sue Allison worked for two years as a London-based freelance writer after graduating from McGill University. She then moved to New York, where she served in various roles with* Life *magazine; when that folded she earned an MFA from the Vermont College of Fine Arts. She is the author of a book on London's Bloomsbury group, and her essays and stories have appeared in a wide variety of publications. "Taking a Reading" first appeared in* Mid-American Review *and was selected by Mary Oliver for* The Best American Essays 2009.

A YARD, A PACE, a foot, a fathom. How beautiful the language of measurement is, and we're not even talking iambs* yet. A fifth, a finger, a jigger, a drop, a dram, a grain, a scruple. A scruple is twenty grains, or twenty barley cornes. It is as small as a pebble. If you have three, you have a dram. First scruples comprise arithmetic degrees and are divided into seconds. A fluid dram takes sixty minims. Add twenty more minims, at minimum, and you have a teaspoon.

---

*Iambs are units of measurement for beats and syllables in poetry.

*Source:* Best American Essays, 2009, Sue Allison, *Taking a Reading* (2009).

My husband's foot is twelve inches long, but mine only seven, making it useless for counting off the length of a carpet or a couch. The yard we have together is bigger than the yard around the house I lived in as a child, and yet is still a yard. If my husband's foot was 660 times what it is, it would be a perfect furlong, but fathom is my favorite. It's how tall my husband is.

A span, a palm, a hand, a nail, an ohm, a knot, a stadion. A stadion was Greek for 622 feet, Roman for 606, not an inch more or less. It was a distance before it was a theater of sport or massacre. The distance between two thumbs is infinite, whether touching or not. A cranberry bushel is bigger than a bushel and a petroleum barrel is bigger than a barrel. What is a bushel and what a barrel when the cranberries are on the bush and the petroleum below ground? A gill is a half of a cup. I have read many recipes that called for half a cup, but none that ever called for a gill, which is never half empty nor half full but all there is when there's a gill.

Carat, candela, caliber, Kelvin, case. A chain is precisely 66 feet divided into precisely 100 links. It is also what is around my neck holding a small diamond heart which I've kept clasped since receiving it some anniversaries ago. It cannot hold a ship to shore, but holds a great deal more. A decibel is barely audible, it taking ten to work up to a light whisper, and who's to say whose whisper we should use. Could I be the Greenwich* of sound? An ell does not come before an em. I don't know why you use hands to measure horses. I mean, how could you possibly? My hand or yours? Two hogsheads make a pipe, though the quantity of a hogshead depends on what it is in it, molasses, say, or ale, as well as where it is meted out: London or an ordinary country shire.

A quintal, a quire, a case, a ream. A ream is a lot of paper, sold and purchased blank. Written on, it's a book.

## Reflections and Responses

1. Consider the issue of voice in this essay. Is it an informative, objective piece of writing, a personal, subjective one, or something in between? Where does the author insert herself into the prose, and where is it detached? Why is this tension between analysis and personal voice important in an essay about measurement?

---

*Greenwich, England, is the traditional home of "mean time," the time of day against which other world time zones are measured.

2. One paragraph of this essay begins with the sentence "Carat, candela, caliber, Kelvin, case." Allison never defines or reflects directly on these terms. Look them up if you don't know their meanings. Why does Allison begin the paragraph with these five units of measurement? What is their significance, and what is the effect within the essay of listing them here?

3. What is the meaning of the last sentence of the essay? How does a ream of blank paper contrast with a book? What is Allison implying by the similarity between the two, and what does the transformation say about the importance of point of view to meaning? What are the two meanings of "taking a reading" in the title, and how might they both relate to this final sentence?

ANNIE DILLARD

# The Stunt Pilot

*Creative expression can take many forms; it need not refer only to literature, painting, or music. We can find creativity in craft and design, in the movements of dancers and athletes, and even—as the following essay reveals—in the aerobatics of a stunt pilot. Observing the breathtaking dives and spins, the "loops and arabesques" of a celebrated pilot, Annie Dillard is struck by their resemblance to artistic expression. She finds in the pilot's use of space a new kind of beauty, one that seems to encompass all the arts—poetry, painting, music, sculpture: "The black plane dropped spinning, and flattened out spinning the other way; it began to carve the air into forms that built wildly and musically on each other and never ended."*

*Annie Dillard is one of America's preeminent essayists, someone for whom, as she puts it, the essay is not an occasional piece but her "real work." Her many award-winning books of essays and nonfiction include* Pilgrim at Tinker Creek, *which won the Pulitzer Prize for General Nonfiction in 1975;* Holy the Firm *(1977);* Living by Fiction *(1982);* Teaching a Stone to Talk *(1982);* An American Childhood *(1987);* The Writing Life *(1989); and* For the Time Being *(1999). Dillard has taught creative writing at Wesleyan University in Middletown, Connecticut, and currently lives in Key West, Florida. Dillard has also published two novels,* The Living *(1992) and* The Maytrees *(2007). "The Stunt Pilot" originally appeared in* Esquire *(1989) and was selected by Justin Kaplan for* The Best American Essays *1990.*

Dave Rahm lived in Bellingham, Washington, north of Seattle. Bellingham, a harbor town, lies between the alpine North Cascade Mountains and the San Juan Islands in Haro Strait above Puget Sound. The latitude is that of Newfoundland. Dave Rahm was a stunt pilot, the air's own genius.

In 1975, with a newcomer's willingness to try anything once, I attended the Bellingham Air Show. The Bellingham airport was a wide clearing in a forest of tall Douglas firs; its runways suited small planes. It was June. People wearing blue or tan zipped jackets stood loosely on the concrete walkways and runways outside the coffee shop. At that latitude in June, you stayed outside because you could, even most of the night, if you could think up something to do. The sky did not darken until ten o'clock or so, and it never got very dark. Your life parted and opened in the sunlight. You tossed your dark winter routines, thought up mad projects, and improvised everything from hour to hour. Being a stunt pilot seemed the most reasonable thing in the world; you could wave your arms in the air all day and night, and sleep next winter.

I saw from the ground a dozen stunt pilots; the air show scheduled them one after the other, for an hour of aerobatics. Each pilot took up his or her plane and performed a batch of tricks. They were precise and impressive. They flew upside down, and straightened out; they did barrel rolls, and straightened out; they drilled through dives and spins, and landed gently on a far runway.

For the end of the day, separated from all other performances of every sort, the air show director had scheduled a program titled "Dave Rahm." The leaflet said that Rahm was a geologist who taught at Western Washington University. He had flown for King Hussein in Jordan. A tall man in the crowd told me Hussein had seen Rahm fly on a visit the king made to the United States; he had invited him to Jordan to perform at ceremonies. Hussein was a pilot, too. "Hussein thought he was the greatest thing in the world."

Idly, paying scant attention, I saw a medium-sized, rugged man dressed in brown leather, all begoggled, climb in a black biplane's open cockpit. The plane was a Bücker Jungman, built in the thirties. I saw a tall, dark-haired woman seize a propeller tip at the plane's nose and yank it down till the engine caught. He was off; he climbed high over the airport in his biplane, very high until he was barely visible as a mote, and then seemed to fall down the air, diving headlong, and streaming beauty in spirals behind him.

The black plane dropped spinning, and flattened out spinning the other way; it began to carve the air into forms that built wildly and musically on each other and never ended. Reluctantly, I started paying attention. Rahm drew high above the world an inexhaustibly glorious line; it piled over our heads in loops and arabesques. It was like a Saul Steinberg* fantasy; the plane was the pen. Like Steinberg's contracting and billowing pen line, the line Rahm spun moved to form new, punning shapes from the edges of the old. Like a Klee† line, it smattered the sky with landscapes and systems.

The air show announcer hushed. He had been squawking all day, and now he quit. The crowd stilled. Even the children watched dumbstruck as the slow, black biplane buzzed its way around the air. Rahm made beauty with his whole body; it was pure pattern, and you could watch it happen. The plane moved every way a line can move, and it controlled three dimensions, so the line carved massive and subtle slits in the air like sculptures. The plane looped the loop, seeming to arch its back like a gymnast; it stalled, dropped, and spun out of it climbing; it spiraled and knifed west on one side's wings and back east on another; it turned cart-wheels, which must be physically impossible; it played with its own line like a cat with yarn. How did the pilot know where in the air he was? If he got lost, the ground would swat him.

Rahm did everything his plane could do: tailspins, four-point rolls, flat spins, figure eights, snap rolls, and hammerheads. He did pirouettes on the plane's tail. The other pilots could do these stunts too, skillfully, one at a time. But Rahm used the plane inexhaustibly, like a brush marking thin air.

His was pure energy and naked spirit. I have thought about it for years. Rahm's line unrolled in time. Like music, it split the bulging rim of the future along its seam. It pried out the present. We watchers waited for the split-second curve of beauty in the present to reveal itself. The human pilot, Dave Rahm, worked in the cockpit right at the plane's nose; his very body tore into the future for us and reeled it down upon us like a curling peel.

Like any fine artist, he controlled the tension of the audience's longing. You desired, unwittingly, a certain kind of roll or climb, or a return to a certain portion of the air, and he fulfilled your hope slantingly, like a poet, or evaded it until you thought you would burst, and then fulfilled it surprisingly, so you gasped and cried out.

The oddest, most exhilarating and exhausting thing was this: he never quit. The music had no periods, no rests or endings;

---

*Saul Steinberg: Contemporary artist (1914–1999) who also created numerous covers for *The New Yorker* magazine.

†Klee: Paul Klee (1879–1940), a Swiss artist known for his highly distinctive abstract paintings.

the poetry's beautiful sentence never ended; the line had no finish; the sculptured forms piled overhead, one into another without surcease. Who could breathe, in a world where rhythm itself had no periods?

It had taken me several minutes to understand what an extraordinary thing I was seeing. Rahm kept all that embellished space in mind at once. For another twenty minutes I watched the beauty unroll and grow more fantastic and unlikely before my eyes. Now Rahm brought the plane down slidingly, and just in time, for I thought I would snap from the effort to compass and remember the line's long intelligence; I could not add another curve. He brought the plane down on a far runway. After a pause, I saw him step out, an ordinary man, and make his way back to the terminal.

The show was over. It was late. Just as I turned from the runway, something caught my eye and made me laugh. It was a swallow, a blue-green swallow, having its own air show, apparently inspired by Rahm. The swallow climbed high over the runway, held its wings oddly, tipped them, and rolled down the air in loops. The inspired swallow. I always want to paint, too, after I see the Rembrandts. The blue-green swallow tumbled precisely, and caught itself and flew up again as if excited, and looped down again, the way swallows do, but tensely, holding its body carefully still. It was a stunt swallow.

I went home and thought about Rahm's performance that night, and the next day, and the next.

I had thought I knew my way around beauty a little bit. I knew I had devoted a good part of my life to it, memorizing poetry and focusing my attention on complexity of rhythm in particular, on force, movement, repetition, and surprise, in both poetry and prose. Now I had stood among dandelions between two asphalt runways in Bellingham, Washington, and begun learning about beauty. Even the Boston Museum of Fine Arts was never more inspiriting than this small northwestern airport on this time-killing Sunday afternoon in June. Nothing on earth is more gladdening than knowing we must roll up our sleeves and move back the boundaries of the humanly possible once more.

Later I flew with Dave Rahm; he took me up. A generous geographer, Dick Smith, at Western Washington University, arranged it, and came along. Rahm and Dick Smith were colleagues at the university. In geology, Rahm had published two books and many articles. Rahm was handsome in a dull sort of way, blunt-featured, wide-jawed, wind-burned, keen-eyed, and taciturn. As anyone would expect. He was forty. He wanted to show me the Cascade Mountains; these enormous peaks, only fifty miles from the coast, rise over nine thousand feet; they are heavily glaciated. Whatcom County has more glaciers than the lower forty-eight states combined; the Cascades make the Rocky Mountains look like hills. Mount Baker is volcanic, like most Cascade peaks. That year, Mount Baker was acting up. Even from my house at the shore I could see, early in the morning on clear days, volcanic vapor rise near its peak. Often the vapor made a cloud that swelled all morning and hid the snows. Every day the newspapers reported on Baker's activity: Would it blow? (A few years later, Mount St. Helens did blow.)

Rahm was not flying his trick biplane that day, but a faster enclosed plane, a single-engine Cessna. We flew from a bumpy grass airstrip near my house, out over the coast and inland. There was coastal plain down there, but we could not see it for clouds. We were over the clouds at five hundred feet and inside them too, heading for an abrupt line of peaks we could not see. I gave up on everything, the way you do in airplanes; it was out of my hands. Every once in a while Rahm saw a peephole in the clouds and buzzed over for a look. "That's Larsen's pea farm," he said, or "That's Nooksack Road," and he changed our course with a heave.

When we got to the mountains, he slid us along Mount Baker's flanks sideways.

Our plane swiped at the mountain with a roar. I glimpsed a windshield view of dirty snow traveling fast. Our shaking, swooping belly seemed to graze the snow. The wings shuddered; we peeled away and the mountain fell back and the engines whined. We felt flung, because we were in fact flung; parts of our faces and internal organs trailed pressingly behind on the curves. We came back for another pass at the mountain, and another. We dove at the snow headlong like suicides; we jerked up, down, or away at the last second, so late we left our hearts, stomachs, and lungs behind. If I forced myself to hold my heavy head up against the G's,* and to raise my eyelids, heavy as barbells, and to notice what I saw, I could see the wrinkled green crevasses cracking the glaciers' snow.

Pitching snow filled all the windows, and shapes of dark rock. I had no notion which way was up. Everything was black or gray or

*G's: A measure of gravitational force.

white except the fatal crevasses; everything made noise and shook. I felt my face smashed sideways and saw rushing abstractions of snow in the windshield. Patches of cloud obscured the snow fleetingly. We straightened out, turned, and dashed at the mountainside for another pass, which we made, apparently, on our ear, an inch or two away from the slope. Icefalls and cornices jumbled and fell away. If a commercial plane's black box, such as the FAA painstakingly recovers from crash sites, could store videotapes as well as pilots' last words, some videotapes would look like this: a mountainside coming up at the windows from all directions, ice and snow and rock filling the screen up close and screaming by.

Rahm was just being polite. His geographer colleague wanted to see the fissure on Mount Baker from which steam escaped. Everybody in Bellingham wanted to see that sooty fissure, as did every geologist in the country; no one on earth could fly so close to it as Rahm. He knew the mountain by familiar love and feel, like a face; he knew what the plane could do and what he dared to do.

When Mount Baker inexplicably let us go, he jammed us into cloud again and soon tilted. "The Sisters!" someone shouted, and I saw the windshield fill with red rock. This mountain looked infernal, a drear and sheer plane of lifeless rock. It was red and sharp; its gritty blades cut through the clouds at random. The mountain was quiet. It was in shade. Careening, we made sideways passes at these brittle peaks too steep for snow. Their rock was full of iron, somebody shouted at me then or later; the iron had rusted, so they were red. Later, when I was back on the ground, I recalled that, from a distance, the two jagged peaks called the Twin Sisters looked translucent against the sky; they were sharp, tapered, and fragile as arrowheads.

I talked to Rahm. He was flying us out to the islands now. The islands were fifty or sixty miles away. Like many other people, I had picked Bellingham, Washington, by looking at an atlas. It was clear from the atlas that you could row in the salt water and see snow-covered mountains; you could scale a glaciated mountainside with an ice ax in August, skirting green crevasses two hundred feet deep, and look out on the islands in the sea. Now, in the air, the clouds had risen over us; dark forms lay on the glinting water. There was almost no color to the day, just blackened green and some yellow. I knew the islands were forested in dark Douglas firs the size of skyscrapers. Bald eagles scavenged on the beaches; robins the size of herring gulls sang in the clearings. We made our way out to the islands through the layer of air between the curving planet and its held, thick clouds.

"When I started trying to figure out what I was going to do with my life, I decided to become an expert on mountains. It wasn't much to be, it wasn't everything, but it was something. I was going to know everything about mountains from every point of view. So I started out in geography." Geography proved too pedestrian for Rahm, too concerned with "how many bushels of wheat an acre." So he ended up in geology. Smith had told me that geology departments throughout the country used Rahm's photographic slides—close-ups of geologic features from the air.

"I used to climb mountains. But you know, you can get a better feel for a mountain's power flying around it, flying all around it, than you can from climbing it tied to its side like a flea."

He talked about his flying performances. He thought of the air as a line, he said. "This end of the line, that end of the line—like a rope." He improvised. "I get a rhythm going and stick with it." While he was performing in a show, he paid attention, he said, to the lighting. He didn't play against the sun. That was all he said about what he did.

In aerobatic maneuvers, pilots pull about seven positive G's on some stunts and six negative G's on others. Some gyrations push; others pull. Pilots alternate the pressures carefully, so they do not gray out or black out.

Later I learned that some stunt pilots tune up by wearing gravity boots. These are boots made to hook over a doorway; wearing them, you hang in the doorway upside down. It must startle a pilot's children to run into their father or mother in the course of their home wanderings—the parents hanging wide-eyed, upside down in the doorway like a bat.

We were landing; here was the airstrip on Stuart Island—that island to which Ferrar Burn* was dragged by the tide. We put down, climbed out of the plane, and walked. We wandered a dirt track through fields to a lee shore where yellow sandstone ledges slid into the sea. The salt chuck, people there called salt water. The sun came out. I caught a snake in the salt chuck; the snake, eighteen inches long, was swimming in the green shallows.

I had a survivor's elation. Rahm had found Mount Baker in the clouds before Mount Baker found the plane. He had wiped it

---

*Ferrar Burn: A resident of the San Juan Islands in northwest Washington who became a local legend after struggling with severe tides to bring in a floating log of Alaska cedar that he had tied to his rowboat. Dillard recounts the story in the chapter that precedes this one in her book, *The Writing Life*.

with the fast plane like a cloth and we had lived. When we took off from Stuart Island and gained altitude, I asked if we could turn over—could we do a barrel roll? The plane was making a lot of noise, and Dick Smith did not hear any of this, I learned later. "Why not?" Rahm said, and added surprisingly, "It won't hurt the plane." Without ado he leaned on the wheel and the wing went down and we went somersaulting over it. We upended with a roar. We stuck to the plane's sides like flung paint. All the blood in my body bulged on my face; it piled between my skull and skin. Vaguely I could see the chrome sea twirling over Rahm's head like a baton, and the dark islands sliding down the skies like rain.

The G's slammed me into my seat like thugs and pinned me while my heart pounded and the plane turned over slowly and compacted each organ in turn. My eyeballs were newly spherical and full of heartbeats. I seemed to hear a crescendo; the wing rolled shuddering down the last 90 degrees and settled on the flat. There were the islands, admirably below us, and the clouds, admirably above. When I could breathe, I asked if we could do it again, and we did. He rolled the other way. The brilliant line of the sea slid up the side window bearing its heavy islands. Through the shriek of my blood and the plane's shakes I glimpsed the line of the sea over the windshield, thin as a spear. How in performance did Rahm keep track while his brain blurred and blood roared in his ears without ceasing? Every performance was a tour de force and a show of will, a *Machtspruch*.* I had seen the other stunt pilots straighten out after a trick or two; their blood could drop back and the planet simmer down. An Olympic gymnast, at peak form, strings out a line of spins ten stunts long across a mat, and is hard put to keep his footing at the end. Rahm endured much greater pressure on his faster spins using the plane's power, and he could spin in three dimensions and keep twirling till he ran out of sky room or luck.

When we straightened out, and had flown straightforwardly for ten minutes toward home, Dick Smith, clearing his throat, brought himself to speak. "What was that we did out there?"

"The barrel rolls?" Rahm said. "They were barrel rolls." He said nothing else. I looked at the back of his head; I could see the serious line of his cheek and jaw. He was in shirtsleeves, tanned, strong-wristed. I could not imagine loving him under any circumstance; he was alien to me, unfazed. He looked like GI Joe. He flew with that matter-of-fact, bored gesture pilots use. They click

*Machtspruch: German, meaning "power speech."

overhead switches and turn dials as if only their magnificent strength makes such dullness endurable. The half circle of wheel in their big hands looks like a toy they plan to crush in a minute; the wiggly stick the wheel mounts seems barely attached.

A crop-duster pilot in Wyoming told me the life expectancy of a crop-duster pilot is five years. They fly too low. They hit buildings and power lines. They have no space to fly out of trouble, and no space to recover from a stall. We were in Cody, Wyoming, out on the north fork of the Shoshone River. The crop duster had wakened me that morning flying over the ranch house and clearing my bedroom roof by half an inch. I saw the bolts on the wheel assembly a few feet from my face. He was spraying with pesticide the plain old grass. Over breakfast I asked him how long he had been dusting crops. "Four years," he said, and the figure stalled in the air between us for a moment. "You know you're going to die at it someday," he added. "We all know it. We accept that; it's part of it." I think now that, since the crop duster was in his twenties, he accepted only that he had to say such stuff; privately he counted on skewing the curve.

I suppose Rahm knew the fact too. I do not know how he felt about it. "It's worth it," said the early French aviator Mermoz. He was Antoine de Saint-Exupéry's friend. "It's worth the final smashup."

Rahm smashed up in front of King Hussein, in Jordan, during a performance. The plane spun down and never came out of it; it nosedived into the ground and exploded. He bought the farm. I was living then with my husband out on that remote island in the San Juans, cut off from everything. Battery radios picked up the Canadian Broadcasting Company out of Toronto, half a continent away; island people would, in theory, learn if the United States blew up, but not much else. There were no newspapers. One friend got the Sunday *New York Times* by mail boat on the following Friday. He saved it until Sunday and had a party, every week; we all read the Sunday *Times* and no one mentioned that it was last week's.

One day, Paul Glenn's brother flew out from Bellingham to visit; he had a seaplane. He landed in the water in front of the cabin and tied up to our mooring. He came in for coffee, and he gave out news of this and that, and—Say, did we know that stunt pilot Dave Rahm had cracked up? In Jordan, during a performance: he never came out of a dive. He just dove right down into the ground, and his wife was there watching. "I saw it on CBS News last night." And then—with a sudden sharp look at my filling eyes—"What, did you know him?" But no, I did not know him. He took me up once. Several years ago. I admired his flying. I had thought that danger was the safest thing in the world, if you went about it right.

Later, I found a newspaper. Rahm was living in Jordan that year; King Hussein invited him to train the aerobatics team, the Royal Jordanian Falcons. He was also visiting professor of geology at the University of Jordan. In Amman that day he had been flying a Pitt Special, a plane he knew well. Katy Rahm, his wife of six months, was sitting beside Hussein in the viewing stands, with her daughter. Rahm died performing a Lomcevak combined with a tail slide and hammerhead. In a Lomcevak, the pilot brings the plane up on a slant and pirouettes. I had seen Rahm do this: the falling plane twirled slowly like a leaf. Like a ballerina, the plane seemed to hold its head back stiff in concentration at the music's slow, painful beauty. It was one of Rahm's favorite routines. Next the pilot flies straight up, stalls the plane, and slides down the air on his tail. He brings the nose down—the hammerhead—kicks the engine, and finishes with a low loop.

It is a dangerous maneuver at any altitude, and Rahm was doing it low. He hit the ground on the loop; the tail slide had left him no height. When Rahm went down, King Hussein dashed to the burning plane to pull him out, but he was already dead.

A few months after the air show, and a month after I had flown with Rahm, I was working at my desk near Bellingham, where I lived, when I heard a sound so odd it finally penetrated my concentration. It was the buzz of an airplane, but it rose and fell musically, and it never quit; the plane never flew out of earshot. I walked out on the porch and looked up: it was Rahm in the black and gold biplane, looping all over the air. I had been wondering about his performance flight: could it really have been so beautiful? It was, for here it was again. The little plane twisted all over the air like a vine. It trailed a line like a very long mathematical proof you could follow only so far, and then it lost you in its complexity. I saw Rahm flying high over the Douglas firs, and out over the water, and back over farms. The air was a fluid, and Rahm was an eel.

It was as if Mozart could move his body through his notes, and you could walk out on the porch, look up, and see him in periwig and breeches, flying around in the sky. You could hear the music as he dove through it; it streamed after him like a contrail.

I lost myself; standing on the firm porch, I lost my direction and reeled. My neck and spine rose and turned, so I followed the plane's line kinesthetically. In his open-cockpit black plane, Rahm demonstrated curved space. He slid down ramps of air, he vaulted and wheeled. He piled loops in heaps and praised height. He unrolled the scroll of air, extended it, and bent it into Möbius strips; he furled line in a thousand new ways, as if he were inventing a script and writing it in one infinitely recurving utterance until I thought the bounds of beauty must break. From inside, the looping plane had sounded tinny, like a kazoo. Outside, the buzz rose and fell to the Doppler effect as the plane looped near or away. Rahm cleaved the sky like a prow and tossed out time left and right in his wake. He performed for forty minutes; then he headed the plane, as small as a wasp, back to the airport inland. Later I learned Rahm often practiced acrobatic flights over this shore. His idea was that if he lost control and was going to go down, he could ditch in the salt chuck, where no one else would get hurt.

If I had not turned two barrel rolls in an airplane, I might have fancied Rahm felt good up there, and playful. Maybe Jackson Pollock felt a sort of playfulness, in addition to the artist's usual deliberate and intelligent care. In my limited experience, painting, unlike writing, pleases the senses while you do it, and more while you do it than after it is done. Drawing lines with an airplane, unfortunately, tortures the senses. Jet bomber pilots black out. I knew Rahm felt as if his brain were bursting his eardrums, felt that if he let his jaws close as tight as centrifugal force pressed them, he would bite through his lungs.
"All virtue is a form of acting," Yeats said. Rahm deliberately turned himself into a figure. Sitting invisible at the controls of a distant airplane, he became the agent and the instrument of art and invention. He did not tell me how he felt when we spoke of his performance flying; he told me instead that he paid attention to how his plane and its line looked to the audience against the lighted sky. If he had noticed how he felt, he could not have done the work. Robed in his airplane, he was as featureless as a priest. He was lost in his figural aspect like an actor or a king. Of his flying, he had said only, "I get a rhythm and stick with it." In its reticence, this statement reminded me of Veronese's* "Given a large canvas, I enhanced it as I saw fit." But Veronese was ironic,

*Veronese: Paolo Veronese (1528–1588), famous Venetian painter.

and Rahm was not; he was as literal as an astronaut; the machine gave him tongue.

When Rahm flew, he sat down in the middle of art and strapped himself in. He spun it all around him. He could not see it himself. If he never saw it on film, he never saw it at all—as if Beethoven could not hear his final symphonies not because he was deaf but because he was inside the paper on which he wrote. Rahm must have felt it happen, that fusion of vision and metal, motion and idea. I think of this man as a figure, a college professor with a PhD upside down in the loud band of beauty. What are we here for? *Propter chorum,* the monks say: for the sake of the choir.

"Purity does not lie in separation from but in deeper penetration into the universe," Teilhard de Chardin* wrote. It is hard to imagine a deeper penetration into the universe than Rahm's last dive in his plane, or than his inexpressible wordless selfless line's inscribing the air and dissolving. Any other art may be permanent. I cannot recall one Rahm sequence. He improvised. If Christo[†] wraps a building or dyes a harbor, we join his poignant and fierce awareness that the work will be gone in days. Rahm's plane shed a ribbon in space, a ribbon whose end unraveled in memory while its beginning unfurled as surprise. He may have acknowledged that what he did could be called art, but it would have been, I think, only in the common misusage, which holds art to be the last extreme of skill. Rahm rode the point of the line to the possible; he discovered it and wound it down to show. He made his dazzling probe on the run. "The world is filled, and filled with the Absolute," Teilhard de Chardin wrote. "To see this is to be made free."

---

*Teilhard de Chardin: Pierre Teilhard de Chardin (1881–1953), a noted paleontologist and Catholic priest whose most famous book, *The Phenomenon of Man,* attempts to bridge the gap between science and religion.

†Christo: A contemporary Bulgarian artist known for staging spectacular environmental effects.

## *Reflections and Responses*

1. How does Dillard establish a connection between stunt piloting and artistic performance? Identify the various moments in her essay when she makes such a connection. What do these moments have in common? What images do they share?

2. Note that Dillard doesn't wait until the very end of her essay to introduce Rahm's death. Why do you think she avoids this kind of climax? What advantage does this give her?

3. "The Stunt Pilot" also appears as an untitled chapter in Dillard's book *The Writing Life*. Why is this an appropriate context for the essay? What does the essay tell us about expression and composition?

BRIAN DOYLE

# *Joyas Voladoras*

*Certain essays are composed like poetry, with a lyric intensity in which every word, every phrase, and every image seems critical. Such essays are usually quite short (often only a few paragraphs) since, for one thing, it is extremely difficult to sustain such verbal intensity over many pages, and for another, if extended too long, the style could become tiresome. Critics sometimes call such works "prose poems," suggesting that their prose style is enriched by such poetic characteristics as cadence and imagery. Attention to the sound of the prose and its phrasal rhythms is crucial, as is metaphorical originality. Suggestiveness of the theme is often favored over explicit statement. All of these literary characteristics can be seen in Brian Doyle's "Joyas Voladoras" as he looks lyrically into matters of the heart ranging from hummingbirds to humans.*

*Brian Doyle is the editor of* Portland Magazine *at the University of Portland, in Oregon. He is the author of six collections of essays, among them* Spirited Men *(about writers and musicians, 2004) and* Leaping *(about everything else, 2003). His most recent books are* The Wet Engine *(2005), about the "muddle & music of hearts,"* The Grail *(2006), about a year in an Oregon vineyard; a collection of poems,* Epiphanies & Elegies *(2006); a novel,* Mink Run *(2010); a collection of short fiction,* Bin Laden's Bald Spot & Other Stories; *and an essay collection,* Grace Notes *(2011). "Joyas Voladoras"—which means "flying jewels," the name the first Spanish explorers gave to hummingbirds—originally appeared in* The American Scholar *and was selected by Susan Orlean for* The Best American Essays 2005.

Consider the hummingbird for a long moment. A hummingbird's heart beats ten times a second. A hummingbird's heart is the size of a pencil eraser. A hummingbird's heart is a lot of the hummingbird. *Joyas voladoras,* flying jewels, the first white explorers in the

*Source:* "Joyas Voladoras," by Brian Doyle, as appeared in *The American Scholar.* Reprinted by permission of Brian Doyle.

Americas called them, and the white men had never seen such creatures, for hummingbirds came into the world only in the Americas, nowhere else in the universe, more than three hundred species of them whirring and zooming and nectaring in hummer time zones nine times removed from ours, their hearts hammering faster than we could clearly hear if we pressed our elephantine ears to their infinitesimal chests.

Each one visits a thousand flowers a day. They can dive at sixty miles an hour. They can fly backward. They can fly more than five hundred miles without pausing to rest. But when they rest they come close to death: on frigid nights, or when they are starving, they retreat into torpor, their metabolic rate slowing to a fifteenth of their normal sleep rate, their hearts sludging nearly to a halt, barely beating, and if they are not soon warmed, if they do not soon find that which is sweet, their hearts grow cold, and they cease to be. Consider for a moment those hummingbirds who did not open their eyes again today, this very day, in the Americas: bearded helmetcrests and booted racket-tails, violet-tailed sylphs and violet-capped woodnymphs, crimson topazes and purple-crowned fairies, red-tailed comets and amethyst woodstars, rainbow-bearded thornbills and glittering-bellied emeralds, velvet-purple coronets and golden-bellied star-frontlets, fiery-tailed awlbills and Andean hillstars, spatuletails and pufflegs,* each the most amazing thing you have never seen, each thunderous wild heart the size of an infant's fingernail, each mad heart silent, a brilliant music stilled.

Hummingbirds, like all flying birds but more so, have incredible enormous immense ferocious metabolisms. To drive those metabolisms they have racecar hearts that eat oxygen at an eyepopping rate. Their hearts are built of thinner, leaner fibers than ours. Their arteries are stiffer and more taut. They have more mitochondria in their heart muscles—anything to gulp more oxygen. Their hearts are stripped to the skin for the war against gravity and inertia, the mad search for food, the insane idea of flight. The price of their ambition is a life closer to death; they suffer more heart attacks and aneurysms and ruptures than any other living creature. It's expensive to fly. You burn out. You fry the machine. You melt the engine. Every creature on earth has approximately two billion

---

*A list of some species of hummingbirds; the majority of hummingbirds are found in the tropics. Only one species is commonly seen in the eastern region of the United States: the ruby-throated hummingbird.

heartbeats to spend in a lifetime. You can spend them slowly, like a tortoise, and live to be two hundred years old, or you can spend them fast, like a hummingbird, and live to be two years old.

The biggest heart in the world is inside the blue whale. It weighs more than seven tons. It's as big as a room. It *is* a room, with four chambers. A child could walk around in it, head high, bending only to step through the valves. The valves are as big as the swinging doors in a saloon. This house of a heart drives a creature a hundred feet long. When this creature is born it is twenty feet long and weighs four tons. It is waaaaay bigger than your car. It drinks a hundred gallons of milk from its mama every day and gains two hundred pounds a day, and when it is seven or eight years old it endures an unimaginable puberty and then it essentially disappears from human ken, for next to nothing is known of the mating habits, travel patterns, diet, social life, language, social structure, diseases, spirituality, wars, stories, despairs, and

*Denis Scott/Corbis*

arts of the blue whale. There are perhaps ten thousand blue whales
in the world, living in every ocean on earth, and of the largest
mammal who ever lived we know nearly nothing. But we know
this: the animals with the largest hearts in the world generally travel
in pairs, and their penetrating moaning cries, their piercing yearning tongue, can be heard underwater for miles and miles.

Mammals and birds have hearts with four chambers. Reptiles and
turtles have hearts with three chambers. Fish have hearts with two
chambers. Insects and mollusks have hearts with one chamber.
Worms have hearts with one chamber, although they may have as
many as eleven single-chambered hearts. Unicellular bacteria have
no hearts at all; but even they have fluid eternally in motion, washing from one side of the cell to the other, swirling and whirling.
No living being is without interior liquid motion. We all churn
inside.

So much held in a heart in a lifetime. So much held in a heart in a
day, an hour, a moment. We are utterly open with no one, in the
end—not mother and father, not wife or husband, not lover, not
child, not friend. We open windows to each but we live alone in
the house of the heart. Perhaps we must. Perhaps we could not

bear to be so naked, for fear of a constantly harrowed heart. When young we think there will come one person who will savor and sustain us always; when we are older we know this is the dream of a child, that all hearts finally are bruised and scarred, scored and torn, repaired by time and will, patched by force of character, yet fragile and rickety forevermore, no matter how ferocious the defense and how many bricks you bring to the wall. You can brick up your heart as stout and tight and hard and cold and impregnable as you possibly can and down it comes in an instant, felled by a woman's second glance, a child's apple breath, the shatter of glass in the road, the words "I have something to tell you," a cat with a broken spine dragging itself into the forest to die, the brush of your mother's papery ancient hand in the thicket of your hair, the memory of your father's voice early in the morning echoing from the kitchen where he is making pancakes for his children.

## Reflections and Responses

1. A common poetic device used often in prose is known as *anaphora*. In prose it is often seen as the repetition of the same words (sometimes with slight variations) at the start of a sentence or clause. Try underlining the use of anaphora in Doyle's short essay. How many examples do you find? Select one sequence of examples and try to explain the effect this device has on your response to the essay.

2. Why do you think Doyle contrasts the hearts of hummingbirds and blue whales? What physical details does he introduce to make you aware of their relative sizes? To what extent do his descriptive details of both creatures' hearts surprise you? What expressions do you find especially original or imaginative?

3. What happens when you reach the final paragraph? In what ways does an essay that at first appeared to be about creatures great and small suddenly turn into an essay about human nature? What has happened to the word *heart*? Do you think "Joyas Voladoras" could be considered a personal essay, even a private one? How would you account for all the specific details that the author introduces in the concluding paragraph, apparently to support a generalization about the human heart?

KITTY BURNS FLOREY

# Sister Bernadette's Barking Dog

*It's said that we live in an increasingly visual culture, surrounded by imagery everywhere we turn. Our phones now have cameras; our computer screen is a collage of icons and flashing screen savers; our information often comes in colorful layouts and graphical formats. Yet one form of visualization has disappeared: We no longer picture sentences. The days are long gone, as Kitty Burns Florey reminds us in "Sister Bernadette's Barking Dog," when elementary school students learned the rules of grammar and parts of speech through the use of visual diagrams. "The diagram," Florey vividly remembers, "was a bit like art, a bit like mathematics. It was much more than words uttered or words written: it was a picture of language."*

*Kitty Burns Florey is the author of ten novels, most recently* The Writing Master *(2011),* The Sleep Specialist *(2007), and* Solos *(2004). In 2009, she published* Script and Scribble: The Rise and Fall of Handwriting. *Her short stories and essays have been published in the* New York Times, Harper's Magazine, The North American Review, The Greensboro Review, *and* House Beautiful. *"Sister Bernadette's Barking Dog" was reprinted from* Harper's Magazine *(a version also appeared in* The Vocabula Review*) and was selected by Susan Orlean for* The Best American Essays 2005. *Readers who enjoy this essay will surely enjoy the expanded book-length treatment of this subject in* Sister Bernadette's Barking Dog: The Quirky History and Lost Art of Diagramming Sentences *(2006).*

Diagramming sentences is one of those lost skills, like darning socks or playing the sackbut, that no one seems to miss. Invented, or at least codified, in an 1877 text called *Higher Lessons in English,* by Alonzo Reed and Brainerd Kellogg, it swept through American public schools like the measles, and was embraced by teachers

*Source:* "Sister Bernadette's Barking Dog," by Kitty Burns Florey. Originally appeared in *Harper's Magazine,* December, 2004. Reprinted by permission of the author.

as the way to reform students who were engaged in "the cold-blooded murder of the English tongue" (to take Henry Higgins* slightly out of context). By promoting the beautifully logical rules of syntax, diagramming would root out evils like "it's me" and "I ain't got none," until everyone wrote like Ralph Waldo Emerson, or at least James Fenimore Cooper.

In my own youth, many years after 1877, diagramming was still serious business. I learned it in the sixth grade from Sister Bernadette. I can still see her: a tiny nun with a sharp pink nose, confidently drawing a dead-straight horizontal line like a highway across the blackboard, flourishing her chalk in the air at the end of it, her veil flipping out behind her as she turned back to the class. "We begin," she said, "with a straight line." And then, in her firm and saintly script, she put words on the line, a noun and a verb—probably something like *dog barked.* Between the words she drew a short vertical slash, bisecting the line. Then she made a road that forked off at an angle—a short country lane under the word *dog*—and on it she wrote *The.*

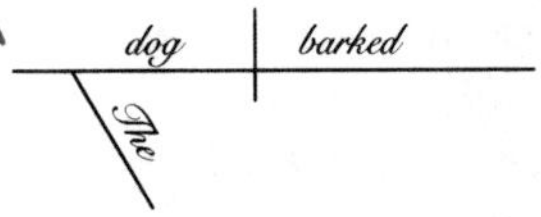

*[handwritten: This actually looks like a good method]*

| | *dog* | *barked* |
|---|---|---|
| *The* | | |

That was it: subject, predicate, and the little modifying article that civilized the sentence—all of it made into a picture that was every bit as clear and informative as an actual portrait of a beagle in midwoof. The thrilling part was that this was a picture not of the animal but of the words that stood for the animal and its noises. It was a representation of something both concrete and abstract. The diagram was a bit like art, a bit like mathematics. It was much more than words uttered or words written: it was a picture of language.

I was hooked. So, it seems, were many of my contemporaries. Among the myths that have attached themselves to memories of being educated in the fifties is the notion that activities like diagramming sentences (along with memorizing poems and adding long columns of figures without a calculator) were pointless and monotonous. I thought diagramming was fun, and most of my friends who were subjected to it look back with varying degrees

*[handwritten: It is not fun for me]*

---

*\*Henry Higgins* is the leading character in George Bernard Shaw's famous play *Pygmalion* (1912), which was made into the popular musical comedy *My Fair Lady.* A phonetics professor, Higgins wins a bet that he can transform Liza Doolittle's accent into such perfect-sounding English that she could be mistaken for a duchess.

*[handwritten left margin: I hate when people say ain't]*

of delight. Some of us were better at it than others, but it was considered a kind of treat, a game that broke up the school day. You took a sentence, threw it against the wall, picked up the pieces, and put them together again, slotting each word into its pigeonhole. When you got it right, you made order and sense out of what we used all the time and took for granted: sentences.

Gertrude Stein,* of all people, was a great fan of diagramming. "I really do not know that anything has ever been more exciting than diagramming sentences," she wrote in the early 1930s. "I like the feeling the everlasting feeling of sentences as they diagram themselves."

In my experience they didn't exactly diagram themselves; they had to be coaxed, if not wrestled. But—the feeling the everlasting feeling: if Gertrude Stein wasn't just riffing on the words, the love-song sound of them, she must have meant the glorious definiteness of the process. I remember loving the look of the sentences, short or long, once they were tidied into diagrams—the curious maplike shapes they made, the way the words settled primly along their horizontals like houses on a road, the way some roads were culs-de-sac and some were long meandering interstates with many exit ramps and scenic lookouts. And the clarity of it all, the ease with which—once they were laid open, their secrets exposed—those sentences could be comprehended.

On a more trivial level, part of the fun was being summoned to the blackboard to show off. There you stood, chalk in hand, while, with a glint in her eye, Sister Bernadette read off an especially tricky sentence. Compact, fastidious handwriting was an asset. A good spatial sense helped you arrange things so that the diagram didn't end up with the words jammed together against the edge of the blackboard like commuters in a subway car. The trick was to think fast, write fast, and not get rattled if you failed in the attempt.

As we became more proficient, the tasks got harder. There was great appeal in the Shaker-like simplicity of sentences like *The dog chased a rabbit* (subject, predicate, direct object), with their plain, no-nonsense diagrams:

*(Handwritten margin notes: "the map can get very long." and "your first instinct is usually right")*

---

**\*Gertrude Stein** (1874–1946) was a prolific novelist and essayist known for her experimental and innovative prose. She wrote extensively on the subject of composition and today is perhaps best known for her best-selling book *The Autobiography of Alice B. Toklas* (1933).

But there were also lovable subtleties, like the way the line that set off a predicate adjective slanted back like a signpost toward the subject it modified:

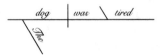

Or the thorny rosebush created by diagramming a prepositional phrase modifying another prepositional phrase:

This one is
very confusing
to me

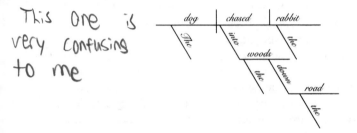

Or the elegant absence of the preposition when using an indirect object, indicated by a short road with no house on it:

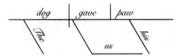

The missing preposition—in this case *to*—could also be placed on that road in parentheses, but this always seemed to me a clumsy solution, right up there with explaining a pun. In a related situation, however, the void where the subject of an imperative sentence would go was better filled, to my mind, with the graphic and slightly menacing parenthesized pronoun, as in:

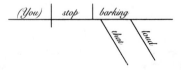

Questions were a special case. For diagramming, they had to be turned inside out, the way a sock has to be eased onto a foot: *What is the dog doing?* transformed into the more dramatic *The dog is doing what?*

Mostly we diagrammed sentences out of a grammar book, but sometimes we were assigned the task of making up our own, taking pleasure in coming up with wild Proustian* wanderings that—kicking and screaming—had to be corralled, harnessed, and made to trot into the barn in neat rows.

Part of the fun of diagramming sentences was that it didn't matter what they said. The dog could bark, chew gum, play chess—in the world of diagramming, sentences weren't about meaning so much as they were about subject, predicate, object, and their various dependents or modifiers. If they were diagrammed properly, they always illustrated correct syntax, no matter how silly their content. We hung those sentences out like a wash until we understood every piece of them. We could see for ourselves the difference between *who* and *whom.* We knew what an adverb was, and we knew where in a sentence it went, and why it went there. We were aware of dangling modifiers because we could see them, quite literally, dangle.

*this would make it fun for kids*

Today, diagramming is not exactly dead, but for many years it has been in sharp decline. This is partly because diagramming sentences seems to double the task of the student, who has to learn a whole new set of rules—where does that pesky line go, and which way does it slant?—in order to illustrate a set of rules that, in fact, has been learned pretty thoroughly simply by immersion in the language from birth. It's only the subtleties that are difficult—*who* versus *whom,* adjective versus adverb, *it's I* versus *it's me*—and most of those come from the mostly doomed attempt, in the early days of English grammar, to stuff English into the well-made boxes of Latin and Greek, which is something like forcing a struggling cat into the carrier for a trip to the vet.

*it would be somewhat confusing for kids to learn*

Another problem is that teachers—and certainly students—have become more willing to accept the idea that the sentences that

---

*****Proustian:** A reference to the prose style of the influential French novelist Marcel Proust (1871–1922), who was known for his fluid and meandering sentences.

can be popped into a diagram aren't always sentences anyone wants to write. One writer friend of mine says that she disliked diagramming because it meant "forcing sentences into conformity." And indeed language can be more supple and interesting than the patterns that perfect syntax forces on it. An attempt to diagram a sentence by James Joyce, or one by Henry James (whose style H. G. Wells compared so memorably to "a magnificent but painful hippopotamus resolved at any cost ... upon picking up a pea"), will quickly demonstrate the limitations of Sister Bernadette's methods. Diagramming may have taught us to write more correctly—and maybe even to think more logically—but I don't think anyone would claim that it taught us to write well. And besides, any writer knows that the best way to learn to write good sentences is not to diagram them but to read them.

Still, like pocket watches and Gilbert and Sullivan operas, diagramming persists, alternately reviled and championed by linguists and grammarians. It can be found in university linguistics courses and on the Web sites of a few diehard enthusiasts. There are teachers' guides, should any teacher want one; it's taught in ESL courses and in progressive private schools. There's a video, *English Grammar: The Art of Diagramming Sentences,* that features a very 1950s-looking teacher named Miss Lamb working at a blackboard. There's even a computer program, apparently, that diagrams.

Sometimes, on a slow subway or a boring car trip, I mentally diagram a sentence, just as I occasionally try to remember the declension of *hic, haec, hoc* or the words to the second verse of "The Star-Spangled Banner." I have no illusions that diagramming sentences in my youth did anything for me, practically speaking. But in an occasional fit of nostalgia, I like to bring back those golden afternoons when

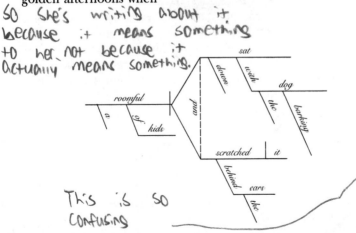

## Reflections and Responses

1. Note the author's use of figurative language throughout the essay. For example, she recalls Sister Bernadette "confidently drawing a dead-straight horizontal line like a highway across the blackboard...." Why is the horizontal line likened to a "highway"? Why is it an appropriate metaphor? How does the author continue this metaphor throughout the essay?

2. Besides the extensive use of figurative language, what other elements does Florey employ to emphasize the role of visualization? How does the idea of art and perception enter into her love of diagramming? How does it help her appreciate the architecture of a sentence?

3. After reading Kitty Burns Florey's nostalgic tribute to diagramming, do you think diagramming is an effective method for learning English grammar that ought to be restored? Why or why not? What advantages do you see in learning to diagram? What are the limitations of this method? In what ways does Florey cover both the advantages and the limitations in her essay? Can you restore her final sentence to the way it would have originally read had she not diagrammed it?

"A roomful of kids sat down with the barking dog, and scratched it behind the ears."

PATRICIA HAMPL

# The Dark Art of Description

*There is so much meaning in this title after reading it.*

*Patricia Hampl is a writer who also teaches writing, and "The Dark Art of Description" is in many ways an essay about what she's learned from her students. At two critical points in this well-crafted essay, which careens smoothly between exposition and narrative, her students address the problem of writing about oneself when one's life is boring—when there doesn't seem to be much to write. Hampl has concluded that the basis of modern memoir is that "fundamentally it isn't about having a more interesting life than someone else." An important illustration of her point is the power of description, especially visual description, in memoir. But her rumination on this link leads to a meditation on the power of description itself—not merely an ornamental picturing of things, description can be the key to storytelling. "Description, written from the personal voice of my own perception," Hampl writes, "proved even to be the link with the world's story, with history itself."*

*Patricia Hampl is Regents Professor and McKnight Distinguished Professor at the University of Minnesota in Minneapolis and has written critically acclaimed fiction, poetry, essays, and autobiography. Her books include* A Romantic Education *(1981),* Virgin Time: In Search of the Contemplative Life *(1992),* I Could Tell You Stories: Sojourns in the Land of Memory *(1999), and* Blue Arabesque: A Search for the Sublime *(2006). Her most recent book is* The Florist's Daughter, *which was selected by the* New York Times *as one of the one hundred notable books of 2007. "The Dark Art of Description" originally appeared in* The Iowa Review *and was selected by Mary Oliver for* The Best American Essays *2009.*

I was coming down the last lap of my most recent book, a memoir about my mother and father, and I was painfully aware of just how specific every bit of writing is, full of choices and chances, not

*Source:* Patricia Hampl, The Dark Art of Description. Reprinted by permission of Marly Rusoff and Associates.

theoretical at all, not the business of sweeping statements or smart ideas about "form" or "genre" or anything remotely theoretical. Just subject-verb-object and the hope of meaning.

Two nights away from the finish of my book, I was working late. I looked away from the computer screen for a moment and there was my dog staring at me intently. She was on the verge of speech. I could see it. *Come to bed.* Her eyes said this clearly. It was almost 2 A.M. and for the past four hours I've been obsessively changing commas to dashes and then back again to commas with the obsessive focus only a fanatic can sustain.

You've become a crazy person again, I said right out loud. The dog padded away.

The great short story writer J.F. Powers was once asked how things were going by a colleague in the corridor at their university. Powers allowed that it had been a tough day—"I spent the morning trying to decide whether to have my character call his friend *pal* or *chum*," he said.

That's where I often find myself—thinking how important the choice of *pal* or *chum* is, how whatever truth writing lays claim to resides in a passion for just such quite mad distinctions. This monomania* is what a friend of mine calls the 600-pound gorilla of a book. Once the 600-pound gorilla gets hold of you, you're his (or hers). "Those last weeks of finishing a book are a world in themselves," he said. "I think that gorilla is the reason most of us write—it's a real high, but it's also a subconscious agreement not to be available or even normal for as long as it takes."

But as soon as you—or I, anyway—break away from the gorilla's embrace of a particular book, those big, rangy theoretical questions begin to make their approach again. Maybe this is especially true of memoir, the odd enterprise of "writing a life" that has captivated our literary life for the last two decades or so. We tend to think of the novel as the classic narrative form—ever evolving, but familiar, its stately provenance long the preserve of academic interest and the center of trade publishing. Whereas the memoir seems new or somehow "modern," a rather suspect literary upstart. And therefore a form that invites interrogation.

But strictly speaking, autobiography is a genre far older than the novel, and is hard-wired into Western literary history. Perhaps from that first injunction of the oracle at Delphi—*Know thyself*—Western culture has been devoted to the exploration

---

*Monomania: An obsession with, or fixation on, one idea or object.

of the individual consciousness and the unspooling of the individual life.

That commandment to *know thyself* was central to antiquity. Plato uttered a version of it; Cicero used it in a tract on the development of social concord. It was such a pillar of cultural, even spiritual value that in the early Christian period Clement of Alexandria felt compelled to claim that the saying had been borrowed by the Greeks from scripture, thus binding the two developing spiritualities—pagan and monotheistic—together in a seamless endeavor.

Closer to modernity, Goethe is supposed to have said with a shudder, "Know thyself? If I knew myself, I'd run away." And Andre Gide probably expressed this revulsion best: "Know thyself! A maxim as pernicious as it is ugly. Whoever observes himself arrests his own development. A caterpillar who wanted to know itself well would never become a butterfly."

But the strongest indictment of the form I have ever encountered came from a student in Indiana who had been conscripted by his Freshman Comp teacher to attend a reading I gave some years ago. He sprawled in his chair with its baseball cap on backwards, his eloquent body language making it clear he was far, far away. Can't win them all, I decided, and carried on, my eye straying back to him like a tongue drawn to the absence of a just-pulled tooth. During the Q&A I fielded the decorous questions the students posed. And then, suddenly, apparently in response to something I'd said, my anti-hero sat bolt upright, and was waving his hand urgently, his face alight with interest. Ah—a convert. I called on him, smiling.

"I get it," he said. "Nothin's ever happened to you—and you write books about it."

He was right, of course. And in pronouncing this acute literary critical remark, he touched on the most peculiar aspect of the rise of the memoir in our times—namely, that fundamentally it isn't about having a more interesting life than someone else. True, there is a strand of autobiographical writing that relies on the documentation of extraordinary circumstances, lives lived in extremity, often at great peril. But such memoirs have always been part of literary history. What characterizes the rise of memoir in recent times is precisely the opposite condition—not a gripping "narrative arc," but the quality of voice, the story of perception rather than action.

The self is not the subject of memoir, in this kind of book, but its instrument. And the work of the self is not to "narrate" but to describe. There is something fundamentally photographic about memoir, photographic rather than cinematic. Not a story, but a series of tableaus we are given to consider. No memoirist is surprised by the absences and blanks in action, for another unavoidable quality of autobiography as I am thinking of it—as lyrical quest literature—is that it is as much about reticence as it is about revelation.

It is often remarked that the advent of the movies and the ever faster pace of modern life have conspired to make description a less essential part of prose narrative in our own times. We don't need to be told what things look like—we are inundated with images, pictures, moving or static. In this view, we need the opposite of the photographic quality so beloved of nineteenth century descriptive writing in which the landscape is rolled out, sentence after sentence, the interior of a room and the interior of the character's mind are meticulously presented.

We require writing, instead, that subsumes description, leaps right over it to frame episode and to create the much sought-after "narrative arc." The motto—even the mantra—of this narrative model is of course the commandment of introductory fiction writing workshops: *Show, don't tell.*

But as recent memoir writing shows, descriptive writing abounds. And it proves, finally, not to be about the object described. Or not only. Description in memoir is where the consciousness of the writer and the material of the story are established in harmony, where the self is lost in the material, in a sense. In fiction of the show-don't-tell variety narrative scenes that "show" and dutifully do not "tell," are advanced by volleys of dialogue in which the author's presence is successfully obscured by the dramatic action of the dialogue of his characters. But in description we hear and feel the absorption of the author in the material. We sense the presence of the creator of the scene.

This personal absorption is what we mean by "style." It is strange that we would choose so oddly surfacey a word—style—for this most soulful aspect of writing. We could, perhaps more exactly, call this relation between consciousness and its subject "integrity." What else is the articulation of perception?

Style is a word usually claimed by fashion and the most passing aesthetic values. But maybe that's as it should be because style in writing is terribly perishable. It can rot—that is what we mean when we recognize writing to be "precious," for example. But at its best and most essential, style is the register between a writer's consciousness and the material he is committed to wrestling to the page. It is the real authority of a writer, more substantial than plot, less ego-dependent than voice.

In 1951, Alfred Kazin published his memoir of his boyhood in Brooklyn, *A Walker in the City,* the book that establishes modern

*[handwritten margin note: It would be hard having to write a memoir and show, but not tell.]*

American memoir. The critic Leslie Fiedler admired the book but was also frustrated by it. It "perversely refuses to be a novel," he said with some annoyance, as if Kazin's book, deeply dependent on descriptive writing, were refusing to behave. And it was. It was refusing to obey the commandment to Show, don't tell.

When you read "The Block and Beyond," a much-anthologized chapter from Kazin's memoir, it is impossible to discuss the main characters and certainly not its plot or even its narrative structure. It is a rhapsodic evocation of a place and time. And once read, it is impossible to forget, as indelible and inevitable as a poem.

What Kazin was able to do—what every memoirist can attempt—in liberating himself from the rigid demands of show-don't-tell narrative was to enter into reflection, into speculation, into interpretation, and to use the fragment, the image, the vignette, rather than narratively linked scenes to form his world and his book. He was able to show *and* tell. To write a story and write an essay—all in the same tale, braided and twined together. The root of this double power lies in description.

\* \* \*

I was one of those enthralled teenage readers of long nineteenth-century English novels. I toiled my way through dense descriptions of gloomy heaths and bogs to get to the airy volleys of dialogue that lofted back and forth down the page to give me what I wanted—would Jane\* and Mr. Rochester … or would they not? Would Dorothea Brooke awaken—would Mr. Lydgate? I didn't relish the descriptive passages. I endured them. Just as Jane and Dorothea endured their parched lives, as if these endless descriptive passages were the desert to be crossed before the paradise of dialogue and the love story could be entered.

Yet all this description was, after all, the *world* of the book—not simply because it gave the book "a sense of place" as the old literary cliché puts it. It wasn't a "sense of place" I cared about in these passages, but the meeting place of perception with story—the place where someone *claimed* the story, where I could glimpse the individual consciousness, the creator of the scene. The person pulling the wires and making Jane and Dorothea move. I was looking, I suppose, for a sign of intimacy with the invisible author. That

---

\***Jane … Lydgate:** Jane and Mr. Rochester are characters from Charlotte Brontë's *Jane Eyre;* Dorothea and Lydgate from George Eliot's *Middlemarch,* both influential nineteenth-century novels by British women.

"dear reader" moment so familiar in nineteenth century novels—
think of Thackeray pausing to have a chat with the reader—with
you!—about how to live on nothing a year. Think of George Eliot
breaking off to describe the furnishings of Dorothea's ardent mind.

Henry James* is probably the crown prince of nineteenth century describers, a *flâneur* of the sentence, a lounge lizard of the
paragraph, taking his own sweet time to unfurl an observation,
smoking the cheroot of his thought in the contemplative after-
dinner puffery of a man who knows how to draw out the pleasure
of his rare tobacco. Or—because James himself never hesitates
to pile up opposing figures of speech until he has sliced his
thought to the refracted transparency he adores—maybe I'll just
switch metaphors and say that James sits mildly at his torture apparatus, turning the crank in meticulously calibrated movements as
the reader lies helplessly strained upon the rack of his ever-
expanding sentences, the exquisite pain of the lengthening
description almost breaking the bones of attention. In short (as
James often says after gassing on for a nice fat paragraph or two
on the quality of a Venetian sunset or the knowing lift of a European eyebrow glimpsed across a table by an artless American ingé-
nue), in short, he loves to carry on.

Carrying on, I was discovering, is what it is to describe. A lot. At
length. To trust description above plot, past character development, and even theme. To understand that to describe is both humbler and more essential than to think of compositional
imponderables such as "voice" or to strain toward superstructures
like "narrative arc." To trust that the act of description will *find*
voice and out of its streaming attention will take hold of narration.

By the time I was considering all of this, I had passed from being
a reader and had become that more desperate literary type—a writer
trying to figure out how to do it myself. I had no idea how to "sustain
a narrative," and didn't even understand at the time (the late 1970s)
that I was writing something called "a memoir." Yet when I read
*Speak, Memory* by Vladimir Nabokov[†] and later read his command—
*Caress the detail, the divine detail*—I knew I had found the motto I could
live by, the one that prevailed over "Show, Don't Tell."

Perhaps only someone as thoroughly divested of his paradise as
Nabokov had been of his boyhood Russia and his family, his native

---

*Henry James: A nineteenth- and early-twentieth-century American-born British
novelist famous for his expansive prose style.

[†]Vladimir Nabokov: A twentieth-century Russian-born American novelist. *Speak,
Memory* was his memoir.

language and all his beloved associations and privileged expectations, could enshrine the detail, the fragment, as the divinity of his
literary religion, could trust the truths to be found in the DNA of
detail, attentively rendered in ardent description. The dutiful
observation that is the yeoman's work of description finally
ascended, Nabokov demonstrated, to the transcendent reality of
literature, to metaphor itself.

Nabokov was asked in an interview if his characters ever "took
over." He replied icily that *his* characters were his galley slaves.

Yet when it was a matter of locating the godhead of literary
endeavor, even a writer as unabashedly imperious as Nabokov
did not point to himself and his intentions but to the lowly detail.
*Caress the detail, the divine detail.* Next to grand conceptions like
plot, which is the legitimate government of most stories, or character, which is the crowned sovereign, the detail looks like a ragged peasant with a half-baked idea of revolution and a crazy, sure
glint in its eye. But here, according to Nabokov, resides divinity.

Henry James put his faith in something at least as insubstantial.
"If one was to undertake to ... report with truth on the human
scene," he wrote, "it could but be because notes had been from
the cradle the ineluctable consequence of one's greatest inward
energy ... to take them was as natural as to look, to think, to feel,
to recognize, to remember." He considered his habit the basis of
literature and called it "the rich principle of the Note."

Such "notes" are of course details, observations. Description. In
attending to these details, in the act of description, the more
dynamic aspects of narrative have a chance to reveal themselves—
not as "action" or "conflict" or any of the theoretical and technical
terms we persist in thinking of as the sources of form. Rather,
description gives the authorial mind a place to be in relation with
the reality of the world.

It was surely this desire for the world—that is for the world's
memoir, which is history—that drew me to memoir, that seemingly personal form. And it was to description I tended, not to narrative, not to story. Maybe the root of the desire to write is always
lost—properly lost—in the non-literary earth of our real lives. And
craft, as we think of it, is just the jargon we give to that darker,
earthier medium.

I know it was my mother who was the storyteller in our house.
I was her audience. Her dear reader, in a way. I dimly—and sometimes bitterly—understood that nothing much was happening in
our modest Midwestern lives, yet I clung to the drama with which
she infused every vignette, every encounter at the grocery store.

And when I sought to make sense of the world that kept slipping *I agree.* away to the past, to loss and forgetfulness, when I protested *if you* inwardly at that disappearance, it was to description I instinctively *read other* turned. Coming from a background in poetry and therefore *work that* being a literalist, it didn't occur to me to copy other prose writers. *you will* It I wanted to learn to write descriptively, I needed—what else?— *subconsciously* pictures. *copy them*

I took myself off to the Minneapolis Institute of Arts and plunked myself down in front of a Bonnard.* I wrote the painting. Described it. I went home and looked at a teacup on my table— I wrote that too. Still life descriptions that ran on for several pages. I wrote and wrote, describing my way through art galleries and the inadvertent still lives of my house and my memory, my grandmother's garden, her Sunday dinners.

To my growing astonishment, these long descriptive passages, sometimes running two, three pages or longer, had a way of sheering off into narrative after all. The teacup I was describing had been given to me by my mother. And once I thought of the fact that she had bought these cups, made in Czechoslovakia, as a bride just before the Second World War, I was writing about that war, about my mother and her later disappointments which somehow were—and were not—part of this fragile cup. Description—which had seemed like background in novels, static and inert as a butterfly pinned to the page of my notebook, proved to be a dynamic engine that stoked voice and even more propelled the occasional narrative arc. Description, written from the personal voice of my own perception, proved even to be the link with the world's story, with history itself. Here was my mother's teacup, made in Czechoslovakia before the War, and here, therefore, was not only my mother's heartbreak but Europe's. The detail was surely divine, offering up miracle after miracle of connections out of the faithful consideration of the fragments before me.

We sense this historical power at the heart of autobiographical writing in the testaments from the Holocaust, from the Gulag, from every marginal and abused life that has found the courage to speak its truth which is often its horror, to preserve its demonic details—and in so doing has seen them become divine. Nadezhda Mandelstam, Anne Frank, Primo Levi—to name only a very few. In

*read her book*

---

time we will, surely, see such documents from Guantanamo* and the unknown places of extreme rendition.

The history of whole countries, of an entire era and even lost populations depends sometimes on a little girl faithfully keeping her diary. The great contract of literature consists in this: you tell me your story and somehow I get my story. If we are looking for another reason to explain the strangely powerful grip of the first-person voice on contemporary writing perhaps we need look no farther than the power of Anne Frank's equation—that to write one's life enables the world to preserve its history.

But what of lives lived in the flyover? Lives that don't have that powerful, if terrible, historical resonance of radical suffering. Ordinary lives, in a word. Alfred Kazin's life—or yours. And certainly mine in middling Minnesota in the middle of the twentieth century. Why bother to describe it? Because of course, all details are divine, not just Nabokov's. In fact, perhaps the poorer the supposed value, the more the detail requires description to assure its divinity.

Which brings me to—if not a story, at least a fragment, a vignette. Early in my teaching life, I went (foolishly) through a killer snowstorm in Minneapolis to get to my University office because I had student conferences scheduled. By the time I arrived, the University had closed and the campus was empty, whipped by white shrouds of blizzard snow, the wind whistling down the Mall. I sat in my office in the empty building, cursing my ruinous work ethic, and wondering if the buses would keep running so I could get home.

Then a rap on my office door. I opened it and there, like an extra out of *Doctor Zhivago*,[†] stood my 11 A.M. appointment, a quiet sophomore named Tommy.

He looked anxious. He was really glad I was there, he said, because he had a big problem with the assignment. I had asked the students to write short autobiographies. "I just can't write anything about my life," he said miserably, his head down, his overshoes puddling on the floor.

I waited for the disclosure. What would it be—child abuse, incest, what murder or mayhem could this boy not divulge? What had brought him trooping through the blizzard to get help with his life story? How would I get him to Student Counseling?

---

*Handwritten marginal notes (left margin):*
This is sadly true. Normal people's lives always get skipped over because nothing happened to them, they didn't do anything extraordinary.

Glad to hear she was a good teacher and caring for his students.

---

*Guantanamo: Guantánamo Bay, Cuba, is the site of a controversial American detention center for accused terrorists opened after 9/11.

[†]*Doctor Zhivago*: A 1965 American movie based on Boris Pasternak's novel.

"See, I come from Fridley," he said, naming one of the nowhere-suburbs sprawling drearily beyond the freeway north of Minneapolis. I stared at him. I didn't, for a moment, comprehend that this was the dark disclosure, this the occasion of his misery: being from Fridley meant, surely, that he had nothing worth writing about.

There it was again—nothin' had ever happened to him and I was asking him to write about it.

"I have good news for you, Tommy," I said. "The field's wide open—nobody has told what it's like to grow up in Fridley yet. It's all yours."

All he needed to do was sit down and describe. And because the detail is divine, if you caress it into life, you find the world you have lost or ignored, the world ruined or devalued. The world you alone can bring into being, bit by broken bit. Your voice, your style—which is to say your integrity. *very dark, but softly true ending.*

## Reflections and Responses

1. How would you categorize "The Dark Art of Description"? Is it a memoir? (It does, after all, contain a rich personal story.) Or is it an expository essay aimed at making a point about writing? Is it some sort of hybrid? Do you think it is a particularly descriptive essay itself? How does the way the essay straddles description, narrative, and argument help advance its agenda?

2. Hampl writes that when she "tried to make sense of the world that kept slipping away into the past, to loss and forgetfulness, when I protested inwardly at that disappearance, it was to description that I instinctively turned." Do you think her assessment of her life—or the life of her student from Fridley—as relatively uneventful is earnest? Or is she suggesting in this paragraph that there can be more narrative to a story than meets the eye?

3. Parse the essay's title: Why does Hampl call description a "Dark Art"? Is there something almost sinister about the way an image can conceal or bolster a story?

AMY LEACH

# *You Be the Moon*

*Nature has always provided us with metaphors for own lives, insignificant as the magnitude of the cosmos may make our existence seem. In her essay "You Be the Moon," Amy Leach works the metaphors both ways: Her lush, dancing description of the surface of the moon draws from allegories of the human experience on earth, but it also seems crafted to teach us something about ourselves: The moon's solitary movements, and the rocky, unforgiving face covering a mysterious inner world seem immediately like parables designed for us. In an essay that is at once informative and beautifully illustrative, Leach blurs the boundaries between science writing, ruminative contemplation of inner experience, and even the personal essay.*

*Amy Leach is a graduate of the University of Iowa MFA program, and has won two prestigious literary awards—a Rona Jaffe Award in 2008 and in 2010 a Whiting Writers' Award for nonfiction. Her essays have appeared in the* Iowa Review, The Massachusetts Review, Orion, The Wilson Quarterly, *and many other periodicals. She is the author of the essay collection* Things That Are *(2012). "You Be the Moon" originally appeared in* A Public Space *and was selected for* The Best American Essays 2009 *by Mary Oliver.*

THERE IS AN ALTITUDE above every planet where a moon can orbit forevermore. In millions of miles of ups and downs, there is one narrow passageway of permanence. If a moon can reach this groove, it will never crash down like masonry nor drift away like a mood; it will be inalienable; it will circle its planet at the exact speed that the planet rotates, always over

*Source:* Amy Leach, "Sail On My Little Honeybee" in *Things That Are* (Minneapolis: Milkweed Editions, 2012). Copyright © 2012 by Amy Leach. Reprinted with permission of Milkweed Editions, www.milkweed.org, and Canongate Books Ltd for the UK.

one site, like the Badlands or Brazzaville or the Great Red Spot,* so that the planet neither drags the moon faster nor slows it down. Moons not locked into this synchronous orbit are being perturbed either up or down. The law is stringent about this; there are no clauses; and all moons are dutiful followers of the law. But, as all good followers of the law discover in the end, unless you happen to roll onto a track precisely 18,254 miles above your planet, the law ejects you or dashes you down. One moon in our solar system has achieved synchronous orbit, being pledged forever to its planet—Pluto's moon Charon. The other 168 moons have not.

Mars has two small moons whose names mean "panic" and "terror." Phobos looks like a potato that experienced one terrible, and many average, concussions. Phobos hurtles around Mars every eight hours, which is three times faster than Mars rotates, which means Mars pulls it back and slows it down. Slowing down makes a moon lose height; in the end Phobos will smite its planet, or else get wrenched apart by gravity into a dusty ring of aftermath. Mars's other moon, Deimos, is a slow and outer moon; an outer and outer moon; someday it will be a scrap moon, rattling around in the outer darkness, where drift superannuated spacecraft and exhausted starlets.

So fast moons slow down and slow moons speed up, and only during excerpts of time do planetary dalliances appear permanent. Our moon through many excerpts—the Moon—is a slow moon. Thus it is speeding up, thus it is falling up, coming off like a wheel, at one and a half inches per year. Let us now reflect upon the Moon; for the Moon has long reflected upon us. To get an idea of the relationship between the Earth and the Moon and the Sun, find two friends and have the self-conscious one with lots of atmosphere be the Earth and the coercive one be the Sun. And you be the Moon, if you are periodically luminous and sometimes unobservable and your inner life has petered out. Then find a large field and take three steps from the Earth, and have the Sun go a quarter mile away.

For an idea of how long your light takes to reach Earth, sing one line from a song, such as "Sail on, my little firefly," and that is how long moonlight takes. The Earth can sing the same line back to you, to represent earthlight. "Sail on, my little firefly." As for the Sun, he should sing as lustily as sunlight; have him discharge the song "I Gave Her Cakes and I Gave Her Ale," which is eight

*Brazzaville is the capital and largest city of the Republic of Congo in Africa; the Great Red Spot is a gigantic storm persistently raging in the atmosphere of Jupiter.

minutes long, which is how long sunlight takes to reach the Earth. Also the Earth may sing to the Sun, and the Sun to the Moon, and the Moon to the Sun, songs of representative length.

Now keep singing and everybody spin and the smaller two of you orbit the next largest rotundity. Now as you, the Moon, go around the Earth, do not circle perfectly, as if you were a mill horse, or an idea. You are not an idea; you make the Earth's heavy blue waters heave up and down! Circle asymmetrically, then, like a small coplanet; truly you and the Earth *both* orbit the center of your combined mass, called the barycenter. Of course, if you and the Earth were equal in bulk, the barycenter would lie exactly between you; you and the Earth would pass your lives in social equilibrium, like the rooster and the pig on the carousel. However, as the Earth is eighty-one times more massive than the Moon, the barycenter is eighty-one times closer to the Earth: thus the barycenter is *inside the Earth*, though not at its *center*. This means that the Earth orbits a point inside itself. The Earth is a self-revolver, nodding slightly to the swooping Moon.

Now the Earth does not *look* eighty-one times as massive as the Moon—in fact it is just four times as wide. To address this perceptual difficulty we will interrupt our lunar reenactment and consult philosophy. Let us refer to our index of philosophies and select one known as Interiorism, which says that truth is to be known by introspection. To discover why the Earth acts so central and the Moon so obsequious, let us not measure yards but consider inward differences. The Earth is not gigantic and the Moon is not slight, but the Earth has a core and the Moon does not. Or rather, if the Moon has a core, it is undetectably small and inert, like a frozen mouse.

How do we know that the Moon has a mousy core? Who has ever really been a Lunar Interiorist? Here we shall invent a philosophy and call it Imaginative Exteriorism, wherein by looking at the exterior, we *imagine* the interior; for the face often tattles on the heart, and an empty surface may bespeak an empty center (though this is not true of alligator eggs). The Moon has a stony face, while the Earth's face is a slaphappy burlesque, screaming flocks of peacocks here, and cloudbursts there, and spriggy merriment everywhere. Such an exhibition is possible only if inside itself the Earth has a core whose nickel density enables the planet not only to sport a moon but also to hold on to tiny flighty molecules. For these bouncing shimmying molecules are Earth's genius, and they are harder to keep than moons. Cloudland has a core of adamant.*

---

*Alligator eggs** have a rocky appearance; **adamant** is an ancient word for a very hard stone or metal.

On behalf of those who feel vacant and uninhabited, to whom nothing occurs, who look up day and night from chalky dust into unrefracted blackness, who watch their plush, blue-headed neighbors yielding splashy gullies and snow devils and excitable vespiaries and backsliding pinnipeds and heady cauliflowers and turtle centuplets and rosy squirrelfish swarming through Rapture Reefs—on behalf of unprofitable individuals everywhere, is the Moon ordained to ever be a shabby waste of rubbled regolith?* Could it never scrabble together a genius like the Earth's?

What about molecule trustees, like the Sun? The solar wind blasts a plasma of particles throughout the solar system; could not some of these particles accrue upon the Moon? For not *all* atoms are wiggle-away; xenon, for example, is heavy and slow. It would make a nicely noncombustible atmosphere, of glowing lavender hue, and would make sound possible, albeit slow, so everyone's voice would drop several octaves and everyone would sound like walruses. And xenon is an anesthetic, so inhabitants would be blithe and amenable to dentistry. But the wind that bringeth the elements taketh them away;† the atmosphere on the Moon is thinner than the thinnest vacuum we can contrive.

Haloes cannot be affixed to the head with pins and clips. Marañón‡ forests, hosting spinetail birds and purple-backed sunbeams and gray-bellied comets and velvet-fronted euphonias and long-tailed weasels, cannot be administered from without. Glory cannot be administered from without. Glory will only coalesce on a body wherein throbs a fiery, molten, mad-stallion heart so dreadfully dense, so inescapably attractive, that it matters little the circumference of the frame.

Of course if your heart is *too* fervent, you will become an attractive incinerator, like the Sun, glorious but no pleasure boat. The glory of the Sun is violent and uninflected; its features are all flames and its sounds are all explosions. The Sun is so loud, like a million bombs all the time, that fine-spun sounds cannot be heard, like birds wading or figs tumbling or the muttering of

---

*Vespiaries** are colonies of wasps or hornets; **pinnipeds** describes the family of fin-footed mammals including walruses and sea lions; **regolith** is a layer of loose rocky material usually used to describe the moon's surface.

†**But the wind that bringeth the elements taketh them away:** a reference to the Book of Job in the Old Testament (Job 1:21): "The Lord gave, and the Lord hath taken away; blessed be the name of the Lord."

‡**Marañón** is a province in Northern Peru.

mathematicians. On the Sun all private qualities disappear into the main loud yellowness.

Nothing makes a sound on the Moon and nothing ever could: not a harpsichordist, not a shattering tureen of mangel-wurzel* stew, not the pebble-sized meteoroids that whang down at seventy-eight thousand miles an hour and heat the ground so hot it glows like a little piece of star; not the huge meteoroids that fracture the bedrock, forming craters two hundred miles across, creating new rings of mountains, making the Moon to tremble on and on—since it doesn't have a sturdy core, the Moon is very convulsible; once atremble, it stays atremble. But it fractures and trembles and glows in absolute silence, for sound is like birds and cannot travel without air.

From looking at its face we had inferred that the Moon's heart is small and dead; but this is not to say that its face has no properties; not even the most stuporous face has no properties. The moonscape is pleated and rumpled, with rills and ridges and craters and crevices and darknesses and brightnesses. Except for some meteor-made bruises, though, its features have not changed for three billion years; they are memorials of an ancient vim. Once the Moon was welling up from inside, jutting into volcanoes from the force of its own melting, cracking at the rind from its deep inner shifts. Now it wears the same glassy expression eon after eon, like a taxidermied antelope. The Moon is a never-brimming eye, a never-whistling tea-kettle, and it shadows the very flower of planets.

There are several kinds of orbits in the orbit catalogue. One is an interrupted orbit, which describes the path of a dumpling flung from a window, the ground being the interrupter of the dumpling's orbit. Another is known as an open orbit, where an unaffiliated traveling object gets pulled to another body, curves around it, and flies away, never to return, like a minute. It is just a gravitational encounter and it merely redirects the object. The other kind of orbit is where a rock, after ages of streaking obliviously past acquisitive black holes and great gassy moon-catchers like Jupiter, happens to come close to a small motor-hearted globe, close enough to feel its influence, to be drawn closer, to make a circle around it, and another and another, and never thereafter to stop, not for billions of years. Once it was its own, and now it is a foundling. This wrapping of the one around the other is called a closed orbit.

---

*A **tureen** is a serving dish for stews, often made of porcelain; **mangel-wurzel** is a kind of beet.

In truth, the beginning of the Moon is a secret. Maybe a piece of Earth broke off and went into orbit, maybe the Moon was begotten by a terrible collision, or maybe it really was a drifter snatched from its onward way. However the Moon began, here is how the Moon will finish: in a billion years the Earth will have nudged it far enough away that it will look 15 percent smaller; in three billion years it will look smaller still; in five billion years the Sun will become a red giant and swallow its children up. The Earth's involvement with the Moon will not last long enough to end.

The disposition of the universe—that crazy wheelwright*— designates that we live on a wheel, with wheels for associates and wheels for luminaries, with days like wheels and years like wheels and shadows that wheel around us night and day; as if by turning and turning, things could come round right. For the moment, if you are still in the field of feathery grass where you were playing the Moon, you might look back at your footprints. The Sun spins in place so his path is just a point; and the Earth leaves a long ellipse around the Sun; but your path is a convoluted zigzag, for you loop around a looping planet. Your trajectory is something like the trajectory of sea ducks. Little harlequin sea ducks swim over the oscillating waves of the sea, diving down into the cold, gray-green waters to unfasten limpets and blue mussels from their rocks, swinging back up into the rough winter waves, the sea itself rolling up and down under the spell of the sailing Moon.

## Reflections and Responses

1. The title of the essay comes from a remark that's made almost offhand in Leach's thought experiment, and yet it aptly summarizes the major ideas in the essay. How does "You Be the Moon" stand for what Leach is challenging us to do? Is she actually asking us to imagine ourselves as the celestial body—or vice versa— or simply prompting us to move closer in our minds to the unimaginable reach of the natural world? Why does she ask us to "be the moon" in this essay?

2. Describe Leach's stylistic use of metaphors and similes in the essay. What does she achieve by explaining the phenomena of

*A **wheelwright** is a person who builds or repairs wheels; why does Leach refer to the universe as one?

the moon and its movements by way of so many terrestrial illustrations and analogies? Pick a few of her uses of figurative language, and describe why they work (or don't work). As a whole, how do these examples advance the major point or points of the essay?

3. Explain what Leach means about the interior and exterior of the moon. How are we supposed to use the lunar surface to see what's inside? What still remains a mystery about the core of moons and planets? How does Leach relate this dichotomy between appearance and internal reality to our human experience? Do you agree with the point she's making? Why or why not?

ARIEL LEVY

# The Lesbian Bride's Handbook

*In 2009, the New York state legislature took steps toward legalizing same-sex marriage. Two years earlier, Ariel Levy and her partner got married anyway. But how did the fact that their wedding was not sanctioned by civil society affect the wedding itself? Instead of a ponderous argument on the merits of gay marriage, Levy writes a light, comic essay on planning the nuptials, considering questions from what a gay bride should wear to what the couple should even call the ceremony. In the process, Levy begins to wonder if her wedding (which she calls a "party about love") is real, or just a parody of heterosexual marriage—and what that means about her relationship and her identity. In trying to please her future mother-not-quite-in-law, Levy realizes that "[i]t was my secret wish that if my party about love was as flawless as the gowns in that store, it would subsume the humiliation of its own existence … subsume the horror of my homosexuality."*

*Ariel Levy's work has appeared in the* Washington Post, Vogue, *and* Slate, *among other publications. She's also the author of* Female Chauvinist Pigs: Women and the Rise of Raunch Culture *(2005), which criticizes the modern feminist establishment. She was a contributing editor for twelve years at* New York *magazine, where "The Lesbian Bride's Handbook" first appeared; it was selected by Adam Gopnik for* The Best American Essays 2008. *Since 2008 she's been a staff writer at* The New Yorker.

What is the right thing to wear to a wedding? Women have been asking themselves this question for generations and, I suppose, coming up with many of the same answers as I have. Black and gray, the colors I usually wear, are obviously too somber. Red is a bad idea: too garish, too iconic—the whore instead of the virgin—and, as a saleswoman at Saks explained to me, one doesn't want to draw attention away from the bride. But then I am the bride. Sort of.

*Source:* Ariel Levy, *The Lesbian Bride's Handbook.* Reprinted by permission of the author.

For several months, admitting that detail filled me with a flickering dread. I knew what would inevitably follow: "Why aren't you wearing white?" Eventually, I realized that, obviously, I could just tell Katie at Barneys or Jen at Chloé, "Because I prefer color." But at first, I felt compelled to tell the whole mortifying truth: "Because it's a gay wedding." Or, if I couldn't quite get those words out of my mouth: "Because it's not a real wedding."

A real wedding was not something I was raised to want. My parents were bohemians of a sort, and real weddings were like real jobs: square. As my mother has managed to mention on numerous occasions, she would have liked to elope, but to please her parents, there was a modest reception; she told them to do whatever they wanted and that she and my father would show up. When Amy and I announced that we intended to have a wedding—not a real wedding, of course, but something festive, something that expressed the scale of our glee—my mother's response was less than gushing. "How can you feel okay about spending all that money on one day?" she wanted to know.

Naturally, I yelled at her for saying that, but the truth is I didn't. By the time things starting getting specific and estimated costs of various things started combining to form enormous estimated sums, money was only one of many things I did not feel okay about. I did not feel okay about the word marriage, for instance, partly because it didn't describe a legal option for me, and partly because the closer that something quite like it loomed the less it

seemed like an attractive condition with which to be afflicted. (This was relatively easy to sidestep, at least in a technical sense: Our invitations promised "a party about love," and you can't really argue with that.) I also didn't feel okay about spending all my free time on the phone with the flower guy and the tent man, or about making little checklists of who was coming, and who was not coming, and who was staying at the Goodstone Inn. And I definitely did not feel okay about telling the sales staff of half the better clothing retailers in New York City that I needed something fetching to wear to my big fat gay wedding.

Now that I know what is involved in throwing such an event, it is difficult to remember exactly how we decided to do so ... hard to retrace the steps that led to my standing in front of a three-way mirror in a $3,700 canary-yellow Donna Karan trapeze dress, completely panicked, knowing that soon, very soon, everyone I knew and loved would be joining me for this hell of my own making, this festival of gayness and commitment.

All I can say for sure is that it started on the blackout.* When I met Amy on a friend's balcony that night, I never wanted the lights to come back on. With all the stoplights dead, traffic moved on the streets below to its own ghostly, unpredictable rhythm—everything was different. The idea that we wouldn't be together from then on seemed unnatural, almost immediately. And so it was unsurprising that despite the considerable obstacles of other relationships and opposite coasts, eventually we had one life. We were pretty pleased with ourselves. "Look!" we wanted to say to everyone. "Look how fun! Look what's possible! Let's have a cocktail!" We would celebrate with our friends—our families, even. There should be music and dancing. We'd need hyacinths and shrimps! Let the wild rumpus begin.

I am not a total idiot. I always had the sense to say no wedding cake, no officiant, no first dance, no here comes the bride, no *Times* announcement, and absolutely no white dress. Who are we kidding? And why? We just wanted a big, awesome party where everyone could meet and go bananas. It's a special opportunity, you know: The only other time everyone you love will assemble in one place is at your funeral. (At most weddings, some people you don't actually love will also be in attendance. But the silver lining of my parents' being irreverent and Amy's parents' being in denial is that we didn't have to invite anyone we didn't want

---

*__The blackout:__ New York City, along with much of the northeast, suffered a major, day-long blackout in August 2003.

to.) The thing is, though, you have to serve *something*, and you can't very well go naked. You can call it a party about love all you want, but you still have to make all the same decisions that every other bride has to make, and you have to make them very carefully unless you want everyone you know to schlep to some crummy party in the middle of nowhere.

And I do not believe in crummy parties. I believe in glamour. I believe that when you are on your deathbed clinging to the murk of your memories, some will stay with you purely on the power of atmosphere: the way a punch bowl looked surrounded by daisies at your 5th-birthday party, the feel of a certain set of blue sheets the first time you traveled alone. There was no way I was going to let this thing be shoddy—some pathetic hers-and-hers imitation of the real thing or some vaguely patchouli-scented *ceremony*. If I was going to have a party about love, it was going to be the classiest party about love ever. I did not experience this imperative as relaxing.

This was not the first large, square, optional ceremony I'd insisted on having despite my mother's warnings. As a 10-year-old, I decided that I wanted to have a bat mitzvah. I was the only kid in the history of Westchester County who *demanded* Hebrew school. And as I stood in front of the racks of red at Bergdorf Goodman, I recalled the feeling I'd had at some point in my preteen Jewish odyssey when I looked down at the sacred ancient letters on the scroll: *What have I done?*

But in both cases, by the time the magnitude of my folly revealed itself to me, it was way, way too late to undo. As my stepmother put it with terrifying accuracy when we went to see how many cocktail tables would fit on the porch of the house where she and my dad live in the Blue Ridge Mountains, "This horse is out of the gate." It was too late to cancel those lovely and meticulously worded invitations. Too late to tell Amy's 80-year-old father, a man who served in MacArthur's honor guard after World War II, that the vibratingly tense dinner at which we'd declared our intention to *faux* wed was a waste of a good steak and two hours of his remaining time on planet Earth. It was too late to do anything but find a dress.

Normally, I love clothes. Really love them. I feel about clothes the way I feel about flowers: They sing to me. But I understand tulips and boots; I understand little jackets. I am a stranger to formalwear. The first dress I brought home was a kind of Grecian muumuu in a cheery shade of coral. It looked like something Mrs. Robinson would have worn to a pool party in *The Graduate*. "Chic, right?" I said to Amy. "Perky and festive."

She appeared confused. "You want to wear a nightgown to our wedding?"

"It's not a wedding!" I shrieked. "It's a party about love!"

Amy rolled her eyes. "I didn't realize it was a pajama party about love."

Back it went. A few days later, I modeled a low-cut pale-gold dress with spaghetti straps and a gauzy skirt from Missoni. "Nice!" said Amy. "You look like a fancy hooker. In Capri." This was not the look I wanted.

Then one day, I went to a doctor's appointment uptown. It was a sunny spring morning and I wore sneakers and track pants so I could walk home to the East Village when it was over. Amy was at Jussara Lee, the custom shop on Little West 12th Street where she was having her suit made for the big event, the P.A.L. As I made my way down Madison Avenue, I envied her. (And by envied I mean, obviously, resented.) *Of course* Amy would wear a suit; Amy always wears a suit. Everything about this situation seemed simpler for her—she was neither ambivalent nor insane, while I was rapidly flipping my lid. She didn't care about how uncool it was that we were doing this; Amy has always been cool. While I obsessed about how lame it was to seek public acceptance, to crave ritual, and grew queasy at the mention of marriage, Amy was excited.

Then something in a shop window caught my eye. A dress the color of grass, the shape of a mermaid. A dress that would flash before your eyes on your deathbed and in your dreams. I could no longer think about being cool or being mortified or being heteronormative. I could no longer think. The doorman looked at my sneakers skeptically as I shuffled past him into the Carolina Herrera boutique.

"Hello," I said to the salesgirl, a water lily of a woman. "I need a dress to wear to my wedding. I do not want to wear white. I want to wear that one."

"A gown," she told me. "That one is a gown."

I stood still in my sneakers. "Great."

If you are unfamiliar with the price points at Carolina Herrera, here's a good way to get a sense of them: Think of the absolute most you can imagine an article of clothing costing. Now triple that. I must have tried on a hundred-thousand dollars' worth of fabric that day. But every dress was exquisite, astounding. Each one made me look thinner and more expensive. And then the saleswoman brought me something I would never have even looked twice at: It was made of pale-blue oxford cloth with ribbons for straps and a corseted bodice. The skirt was tight at the top and then exploded with volume and hand-painted floral appliqués. When I put it on, I appeared to be in full bloom. "There's your bouquet," she said.

"I'll take it."

If my mother knew how much money I paid for that dress, I do believe she would disown me. But I wasn't thinking about my mother when the seamstress started pinning me in. I was thinking about Amy's.

Like me, Mrs. Norquist was a journalist before she got married. Like me, she is a chatterbox and a gardener. And like me, she is a clotheshorse. But that's it. Mrs. Norquist is a staunch conservative and a churchgoer, as are two of the three sons she raised. (Her oldest, Bruce, is an Evangelical minister, and her youngest, Todd, works for the creationist movement.) When Amy came out in college (two decades ago), Mrs. Norquist didn't speak to her for a year. In fact, as much as she likes to gab, Mrs. Norquist does not talk about anything that really bothers her, except to say the words "Oh, honestly." She likes to talk about who's had a baby and who's been on a trip, and she likes to talk about weddings, a lot. She talks about weddings as much as my mother talks about shiatsu. Where my family is freaky and loose, foulmouthed and freewheeling, Mrs. Norquist is nurturing and restrained, a woman who makes toasted cheese sandwiches and tomato soup. I fell for her immediately.

When we go to visit Amy's parents, generally Amy and her dad watch sports, and Mrs. Norquist and I drink tea and look at fashion magazines together. This is not something I find boring. It is a shared passion and a neutral territory—we avoid discussing politics, sexuality, ethnicity, and religion (except once, when I let loose an "oy vey" and she said, "What?" And I said, "That's what my people say when we mean 'Oh, honestly.'"). Fashion is what we agree upon, the thing we share besides Amy (who does not look at fashion magazines, unless maybe there were a special issue on man-tailored suits). "That's a darling heel!" Mrs. Norquist will say. "It would be good in a dark suede," I reply. It's honest communication. We are both ourselves when we talk about clothes, telling each other, for once, the whole truth.

When I saw myself in the mirror in that blue gown with its graceful silhouette and giddy flowers, I could hear Mrs. Norquist gasping and saying, "Isn't that gorgeous!" It was my secret wish that she would look at it and see in our lives sparkle instead of shame. It was my secret wish that if my party about love was as flawless as the gowns in that store, it would subsume the humiliation of its own existence … subsume the horror of my homosexuality.

"What do you care what other people think?" is what my own
mother would say, of course—has said, many times over the course
of my life. And that is the difference between us. My mother is a
woman who moved to Cape Cod on a whim. Who has giant green
marbles stuck in the plaster of her walls for decoration and an
extensive collection of Buddha-like objects she has amassed in her
travels through China, Tibet, and the gift shops of the lower cape.
She wears pajamas to work and is nicknamed Rocky and was, in her
day, a pretty serious practitioner of non-monogamy. My mother is
(still) a bad-ass, because she just doesn't give a shit what anybody
else thinks. I care what everybody thinks. So does Mrs. Norquist.
I am not sure which one of them I find more mysterious.

I'm not going to lie to you: My gay wedding rocked. My oldest
friend, Jesse, played "Crimson and Clover" on his electric guitar
when we walked down the mountain, and I can still feel the
sound of that song reverberating in my chest. My mother wore
high heels and makeup for the first time I can remember and
danced until one in the morning. There were these amazing
pink margaritas everyone kept drinking. Mrs. Norquist gave Amy
the handkerchief her mother gave her on her wedding day:
"Something blue," she said, and that's all she said on the subject.
That and "Isn't that gorgeous!" when she saw my gown. She still
can't quite bring herself to call what happened in September a
wedding. But then, for a long time, neither could I.

The dress is still hanging in my closet, which has less to do with
my being sentimental than it does with eBay's being really complicated. I can't imagine that I'll ever wear it again, partly because
mine is not a black-tie life, and also because I doubt very much
that I could get back into it. (When conservatives discuss the perils
of gay marriage, they fail to mention its most pernicious consequence: Gay marriage, like all marriage, is extremely fattening.)
One of these days I'll sell it, though: That thing cost a fortune,
and who could feel okay about keeping something so expensive
hanging in a garment bag? Amy I'm keeping.

## Reflections and Responses

1. "I believe," Levy writes, "that when you are on your deathbed
clinging to the murk of your memories, some will stay with you
purely on the power of atmosphere." What does she mean by

this, and how does the story of her wedding confirm her point? Notice that in an essay about a wedding, there's only a little more than a paragraph about the wedding itself; how does that brief description, contrasted with a long meditation about planning for the event, illustrate (or subvert) Levy's ideas about the meaning of ceremonies?

2. Levy stays away from the politics of gay marriage for the most part, but does forward something of an emotional argument for it in the scenes with Mrs. Norquist. How is the form of Levy's essay more (or less) effective than a politically oriented argument for gay marriage?

3. Levy uses humor, especially about the cost of the ceremony, the stresses of planning it, how "fattening" it is, etc., throughout her essay. Identify some of Levy's jokes and consider their function. Do they serve some purpose in the essay? Think especially about the tradition of similar wedding-themed humor in the context of traditional, straight weddings. Is Levy suggesting that her wedding is—or that she wants it to be—despite what she tells store clerks, a "real wedding"?

ALAN LIGHTMAN

# The Accidental Universe

*"The history of science," writes physicist Alan Lightman, "can be viewed as the recasting of phenomena that were once thought to be accidents as phenomena that can be understood in terms of fundamental causes and principles." Gradually, according to this model, science can come to explain more and more about the world we live in, and demonstrate that many natural events that may appear mysterious are actually the consequences of immutable natural laws. Yet this comfortable view of how science works may be coming to an end, argues Lightman, as he explores new scientific findings that "have led some of the world's premier physicists to propose that our universe is only one of an enormous number of universes" that these physicists call a "multiverse." In "The Accidental Universe" Lightman investigates the bewildering possibilities of multiple universes and what that theory suggests about the one we inhabit.*

*Alan Lightman is a novelist, essayist, and physicist, with a PhD in theoretical physics. He has served on the faculties of Harvard University and MIT and was the first person to receive dual faculty appointments at MIT in science and in the humanities. Lightman's* Einstein's Dreams *(1993) was an international bestseller and has been translated into 30 languages. His novel* The Diagnosis *(2000) was a finalist for the National Book Award in fiction. His latest book is* Mr g, *a novel about the creation as told by God. "The Accidental Universe" originally appeared in* Harper's Magazine *and was selected by David Brooks for* The Best American Essays 2012.

In the fifth century B.C., the philosopher Democritus proposed that all matter was made of tiny and indivisible atoms, which came in various sizes and textures—some hard and some soft, some smooth and some thorny. The atoms themselves were taken as givens. In the nineteenth century, scientists discovered

*Source:* Best American Essays, 2011, Alan Lightman, *The Accidental Universe.*

that the chemical properties of atoms repeat periodically (and created the periodic table to reflect this fact), but the origins of such patterns remained mysterious. It wasn't until the twentieth century that scientists learned that the properties of an atom are determined by the number and placement of its electrons, the subatomic particles that orbit its nucleus. And we now know that all atoms heavier than helium were created in the nuclear furnaces of stars.

The history of science can be viewed as the recasting of phenomena that were once thought to be accidents as phenomena that can be understood in terms of fundamental causes and principles. One can add to the list of the fully explained: the hue of the sky, the orbits of planets, the angle of the wake of a boat moving through a lake, the six-sided patterns of snowflakes, the weight of a flying bustard, the temperature of boiling water, the size of raindrops, the circular shape of the sun. All these phenomena and many more, once thought to have been fixed at the beginning of time or to be the result of random events thereafter, have been explained as *necessary* consequences of the fundamental laws of nature—laws discovered by human beings.

This long and appealing trend may be coming to an end. Dramatic developments in cosmological findings and thought have led some of the world's premier physicists to propose that our universe is only one of an enormous number of universes with wildly varying properties, and that some of the most basic features of our particular universe are indeed mere *accidents*—a random throw of the cosmic dice. In which case, there is no hope of ever explaining our universe's features in terms of fundamental causes and principles.

It is perhaps impossible to say how far apart the different universes may be, or whether they exist simultaneously in time. Some may have stars and galaxies like ours. Some may not. Some may be finite in size. Some may be infinite. Physicists call the totality of universes the "multiverse." Alan Guth, a pioneer in cosmological thought, says that "the multiple-universe idea severely limits our hopes to understand the world from fundamental principles." And the philosophical ethos of science is torn from its roots. As put to me recently by Nobel Prize–winning physicist Steven Weinberg, a man as careful in his words as in his mathematical calculations, "We now find ourselves at a historic fork in the road we travel to understand the laws of nature. If the multiverse idea is correct, the style of fundamental physics will be radically changed."

The scientists most distressed by Weinberg's "fork in the road" are theoretical physicists. Theoretical physics is the deepest and purest branch of science. It is the outpost of science closest to philosophy, and religion. Experimental scientists occupy themselves with observing and measuring the cosmos, finding out what stuff exists, no matter how strange that stuff may be. Theoretical physicists, on the other hand, are not satisfied with observing the universe. They want to know *why*. They want to explain all the properties of the universe in terms of a few fundamental principles and parameters. These fundamental principles, in turn, lead to the "laws of nature," which govern the behavior of all matter and energy. An example of a fundamental principle in physics, first proposed by Galileo in 1632 and extended by Einstein in 1905, is the following: All observers traveling at constant velocity relative to one another should witness identical laws of nature. From this principle, Einstein derived his theory of special relativity. An example of a fundamental parameter is the mass of an electron, considered one of the two dozen or so "elementary" particles of nature. As far as physicists are concerned, the fewer the fundamental principles and parameters, the better. The underlying hope and belief of this enterprise has always been that these basic principles are so restrictive that only one, self-consistent universe is possible, like a crossword puzzle with only one solution. That one universe would be, of course, the universe we live in. Theoretical physicists are Platonists. Until the past few years, they agreed that the entire universe, the one universe, is generated from a few mathematical truths and principles of symmetry, perhaps throwing in a handful of parameters like the mass of the electron. It seemed that we were closing in on a vision of our universe in which everything could be calculated, predicted, and understood.

However, two theories in physics, eternal inflation and string theory, now suggest that the *same* fundamental principles from which the laws of nature derive may lead to many *different* self-consistent universes, with many different properties. It is as if you walked into a shoe store, had your feet measured, and found that a size 5 would fit you, a size 8 would also fit, and a size 12 would fit equally well. Such wishy-washy results make theoretical physicists extremely unhappy. Evidently, the fundamental laws of nature do not pin down a single and unique universe. According to the current thinking of many physicists, we are living in one of a vast number of universes. We are living in an accidental universe. We are living in a universe uncalculable by science.

"Back in the 1970s and 1980s," says Alan Guth, "the feeling was that we were so smart, we almost had everything figured out."

What physicists had figured out were very accurate theories of three of the four fundamental forces of nature: the strong nuclear force that binds atomic nuclei together, the weak force that is responsible for some forms of radioactive decay, and the electro-magnetic force between electrically charged particles. And there were prospects for merging the theory known as quantum physics with Einstein's theory of the fourth force, gravity, and thus pulling all of them into the fold of what physicists called the Theory of Everything, or the Final Theory. These theories of the 1970s and 1980s required the specification of a couple dozen parameters corresponding to the masses of the elementary particles, and another half dozen or so parameters corresponding to the strengths of the fundamental forces. The next step would then have been to derive most of the elementary particle masses in terms of one or two fundamental masses and define the strengths of all the funda-mental forces in terms of a single fundamental force.

There were good reasons to think that physicists were poised to take this next step. Indeed, since the time of Galileo, physics has been extremely successful in discovering principles and laws that have fewer and fewer free parameters and that are also in close agreement with the observed facts of the world. For example, the observed rotation of the ellipse of the orbit of Mercury, 0.012 degrees per century, was successfully calculated using the theory of general relativity, and the observed magnetic strength of an electron, 2.002319 magnetons, was derived using the theory of quantum electrodynamics. More than any other science, physics brims with highly accurate agreements between theory and experiment.

Guth started his physics career in this sunny scientific world. Now sixty-four years old and a professor at MIT, he was in his early thirties when he proposed a major revision to the Big Bang theory, something called inflation. We now have a great deal of evidence suggesting that our universe began as a nugget of extremely high density and temperature about 14 billion years ago and has been expanding, thinning out, and cooling ever since. The theory of inflation proposes that when our universe was only about a trillionth of a trillionth of a trillionth of a second old, a peculiar type of energy caused the cosmos to expand very rapidly. A tiny fraction of a second later, the universe returned to the more leisurely rate of expansion of the standard Big Bang model. Inflation solved a number of outstanding problems in cos-mology, such as why the universe appears so homogeneous on large scales.

When I visited Guth in his third-floor office at MIT one cool day in May, I could barely see him above the stacks of paper and empty Diet Coke bottles on his desk. More piles of paper and dozens of magazines littered the floor. In fact, a few years ago Guth won a contest sponsored by the *Boston Globe* for the messiest office in the city. The prize was the services of a professional organizer for one day. "She was actually more a nuisance than a help. She took piles of envelopes from the floor and began sorting them according to size." He wears aviator-style eyeglasses, keeps his hair long, and chain-drinks Diet Cokes. "The reason I went into theoretical physics," Guth tells me, "is that I liked the idea that we could understand everything—i.e., the universe—in terms of mathematics and logic." He gives a bitter laugh. We have been talking about the multiverse.

While challenging the Platonic dream of theoretical physicists, the multiverse idea does explain one aspect of our universe that has unsettled some scientists for years: according to various calculations, if the values of some of the fundamental parameters of our universe were a little larger or a little smaller, life could not have arisen. For example, if the nuclear force were a few percentage points stronger than it actually is, then all the hydrogen atoms in the infant universe would have fused with other hydrogen atoms to make helium, and there would be no hydrogen left. No hydrogen means no water. Although we are far from certain about what conditions are necessary for life, most biologists believe that water is necessary. On the other hand, if the nuclear force were substantially weaker than what it actually is, then the complex atoms needed for biology could not hold together. As another example, if the relationship between the strengths of the gravitational force and the electromagnetic force were not close to what it is, then the cosmos would not harbor any stars that explode and spew out life-supporting chemical elements into space or any other stars that form planets. Both kinds of stars are required for the emergence of life. The strengths of the basic forces and certain other fundamental parameters in our universe appear to be "fine-tuned" to allow the existence of life. The recognition of this fine-tuning led British physicist Brandon Carter to articulate what he called the anthropic principle, which states that the universe must have the parameters it does because we are here to observe it. Actually, the word *anthropic*, from the Greek for "man," is a misnomer: if these fundamental parameters were much different from what they are, it is not only human beings who would not exist. No life of any kind would exist.

If such conclusions are correct, the great question, of course, is *why* these fundamental parameters happen to lie within the range needed for life. Does the universe care about life? Intelligent design is one answer. Indeed, a fair number of theologians, philosophers, and even some scientists have used fine-tuning and the anthropic principle as evidence of the existence of God. For example, at the 2011 Christian Scholars' Conference at Pepperdine University, Francis Collins, a leading geneticist and director of the National Institutes of Health, said, "To get our universe, with all of its potential for complexities or any kind of potential for any kind of life-form, everything has to be precisely defined on this knife edge of improbability.... [Y]ou have to see the hands of a creator who set the parameters to be just so because the creator was interested in something a little more complicated than random particles."

Intelligent design, however, is an answer to fine-tuning that does not appeal to most scientists. The multiverse offers another explanation. If there are countless different universes with different properties—for example, some with nuclear forces much stronger than in our universe and some with nuclear forces much weaker—then some of those universes will allow the emergence of life and some will not. Some of those universes will be dead, lifeless hulks of matter and energy, and others will permit the emergence of cells, plants and animals, minds. From the huge range of possible universes predicted by the theories, the fraction of universes with life is undoubtedly small. But that doesn't matter. We live in one of the universes that permits life because otherwise we wouldn't be here to ask the question.

The explanation is similar to the explanation of why we happen to live on a planet that has so many nice things for our comfortable existence: oxygen, water, a temperature between the freezing and boiling points of water, and so on. Is this happy coincidence just good luck, or an act of Providence, or what? No, it is simply that we could not live on planets without such properties. Many other planets exist that are not so hospitable to life, such as Uranus, where the temperature is −371 degrees Fahrenheit, and Venus, where it rains sulfuric acid.

The multiverse offers an explanation to the fine-tuning conundrum that does not require the presence of a Designer. As Steven Weinberg says: "Over many centuries science has weakened the hold of religion, not by disproving the existence of God but by invalidating arguments for God based on what we observe in the natural world. The multiverse idea offers an explanation of why we find ourselves in a universe favorable to life that does not rely on the benevolence of a creator, and so if correct will leave still less support for religion."

Some physicists remain skeptical of the anthropic principle and the reliance on multiple universes to explain the values of the fundamental parameters of physics. Others, such as Weinberg and Guth, have reluctantly accepted the anthropic principle and the multiverse idea as together providing the best possible explanation for the observed facts.

If the multiverse idea is correct, then the historic mission of physics to explain all the properties of our universe in terms of fundamental principles—to explain why the properties of our universe must *necessarily* be what they are—is futile, a beautiful philosophical dream that simply isn't true. Our universe is what it is because we are here. The situation could be likened to a school of intelligent fish who one day began wondering why their world is completely filled with water. Many of the fish, the theorists, hope to prove that the entire cosmos necessarily has to be filled with water. For years, they put their minds to the task but can never quite seem to prove their assertion. Then, a wizened group of fish postulates that maybe they are fooling themselves. Maybe there are, they suggest, many other worlds, some of them completely dry, and everything in between.

The most striking example of fine-tuning, and one that practically demands the multiverse to explain it, is the unexpected detection of what scientists call dark energy. Little more than a decade ago, using robotic telescopes in Arizona, Chile, Hawaii, and outer space that can comb through nearly a million galaxies a night, astronomers discovered that the expansion of the universe is accelerating. As mentioned previously, it has been known since the late 1920s that the universe is expanding; it's a central feature of the Big Bang model. Orthodox cosmological thought held that the expansion is slowing down. After all, gravity is an attractive force; it pulls masses closer together. So it was quite a surprise in 1998 when two teams of astronomers announced that some unknown force appears to be jamming its foot down on the cosmic accelerator pedal. The expansion is speeding up. Galaxies are flying away from each other as if repelled by antigravity. Says Robert Kirshner, one of the team members who made the discovery: "This is not your father's universe." (In October, members of both teams were awarded the Nobel Prize in Physics.)

Physicists have named the energy associated with this cosmological force dark energy. No one knows what it is. Not only invisible, dark energy apparently hides out in empty space. Yet, based on our observations of the accelerating rate of expansion, dark energy constitutes a whopping three quarters of the total energy of the universe. It is the invisible elephant in the room of science.

The amount of dark energy, or more precisely the amount of dark energy in every cubic centimeter of space, has been calculated to be about one hundred-millionth ($10^{-8}$) of an erg per cubic centimeter. (For comparison, a penny dropped from waist-high hits the floor with an energy of about three hundred thousand—that is, $3 \times 10^5$—ergs.) This may not seem like much, but it adds up in the vast volumes of outer space. Astronomers were able to determine this number by measuring the rate of expansion of the universe at different epochs—if the universe is accelerating, then its rate of expansion was slower in the past. From the amount of acceleration, astronomers can calculate the amount of dark energy in the universe.

Theoretical physicists have several hypotheses about the identity of dark energy. It may be the energy of ghostly subatomic particles that can briefly appear out of nothing before self-annihilating and slipping back into the vacuum. According to quantum physics, empty space is a pandemonium of subatomic particles rushing about and then vanishing before they can be seen. Dark energy may also be associated with an as-yet-unobserved force field called the Higgs field, which is sometimes invoked to explain why certain kinds of matter have mass. (Theoretical physicists ponder things that other people do not.) And in the models proposed by string theory, dark energy may be associated with the way in which extra dimensions of space—beyond the usual length, width, and breadth—get compressed down to sizes much smaller than atoms, so that we do not notice them.

These various hypotheses give a fantastically large range for the *theoretically possible* amounts of dark energy in a universe, from something like $10^{115}$ ergs per cubic centimeter to $-10^{115}$ ergs per cubic centimeter. (A negative value for dark energy would mean that it acts to *decelerate* the universe, in contrast to what is observed.) Thus, in absolute magnitude, the amount of dark energy actually present in our universe is either very, very small or very, very large compared with what it could be. This fact alone is surprising. If the theoretically possible positive values for dark energy were marked out on a ruler stretching from here to the sun, with zero at one end of the ruler and $10^{115}$ ergs per cubic centimeter at the other end, the value of dark energy actually found in our universe ($10^{-8}$ ergs per cubic centimeter) would be closer to the zero end than the width of an atom.

On one thing most physicists agree: If the amount of dark energy in our universe were only a little bit different than what it actually is, then life could never have emerged. A little more and the universe would accelerate so rapidly that the matter in the young cosmos could never pull itself together to form stars and thence form the complex atoms made in stars. And, going into negative values of dark energy, a little less and the universe would decelerate so rapidly that it would recollapse before there was time to form even the simplest atoms.

Here we have a clear example of fine-tuning: out of all the possible amounts of dark energy that our universe might have, the actual amount lies in the tiny sliver of the range that allows life. There is little argument on this point. It does not depend on assumptions about whether we need liquid water for life or oxygen or particular biochemistries. As before, one is compelled to ask the question: Why does such fine-tuning occur? And the answer many physicists now believe: The multiverse. A vast number of universes may exist, with many different values of the amount of dark energy. Our particular universe is one of the universes with a small value, permitting the emergence of life. We are here, so our universe must be such a universe. We are an accident. From the cosmic lottery hat containing zillions of universes, we happened to draw a universe that allowed life. But then again, if we had not drawn such a ticket, we would not be here to ponder the odds.

The concept of the multiverse is compelling not only because it explains the problem of fine-tuning. As I mentioned earlier, the possibility of the multiverse is actually predicted by modern theories of physics. One such theory, called eternal inflation, is a revision of Guth's inflation theory developed by Andrei Linde, Paul Steinhardt, and Alex Vilenkin in the early and mid-1980s. In regular inflation theory, the very rapid expansion of the infant universe is caused by an energy field, like dark energy, that is temporarily trapped in a condition that does not represent the lowest possible energy for the universe as a whole—like a marble sitting in a small dent on a table. The marble can stay there, but if it is jostled it will roll out of the dent, roll across the table, and then fall to the floor (which represents the lowest possible energy level). In the theory of eternal inflation, the dark energy field has many different values at different points of space, analogous to lots of marbles sitting in lots of dents on the cosmic table. Moreover, as space expands rapidly, the number of marbles increases. Each of these marbles is jostled by the random processes inherent in quantum mechanics, and some of the marbles will begin rolling across the table and onto the floor. Each marble starts a new Big Bang, essentially a new universe. Thus, the original, rapidly expanding universe spawns a multitude of new universes, in a never-ending process.

String theory, too, predicts the possibility of the multiverse. Originally conceived in the late 1960s as a theory of the strong nuclear force but soon enlarged far beyond that ambition, string theory postulates that the smallest constituents of matter are not subatomic particles like the electron but extremely tiny one-dimensional "strings" of energy. These elemental strings can vibrate at different frequencies, like the strings of a violin, and the different modes of vibration correspond to different fundamental particles and forces. String theories typically require seven dimensions of space in addition to the usual three, which are compacted down to such small sizes that we never experience them, like a three-dimensional garden hose that appears as a one-dimensional line when seen from a great distance. There are, in fact, a vast number of ways that the extra dimensions in string theory can be folded up, and each of the different ways corresponds to a different universe with different physical properties.

It was originally hoped that from a theory of these strings, with very few additional parameters, physicists would be able to explain all the forces and particles of nature—all of reality would be a manifestation of the vibrations of elemental strings. String theory would then be the ultimate realization of the Platonic ideal of a fully explicable cosmos. In the past few years, however, physicists have discovered that string theory predicts not a unique universe but a huge number of possible universes with different properties. It has been estimated that the "string landscape" contains $10^{500}$ different possible universes. For all practical purposes, that number is infinite.

It is important to point out that neither eternal inflation nor string theory has anywhere near the experimental support of many previous theories in physics, such as special relativity or quantum electrodynamics, mentioned earlier. Eternal inflation or string theory, or both, could turn out to be wrong. However, some of the world's leading physicists have devoted their careers to the study of these two theories.

Back to the intelligent fish. The wizened old fish conjecture that there are many other worlds, some with dry land and some with water. Some of the fish grudgingly accept this explanation. Some feel relieved. Some feel like their lifelong ruminations have been pointless. And some remain deeply concerned. Because there is no way they can prove this conjecture. That same uncertainty disturbs many physicists who are adjusting to the idea of the multiverse. Not only must we accept that basic properties of our universe are accidental and uncalculable. In addition, we must believe in the existence of many other universes. But we have no conceivable way of observing these other universes and cannot prove their existence. Thus, to explain what we see in the world and in our mental deductions, we must believe in what we cannot prove.

Sound familiar? Theologians are accustomed to taking some beliefs on faith. Scientists are not. All we can do is hope that the same theories that predict the multiverse also produce many other predictions that we can test here in our own universe. But the other universes themselves will almost certainly remain a conjecture.

"We had a lot more confidence in our intuition before the discovery of dark energy and the multiverse idea," says Guth. "There will still be a lot for us to understand, but we will miss out on the fun of figuring everything out from first principles."

One wonders whether a young Alan Guth, considering a career in science today, would choose theoretical physics.

## Reflections and Responses

1. One of the major skills of a talented science writer is to find analogies to help readers understand unfamiliar and difficult concepts. Identify a few of Lightman's analogies. How do they help illustrate the concept of a "multiverse"? Do you find them effective? Why or why not?

2. Note that Lightman's essay is also part profile. Who is Alan Guth and of what importance is he to Lightman's essay? Since Lightman himself is a physicist, why do you think he relies on the interview with Guth throughout his essay?

3. In what ways does "fine-tuning" lead some to believe in a God or intelligent design? How does the theory of a "multiverse" explain "fine-tuning"? What is Lightman saying about the "multiverse" in his final paragraphs? What connection does he make between science and theology?

JOYCE CAROL OATES

# *They All Just Went Away*

*The essay has long been the perfect form for the reflective mind. In the hands of a great writer, the process of reflection can be stimulated by a single incident or image and then veer off in so many different directions that, by the end of the essay, the reader is amazed at how much ground has been covered. "They All Just Went Away" does everything a superb reflective essay can do because it moves from the personal eccentricities of a lonely young girl who finds herself drawn to abandoned houses and desolate families into a consideration of American art, class boundaries, sexual abuse, and strange erotic attachments. It is not a cheerful or placid piece of writing, however. "As I am not drawn to art that makes me feel good, comfortable, or at ease," Joyce Carol Oates writes, "so I am not drawn to essays that 'smile,' except in the context of larger, more complex ambitions."*

*One of the country's most distinguished authors, Joyce Carol Oates has published over two dozen novels and numerous collections of poems, plays, short stories, criticism, and essays. Equipped with her work alone, the scholar and essayist Henry Louis Gates Jr. claimed, a future archaeologist could "easily piece together the whole postwar America." The recipient of countless literary awards, she was at thirty-one the youngest writer ever to receive the prestigious National Book Award for fiction when her novel* them *was chosen in 1969. She currently teaches writing at Princeton University. Among her most recent works of fiction are* Blonde *(2000),* I'll Take You There *(2002),* The Tattooed Girl *(2003),* The Falls *(2004),* Missing Mom *(2005),* Black Girl/White Girl *(2006),* The Gravedigger's Daughter *(2007),* My Sister, My Love *(2008),* Dear Husband: Stories *(2009),* The Cornmaiden and Other Nightmares *(2011), and* Mudwoman *(2012). In 2011 she published* A Widow's Story: A Memoir. *"They All*

*Source:* "They All Just Went Away" by Joyce Carol Oates. First published in *The New Yorker.* Copyright © 1996 by The Ontario Review, Inc. Reprinted by permission of the author.

*Just Went Away" originally appeared in* The New Yorker *(1995) and was selected by Geoffrey C. Ward for* The Best American Essays 1996.

I must have been a lonely child. Until the age of twelve or thirteen, my most intense, happiest hours were spent tramping desolate fields, woods, and creek banks near my family's farmhouse in Millersport, New York. No one knew where I went. My father, working most of the day at Harrison's, a division of General Motors in Lockport, and at other times preoccupied, would not have asked; if my mother asked, I might have answered in a way that would deflect curiosity. I was an articulate, verbal child. Yet I could not have explained what drew me to the abandoned houses, barns, silos, corncribs. A hike of miles through fields of spiky grass, across outcroppings of shale as steeply angled as stairs, was a lark if the reward was an empty house.

Some of these houses had been inhabited as "homes" fairly recently—they had not yet reverted to the wild. Others, abandoned during the Depression, had long since begun to rot and collapse, engulfed by vegetation (trumpet vine, wisteria, rose of Sharon, willow) that elsewhere, on our property for instance, was kept neatly trimmed. I was drawn to both kinds of houses, though the more recently inhabited were more forbidding and therefore more inviting.

To push open a door into such silence: the absolute emptiness of a house whose occupants have departed. Often, the crack of

Cindy Creighton/iStockphoto.com

broken glass underfoot. A startled buzzing of flies, hornets. The slithering, ticklish sensation of a garter snake crawling across floorboards.

Left behind, as if in haste, were remnants of a lost household. A broken toy on the floor, a baby's bottle. A rain-soaked sofa, looking as if it has been gutted with a hunter's skilled knife. Strips of wallpaper like shredded skin. Smashed crockery, piles of tin cans; soda, beer, whiskey bottles. An icebox, its door yawning open. Once, on a counter, a dirt-stiffened rag that, unfolded like precious cloth, revealed itself to be a woman's cheaply glamorous "see-through" blouse, threaded with glitter-strips of gold.

This was a long time ago, yet it is more vivid to me than anything now.

This was when I was too young to think the house is the mother's body, you have been expelled and are forbidden now to reenter.

Always, I was prepared to see a face at a high, empty window. A woman's hand uplifted in greeting, or in warning. *Hello! Come in! Stay away! Run! Who are you?* A movement in the corner of my eye: the blurred motion of a person passing through a doorway, or glimpsed through a window. There might be a single shriek of laughter from a barn—piercing as a bird's cry. Murmurous, teasing voices confused with wind rippling through tall, coarse, gone-to-seed grass. Voices that, when you pause to listen, fade immediately and are gone.

The sky in such places of abandonment was always of the hue and brightness of tin, as if the melancholy rural poverty of tin roofs reflected upward.

A house: a structural arrangement of space, geometrically laid out to provide what are called rooms, these divided from one another by verticals and horizontals called walls, ceilings, floors. The house contains the home but is not identical with it. The house anticipates the home and will very likely survive it, reverting again simply to house when home (that is, life) departs. For only where there is life can there be home.

I have never found the visual equivalent of these abandoned farmhouses of upstate New York, of northern Erie County, in the area of the long, meandering Tonawanda Creek and the Barge Canal. You think most immediately of the canvases of Edward Hopper: those dreamily stylized visions of a lost America, houses never depicted as homes, and human beings, if you look closer, never depicted as other than mannequins. For Hopper is not a realist but a surrealist. His dreams are of the ordinary, as if, even in imagination, the artist were trapped in an unyielding daylight consciousness. There seems almost a kind of rage, a revenge against such restraints, in Hopper's studied, endlessly repeated *simplicity*. By contrast, Charles Burchfield, with his numerous oils and watercolors—frequently of upstate New York landscapes, houses, and farms—rendered the real as visionary and luminous, suffused with a Blakean rapture and a kind of radical simplicity, too. Then there are the shimmering New England barns, fields, and skies of our contemporary Wolf Kahn—images evoked by memory, almost on the verge of dissolution. But the "real"—what assaults the eye before the eye begins its work of selection—is never on the verge of dissolution, still less of appropriation. The real is raw, jarring, unexpected, sometimes trashy, sometimes luminous. Above all, the real is arbitrary. For to be a realist (in art or in life) is to acknowledge that all things might be other than they are. That there is no design, no intention, no aesthetic or moral or teleological imprimatur but, rather, the equivalent of Darwin's great vision of a blind, purposeless, ceaseless evolutionary process that yields no "products"—only temporary strategies against extinction.

Yet, being human, we think, To what purpose these broken-off things, if not to be gathered up, at last, in a single ecstatic vision?

There is a strange and profound and unknowable reality to these abandoned houses where jealously guarded, even prized possessions have become mere trash: windowpanes long ago smashed, and the spaces where they had been festooned with cobwebs, and cobwebs brushing against your face, catching in your hair like caresses. The peculiar, dank smell of wood rot and mildew, in one of the houses I most recall that had partly burned down, the smell of smoke and scorch, in early summer pervading even the lyric smell of honeysuckle—these haunting smells, never, at the time of experiencing, given specific sources, names.

Where a house has been abandoned—unworthy of being sold to new tenants, very likely seized by the county for default on taxes and the property held in escrow—you can be sure there has been a sad story. There have been devastated lives. Lives to be spoken of pityingly. How they went wrong. Why did she marry him, why did she stay with him? Just desperate people. Ignorant. Poor white trash. Runs in the family. A wrong turn.

Shall I say for the record that ours was a happy, close-knit, and unextraordinary family for our time, place, and economic status? Yet what was vividly real in the solid-built old farmhouse that contained my home (my family consisted of my father, mother, younger brother, grandfather, and grandmother, who owned the property—a slow-failing farm whose principal crop had become Bartlett pears by the time I was a girl) was of far less significance to me than what was real elsewhere. A gone-to-seed landscape had an authority that seemed to me incontestable: the powerful authority of silence in houses from which the human voice had vanished. For the abandoned house contained the future of any house—the lilac tree pushing through the rotted veranda, hornets' nests beneath eaves, windows smashed by vandals, human excrement left to dry on a parlor floor once scrubbed on hands and knees.

The abandoned, the devastated, was the profound experience, whereas involvement in family life—the fever, the bliss, the abrasions, the infinite distractions of human love—was so clearly temporary. Like a television screen upon which antic images (at this time, in the fifties, minimally varying gradations of gray) appear fleetingly and are gone.

I have seemed to suggest that the abandoned houses were all distant from our house, but in fact the one that had been partly gutted by fire—which I will call the Weidel house—was perhaps a half mile away. If you drove, turning right off Transit Road, which was our road, onto the old Creek Road, it would have been a distance of a mile or more, but if you crossed through our back potato field and through the marshy woods which no one seemed to own, it was a quick walk.

The Weidels' dog, Slossie, a mixed breed with a stumpy, energetic tail and a sweet disposition, sand-colored, rheumy-eyed, as hungry for affection as for the scraps we sometimes fed her, trotted over frequently to play with my brother and me. Though, strictly speaking, Slossie was not wanted at our house. None of the Weidels were wanted.

The "Weidel house," it would be called for years. The "Weidel property." As if the very land—which the family had not owned in any case, but only rented, partly with county-welfare support—were somehow imprinted with that name, a man's identity. Or infamy.

For tales were told of the father who drank, beat and terrorized his family, "did things to" his daughters, and finally set the house on fire and fled and was arrested, disappearing forever from the proper, decent life of our community. There was no romance in Mr. Weidel, whom my father knew only slightly and despised as a drinker, and as a wife- and child-beater. Mr. Weidel was a railway worker in Lockport, or perhaps an ex-railway worker, for he seemed to work only sporadically, though he always wore a railwayman's cap. He and his elder sons were hunters, owning a shotgun among them and one or two deer rifles. His face was broad, fair, vein-swollen, with a look of flushed, alcoholic reproach. He was tall and heavyset, with graying black whiskers that sprouted like quills. His eyes had a way of swerving in their sockets, seeking you out when you could not slip away quickly enough. *H'lo there, little Joyce! Joycie! Joycie Oates, h'lo!* He wore rubber boots that flapped, unbuckled, about his feet.

Mrs. Weidel was a faded-pretty, apologetic woman with a body that seemed to have become bloated, as with a perpetual pregnancy. Her bosom had sunk to her waist. Her legs were encased, sausagelike, in flesh-colored support hose. *How can that woman live with him? That pig.* There was disdain, disgust, in this frequent refrain. *Why doesn't she leave him? Did you see that black eye? Did you hear them the other night? Take the girls away, at least.* It was thought that she could, for Mrs. Weidel was the only one in the family who seemed to work at all regularly. She was hired for seasonal canning in a tomato factory in lower Lockport and may have done housecleaning in the city.

A shifting household of relatives and rumored "boarders" lived in the Weidel house. There were six Weidel children, four sons and two daughters. Ruth was a year older than I, and Dorothy two years younger. There was an older brother of Mr. Weidel's, who walked with a cane and was said to be an ex-convict, from Attica. The eldest Weidel son, Roy, owned a motorcycle, and friends of his often visited, fellow bikers. There were loud parties, frequent disputes, and tales of Mr. Weidel's chasing his wife with a butcher knife, a claw hammer, the shotgun, threatening to "blow her head off." Mrs. Weidel and the younger children fled outdoors in terror and hid in the hayloft. Sheriff's deputies drove out to the house, but no charges were ever pressed against Mr. Weidel. Until the fire, which was so public that it couldn't be denied.

There was the summer day—I was eleven years old—that Mr. Weidel shot Slossie. We heard the poor creature yelping and whimpering for what seemed like hours. When my father came home from work, he went to speak to Mr. Weidel, though my mother begged him not to. By this time, the dog had dragged herself beneath the Weidels' house to die. Mr. Weidel was furious at the intrusion, drunk, defensive—Slossie was his goddam dog, he said, she'd been getting in the way, she was "old." But my father convinced him to put the poor dog out of her misery. So Mr. Weidel made one of his sons drag Slossie out from beneath the house, and he straddled her and shot her a second time, and a third, at close range. My father, who'd never hunted, who'd never owned a gun, backed off, a hand over his eyes.

Afterward, my father would say of that day that walking away from that drunken son of a bitch with a rifle in his hands was about the hardest thing he'd ever done. He'd expected a shot between his shoulders.

The fire was the following year, around Thanksgiving.

After the Weidels were gone from Millersport and the house stood empty, I discovered Slossie's grave. I'm sure it was Slossie's grave. It was beyond the dog hutch, in the weedy back yard, a sunken patch of earth measuring about three feet by four with one of Mrs. Weidel's big whitewashed rocks at the head.

Morning glories grew in clusters on the posts of the front porch. Mrs. Weidel had planted hollyhocks, sunflowers, and trumpet vine in the yard. Tough, weedlike flowers that would survive for years.

It had been said of Ruth and her sister Dorothy that they were "slow." Yet Ruth was never slow to fly into a rage when she was teased by neighborhood boys or by her older brothers. She waved her fists and stammered obscenities, words that stung like hail. Her face darkened with blood, and her full, thick lips quivered with a strange sort of pleasure. How you loved to see Ruth Weidel fly into one of her rages; it was like holding a lighted match to flammable material.

The Weidel house was like any other rundown woodframe house, said by my grandfather to have been "thrown up" in the 1920s. It had no cellar, only a concrete-block foundation—an emptiness that gradually filled with debris. It had an upstairs with several small bedrooms. There was no attic. No insulation. Steep, almost vertical stairs. The previous tenant had started to construct a front porch of raw planks, never completed or painted. (Though Mrs. Weidel added "touches" to the porch—chairs, a woven-rush rug, geraniums in flowerpots.) The roof of the house was made of sheets of tin, scarred and scabbed like skin, and the front was covered in simulated-brick asphalt siding pieced together from lumberyard scraps. All year round, a number of the windows were covered in transparent duct tape and never opened. From a distance, the house was the fading dun color of a deer's winter coat.

Our house had an attic and a cellar and a deep well and a solid cement foundation. My father did all the carpentry on our house, most of the shingling, the painting, the masonry. I would not know until I was an adult that he'd come from what's called a "broken home" himself—what an image, luridly visual, of a house literally broken, split in two, its secrets spilled out onto the ground for all to see, like entrails.

My mother, unlike Mrs. Weidel, had time to houseclean. It was a continuous task, a mother's responsibility. My mother planted vegetables, strawberries, beds of flowers. Petunias and pansies and zinnias. Crimson peonies that flowered for my birthday, in mid-June.

I remember the night of the fire vividly, as if it had been a festive affair to which I'd been invited.

There was the sound of a siren on the Creek Road. There were shouts, and an astonishing burst of flame in the night, in the direction of the Weidel house. The air was moist, and reflected and magnified the fire, surrounding it like a nimbus. My grandparents would claim there had never been such excitement in Millersport, and perhaps that was true. My father dressed hurriedly and went to help the firefighters, and my mother and the rest of us watched from upstairs windows. The fire began at about 1 A.M., and it would be past 4 A.M. before my seven-year-old brother and I got back to bed.

Yet what was so exciting an event was, in fact, an ending, with nothing to follow. Immediately afterward, the Weidels disappeared from Millersport and from our lives. It was said that Mr. Weidel fled "as a fugitive" but was captured and arrested the next day, in Buffalo. The family was broken up, scattered, the younger children placed in foster homes. That quickly, the Weidels were gone.

For a long time, the smell of wood smoke, scorch, pervaded the air of Millersport, the fresh, damp smell of earth sullied by its presence. Neighbors complained that the Weidel house should be razed at the county's expense, bulldozed over, and the property sold. But nothing was done for years. Who knows why? When I went away to college, the old falling-down house was still there.

How swiftly, in a single season, a human habitation can turn wild. The bumpy cinder driveway over which the eldest Weidel son had ridden his motorcycle was soon stippled with tall weeds.

What had happened to Roy Weidel? It was said he'd joined the navy. No, he had a police record and could not have joined the navy. He'd disappeared. Asked by the police to give a sworn statement about the night of his father's "arson," he'd panicked and fled.

Signs were posted—NO TRESPASSING, THIS PROPERTY CONDEMNED BY ERIE CO.—and they, too, over a period of months, became shabby and faded. My parents warned me never to wander onto the Weidel property. There was a well with a loose-fitting cover, among other dangers. As if I would fall into a well! I smiled to think how little my parents knew me. How little anyone knew me.

Have I said that my father never struck his children, as Mr. Weidel struck his? And did worse things to them, to the girls sometimes, it was whispered. Yes, and Mrs. Weidel, who seemed so soft and apologetic and sad, she too had beaten the younger children when she'd been drinking. County social workers came around to question neighbors, and spread the story of what they learned along the way.

In fact, I may have been disciplined, spanked, a few times. Like most children, I don't remember. I remember Mr. Weidel spanking his children until they screamed (though I wasn't a witness, was I?), but I don't remember being spanked by my parents, and in any case, if I was, it was no more than I deserved.

I'd seen Mr. Weidel urinating once at the roadside. The loose-flying skein of the kerosene he'd flung around the house before setting the fire must have resembled the stream of his urine, transparent and glittering. But they laughed, saying Mr. Weidel had been too drunk, or too careless, to have done an adequate job of sprinkling kerosene through the downstairs of the house. Wasn't it like him, such a slovenly job. Only part of the house had burned, a wall of the kitchen and an adjoining woodshed.

Had Mr. Weidel wanted to burn his family alive in their beds? Mrs. Weidel testified no, they'd all been awake, they'd run out into the yard before the fire began. They'd never been in any danger, she swore. But Mr. Weidel was indicted on several counts of attempted murder, along with other charges.

For so many years the Weidel house remained standing. There was something defiant about it, like someone who has been mortally wounded but will not die. In the weedy front yard, Mrs. Weidel's display of whitewashed rocks and plaster-of-Paris gnomes and the clay pedestal with the shiny blue glass ball disappeared from view within a year or so. Brambles grew everywhere. I forced myself to taste a small bitter red berry but spat it out, it made my mouth pucker so.

What did it mean that Erie County had "condemned" the Weidel property? The downstairs windows were carelessly boarded over, and both the front and rear doors were unlocked, collapsing on their hinges. Broken glass underfoot and a sickish stench of burn, mildew, decay. Yet there were "touches"—on what remained of a kitchen wall, a Holstein calendar from a local feed store, a child's crayon drawing. Upstairs, children's clothes, socks and old shoes heaped on the floor. I recognized with a thrill of repugnance an old red sweater of Ruth's, angora-fuzzy. There were broken Christmas tree ornaments, a naked pink plastic doll. Toppled bedsprings, filthy mattresses streaked with yellow and rust-colored stains. The mattresses looked as if they'd been gutted, their stuffing strewn about. The most terrible punishment, I thought, would be to be forced to lie down on such a mattress.

I thought of Mrs. Weidel, her swollen, blackened eyes, her bruised face. Shouts and sirens in the night, the sheriff's patrol car. But no charges filed. The social worker told my mother how Mrs. Weidel had screamed at the county people, insisting her husband hadn't done anything wrong and shouldn't go to jail. The names she'd called them! Unrepeatable.

She was the wife of that man, they'd had babies together. The law had no right to interfere. The law had nothing to do with them.

As a woman and as a writer, I have long wondered at the wellsprings of female masochism. Or what, in despair of a more subtle, less reductive phrase, we can call the congeries of predilections toward self-hurt, self-erasure, self-repudiation in women. These predilections are presumably "learned"—"acquired"—but perhaps also imprinted in our genes, of biological necessity, neurophysiological fate, predilections that predate culture. Indeed, may shape culture. Do not say, "Yes, but these are isolated, peripheral examples. These are marginal Americans, uneducated. They tell us nothing about ourselves." They tell us everything about ourselves, and even the telling, the exposure, is a kind of cutting, an inscription in the flesh.

Yet what could possibly be the evolutionary advantage of self-hurt in the female? Abnegation in the face of another's cruelty? Acquiescence to another's will? This loathsome secret that women do not care to speak of, or even acknowledge.

Two or three years later, in high school, twelve miles away in a consolidated district school to which, as a sophomore, I went by school bus, Ruth Weidel appeared. She was living now with relatives in Lockport. She looked, at sixteen, like a woman in her twenties; big-breasted, with full, strong thighs and burnished-brown hair inexpertly bleached. Ruth's homeroom was "special education," but she took some classes with the rest of us. If she

recognized me, in our home economics class, she was careful to
give no sign.

There was a tacit understanding that "something had happened" to Ruth Weidel, and her teachers treated her guardedly.
Ruth was special, the way a handicapped person is special. She
was withdrawn, quiet; if still prone to violent outbursts of rage,
she might have been on medication to control it. Her eyes, like
her father's, seemed always about to swerve in their sockets. Her
face was round, fleshy, like a pudding, her nose oily-pored. Yet she
wore lipstick, she was "glamorous"—almost. In gym class, Ruth's
large breasts straining against her T-shirt and the shining rippled
muscles and fatty flesh of her thighs were amazing to us; we were
so much thinner and less female, so much younger.

I believed that I should protect Ruth Weidel, so I told none of
the other students about her family. Even to Ruth, for a long time
I pretended not to know who she was. I can't explain how Ruth
could have possibly believed me, yet this seems to have been so.
Quite purposefully, I befriended Ruth. I thought her face would
lose its sallow hardness if she could be made to smile, and so it
became a kind of challenge to me to induce Ruth Weidel to
smile. She was lonely and miserable at school, and flattered by
my attention. For so few "normal" girls sought out "specialed"
girls. At first she may have been suspicious, but by degrees she
became trusting. I thought of Slossie: trust shows in the eyes.

I sat with Ruth at lunch in the school cafeteria and eventually
I asked her about the house on the old Creek Road, and she lied
bluntly, to my face, insisting that an uncle of hers had owned that
house. She'd only visited a few times. She and her family. I asked,
"How did the fire start?" and Ruth said, slowly, each word sucked
like a pebble in the mouth, "Lightning. Lightning hit it. One night
in a storm." I asked, "Are you living with your mother now, Ruth?"
and Ruth shrugged, and made a face, and said, "She's OK. I see
her sometimes." I asked about Dorothy. I asked where Mrs. Weidel
was. I said that my mother had always liked her mother, and
missed her when she went away. But Ruth seemed not to hear.
Her gaze had drifted. I said, "Why did you all move away?" Ruth
did not reply, though I could hear her breathing hard. "Why did
you abandon your house? It could have been fixed. It's still there.
Your mom's hollyhocks are still there. You should come out and
see it sometime. You could visit me." Ruth shrugged, and laughed.
She gave me a sidelong glance, almost flirtatiously. It was startling
to see how good-looking she could be, how sullen-sexy; to know
how men would stare at her who would never so much as glance

at a girl like me. Ruth said slowly, as if she'd come to a final, adamant conclusion to a problem that had long vexed her, "They all just went away."

Another time, after lunch with Ruth, I left a plastic change purse with a few coins in it on the ledge in one of the girls' lavatories, where Ruth was washing her hands. I don't recall whether I left it on purpose or not. But when I returned, after waiting for Ruth to leave the lavatory, the change purse was gone.

Once or twice, I invited Ruth Weidel to come home with me on the school bus some afternoon, to Millersport, to have supper with my family and stay the night. I must not have truly believed she might accept, for my mother would have been horrified and would have forced me to rescind the invitation. Ruth had hesitated, as if she wanted to say yes, wanted very badly to say yes, but finally she said, "No. I guess I better not."

## Reflections and Responses

1. How does Joyce Carol Oates introduce the issue of class into the essay? How does her background differ from Ruth Weidel's? How would you describe her attitude toward the Weidel family? Why is she drawn to them? What does she find attractive about them?

2. How can you account for the abrupt introduction in the ninth paragraph of houses as the subject for famous American painters? Why do you think the author suddenly interjected this information? What does it contribute to the essay as a whole?

3. Where does the essay's title come from? Why do you think Joyce Carol Oates used this expression as the title? What does it suggest about the overall experience of the essay?

DAVID SEDARIS

# This Old House

*Describing one's childhood house is such a common subject for a personal essay it has become a cliché. After all, what can be a more tangible manifestation of one's relationship to the past than one's memories of the house one grew up in? In this essay humorist David Sedaris subverts the trope, almost completely glossing over his practical parents' suburban house, where furniture was chosen "for its durability rather than for its beauty." In its place he ruminates on a house where he rented a room as a young adult—an older, dingier place filled with antiques and characters so eccentric and colorful they seem to come from television. In particular, Sedaris forms a bond with his landlady Rosemary, a maternal figure who stokes his romanticization of the past. But as Sedaris explores his old house, he considers its bizarre and profound alienation. "The idea was that we were different, not like the rest of America, with its Fuzzbusters and shopping malls and rotating shower-heads," he writes. And he quotes Rosemary: " 'If it's not new and shiny, they don't want anything to do with it.... . Give them the Liberty Bell and they'd bitch about the crack. That's how folks are nowadays.' "*

*David Sedaris is perhaps the most popular humor writer in America. He is best known for his sardonic reflections on his childhood, reflections that often involve biting social commentary. He contributes frequently to* The New Yorker, *where "This Old House" first appeared, and to* This American Life *on National Public Radio. His collections include* Barrel Fever *(1994),* Naked *(1997),* Holidays on Ice *(1997),* Me Talk Pretty One Day *(2000),* Dress Your Family in Corduroy and Denim *(2004),* When You Are Engulfed in Flames *(2008), and* Squirrel Seeks Chipmunk: A Modern Bestiary *(2010). "This Old House" was selected by Adam Gopnik for* The Best American Essays 2008.

*Source:* From *When You are Engulfed in Flames* by David Sedaris. Copyright © 2008 by David Sedaris. By permission of Little, Brown and Company and Don Gongdon Associates, Inc.

When it came to decorating her home, my mother was nothing if not practical. She learned early on that children will destroy whatever you put in front of them, so for most of my youth our furniture was chosen for its durability rather than for its beauty. The one exception was the dining-room set, which my parents bought shortly after they were married. Should a guest eye the buffet for longer than a second, my mother would notice and jump in to prompt a compliment. "You like it?" she'd ask. "It's Scandinavian!" This, we learned, was the name of a region—a cold and forsaken place where people stayed indoors and plotted the death of knobs.

The buffet, like the table, was an exercise in elegant simplicity. The set was made of teak, and had been finished with tung oil. This brought out the character of the wood, allowing it, at certain times of day, to practically glow. Nothing was more beautiful than our dining room, especially after my father covered the walls with cork. It wasn't the kind you use on bulletin boards but something coarse and dark, the color of damp pine mulch. Light the candles beneath the chafing dish, lay the table with the charcoal-textured dinnerware we hardly ever used, and you had yourself a real picture.

This dining room, I liked to think, was what my family was all about. Throughout my childhood, it brought me great pleasure, but then I turned sixteen and decided that I didn't like it anymore. What happened was a television show,* a weekly drama about a close-knit family in Depression-era Virginia. The family didn't have a blender or a country-club membership, but they did have one another—that and a really great house, an old one, built in the twenties or something. All their bedrooms had slanted clapboard walls and oil lamps that bathed everything in fragile golden light. I wouldn't have used the word "romantic," but that's how I thought of it.

"You think those prewar years were cozy?" my father once asked. "Try getting up at 5 A.M. to sell newspapers on the snow-covered streets. That's what I did and it stunk to high heaven."

"Well," I told him, "I'm just sorry that you weren't able to appreciate it."

Like anyone nostalgic for a time he didn't live through, I chose to weed out the little inconveniences: polio, say, or the thought of eating stewed squirrel. The world was simply grander back then, somehow more civilized, and nicer to look at. Wasn't it crushing to live in a house no older than our cat?

"No," my father said. "Not at all."

---

*A television show: The allusion is to *The Waltons,* a popular 1960s TV series.

My mother felt the same: "Boxed in by neighbors, having to walk through my parents' bedroom in order to reach the kitchen. If you think that was fun, you never saw your grandfather with his teeth out."

They were more than willing to leave their pasts behind them, and reacted strongly when my sister Gretchen and I began dragging it home. "The *Andrews* Sisters*?" my father groaned. "What the hell do you want to listen to them for?"

When I started buying clothes from Goodwill, he really went off, and for good reason, probably. The suspenders and knickers were bad enough, but when I added a top hat he planted himself in the doorway and physically prevented me from leaving the house. "It doesn't make sense," I remember him saying. "That hat with those pants, worn with the damn platform shoes ..." His speech temporarily left him, and he found himself waving his hands, no doubt wishing that they held magic wands. "You're just ... a mess is what you are."

The way I saw it, the problem wasn't my outfit but my context. Sure I looked out of place beside a Scandinavian buffet, but put me in the proper environment and I'd undoubtedly fit right in.

"The environment you're looking for is called a psychiatric hospital," my father said. "Now give me the damn hat before I burn it off."

I longed for a home where history was respected—and, four years later, I finally found one. This was in Chapel Hill, North Carolina. I'd gone there to visit an old friend from high school— and because I was between jobs, and had no real obligations, I decided to stay for a while and maybe look for some dishwashing work. The restaurant that hired me was a local institution, all dark wood and windowpanes the size of playing cards. The food was O.K., but what the place was really known for was the classical music that the man in charge, someone named Byron, pumped into the dining room. Anyone else might have thrown in a compilation tape, but he took his responsibilities very seriously, and planned each meal as if it were an evening at Tanglewood. I hoped that dishwashing might lead to a job in the dining room, busing tables, and, eventually, waiting on them, but I kept these aspirations to myself. Dressed as I was, in jodhpurs and a smoking jacket, I should have been grateful that I was hired at all.

After getting my first paycheck, I scouted out a place to live. My two requirements were that it be cheap and close to where

---

*The Andrews Sisters: An enormously popular trio whose career straddled World War II.

I worked, and on both counts I succeeded. I couldn't have dreamed that it would also be old and untouched, an actual boarding house. The owner was adjusting her "Room for Rent" sign as I passed, and our eyes locked in an expression that said, "Hark, stranger, you are one of me!" Both of us looked like figures from a scratchy newsreel: me the unemployed factory worker in tortoiseshell safety glasses and a tweed overcoat two sizes too large, and her, the feisty widow lady, taking in boarders in order to make ends meet. "Excuse me," I called, "but is that hat from the forties?"

The woman put her hands to her head and adjusted what looked like a fistful of cherries spilling from a velveteen saucer. "Why, yes it is," she said. "How canny of you to notice." I'll say that her name was Rosemary Dowd, and, as she introduced herself, I tried to guess her age. What foxed me was her makeup, which was on the heavy side, and involved a great deal of peach-colored powder. From a distance, her hair looked white, but now I could see that it was streaked with yellow, almost randomly, like snow that had been peed on. If she seemed somewhat mannish, it was the fault of her clothing rather than her features. Both her jacket and her blouse were kitted out with shoulder pads, and when they were worn together she could barely fit through the door. This might be a problem for others, but Rosemary didn't get out much. And why would she want to?

I hadn't even crossed the threshold when I agreed to take the room. What sold me was the look of the place. Some might have found it shabby—"a dump," my father would eventually call it— but, unless you ate them, a few thousand paint chips never hurt anyone. The same could be said for the groaning front porch and the occasional missing shingle. It was easy to imagine that the house, set as it was on the lip of a student parking lot, had dropped from the sky, like Dorothy's in *The Wizard of Oz*, but with a second story. Then there was the inside, which was even better. The front door opened into a living room, or, as Rosemary called it, "the parlor." The word was old-fashioned, but fitting. Velvet curtains framed the windows. The walls were papered in a faint, floral pattern, and doilies were everywhere, laid flat on table-tops and sagging like cobwebs from the backs of overstuffed chairs. My eyes moved from one thing to another, and, like my mother with her dining-room set, Rosemary took note of where they landed. "I see you like my davenport," she said, and, "You don't find lamps like that anymore. It's a genuine Stephanie."

It came as no surprise that she bought and sold antiques, or "dab-bled" in them, as she said. Every available surface was crowded with objects: green-glass candy dishes, framed photographs of movie stars, cigarette boxes with monogrammed lids. An umbrella leaned against an open steamer trunk, and, when I observed that its handle was Bakelite, my new landlady unpinned her saucer of cherries and predicted that the two of us were going to get along famously.

And for many months we did. Rosemary lived on the ground floor, in a set of closed-off rooms she referred to as her chambers. The door that led to them opened onto the parlor, and when I stood outside I could sometimes hear her television. This seemed to me a kind of betrayal, like putting a pool table inside the Great Pyramid, but she assured me that the set was an old one—"My 'Model Tee Vee,'" she called it.

My room was upstairs, and in letters home I described it as "hunky-dory." How else to capture my peeling, buckled wallpaper, and the way that it brought everything together. The bed, the desk, the brass-plated floor lamp: it was all there waiting for me, and though certain pieces had seen better days—the guest chair, for instance, was missing its seat—at least everything was uniformly old. From my window I could see the parking lot and, beyond that, the busy road leading to the restaurant. It pleased Rosemary that I worked in such a venerable place. "It suits you," she said. "And don't feel bad about washing dishes. I think even Gable* did it for a while."

"Did he?"

I felt so clever, catching all her references. The other boarder didn't even know who Charlie Chan[†] was, and the guy was half Korean! I'd see him in the hall from time to time—a chemistry major, I think he was. There was a third room as well, but owing to some water damage Rosemary was having a hard time renting it. "Not that I care so much," she told me. "In my business, it's more about quality than quantity."

I moved in at the beginning of January, and throughout that winter my life felt like a beautiful dream. I'd come home at the end of the day and Rosemary would be sitting in the parlor, both of us fully costumed. "Aha!" she'd say. "Just the young man I was looking for." Then she'd pull out some new treasure she'd bought at an estate sale and explain what made it so valuable: "On most of

---

*Gable: Clark Gable was one of the most famous actors in the early period of American cinema.

[†]Charlie Chan: A fictional Chinese American detective created during the 1920s and perennially popular in novels, radio, and movies.

the later Fire King loaf pans, the trademark helmet is etched
rather than embossed."

The idea was that we were different, not like the rest of America, with its Fuzzbusters* and shopping malls and rotating shower-
heads. "If it's not new and shiny, they don't want anything to do
with it," Rosemary would complain. "Give them the Liberty Bell
and they'd bitch about the crack. That's how folks are nowadays.
I've seen it."

There was a radio station in Raleigh that broadcast old programs,
and sometimes at night, when the reception was good, we'd sit on
the davenport and listen to Jack Benny or *Fibber McGee and Molly*.
Rosemary might mend a worn WAC uniform with her old-timey
sewing kit, while I'd stare into the fireplace and wish that it still
worked. Maybe we'd leaf through some old *Look* magazines.
Maybe the wind would rattle the windows and we'd draw a quilt
over our laps and savor the heady scent of mothballs.

I hoped that our lives would continue this way forever, but inevitably the past came knocking. Not the good kind that was collect-
ible but the bad kind that had arthritis. One afternoon in early
April, I returned home from work to find a lost-looking white-
haired woman sitting in the parlor. Her fingers were stiff and
gnarled, so rather than shake hands I offered a little salute. "Sister
Sykes" was how she introduced herself. I thought that was maybe
what they called her in church, but then Rosemary walked out of
her chambers and told me through gritted teeth that this was a
professional name.

"Mother here was a psychic," she explained. "Had herself a tarot
deck and a crystal ball and told people whatever stupid malarkey
they wanted to hear."

"That I did," Sister Sykes said, chuckling.

You'd think that someone who occasionally wore a turban herself would like having a psychic as a mom, but Rosemary was over
it. "If she'd forecast thirty years ago that I'd wind up having to take
care of her, I would have put my head in the oven and killed
myself," she told me.

When June rolled around, the chemistry student graduated, and
his room was rented to a young man I'll call Chaz, who worked on
a road-construction crew. "You know those guys that hold the
flags?" he said. "Well, that's me. That's what I do."

His face, like his name, was chiselled and memorable, and, after
deciding that he was too handsome, I began to examine him for

*Fuzzbusters**: Radar detectors used to evade highway patrol.

flaws. The split lower lip only added to his appeal, so I moved on to his hair, which had clearly been blow-dried, and to the strand of turquoise pebbles visible through his unbuttoned shirt.

"What are you looking at?" he asked, and before I had a chance to blush he started telling me about his ex-girlfriend. They'd lived together for six months, in a little apartment behind Fowler's grocery store, but then she cheated on him with someone named Robby, an asshole who went to U.N.C. and majored in fucking up other people's lives. "You're not one of those college snobs, are you?" he asked.

I probably should have said "No," rather than "Not presently."

"What did you study?" he asked. "Bank robbing?"

"Excuse me?"

"Your clothes," he said. "You and that lady downstairs look like those people from *Bonnie and Clyde,** not the stars but the other ones. The ones who fuck everything up."

"Yes, well, we're individuals."

"Individual freaks," he said, and then he laughed, suggesting that there were no hard feelings. "Anyway, I don't have time to stand around and jaw. A friend and me are hitting the bars."

He'd do this every time: start a conversation and end it abruptly, as if it had been me who was running his mouth. Before Chaz moved in, the upstairs was fairly quiet. Now I heard the sound of his radio through the wall, a rock station that made it all the harder to pretend I was living in gentler times. When he was bored, he'd knock on my door and demand that I give him a cigarette. Then he'd stand there and smoke it, complaining that my room was too clean, my sketches were too sketchy, my old-fashioned bathrobe was too old-fashioned. "Well, enough of this," he'd say. "I have my own life to lead." Three or four times a night this would happen.

As Chaz changed life on the second floor, Sister Sykes changed it on the first. I went to check my mail one morning and found Rosemary dressed just like anyone else her age: no hat or costume jewelry, just a pair of slacks and a ho-hum blouse with unpadded shoulders. She wasn't wearing makeup, either, and had neglected to curl her hair. "What can I tell you?" she said. "That kind of dazzle takes time, and I just don't seem to have any lately." The parlor, which had always been just so, had gone downhill as well. Now there were cans of iced-tea mix sitting on the Victrola, and boxed

---

***Bonnie and Clyde:*** An acclaimed 1967 film by director Arthur Penn about the Great Depression–era bank-robbing duo.

pots and pans parked in the corner where the credenza used to be. There was no more listening to Jack Benny, because that was Sister Sykes's bath time. "The queen bee," Rosemary called her.

Later that summer, just after the Fourth of July, I came downstairs and found a pair of scuffed white suitcases beside the front door. I hoped that someone was on his way out—Chaz, specifically—but it appeared that the luggage was coming rather than going. "Meet my daughter," Rosemary said, this with the same grudging tone she'd used to introduce her mother. The young woman—I'll call her Ava—took a rope of hair from the side of her head and stuck it in her mouth. She was a skinny thing, and very pale, dressed in jeans and a Western-style shirt. "In her own little world," Sister Sykes said.

Rosemary told me later that her daughter had just been released from a mental institution, and though I tried to act surprised, I don't think I was very convincing. It was like she was on acid almost, the way she'd sit and examine something long after it had lost its mystery: an ashtray, a dried-up moth, Chaz's blow-dryer in the upstairs bathroom—everything got equal attention, including my room. There were no lockable doors on the second floor. The keys had been lost years earlier, so Ava just wandered in whenever she felt like it. I'd come home after a full day of work—my clothes smelling of wet garbage, my shoes squishy with dishwater—and find her sitting on my bed, or standing like a zombie behind my door.

"You scared me," I'd say, and she'd stare into my face until I turned away.

The situation at Rosemary's sank to a new low when Chaz lost his job. "I was overqualified," he told me, but, as the days passed, his story became more elaborate, and he felt an ever-increasing urge to share it with me. He started knocking more often, not caring that it was 6 A.M. or well after midnight. "And another thing ..." he'd say, stringing ten separate conversations into one. He got into a fight that left him with a black eye. He threw his radio out the window and then scattered the broken pieces throughout the parking lot.

Late one evening, he came to my door, and when I opened it he grabbed me around the waist and lifted me off the floor. This might sound innocent, but his was not a celebratory gesture. We hadn't won a game or been granted a stay of execution, and carefree people don't call you a "hand puppet of the Dark Lord" when they pick you up without your consent. I knew then that there was something seriously wrong with the guy, but I couldn't put a name to it. I guess I thought that Chaz was too good-looking to be crazy.

When he started slipping notes under my door, I decided it was time to update my thinking. "Now I'm going to *die* and come back on the same day," one of them read. It wasn't just the messages but the writing itself that spooked me, the letters all jittery and butting up against one another. Some of his notes included diagrams, and flames rendered in red ink. When he started leaving them for Rosemary, she called him down to the parlor and told him he had to leave. For a minute or two, he seemed to take it well, but then he thought better of it and threatened to return as a vapor.

"Did he say 'viper'?" Sister Sykes asked.

Chaz's parents came a week later, and asked if any of us had seen him. "He's a schizophrenic, you see, but sometimes he goes off his medication."

I'd thought that Rosemary would be sympathetic, but she was sick to death of mental illness, just as she was sick of old people, and of having to take in boarders to make ends meet. "If he was screwy you should have told me before he moved in," she said to Chaz's father. "I can't have people like that running through my house. What with these antiques, it's just not safe." The man's eyes wandered around the parlor, and through them I saw what he did: a dirty room full of junk. It had never been anything more than that, but for some reason—the heat, maybe, or the couple's heavy, almost contagious sense of despair—every gouge and smudge jumped violently into focus. More depressing still was the thought that I belonged here, that I fit in.

For years, the university had been trying to buy Rosemary's property. Representatives would come to the door, and her accounts of these meetings seemed torn from a late-night movie: "So I said to him, 'But don't you see? This isn't just a house. It's my home, sir. My home.'"

They didn't want the building, of course, just the land. With every passing semester, it became more valuable, and she was smart to hold out for as long as she did. I don't know what their final offer was, but Rosemary accepted it. She signed the papers with a vintage fountain pen, and was still holding it when she came to give me the news. This was in August, and I was lying on my floor, making a sweat angel. A part of me was sad that the house was being sold, but another, bigger part—the part that loved air-conditioning—was more than ready to move on. It was pretty clear that as far as the restaurant was concerned I was never going to advance beyond dishwashing. Then, too, it was hard to live in a college town and not go to college. The students

I saw out my window were a constant reminder that I was just spinning my wheels, and I was beginning to imagine how I would feel in another ten years, when they started looking like kids to me. A few days before I left, Ava and I sat together on the front porch. It had just begun to rain when she turned and asked, "Did I ever tell you about my daddy?"

This was more than I'd ever heard her say, and before continuing she took off her shoes and socks and set them on the floor beside her. Then she drew a hank of hair into her mouth, and told me that her father had died of a heart attack. "Said he didn't feel well and an hour later he just plunked over."

I asked a few follow-up questions, and learned that he had died on November 19, 1963.* Three days after that, the funeral was held, and while riding from the church to the cemetery Ava looked out the window and noticed that everyone she passed was crying. "Old people, college students, even the colored men at the gas station—the soul brothers, or whatever we're supposed to call them now."

It was such an outmoded term, I just had to use it myself. "How did the soul brothers know your father?"

"That's just it," she said. "No one told us until after the burial that Kennedy had been shot. It happened when we were in the church, so that's what everyone was so upset about. The President, not my father."

She then put her socks back on and walked into the parlor, leaving both me and her shoes behind.

When I'd tell people about this later, they'd say, "Oh, come on," because it was all too much, really. An arthritic psychic, a ramshackle house, and either two or four crazy people, depending on your tolerance for hats. Harder to swallow is that each of us was such a cliché. It was as if you'd taken a Carson McCullers† novel, mixed it with a Tennessee Williams play, and dumped all the sets and characters into a single box. I didn't even add that Sister Sykes used to own a squirrel monkey, as it only amounted to overkill. Even the outside world seems suspect here: the leafy college town, the restaurant with its classical music.

I never presumed that Kennedy's death was responsible for Ava's breakdown. Plenty of people endure startling coincidences

---

*November 19, 1963: Three days before the assassination of President John F. Kennedy in Dallas.

†Carson McCullers … TennesseE Williams: Both southern American writers known for their portrayal of the psychology of everyday life.

with no lasting aftereffects, so I imagine that her troubles started years earlier. As for Chaz, I later learned that it was fairly common for schizophrenics to go off their medication. I'd think it strange that the boarding house attracted both him and me, but that's what cheap places do—draw in people with no money. An apartment of my own was unthinkable at that time of my life, and, even if I'd found an affordable one, it wouldn't have satisfied my fundamental need: to live in a communal past, or what I imagined the past to be like—a world full of antiques. What I could never fathom, and still can't, really, is that at one point all those things were new—the wheezing Victrola, the hulking davenport. How were they any different from the eight-track tape player, or my parents' Scandinavian dining-room set? Given enough time, I guess, anything can look good. All it has to do is survive.

## Reflections and Responses

1. Sedaris is best known as a humor writer, and the content of "This Old House" is ostensibly humorous. But the tone of the essay is more ambiguous, floating between zinging one-liners and poignant nostalgia. How would you characterize the overall tone of the essay? How is this hybrid, or at least difficult, tone a particularly effective vehicle for the essay's content?

2. Sedaris concludes by writing "When I'd tell people about this later, they'd say, 'Oh, come on,' because it was all too much, really.... . Even the outside world seems suspect here: the leafy college town, the restaurant with its classical music." What exactly does Sedaris mean is "suspect"? Why does he compare his story to works of fiction? Do you think elements of it might be exaggerated or fictitious? Review the essay for clues that Sedaris may be mixing memoir with fictive, or at least cinematic, elements.

3. Sedaris writes that he considered the TV Waltons' house "romantic." What aspects of the past does Sedaris romanticize, and how do his parents react to this romanticization? How does Sedaris' relationship with his parents play on the typical dynamic between generations? How does this tension add to the humor, and the broader themes, of the essay as a whole?

PATRICIA SMITH

# *Pearl, Upward*

*A person's identity is formed by many factors, but the places we're from are often forces in shaping who we are, and essayists frequently focus on geography as a source of identity. In this essay, Patricia Smith considers her mother through the windows of the two places tugging at her—her native rural Alabama, and Chicago, a metropolis to which hundreds of thousands of African Americans like Smith's mother flocked after World War II, a massive relocation known historically as "The Great Migration." By entering her mother's consciousness, Smith depicts a character drawn like a magnet to the big city, but whose Delta roots still loomed very large both during and after the life-transforming trip.*

*Patricia Smith is the author of five books of poetry, including* Blood Dazzler, *chronicling the tragedy of Hurricane Katrina and a finalist for the 2008 National Book Award, and* Teahouse of the Almighty, *a National Poetry Series selection. Her work has appeared in* Poetry, The Paris Review, TriQuarterly, *and* Best American Poetry 2011. *She is a Pushcart Prize winner and a four-time individual champion of the National Poetry Slam, the most successful poet in the competition's history. Currently, she is a professor at the City University of New York/College of Staten Island, and is on the faculty of both Cave Canem and the Stonecoast MFA program at the University of Southern Maine. "Pearl, Upward" originally appeared in* Crab Orchard Review *and was selected by Edwidge Danticat for* The Best American Essays 2011.

CHICAGO, SAY IT. Push out the three sighs, don't let such a huge wish languish. Her world, so big she didn't know its edges, suddenly not enough. She's heard the dreams out loud, the tales of where money flows, and after you arrive it takes *what, a minute?* to forget that Alabama ever held sugar for you.

*Source:* Best American Essays, 2011, Patricia Smith, Pearl, Upward (2011).

She wants to find a factory where she can work boredom into her fingers. She's never heard a siren razor the dark. She wants Lucky Strikes, a dose of high life every Friday, hard lessons from a jukebox. Wants to wave goodbye to her mama and a God not particular to ugly. Just the word *city* shimmies her. All she needs is a bus ticket, a brown riveted case to hold her dresses, and a waxed bag crammed with smashed slices of white bread and doughy fried chicken splashed with Tabasco. This place, Chicago, is too far to run. But she knows with the whole of her heart that it is what she's been running toward.

Apple cheeks, glorious gap-tooth fills the window of the Greyhound. For the occasion, she has hot-combed her hair into shivering strings and donned a homemade skirt that wrestles with her curves. This deception is what the city asks. I dream her sleeping at angles, her head full and hurting with future, until the bus arrives in the city. Then she stumbles forth with all she owns, wanting to be stunned by some sudden thunder. Tries not to see the brown folks—the whipcloth shoe shiners, the bag carriers—staring at her, searching for some sign, craving a smell of where she came from.

How does a city look when you've never seen it before? Grimace and whisper hover everywhere. It is months before she realizes that no one knows her name. No one says Annie Pearl and means it.

She crafts a life that is dimmer than she'd hoped, in a tenement flat with walls pressing in hard and fat roaches, sluggish with Raid, dropping into her food, writhing on the mattress of her Murphy bed. In daytime, she works in a straight line with other women, her hands moving without her. *Repeat. Repeat.* When her evenings are breezy and free and there is change in her purse, she looks for music that whines, men in sharkskin suits, a little something to scorch her throat. Drawn to the jukebox, she punches one letter, one number, hears her story sung over and over in indigo gravel. And she cries when she hears what has happened to homemade guitars. They've forgotten how much they need the southern moon.

At night when she tries to sleep, Alabama fills her head with a cruel grace, its colors brighter, and its memory impossibly wide. She remembers the drumbeat she once was.

My mother, Annie Pearl Smith, never talks with me of Annie Pearl Connor, the girl she was before she boarded that Greyhound, before she rolled into the city. The South, she insists, was the land of clipped dreaming, ain't got nones and never gon' haves. Alabama only existed to be left behind. It's as if a whole new person was born on that bus, her first full breath straining through exhaust, her first word *Chicago*.

But from her sisters I heard stories of what a raging tomboy she was, how it seemed like she was always running.

Whenever I dream her young, I see red dust on her ankles and feet. Those feet were flat and ashy, steady stomping, the corn on her baby toe raw and peeled back. No shoes could hold them. Those feet were always naked, touched by everything, stones asked her to limp and she didn't. Low branches whipped, sliced her skin, and they urged her to cry and she wouldn't. Blood dripped and etched rivers in rust.

She was a blazing girl, screech raucous and careening, rhymes and games and dares in her throat. Her laugh was a shattering on the air. Playing like she had to play to live, she shoved at what slowed her, steamrolled whatever wouldn't move. Alabama's no fool. It didn't get in her way.

What was down south then, then where she romped and ran? Slant sag porches, pea shuck, twangy box guitars begging under blue moons. Combs spitting sparks, pull horses making back roads tremble, swear-scowling elders with rheumy glares fixed on checkerboards. Cursed futures crammed into cotton pouches with bits of bitterroot and a smoldering song. Tragic men buckling under the weight of the Lord's work, the grim rigidity of His word. The horrid parts of meat stewed sweet and possible. And still, whispers about the disappeared, whole souls lost in the passage.

There was nothing before or beyond just being a southern girl, when there was wind to rip with your body and space to claim. Her braids always undid themselves. She panted staccato, gulped steam, and stopped sometimes to rest her feet in meandering water. But why stop when she was the best reason she knew to whip up the air?

And yes, she also owned that slower face. She could be the porch-swinging girl, good to her mama and fixed on Jesus, precious in white collar ironed stiff and bleached to the point of blue. She could make herself stand patient in that Saturday morning kitchen assembly line, long enough to scrape the scream from chitlins and pass the collards three times under the faucet to rinse away the grit. She could set the places at the table and straight sit through endless meals she doesn't have time to taste.

She wore that face as Saturday night's whole weight was polished and spit-shined for Sunday morning. Twisting in the pew and grimacing when her mother's hand pushed down hard on her thigh in warning. *Girl, how many times I got to tell you God don't like ugly?* To her, righteousness was a mystery that rode the edge of an organ wail. She'd seen the Holy Ghost seep into the old women, watched as their backs cracked, eyes bulged, careful dresses rose up. She wondered how God's hot hand felt in their heads, how they danced in ways so clearly beyond them. Decided there would be time enough for this strange salvation. First she had to be young.

All the time her toes tapped, feet flattened out inside her shoes. The sun called her name and made her heart howl. She was a drumbeat, sometimes slow and thoughtful on deep thick skins, most times asking something, steady asking, needing to know, needing to know *now*, taking flight from that rhythm inside her. Twisting on rusty hinge, the porch door whined for one second 'bout where she was. But that girl was gone.

I dream her brave, unleashed, naughty the way free folks are. Playing and frolicking her fill, flailing tough with cousins and sisters, but running wide, running on purpose, running toward something. She couldn't name this chaos, but she believed it knew her, owned her in a way religion should.

At night, the brooding sky pushed down on her tired head, made her stay in place. She sweated outside the sheets. Kicked. Headed somewhere past this.

Anybody know how a Delta* girl dreams? How the specter of a city rises up in her head and demands its space and time? How borders and boxes are suddenly magic, tenements harbor pulse, and the all there is must be a man with a felt fedora dipped lazily over one eye? She was turning into a woman, tree trunk legs, exclamation just over her heart. Alabama had to strain to hold on.

Oh, her hips were always there, but suddenly they were a startling fluid and boys lined the dust road and she slowed her run to rock them. Soon she was walking in circles. Then she was barely moving at all. Stones asked her to limp and she did. She was scrubbing her feet in river water and searching for shoes.

Chicago.

*Chicago.*

The one word sounded like a secret shared. And, poised in that moment before she discovered the truth, Annie Pearl Connor was catch-in-the-breath beautiful. She was sweet in that space between knowing and not knowing.

Months later, her face pressed against a tenement window, she is a note so incredibly blue only the city could sing it.

---

*The **Delta** refers to the Mississippi Delta, a general geographic region of the South.

She has to believe that love will complete her.

And so she finds him, a man who seems to be what Chicago lied and said it was. He smolders, gold tooth flashing. He promises no permanence. She walks into the circle of his arms and stands very still there. There must be more than this, she believes, and knows she must fill her body with me, that she must claim her place in the north with a child touting her blood. Hot at the thought of creation, she is driven by that American dream of birthing a colorless colored child with no memories whatsoever of the Delta.

It is a difficult delivery, with no knife slipped below the bed to cut the pain. In a room of beeping machines and sterilized silver, she can't get loose. Her legs are bound. Her hands are being held down. She screams, not from pain but from knowing. My mother has just given worry to the world.

There will be no running from this.

This child is a chaos she must name.

## Reflections and Responses

1. How does Smith describe and characterize her mother? Notice that we get few biographical details in the essay. List the information we do learn, and describe what inner characteristics we know she possesses. What is the significance of the subtle ways in which Smith draws her portrait? How does this help us to know Smith's mother?

2. Describe the characteristics of Alabama and Chicago in the essay. Which one do we know more about? Why? What is the image we get of Chicago, and how was this image shaped by Smith's mother's experience? What does Smith tell us about the Delta that both distances us from it and endears us to it as a source of identity?

3. Is the essay in any way about African American identity or the African American experience? Why or why not? Why does Smith suppress the phrase "colored child" until late into the essay? How does this one phrase help readers of different backgrounds identify with the essay as universal, and also narrow it to a particular historical and social focus?

GAY TALESE

# Ali in Havana

*When one of America's leading journalists was assigned to profile one of the world's biggest celebrities on a humanitarian-aid visit to one of the world's most controversial political figures, the result was bound to be a fascinating piece of writing and disclosure. In "Ali in Havana," Gay Talese accompanies the great fighter Muhammad Ali as he travels with his wife and entourage, along with many other visitors, to a reception at Havana's Palace of the Revolution to meet aging communist leader Fidel Castro. What ensues is both comic and poignant, as the magical Ali, stricken with Parkinson's disease, leaves Castro—who has been struggling to keep the small talk flowing—with a very odd parting token. A connoisseur of the unnoticed detail, Talese captures all of the humor, tension, and awkwardness of this nearly surrealistic scene.*

*Gay Talese is one of the founders of the New Journalism, a literary movement that irrevocably altered both the art of reporting and the art of the essay. He is the best-selling author of books about the* New York Times, The Kingdom and the Power *(1969); the inside story of a Mafia family,* Honor Thy Father *(1971); the changing moral values of America,* Thy Neighbor's Wife *(1981); and a historical memoir,* Unto the Sons *(1992). Other nonfiction books include* The Bridge, New York: A Serendipiter's Journey *(1964) and* Fame and Obscurity *(1970). In 2006, he published a memoir,* A Writer's Life. *Talese served as guest editor of* The Best American Essays *1987. "Ali in Havana" originally appeared in* Esquire *and was selected by Ian Frazier for the 1997 volume.*

It is a warm, breezy, palm-flapping winter evening in Havana, and the leading restaurants are crowded with tourists from Europe, Asia, and South America being serenaded by guitarists relentlessly

singing "*Guan-tan-a-mera ... guajira ... Guan-tan-a-mera*"; and at the
Café Cantante there are clamorous salsa dancers, mambo kings,
grunting, bare-chested male performers lifting tables with their
teeth, and turbaned women swathed in hip-hugging skirts, blowing
whistles while gyrating their glistening bodies into an erotic frenzy.
In the café's audience as well as in the restaurants, hotels, and other
public places throughout the island, cigarettes and cigars are
smoked without restraint or restriction. Two prostitutes are smoking
and talking privately on the corner of a dimly lit street bordering the
manicured lawns of Havana's five-star Hotel Nacional. They are
copper-colored women in their early twenties wearing faded minis-
kirts and halters, and as they chat, they are watching attentively
while two men—one white, the other black—huddle over the raised
trunk of a parked red Toyota, arguing about the prices of the boxes
of black-market Havana cigars that are stacked within.

The white man is a square-jawed Hungarian in his mid-thirties,
wearing a beige tropical suit and a wide yellow tie, and he is one of
Havana's leading entrepreneurs in the thriving illegal business of selling top-quality hand-rolled Cuban cigars below the local and international market price. The black man behind the car is a well-built,
baldish, gray-bearded individual in his mid-fifties from Los Angeles
named Howard Bingham; and no matter what price the Hungarian
quotes, Bingham shakes his head and says, "No, no—that's too much!"

"You're crazy!" cries the Hungarian in slightly accented English,
taking one of the boxes from the trunk and waving it in Howard Bingham's face. "These are Cohiba Esplendidos! The best in the world!
You will pay one thousand dollars for a box like this in the States."

"Not me," says Bingham, who wears a Hawaiian shirt with a camera strapped around his neck. He is a professional photographer,
and he is staying at the Hotel Nacional with his friend Muhammad
Ali. "I wouldn't give you more than fifty dollars."

"You really are crazy," says the Hungarian, slicing through the
box's paper seal with his fingernail, opening the lid to reveal a
gleaming row of labeled Esplendidos.

"Fifty dollars," says Bingham.

"A hundred dollars," insists the Hungarian. "And hurry! The
police could be driving around." The Hungarian straightens up
and stares over the car toward the palm-lined lawn and stan-
chioned lights that glow in the distance along the road leading
to the hotel's ornate portico, which is now jammed with people
and vehicles; then he turns and flings a glance back toward the
nearby public street, where he notices that the prostitutes are
now blowing smoke in his direction. He frowns.

"Quick, quick," he says to Bingham, handing him the box. "One hundred dollars."

Howard Bingham does not smoke. He and Muhammad Ali and their traveling companions are leaving Havana tomorrow, after participating in a five-day American humanitarian-aid mission that brought a planeload of medical supplies to hospitals and clinics depleted by the United States' embargo, and Bingham would like to return home with some fine contraband cigars for his friends. But, on the other hand, one hundred is still too much.

"Fifty dollars," says Bingham determinedly, looking at his watch. He begins to walk away.

"O.K., O.K.," the Hungarian says petulantly. "Fifty."

Bingham reaches into his pocket for the money, and the Hungarian grabs it and gives him the Esplendidos before driving off in the Toyota. One of the prostitutes takes a few steps toward Bingham, but the photographer hurries on to the hotel. Fidel Castro is having a reception tonight for Muhammad Ali, and Bingham has only a half hour to change and be at the portico to catch the chartered bus that will take them to the government's headquarters. He will be bringing one of his photographs to the Cuban leader: an enlarged, framed portrait showing Muhammad Ali and Malcolm X walking together along a Harlem sidewalk in 1963. Malcolm X was thirty-seven at the time, two years away from an assassin's bullet; the twenty-one-year-old Ali was about to win the heavyweight title in a remarkable upset over Sonny Liston in Miami. Bingham's photograph is inscribed, To PRESIDENT FIDEL CASTRO, FROM MUHAMMAD ALI. Under his signature, the former champion has sketched a little heart.

Although Muhammad Ali is now fifty-four and has been retired from boxing for more than fifteen years, he is still one of the most famous men in the world, being identifiable throughout five continents; and as he walks through the lobby of the Hotel Nacional toward the bus, wearing a gray sharkskin suit and a white cotton shirt buttoned at the neck without a tie, several guests approach him and request his autograph. It takes him about thirty seconds to write "Muhammad Ali," so shaky are his hands from the effects of Parkinson's syndrome; and though he walks without support, his movements are quite slow, and Howard Bingham and Ali's fourth wife, Yolanda, are following nearby.

Bingham met Ali thirty-five years ago in Los Angeles, shortly after the fighter had turned professional and before he discarded his "slave name" (Cassius Marcellus Clay) and joined the Black

Muslims. Bingham subsequently became his closest male friend and has photographed every aspect of Ali's life: his rise and fall three times as the heavyweight champion; his three-year expulsion from boxing, beginning in 1967, for refusing to serve in the American military during the Vietnam War ("I ain't got no quarrel with them Vietcong"); his four marriages; his fatherhood of nine children (one adopted, two out of wedlock); his endless public appearances in all parts of the world—Germany, England, Egypt (sailing on the Nile with a son of Elijah Muhammad's), Sweden, Libya, Pakistan (hugging refugees from Afghanistan), Japan, Indonesia, Ghana (wearing a dashiki and posing with President Kwame Nkrumah), Zaire (beating George Foreman), Manila (beating Joe Frazier) ... and now, on the final night of his 1996 visit to Cuba, he is en route to a social encounter with an aging contender he has long admired—one who has survived at the top for nearly forty years despite the ill will of nine American presidents, the CIA, the Mafia, and various militant Cuban Americans.

Bingham waits for Ali near the open door of the charter bus that is blocking the hotel's entrance; but Ali lingers within the crowd in the lobby, and Yolanda steps aside to let some people get closer to her husband.

She is a large and pretty woman of thirty-eight, with a radiant smile and a freckled, fair complexion that reflects her interracial ancestry. A scarf is loosely draped over her head and shoulders, her arms are covered by long sleeves, and her well-designed dress in vivid hues hangs below her knees. She converted to Islam from Catholicism when she married Ali, a man sixteen years her senior but one with whom she shared a familial bond dating back to her girlhood in their native Louisville, where her mother and Ali's mother were sisterly soul mates who traveled together to attend his fights. Yolanda had occasionally joined Ali's entourage, becoming acquainted with not only the boxing element but with Ali's female contemporaries who were his lovers, his wives, the mothers of his children; and she remained in touch with Ali throughout the 1970s, while she majored in psychology at Vanderbilt and later earned her master's degree in business at UCLA. Then—with the end of Ali's boxing career, his third marriage, and his vibrant health—Yolanda intimately entered his life as casually and naturally as she now stands waiting to reclaim her place at his side.

She knows that he is enjoying himself. There is a slight twinkle in his eyes, not much expression on his face, and no words forthcoming from this once most talkative of champions. But the mind behind his Parkinson's mask is functioning normally, and he is characteristically committed to what he is doing: he is spelling out his full name on whatever cards or scraps of paper his admirers are handing him. "Muhammad Ali." He does not settle for a time-saving "Ali" or his mere initials. He has never shortchanged his audience.

And in this audience tonight are people from Latin America, Canada, Africa, Russia, China, Germany, France. There are two hundred French travel agents staying at the hotel in conjunction with the Cuban government's campaign to increase its growing tourist trade (which last year saw about 745,000 visitors spending an estimated one billion dollars on the island). There is also on hand an Italian movie producer and his lady friend from Rome and a onetime Japanese wrestler, Antonio Inoki, who injured Ali's legs during a 1976 exhibition in Tokyo (but who warmly embraced him two nights ago in the hotel's lounge as they sat listening to Cuban pianist Chucho Valdes playing jazz on a Russian-made Moskva baby grand); and there is also in the crowd, standing taller than the rest, the forty-three-year-old, six-foot five-inch Cuban heavyweight hero Teófilo Stevenson, who was a three-time Olympic gold medalist, in 1972, 1976 and 1980, and who, on this island at least, is every bit as renowned as Ali or Castro.

Though part of Stevenson's reputation derives from his erstwhile power and skill in the ring (although he never fought Ali), it is also attributable to his not having succumbed to the offers of professional boxing promoters, stubbornly resisting the Yankee dollar—although Stevenson hardly seems deprived. He dwells among his countrymen like a towering Cuban peacock, occupying high positions within the government's athletic programs and gaining sufficient attention from the island's women to have garnered four wives so far, who are testimony to his eclectic taste.

His first wife was a dance instructor. His second was an industrial engineer. His third was a medical doctor. His fourth and present wife is a criminal attorney. Her name is Fraymari, and she is a girlishly petite olive-skinned woman of twenty-three who, standing next to her husband in the lobby, rises barely higher than the midsection of his embroidered guayabera—a tightly tailored, short-sleeved shirt that accentuates his tapered torso, his broad shoulders, and the length of his dark, muscular arms, which once prevented his opponents from doing any injustice to his winning Latin looks.

Stevenson always fought from an upright position, and he maintains that posture today. When people talk to him, his eyes look downward, but his head remains high. The firm jaw of his oval-shaped head seems to be locked at a right angle to his straight-spined back. He is a proud man who exhibits all of his height. But he does listen, especially when the words being directed up at him are coming from the perky little attorney who is his wife. Fraymari is now reminding him that it is getting late—everyone should be on the bus; Fidel may be waiting. Stevenson lowers his eyes toward her and winks. He has gotten the message. He has been Ali's principal escort throughout this visit. He was also Ali's guest in the United States during the fall of 1995; and though he knows only a few words of English, and Ali no Spanish, they are brotherly in their body language.

Stevenson edges himself into the crowd and gently places his right arm around the shoulders of his fellow champion. And then, slowly but firmly, he guides Ali toward the bus.

The road to Fidel Castro's Palace of the Revolution leads through a memory lane of old American automobiles chugging along at about twenty-five miles an hour—springless, pre-embargo Ford coupes and Plymouth sedans, DeSotos and LaSalles, Nashes and Studebakers, and various vehicular collages created out of Cadillac grilles and Oldsmobile axles and Buick fenders patched with pieces of oil-drum metal and powered by engines interlinked with kitchen utensils and pre-Batista lawn mowers and other gadgets that have elevated the craft of tinkering in Cuba to the status of high art.

The relatively newer forms of transportation seen on the road are, of course, non-American products—Polish Fiats, Russian Ladas, German motor scooters, Chinese bicycles, and the glistening, newly imported, air-conditioned Japanese bus from which Muhammad Ali is now gazing through a closed window out toward the street. At times, he raises a hand in response to one of the waving pedestrians or cyclists or motorists who recognize the bus, which has been shown repeatedly on the local TV news conveying Ali and his companions to the medical centers and tourist sites that have been part of the busy itinerary.

On the bus, as always, Ali is sitting alone, spread out across the two front seats in the left aisle directly behind the Cuban driver. Yolanda sits a few feet ahead of him to the right; she is adjacent to the driver and within inches of the windshield. The seats behind her are occupied by Teófilo Stevenson, Fraymari, and the photographer Bingham. Seated behind Ali, and also occupying two seats, is an American screenwriter named Greg Howard, who weighs more than three hundred pounds. Although he has traveled with

Ali for only a few months while researching a film on the fighter's
life, Greg Howard has firmly established himself as an intimate
sidekick, and as such is among the very few on this trip who have
heard Ali's voice. Ali speaks so softly that it is impossible to hear
him in a crowd, and as a result whatever public comments or sen-
timents he is expected to, or chooses to, express are verbalized by
Yolanda, or Bingham, or Teófilo Stevenson, or even at times by
this stout young screenwriter.

"Ali is in his Zen period," Greg Howard has said more than once,
in reference to Ali's quiescence. Like Ali, he admires what he has
seen so far in Cuba—"There's no racism here"—and as a black man
he has long identified with many of Ali's frustrations and confrontations. His student thesis at Princeton analyzed the Newark race riots
of 1967, and the Hollywood script he most recently completed
focuses on the Negro baseball leagues of the pre–World War II
years. He envisions his new work on Ali in the genre of *Gandhi*.

The two-dozen bus seats behind those tacitly reserved for Ali's
inner circle are occupied by the secretary-general of the Cuban
Red Cross and the American humanitarian personnel who have
entrusted him with $500,000 worth of donated medical supplies;
and there are also the two Cuban interpreters and a dozen members of the American media, including the CBS-TV commentator
Ed Bradley and his producers and camera crew from *60 Minutes*.

Ed Bradley is a gracious but reserved individualist who has
appeared on television for a decade with his left earlobe pierced
by a small circular ring—which, after some unfavorable comment
initially expressed by his colleagues Mike Wallace and Andy
Rooney, prompted Bradley's explanation: "It's *my* ear." Bradley
also indulges in his identity as a cigar smoker; and as he sits in
the midsection of the bus next to his Haitian lady friend, he is
taking full advantage of the Communist regime's laissez-faire attitude toward tobacco, puffing away on a Cohiba Robusto, for which
he paid full price at the Nacional's tobacco shop—and which now
exudes a costly cloud of fragrance that appeals to his friend (who
occasionally also smokes cigars) but is not appreciated by the two
California women who are seated two rows back and are affiliated
with a humanitarian-aid agency.

Indeed, the women have been commenting about the smoking
habits of countless people they have encountered in Havana,
being especially disappointed to discover earlier this very day that
the pediatric hospital they visited (and to which they committed
donations) is under the supervision of three tobacco-loving family

physicians. When one of the American women, a blonde from
Santa Barbara, reproached one of the cigarette-smoking doctors
indirectly for setting such a poor example, she was told in effect
that the island's health statistics regarding longevity, infant mortal-
ity, and general fitness compared favorably with those in the
United States and were probably better than those of Americans
residing in the capital city of Washington. On the other hand, the
doctor made it clear that he did not believe that smoking was good
for one's health—after all, Fidel himself had given it up; but
unfortunately, the doctor added, in a classic understatement,
"Some people have not followed him."

Nothing the doctor said appeased the woman from Santa Barbara. She did not, however, wish to appear confrontational at the
hospital's news conference, which was covered by the press; nor
during her many bus rides with Ed Bradley did she ever request
that he discard his cigar. "Mr. Bradley intimidates me," she con-
fided to her California coworker. But he was of course living
within the law on this island that the doctor had called "the cradle
of the best tobacco in the world." In Cuba, the most available
American periodical on the newsstands is *Cigar Aficionado*.

The bus passes through the Plaza de la Revolución and comes
to a halt at a security checkpoint near the large glass doors that
open onto the marble-floored foyer of a 1950s modern building
that is the center of communism's only stronghold in the Western
Hemisphere.

As the bus door swings open, Greg Howard moves forward in his
seat and grabs the 235-pound Muhammad Ali by the arms and
shoulders and helps him to his feet; and after Ali has made his
way down to the metal step, he turns and stretches back into the
bus to take hold of the extended hands and forearms of the 300-
pound screenwriter and pulls him to a standing position. This routine, repeated at each and every bus stop throughout the week, is
never accompanied by either man's acknowledging that he had
received any assistance, although Ali is aware that some passengers
find the pas de deux quite amusing, and he is not reluctant to use
his friend to further comic effect. After the bus had made an earlier stop in front of the sixteenth-century Morro Castle—where Ali
had followed Teófilo Stevenson up a 117-step spiral staircase for a
rooftop view of Havana Harbor—he spotted the solitary figure of
Greg Howard standing below in the courtyard. Knowing that there
was no way the narrow staircase could accommodate Howard's
wide body, Ali suddenly began to wave his arms, summoning
Howard to come up and join him.

Castro's security guards, who know in advance the names of all the bus passengers, guide Ali and the others through the glass doors and then into a pair of waiting elevators for a brief ride that is followed by a short walk through a corridor and finally into a large white-walled reception room, where it is announced that Fidel Castro will soon join them. The room has high ceilings and potted palms in every corner and is sparsely furnished with modern tan leather furniture. Next to a sofa is a table with two telephones, one gray and the other red. Overlooking the sofa is an oil painting of the Viñales Valley, which lies west of Havana; and among the primitive art displayed on a circular table in front of the sofa is a grotesque tribal figure similar to the one Ali had examined earlier in the week at a trinket stand while touring with the group in Havana's Old Square. Ali had then whispered into the ear of Howard Bingham, and Bingham had repeated aloud what Ali had said: "Joe Frazier."

Ali now stands in the middle of the room, next to Bingham, who carries under his arm the framed photograph he plans to give Castro. Teófilo Stevenson and Fraymari stand facing them. The diminutive and delicate-boned Fraymari has painted her lips scarlet and has pulled back her hair in a matronly manner, hoping no doubt to appear more mature than her twenty-three years suggest, but standing next to the three much older and heavier and taller men transforms her image closer to that of an anorexic teenager. Ali's wife and Greg Howard are wandering about within the group that is exchanging comments in muted tones, either in English or Spanish, sometimes assisted by the interpreters. Ali's hands are shaking uncontrollably at his sides; but since his companions have witnessed this all week, the only people who are now paying attention are the security guards posted near the door.

Also waiting near the door for Castro is the four-man CBS camera team, and chatting with them and his two producers is Ed Bradley, without his cigar. There are no ashtrays in this room! This is a most uncommon sight in Cuba. Its implications might be political. Perhaps the sensibilities of the blond woman from Santa Barbara were taken into account by the doctors at the hospital and communicated to Castro's underlings, who are now making a conciliatory gesture toward their American benefactress.

Since the security guards have not invited the guests to be seated, everybody remains standing—for ten minutes, for twenty minutes, and then for a full half hour. Teófilo Stevenson shifts his weight from foot to foot and gazes over the heads of the crowd

toward the upper level of the portal through which Castro is
expected to enter—if he shows up. Stevenson knows from experience that Castro's schedule is unpredictable. There is always a
crisis of some sort in Cuba, and it has long been rumored on
the island that Castro constantly changes the location of where
he sleeps. The identity of his bed partners is, of course, a state
secret. Two nights ago, Stevenson and Ali and the rest were kept
waiting until midnight for an expected meeting with Castro at the
Hotel Biocaribe (to which Bingham had brought his gift photograph). But Castro never appeared. And no explanation was
offered.

Now in this reception room, it is already 9 P.M. Ali continues to
shake. No one has had dinner. The small talk is getting smaller: A
few people would like to smoke. The regime is not assuaging anyone in this crowd with a bartender. It is a cocktail party without
cocktails. There are not even canapés or soft drinks. Everyone is
becoming increasingly restless—and then suddenly there is a collective sigh. The very familiar man with the beard strides into the
room, dressed for guerrilla combat; and in a cheerful, high-
pitched voice that soars beyond his whiskers, he announces, "Buenas noches!"

In an even higher tone, he repeats, "Buenas noches," this time
with a few waves to the group while hastening toward the guest
of honor; and then, with his arms extended, the seventy-year-old
Fidel Castro immediately obscures the lower half of Ali's expres-
sionless face with a gentle embrace and his flowing gray beard.

"I am glad to see you," Castro says to Ali, via the interpreter who
followed him into the room, a comely, fair-skinned woman with a
refined English accent. "I am very, very glad to see you," Castro
continues, backing up to look into Ali's eyes while holding on to
his trembling arms, "and I am thankful for your visit." Castro then
releases his grip and awaits a possible reply. Ali says nothing. His
expression remains characteristically fixed and benign, and his
eyes do not blink despite the flashbulbs of several surrounding
photographers. As the silence persists, Castro turns toward his
old friend Teófilo Stevenson, feigning a jab. The Cuban boxing
champion lowers his eyes and, with widened lips and cheeks, reg-
isters a smile. Castro then notices the tiny brunette standing
beside Stevenson.

"Stevenson, who is this young woman?" Castro asks aloud in
a tone of obvious approval. But before Stevenson can reply,
Fraymari steps forward with a hint of lawyerly indignation: "You
mean you don't remember me?"

Castro seems stunned. He smiles feebly, trying to conceal his confusion. He turns inquiringly toward his boxing hero, but Stevenson's eyes only roll upward. Stevenson knows that Castro has met Fraymari socially on earlier occasions, but unfortunately the Cuban leader has forgotten, and it is equally unfortunate that Fraymari is now behaving like a prosecutor.

"You held my son in your arms before he was one year old!" she reminds him while Castro continues to ponder. The crowd is attentive; the television cameras are rolling.

"At a volleyball game?" Castro asks tentatively.

"No, no," Stevenson interrupts, before Fraymari can say anything more, "that was my former wife. The doctor."

Castro slowly shakes his head in mock disapproval. Then he abruptly turns away from the couple, but not before reminding Stevenson, "You should get name tags."

Castro redirects his attention to Muhammad Ali. He studies Ali's face.

"Where is your wife?" he asks softly. Ali says nothing. There is more silence and turning of heads in the group until Howard Bingham spots Yolanda standing near the back and waves her to Castro's side.

Before she arrives, Bingham steps forward and presents Castro with the photograph of Ali and Malcolm X in Harlem in 1963. Castro holds it up level with his eyes and studies it silently for several seconds. When this picture was taken, Castro had been in control of Cuba for nearly four years. He was then thirty-seven. In 1959, he defeated the U.S.-backed dictator Fulgencio Batista, overcoming odds greater than Ali's subsequent victory over the supposedly unbeatable Sonny Liston. Batista had actually announced Castro's death back in 1956. Castro, then hiding in a secret outpost, thirty years old and beardless, was a disgruntled Jesuit-trained lawyer who was born into a landowning family and who craved Batista's job. At thirty-two, he had it. Batista was forced to flee to the Dominican Republic.

During this period, Muhammad Ali was only an amateur. His greatest achievement would come in 1960, when he received a gold medal in Rome as a member of the United States Olympic boxing team. But later in the sixties, he and Castro would share the world stage as figures moving against the American establishment—and now, in the twilight of their lives, on this winter's night in Havana, they meet for the first time: Ali silent and Castro isolated on his island.

"*Que bien!*" Castro says to Howard Bingham before showing the photograph to his interpreter. Then Castro is introduced by Bingham to Ali's wife. After they exchange greetings through the interpreter, he asks her, as if surprised, "You don't speak Spanish?"

"No," she says softly. She begins to caress her husband's left wrist, on which he wears a $250 silver Swiss Army watch she bought him. It is the only jewelry Ali wears.

"But I thought I saw you speaking Spanish on the TV news this week," Castro continues wonderingly before acknowledging that her voice had obviously been dubbed.

"Do you live in New York?"

"No, we live in Michigan."

"Cold," says Castro.

"Very cold," she repeats.

"In Michigan, don't you find many people that speak Spanish?"

"No, not many," she says. "Mostly in California, New York …" and, after a pause, "Florida."

Castro nods. It takes him a few seconds to think up another question. Small talk has never been the forte of this man who specializes in nonstop haranguing monologues that can last for hours; and yet here he is, in a room crowded with camera crews and news photographers—a talk-show host with a guest of honor who is speechless. But Fidel Castro plods on, asking Ali's wife if she has a favorite sport.

"I play a little tennis," Yolanda says, and then asks him, "Do you play tennis?"

"Ping-Pong," he replies, quickly adding that during his youth he had been active in the ring. "I spent hours boxing … " he begins to reminisce, but before he finishes his sentence, he sees the slowly rising right fist of Muhammad Ali moving toward his chin! Exuberant cheering and handclapping resound through the room, and Castro jumps sideways toward Stevenson, shouting, "*Asesorame!*"—"Help me!"

Stevenson's long arms land upon Ali's shoulders from behind, squeezing him gently; and then, after he releases him, the two ex-champions face each other and begin to act out in slow motion the postures of competing prizefighters—bobbing, weaving, swinging, ducking—all of it done without touching and all of it accompanied by three minutes of ongoing applause and the clicking of cameras, and also some feelings of relief from Ali's friends because, in his own way, he has decided to join them. Ali still says nothing, his face still inscrutable, but he is less remote, less alone, and he does not pull away from Stevenson's

*Hazel Hankin/GalileoPix*

embrace as the latter eagerly tells Castro about a boxing exhibition that he and Ali had staged earlier in the week at the Balado
gym, in front of hundreds of fans and some of the island's up-
and-coming contenders.

Stevenson did not actually explain that it had been merely
another photo opportunity, one in which they sparred openhanded
in the ring, wearing their street clothes and barely touching each
other's bodies and faces; but then Stevenson had climbed out of
the ring, leaving Ali to the more taxing test of withstanding two
abbreviated rounds against one and then another young bully of
grade school age who clearly had not come to participate in a kid-
die show. They had come to floor the champ. Their bellicose little
bodies and hot-gloved hands and helmeted hell-bent heads were
consumed with fury and ambition; and as they charged ahead,
swinging wildly and swaggering to the roars of their teenage friends
and relatives at ringside, one could imagine their future boastings
to their grandchildren: On one fine day back in the winter of '96,
I whacked Muhammad Ali! Except, in truth, on this particular day,
Ali was still too fast for them. He backpedaled and shifted and
swayed, stood on the toes of his black woven-leather pointed
shoes, and showed that his body was made for motion—his
Parkinson's problems were lost in his shuffle, in the thrusts of his
butterfly sting that whistled two feet above the heads of his aspiring
assailants, in the dazzling dips of his rope-a-dope that had con-
founded George Foreman in Zaire, in his ever-memorable style,

which in this Cuban gym moistened the eyes of his ever-observant photographer friend and provoked the overweight screen writer to cry out in a voice that few in this noisy Spanish crowd could understand, "Ali's on a high! Ali's on a high!"

Teófilo Stevenson raises Ali's right arm above the head of Castro, and the news photographers spend several minutes posing the three of them together in flashing light. Castro then sees Fraymari watching alone at some distance. She is not smiling. Castro nods toward her. He summons a photographer to take a picture of Fraymari and himself. But she relaxes only after her husband comes over to join her in the conversation, which Castro immediately directs to the health and growth of their son, who is not yet two years old.

"Will he be as tall as his father?" Castro asks.

"I assume so," Fraymari says, glancing up toward her husband. She also has to look up when talking to Fidel Castro, for the Cuban leader is taller than six feet and his posture is nearly as erect as her husband's. Only the six-foot three-inch Muhammad Ali, who is standing with Bingham on the far side of her husband—and whose skin coloring, oval-shaped head, and burr-style haircut are very similar to her husband's—betrays his height with the slope-shouldered forward slouch he has developed since his illness.

"How much does your son weigh?" Castro continues.

"When he was one year old, he was already twenty-six pounds," Fraymari says. "This is three above normal. He was walking at nine months."

"She still breast-feeds him," Teófilo Stevenson says, seeming pleased.

"Oh, that's very nourishing," agrees Castro.

"Sometimes the kid becomes confused and thinks my chest is his mother's breast," Stevenson says, and he could have added that his son is also confused by Ali's sunglasses. The little boy engraved teeth marks all over the plastic frames while chewing on them during the days he accompanied his parents on Ali's bus tour.

As a CBS boom pole swoops down closer to catch the conversation, Castro reaches out to touch Stevenson's belly and asks, "How much do you weigh?"

"Two hundred thirty-eight pounds, more or less."

"That's thirty-eight more than me," Castro says, but he complains, "I eat very little. Very little. The diet advice I get is never accurate. I eat around fifteen hundred calories—less than thirty grams of protein, less than that."

Castro slaps a hand against his own midsection, which is relatively flat. If he does have a potbelly, it is concealed within his well-tailored uniform. Indeed, for a man of seventy, he seems in fine health. His facial skin is florid and unsagging, his dark eyes dart around the room with ever-alert intensity, and he has a full head of lustrous gray hair not thinning at the crown. The attention he pays to himself might be measured from his manicured fingernails down to his square-toed boots, which are unscuffed and smoothly buffed without the burnish of a lackey's spit shine. But his beard seems to belong to another man and another time. It is excessively long and scraggly. Wispy white hairs mix with the faded black and dangle down the front of his uniform like an old shroud, weather-worn and drying out. It is the beard from the hills. Castro strokes it constantly, as if trying to revive the vitality of its fiber.

Castro now looks at Ali.

"How's your appetite?" he asks, forgetting that Ali is not speaking.

"Where's your wife?" he then asks aloud, and Howard Bingham calls out to her. Yolanda has once more drifted back into the group.

When she arrives, Castro hesitates before speaking to her. It is as if he is not absolutely sure who she is. He has met so many people since arriving, and with the group rotating constantly due to the jostling of the photographers, Castro cannot be certain whether the woman at his side is Muhammad Ali's wife or Ed Bradley's friend or some other woman he has met moments ago who has left him with an unlasting impression. Having already committed a faux pas regarding one of the wives of the two multimarried ex-champions standing nearby, Castro waits for some hint from his interpreter. None is offered. Fortunately, he does not have to worry in this country about the women's vote—or any vote, for that matter—but he does sigh in mild relief when Yolanda reintroduces herself as Ali's wife and does so by name.

"Ah, Yolanda," Castro repeats, "what a beautiful name. That's the name of a queen somewhere."

"In our household," she says.

"And how is your husband's appetite?"

"Good, but he likes sweets."

"We can send you some of our ice cream to Michigan," Castro says. Without waiting for her to comment, he asks, "Michigan is very cold?"

"Oh, yes," she replies, not indicating that they had already discussed Michigan's winter weather.

"How much snow?"

"We didn't get hit with the blizzard," Yolanda says, referring to a storm in January, "but it can get three, four feet—"

Teófilo Stevenson interrupts to say that he had been in Michigan during the previous October.

"Oh," Castro says, raising an eyebrow. He mentions that during the same month he had also been in the United States (attending the United Nations' fiftieth-anniversary tribute). He asks Stevenson the length of his American visit.

"I was there for nineteen days," says Stevenson.

"Nineteen days!" Castro repeats. "Longer than I was."

Castro complains that he was limited to five days and prohibited from traveling beyond New York.

"Well, *comandante*," Stevenson responds offhandedly, in a slightly superior tone, "if you like, I will sometime show you my video."

Stevenson appears to be very comfortable in the presence of the Cuban leader, and perhaps the latter has habitually encouraged this; but at this moment, Castro may well be finding his boxing hero a bit condescending and worthy of a retaliatory jab. He knows how to deliver it.

"When you visited the United States," Castro asks pointedly, "did you bring your wife, the lawyer?"

Stevenson stiffens. He directs his eyes toward his wife. She turns away.

"No," Stevenson answers quietly. "I went alone."

Castro abruptly shifts his attention to the other side of the room, where the CBS camera crew is positioned, and he asks Ed Bradley, "What do you do?"

"We're making a documentary on Ali," Bradley explains, "and we followed him to Cuba to see what he was doing in Cuba and ..."

Bradley's voice is suddenly overwhelmed by the sounds of laughter and handclapping. Bradley and Castro turn to discover that Muhammad Ali is now reclaiming everyone's attention. He is holding his shaky left fist in the air; but instead of assuming a boxer's pose, as he had done earlier, he is beginning to pull out from the top of his upraised fist, slowly and with dramatic delicacy, the tip of a red silk handkerchief that is pinched between his right index finger and thumb.

After he has pulled out the entire handkerchief, he dangles it in the air for a few seconds, waving it closer and closer to the forehead of the wide-eyed Fidel Castro. Ali seems bewitched. He continues to stare stagnantly at Castro and the others, surrounded by applause that he gives no indication he hears. Then he proceeds to place the handkerchief back into the top of his cupped left hand—pecking with the pinched fingers of his right—and then quickly opens his palms toward his audience and reveals that the handkerchief has disappeared.

"Where is it?" cries Castro, who seems to be genuinely surprised and delighted. He approaches Ali and examines his hands, repeating, "Where is it? Where have you put it?"

Everyone who has traveled on Ali's bus during the week knows where he has hidden it. They have seen him perform the trick repeatedly in front of some of the patients and doctors at the hospitals and clinics as well as before countless tourists who have recognized him in his hotel lobby or during his strolls through the town square. They have also seen him follow up each performance with a demonstration that exposes his method. He keeps hidden in his fist a flesh-colored rubber thumb that contains the handkerchief that he will eventually pull out with the fingers of his other hand; and when he is reinserting the handkerchief, he is actually shoving the material back into the concealed rubber thumb, into which he then inserts his own right thumb. When he opens his hands, the uninformed among his onlookers are seeing his empty palms and missing the fact that the handkerchief is tucked within the rubber thumb that is covering his outstretched right thumb. Sharing with his audience the mystery of his magic always earns him additional applause.

After Ali has performed and explained the trick to Castro, he gives Castro the rubber thumb to examine—and, with more zest than he has shown all evening, Castro says, "Oh, let me try it, I want to try—it's the first time I have seen such a wonderful thing!" And after a few minutes of coaching from Howard Bingham, who long ago learned how to do it from Ali, the Cuban leader performs with sufficient dexterity and panache to satisfy his magical ambitions and to arouse another round of applause from the guests.

Meanwhile, more than ten minutes have passed since Ali began his comic routine. It is already after 9:30 P.M., and the commentator Ed Bradley, whose conversation with Castro had been interrupted, is concerned that the Cuban leader might leave the room without responding to the questions Bradley has prepared for his show. Bradley edges close to Castro's interpreter, saying in a voice that is sure to be heard, "Would you ask him if he followed ... was able to follow Ali when he was boxing professionally?"

The question is relayed and repeated until Castro, facing the CBS cameras, replies, "Yes, I recall the days when they were discussing the possibilities of a match between the two of them"— he nods toward Stevenson and Ali—"and I remember when he went to Africa."

"In Zaire," Bradley clarifies, referring to Ali's victory in 1974 over George Foreman. And he follows up: "What kind of impact did he have in this country, because he was a revolutionary as well as ... ?"

"It was great," Castro says. "He was very much admired as a sportsman, as a boxer, as a person. There was always a high opinion of him. But I never guessed one day we would meet here, with this kind gesture of bringing medicine, seeing our children, visiting our polyclinics. I am very glad, I am thrilled, to have the opportunity to meet him personally, to appreciate his kindness. I see he is strong. I see he has a very kind face."

Castro is speaking as if Ali were not in the room, standing a few feet away. Ali maintains his fixed façade even as Stevenson whispers into his ear, asking in English, "Muhammad, Muhammad, why you no speak?" Stevenson then turns to tell the journalist who stands behind him, "Muhammad does speak. He speaks to me." Stevenson says nothing more because Castro is now looking at him while continuing to tell Bradley, "I am very glad that he and Stevenson have met." After a pause, Castro adds, "And I am glad that they never fought."

"He's not so sure," Bradley interjects, smiling in the direction of Stevenson.

"I find in that friendship something beautiful," Castro insists softly.

"There is a tie between the two of them," Bradley says.

"Yes," says Castro. "It is true." He again looks at Ali, then at Stevenson, as if searching for something more profound to say.

"And how's the documentary?" he finally asks Bradley.

"It'll be on *60 Minutes*."

"When?"

"Maybe one month," Bradley says, reminding Castro's interpreter, "This is the program on which the *comandante* has been interviewed by Dan Rather a number of times in the past, when Dan Rather was on *60 Minutes*."

"And who's there now?" Castro wants to know.

"I am," Bradley answers.

"You," Castro repeats, with a quick glance at Bradley's earring. "So you are there—the boss now?"

Bradley responds as a media star without illusions: "I'm a worker."

Trays containing coffee, tea, and orange juice finally arrive, but only in amounts sufficient for Ali and Yolanda, Howard Bingham, Greg Howard, the Stevensons, and Castro—although Castro tells the waiters he wants nothing.

Castro motions for Ali and the others to join him across the room, around the circular table. The camera crews and the rest of the guests follow, standing as near to the principals as they can. But throughout the group there is a discernible restlessness. They have been standing for more than an hour and a half. It is now approaching 10 P.M. There has been no food. And for the vast majority, it is clear that there will also be nothing to drink. Even among the special guests, seated and sipping from chilled glasses or hot cups, there is a waning level of fascination with the evening. Indeed, Muhammad Ali's eyes are closed. He is sleeping.

Yolanda sits next to him on the sofa, pretending not to notice. Castro also ignores it, although he sits directly across the table, with the interpreter and the Stevensons.

"How large is Michigan?" Castro begins a new round of questioning with Yolanda, returning for the third time to a subject they had explored beyond the interest of anyone in the room except Castro himself.

"I don't know how big the state is as far as demographics," Yolanda says. "We live in a very small village [Barrien Springs] with about two thousand people."

"Are you going back to Michigan tomorrow?"

"Yes."

"What time?"

"Two-thirty."

"Via Miami?" Castro asks.

"Yes."

"From Miami, where do you fly?"

"We're flying to Michigan."

"How many hours' flight?"

"We have to change at Cincinnati—about two and a half hours."

"Flying time?" asks Castro.

Muhammad Ali opens his eyes, then closes them.

"Flying time," Yolanda repeats.

"From Miami to Michigan?" Castro continues.

"No," she again explains, but still with patience, "we have to go to Cincinnati. There are no direct flights."

"So you have to take two planes?" Castro asks.

"Yes," she says, adding for clarification, "Miami to Cincinnati—and then Cincinnati to South Bend, Indiana."

"From Cincinnati … ?"

"To South Bend," she says. "That's the closest airport."

"So," Fidel goes on, "it is on the outskirts of the city?"

"Yes."

"You have a farm?"

"No," Yolanda says, "just land. We let someone else do the growing."

She mentions that Teófilo Stevenson has traveled through this part of the Midwest. The mention of his name gains Stevenson's attention.

"I was in Chicago," Stevenson tells Castro.

"You were at their home?" Castro asks.

"No," Yolanda corrects Stevenson, "you were in Michigan."

"I was in the countryside," Stevenson says. Unable to resist, he adds, "I have a video of that visit. I'll show it to you sometime."

Castro seems not to hear him. He directs his attention back to Yolanda, asking her where she was born, where she was educated, when she became married, and how many years separate her age from that of her husband, Muhammad Ali.

After Yolanda acknowledges being sixteen years younger than Ali, Castro turns toward Fraymari and with affected sympathy says that she married a man who is twenty years her senior.

"*Comandante!*" Stevenson intercedes, "I am in shape. Sports keep you healthy. Sports add years to your life and life to your years!"

"Oh, what conflict she has," Castro goes on, ignoring Stevenson and catering to Fraymari—and to the CBS cameraman who steps forward for a closer view of Castro's face. "She is a lawyer, and she does not put this husband in jail." Castro is enjoying much more than Fraymari the attention this topic is now getting from the group. Castro had lost his audience and now has it back and seemingly wants to retain it, no matter at what cost to Stevenson's harmony with Fraymari. Yes, Castro continues, Fraymari had the misfortune to select a husband "who can never settle down…. Jail would be an appropriate place for him."

"*Comandante,*" Stevenson interrupts in a jocular manner that seems intended to placate both the lawyer who is his spouse and the lawyer who rules the country, "I might as well be locked up!"

He implies that should he deviate from marital fidelity, his lawyer wife "will surely put me in a place where she is the only woman who can visit me!"

Everyone around the table and within the circling group laughs. Ali is now awake. The banter between Castro and Stevenson resumes until Yolanda, all but rising in her chair, tells Castro, "We have to pack."

"You're going to have dinner now?" he asks.

"Yes, sir," she says. Ali stands, along with Howard Bingham. Yolanda thanks Castro's interpreter directly, saying, "Be sure to tell him, 'You're always welcome in our home.'" The interpreter quotes Castro as again complaining that when he visits America, he is usually restricted to New York, but he adds, "Things change."

The group watches as Yolanda and Ali pass through, and Castro follows them into the hallway. The elevator arrives, and its door is held open by a security guard. Castro extends his final farewell with handshakes—and only then does he discover that he holds Ali's rubber thumb in his hand. Apologizing, he tries to hand it back to Ali, but Bingham politely protests. "No, no," Bingham says, "Ali wants you to have it."

Castro's interpreter at first fails to understand what Bingham is saying.

"He wants you to keep it," Bingham repeats.

Bingham enters the elevator with Ali and Yolanda. Before the door closes, Castro smiles, waves goodbye, and stares with curiosity at the rubber thumb. Then he puts it in his pocket.

## Reflections and Responses

1. Read Gay Talese's comments "On Certain Magazine Interviews" and "Listening to People Think" (pp. 34–35). How do you think his journalistic procedures in this essay compare to his comments about the art of interviewing?

2. How would you describe Talese's role in the essay? Where does he seem visible? Where does he seem almost invisible? How does he fit himself as a participant or as an observer into different situations?

3. Consider how Talese sets up the drama at the palace reception. How does he build tension? How does he mix both the leading

and minor roles? Why do you think he focuses so closely on the different conversations? What do you think he wants the conversations to convey in general about the overall event? Consider, too, the strange gift Ali leaves with Castro. Do you think the gift can have any larger significance? Do you think Talese finds it significant? What exactly is it, and what might it represent?

# 3

# *The Public Sphere: Advocacy, Argument, Controversy*

ALAN M. DERSHOWITZ

# Shouting "Fire!"

*Artists and performers are not the only ones who explore the boundaries of free expression. Lawyers and judges, too, frequently find themselves struggling to ascertain the limits of free speech. In the following essay, one of America's best-known trial lawyers, Alan M. Dershowitz, takes a close look at one of the most commonly used arguments against free speech, the idea that some speech should be suppressed because it is "just like" falsely shouting fire in a crowded theater. In his investigation into the source of this famous analogy, Dershowitz demonstrates how it has been widely misused and abused by proponents of censorship. Indeed, it was an "inapt analogy even in the context in which it was originally offered." As an expression to suppress expression, the "shouting fire" analogy, Dershowitz maintains, has been "invoked so often, by so many people, in such diverse contexts, that it has become part of our national folk language."*

*Alan M. Dershowitz is Felix Frankfurter Professor of Law at Harvard Law School. He is the author of many books, including* The Best Defense *(1982),* Taking Liberties *(1988),* Chutzpah *(1991),* Contrary to Public Opinion *(1992),* The Abuse Excuse *(1994),* Reasonable Doubts *(1996), and* Sexual McCarthyism *(1998). His most recent books include* Supreme Injustice *(2001),* Letters to a Young Lawyer *(2001),* Why Terrorism Works *(2002),* America on Trial *(2004),* Rights from Wrongs *(2004), and* Preemption: A Knife That Cuts Both Ways *(2006). In 2007 Dershowitz published* Finding Jefferson: A Lost Letter, a Remarkable Discovery, and the First Amendment in an Age of Terrorism *and* Blasphemy: How the Religious Right Is Hijacking the Declaration of Independence. *He published a novel,* The Trials of Zion, *in 2010. In addition to his teaching and writing, Professor Dershowitz is an active criminal defense and civil liberties lawyer.*

*"Shouting 'Fire!'" originally appeared in* The Atlantic *(1989) and was selected by Justin Kaplan for* The Best American Essays *1990.*

When the Reverend Jerry Falwell learned that the Supreme Court had reversed his $200,000 judgment against *Hustler* magazine for the emotional distress that he had suffered from an outrageous parody, his response was typical of those who seek to censor speech: "Just as no person may scream 'Fire!' in a crowded theater when there is no fire, and find cover under the First Amendment, likewise, no sleazy merchant like Larry Flynt should be able to use the First Amendment as an excuse for maliciously and dishonestly attacking public figures, as he has so often done."

Justice Oliver Wendell Holmes's classic example of unprotected speech—falsely shouting "Fire!" in a crowded theater—has been invoked so often, by so many people, in such diverse contexts, that it has become part of our national folk language. It has even appeared—most appropriately—in the theater: in Tom Stoppard's play *Rosencrantz and Guildenstern Are Dead* a character shouts at the audience, "Fire!" He then quickly explains: "It's all right— I'm demonstrating the misuse of free speech." Shouting "Fire!" in the theater may well be the only jurisprudential analogy that has assumed the status of a folk argument. A prominent historian recently characterized it as "the most brilliantly persuasive expression that ever came from Holmes' pen." But in spite of its hallowed position in both the jurisprudence of the First Amendment and the arsenal of political discourse, it is and was an inapt analogy, even in the context in which it was originally offered. It has lately become—despite, perhaps even because of, the frequency and promiscuousness of its invocation—little more than a caricature of logical argumentation.

The case that gave rise to the "Fire!"-in-a-crowded-theater analogy, *Schenck v. United States*, involved the prosecution of Charles Schenck, who was the general secretary of the Socialist party in Philadelphia, and Elizabeth Baer, who was its recording secretary. In 1917 a jury found Schenck and Baer guilty of attempting to cause insubordination among soldiers who had been drafted to fight in the First World War. They and other party members had circulated leaflets urging draftees not to "submit to intimidation" by fighting in a war being conducted on behalf of "Wall Street's chosen few."

Schenck admitted, and the Court found, that the intent of the pamphlets' "impassioned language" was to "influence" draftees to resist the draft. Interestingly, however, Justice Holmes noted that nothing in the pamphlet suggested that the draftees should use unlawful or violent means to oppose conscription: "In form at least [the pamphlet] confined itself to peaceful measures, such as a petition for the repeal of the act" and an exhortation to exercise "your right to assert your opposition to the draft." Many of its most impassioned words were quoted directly from the Constitution.

Justice Holmes acknowledged that "in many places and in ordinary times the defendants, in saying all that was said in the circular, would have been within their constitutional rights." "But," he added, "the character of every act depends upon the circumstances in which it is done." And to illustrate that truism he went on to say:

> The most stringent protection of free speech would not protect a man in falsely shouting fire in a theater, and causing a panic. It does not even protect a man from an injunction against uttering words that may have all the effect of force.

Justice Holmes then upheld the convictions in the context of a wartime draft, holding that the pamphlet created "a clear and present danger" of hindering the war effort while our soldiers were fighting for their lives and our liberty.

The example of shouting "Fire!" obviously bore little relationship to the facts of the Schenck case. The Schenck pamphlet contained a substantive political message. It urged its draftee readers to *think* about the message and then—if they so chose—to act on it in a lawful and nonviolent way. The man who shouts "Fire!" in a crowded theater is neither sending a political message nor inviting his listener to think about what he has said and decide what to do in a rational, calculated manner. On the contrary, the message is designed to force action *without* contemplation. The message "Fire!" is directed not to the mind and the conscience of the listener but, rather, to his adrenaline and his feet. It is a stimulus to immediate *action*, not thoughtful reflection. It is—as Justice Holmes recognized in his follow-up sentence—the functional equivalent of "uttering words that may have all the effect of force."

Indeed, in that respect the shout of "Fire!" is not even speech, in any meaningful sense of that term. It is a *clang* sound, the equivalent of setting off a nonverbal alarm. Had Justice Holmes been more honest about his example, he would have said that freedom of speech does not protect a kid who pulls a fire alarm in the absence of a fire. But that obviously would have been irrelevant to the case at hand. The proposition that pulling an alarm is not protected speech certainly leads to the conclusion that shouting the word "fire" is also not protected. But the core analogy is the nonverbal alarm, and the derivative example is the verbal shout. By cleverly substituting the derivative shout for the core alarm, Holmes made it possible to analogize one set of words to another—as he could not have done if he had begun with the self-evident proposition that setting off an alarm bell is not free speech.

The analogy is thus not only inapt but also insulting. Most Americans do not respond to political rhetoric with the same kind of automatic acceptance expected of schoolchildren responding to a fire drill. Not a single recipient of the Schenck pamphlet is known to have changed his mind after reading it. Indeed, one draftee, who appeared as a prosecution witness, was asked whether reading the pamphlet asserting that the draft law was unjust would make him "immediately decide that you must erase that law." Not surprisingly, he replied, "I do my own thinking." A theatergoer would probably not respond similarly if asked how he would react to a shout of "Fire!"

Another important reason why the analogy is inapt is that Holmes emphasizes the factual falsity of the shout "Fire!" The Schenck pamphlet, however, was not factually false. It contained political opinions and ideas about the causes of the war and about appropriate and lawful responses to the draft. As the Supreme Court recently reaffirmed (in *Falwell v. Hustler*), "The First Amendment recognizes no such thing as a 'false' idea." Nor does it recognize false opinions about the causes of or cures for war.

A closer analogy to the facts of the Schenck case might have been provided by a person's standing outside a theater, offering the patrons a leaflet advising them that in his opinion the theater was structurally unsafe, and urging them not to enter but to complain to the building inspectors. That analogy, however, would not have served Holmes's argument for punishing Schenck. Holmes needed an analogy that would appear relevant to Schenck's political speech but that would invite the conclusion that censorship was appropriate.

Unsurprisingly, a war-weary nation—in the throes of a know-nothing hysteria over immigrant anarchists and socialists—welcomed the comparison between what was regarded as a seditious political pamphlet and a malicious shout of "Fire!" Ironically, the "Fire!" analogy is nearly all that survives from the Schenck case; the ruling itself is almost certainly not good law. Pamphlets of the kind that resulted in Schenck's imprisonment have been circulated with impunity during subsequent wars.

Over the past several years I have assembled a collection of instances—cases, speeches, arguments—in which proponents of censorship have maintained that the expression at issue is "just like" or "equivalent to" falsely shouting "Fire!" in a crowded theater and ought to be banned, "just as" shouting "Fire!" ought to be banned. The analogy is generally invoked, often with self-satisfaction, as an absolute argument-stopper. It does, after all, claim the high authority of the great Justice Oliver Wendell Holmes. I have rarely heard it invoked in a convincing, or even particularly relevant, way. But that, too, can claim lineage from the great Holmes.

Not unlike Falwell, with his silly comparison between shouting "Fire!" and publishing an offensive parody, courts and commentators have frequently invoked "Fire!" as an analogy to expression that is not an automatic stimulus to panic. A state supreme court held that "Holmes' aphorism ... applies with equal force to pornography"—in particular to the exhibition of the movie *Carmen Baby* in a drive-in theater in close proximity to highways and homes. Another court analogized "picketing ... in support of a secondary boycott" to shouting "Fire!" because in both instances "speech and conduct are brigaded." In the famous Skokie case one of the judges argued that allowing Nazis to march through a city where a large number of Holocaust survivors live "just might fall into the same category as one's 'right' to cry fire in a crowded theater."

Outside court the analogies become even more badly stretched. A spokesperson for the New Jersey Sports and Exposition Authority complained that newspaper reports to the effect that a large number of football players had contracted cancer after playing in the Meadowlands—a stadium atop a landfill—were the "journalistic equivalent of shouting fire in a crowded theater." An insect researcher acknowledged that his prediction that a certain amusement park might become roach-infested "may be tantamount to shouting fire in a crowded theater." The philosopher Sidney Hook, in a letter to the *New York Times* bemoaning a Supreme Court decision that required a plaintiff in a defamation action to prove that the offending statement was actually false, argued that the First Amendment does not give the press carte blanche to accuse innocent persons "anymore than the First Amendment protects the right of someone falsely to shout fire in a crowded theater."

Some close analogies to shouting "Fire!" or setting off an alarm are, of course, available: calling in a false bomb threat; dialing 911 and falsely describing an emergency; making a loud, gunlike sound in the presence of the President; setting off a voice-activated sprinkler system by falsely shouting "Fire!" In one case in which the "Fire!" analogy was directly to the point, a creative defendant tried to get around it. The case involved a man who calmly advised an airline clerk that he was "only here to hijack the plane." He was charged, in effect, with shouting "Fire!" in a crowded theater, and his rejected defense—as quoted by the court—was as follows: "If we built fire-proof theaters and let people know about this, then the shouting of 'Fire!' would not cause panic."

Here are some more-distant but still related examples: the recent incident of the police slaying in which some members of an onlooking crowd urged a mentally ill vagrant who had taken an officer's gun to shoot the officer; the screaming of racial epithets during a tense confrontation; shouting down a speaker and preventing him from continuing his speech.

Analogies are, by their nature, matters of degree. Some are closer to the core example than others. But any attempt to analogize political ideas in a pamphlet, ugly parody in a magazine, offensive movies in a theater, controversial newspaper articles, or any of the other expressions and actions catalogued above to the very different act of shouting "Fire!" in a crowded theater is either self-deceptive or self-serving.

The government does, of course, have some arguably legitimate bases for suppressing speech which bear no relationship to shouting "Fire!" It may ban the publication of nuclear-weapon codes, of information about troop movements, and of the identity of undercover agents. It may criminalize extortion threats and conspiratorial agreements. These expressions may lead directly to serious harm, but the mechanisms of causation are very different from that at work when an alarm is sounded. One may also argue—less persuasively, in my view—against protecting certain forms of public obscenity and defamatory statements. Here, too, the mechanisms of causation are very different. None of these exceptions to the First Amendment's exhortation that the government "shall make no law ... abridging the freedom of speech, or of the press" is anything like falsely shouting "Fire!" in a crowded theater; they all must be justified on other grounds.

A comedian once told his audience, during the stand-up routine, about the time he was standing around a fire with a crowd of people and got in trouble for yelling "Theater, theater!" That, I think, is about as clever and productive a use as anyone has ever made of Holmes's flawed analogy.

## Reflections and Responses

1. Consider Dershowitz's analysis of Justice Holmes's decision in the Schenck case. What does Dershowitz find wrong with Holmes's reasoning? In what ways is Holmes's analogy "flawed"?

2. To what kinds of expression does Dershowitz find Holmes's analogy applicable? Go through Dershowitz's examples of protected and unprotected speech. Why is the "falsely shouting fire" analogy appropriate in some instances and not in others?

3. Consider Dershowitz's anecdote in the last paragraph about the comedian who yells "Theater, theater!" What was the comedian expressing? Why does Dershowitz find this response to Holmes's analogy "clever and productive"?

GEORGE GESSERT

# An Orgy of Power

*In May 2004, The New Yorker magazine published shocking photos showing United States military personnel treating prisoners at the Abu Ghraib prison in occupied Baghdad in ways that most people classified immediately as torture. Americans have always prided themselves on the fair treatment of even their worst enemies; consequently the photos appalled the world community and called into question many of the premises on which the invasion of Iraq had been launched the previous year. In this remarkable essay, part personal and part political, George Gessert examines his own reaction to the revelations of Abu Ghraib, and considers the horror of torture itself. Quoting Austrian essayist Jean Améry, Gessert concludes that torture is borne of our "innate drive for unchecked self-expansion," and that the torturers, like their victims, are human beings, "capable of beautiful behavior and terrible behavior, individually and collectively."*

*George Gessert is an artist prominent in the bio-art movement, which uses living matter as a medium. His work has been exhibited widely in the United States, Australia, and Europe. He is the author, most recently, of* Green Light: Toward an Art of Evolution *(2010), and his writing has appeared in several anthologies, including* Biomediale, Art et Biotechnologies, and *The Aesthetics of Care. He is an editor at the journal* Leonardo, *and won a Pushcart Prize in 2005. "An Orgy of Power" was selected by David Foster Wallace for* The Best American Essays 2007.

I am reluctant to write about torture. It holds no special fascination for me—on the contrary, I find the subject repellent. But I did not choose the times I live in, nor do I choose what I am compelled to write. As a writer I am committed to speaking from my own experience, which may seem to counsel silence. I have not been to Iraq,

*Source:* George Gessert, *An Orgy of Power.* Reprinted by permission of the author. George Gessert is an artist and writer. His book, *Green Light,* is forthcoming from MIT Press.

Afghanistan, or Guantánamo Bay. I am not a journalist or an authority on the history of torture. But the perimeters of experience do not end with what is immediate. In today's world, almost everything connects with everything else. The coffee that fuels my editing was raised in Kenya, my shirt was made in China. Reports arrive daily from around the world. The problem is sorting the relevant from the irrelevant, the true from the false, and assigning each bit of information something like its proper weight. These things make learning gradual, writing slow, and these notes very late.

In August 2002, following the battle of Konduz in Afghanistan, I read puzzling reports on the Internet. More than two hundred prisoners taken at Konduz had been found dead in a mass grave. They had died of heat, dehydration, and suffocation after being sealed in metal containers for transport to Shabarghan prison. The U.S. role in the deaths was unclear, and to date has not been properly investigated, although the number of victims is now put at a thousand. However, the U.S. Army's Special Forces seems to have been involved.[1]

The media gave extensive attention to one captive, John Walker Lindh. He was a twenty-one-year-old Californian who had converted to Islam, and trained in Afghanistan to fight the Northern Alliance. He had arrived at the front lines before September 11. We now know that he had no advance knowledge of the attacks on New York and Washington, D.C., and that reports he heard afterward were sketchy. Following his capture he was separated from other prisoners and allegedly tortured.

The accounts that I read at the time said that Lindh had been handcuffed, blindfolded, and photographed. Some of his captors were hostile to him and did not treat a wound in his leg. But how was this torture? I wondered if Lindh's family and lawyer were making exaggerated claims in an attempt to win public sympathy for the young man and save him from the death sentence he could face if charged with aiding the enemy. Only much later did I read that Lindh had had a bullet in his leg, and U.S. agents had left the bullet there while they interrogated him, which had gone on until the wound became "seeping and malodorous." Lindh received death threats, and his hands were cuffed so tightly that he was in intense pain. He was confined in a metal shipping container, and suffered extended exposure to cold.[2]

For almost a year after the battle of Konduz I read sketchy and ambiguous reports of prisoner mistreatment. I was not sure what to make of them. Then came the pictures from Abu Ghraib and overwhelming evidence that detainees had been tortured. They

Getty Images News/Getty Images

*A detainee at Abu Ghraib Prison appears to be intimidated by a U.S. soldier with a trained dog.*

had been tortured not only in Iraq, but in Afghanistan and an archipelago of prisons around the world. Documents surfaced, such as the so-called torture memo of August 1, 2002, showing that very close associates of President Bush, apparently with his full approval, had encouraged torture.[3]

Lions and hyenas kill swiftly. Housecats play with their victims, but only to practice pouncing, not to cause pain. Tapeworms and the shingles virus keep their victims alive as sources of sustenance, not to cause pain. Only humans torture.

In many societies torture was open and acceptable. The Romans made elaborate forms of animal and human torture into public entertainments. During the Inquisition torture served the Church. But from the earliest days of the republic Americans have defined themselves as the people who are opposed to "cruel and unusual punishments." The Eighth Amendment to the Constitution provides a legal groundwork for putting this ideal into practice. By the twentieth century, the United States had become an international leader in outlawing torture. Along the way some Americans engaged in torture, but cruel and unusual punishments, variously defined, have been forbidden for so long as to seem somehow foreign and un-American. Consequently most Americans are unaccustomed to discussing torture, much less torture done with encouragement from the president.

A few days ago a letter appeared in our local newspaper repeating the familiar claim that nothing worse happened at Abu Ghraib than happens in fraternity hazings. This simile has cropped up in local and national media ever since Rush Limbaugh gave it his imprimatur on May 4, 2004, on his show "It's Not About Us; This Is War."

> CALLER: It was like a college fraternity prank that stacked up naked men …
> LIMBAUGH: Exactly. Exactly my point. This is no different than what happens at the Skull and Bones* initiation … I'm talking about people having a good time, these people, you ever heard of emotional release? You ever heard of need to blow off some steam?

No doubt stress relief was a factor in what happened, and not only at Abu Ghraib. An army sergeant, describing events at Camp Mercury, near Fallujah, reported that "everyone in camp knew if you wanted to work out your frustrations you show up" at the PUC tent. PUC, pronounced "puck," stands for person under control, the term that has replaced POW, or prisoner of war, which evokes the Geneva Conventions. As an example of someone working out his frustrations, the sergeant told of a cook who on his day off went to the PUC tent and broke a prisoner's leg with a Louisville Slugger, a metal baseball bat.[4]

I am not shocked by war photographs. They are all too familiar. I have seen too many images of the dead and wounded, too many mutilated children, too many body parts in black-and-white and in color, and far too many grief-stricken survivors. Long ago, without ever making a conscious decision, I became detached. But my automatic defenses did not work with the photographs from Abu Ghraib. Their extraordinary power arose from the novelty of their subject matter, their striking resemblance to pornography, and their absolute authenticity. I doubt that any professional photographer or trained artist could have created such damning images.

---

*Skull and Bones: An exclusive, fraternity-like society at Yale University.

The tormenters are my fellow countrymen and -women. They look like people on the street, and from all reports they are ordinary citizens. But the prisoners, in their fear, anguish, and humiliation, are more immediately recognizable as human beings—even with digitally blanked-out faces.

Of the many photographs from Abu Ghraib (the Pentagon may hold thousands), so far only about two dozen have entered the public realm.[5] After seeing a dozen or so photographs, I began to follow news about torture. This led me to pay attention to how public discussion was being framed. Beginning in March 2004, when the first photographs became public, the media adopted the administration's preferred word, "abuse," to describe what had happened at Abu Ghraib. "Abuse" covers a range of activities, but is not ordinarily used to describe attempted male rape, which is what some of the photographs show. We do not ordinarily call homicide "abuse," and yet one of the photographs is of a man who had evidently been beaten to death. The media could have corrected itself when those reports were confirmed, and when evidence emerged that detainees at Abu Ghraib, Guantánamo Bay, Bagram Air Base, and elsewhere had been forced to maintain stress positions until passing out, reports of cigarettes being put out in a detainee's ears, evidence of blows that liquefied muscles and produced strokes, and of many other clear instances of torture. But even today the media persists in using the unmodified word "abuse." Why? Perhaps reporters and media executives fear the administration. Fear is not unreasonable. The Bush administration has been unsparingly hostile and vindictive toward critics. Or perhaps mainstream reporters and those who manage the media fear the public, the greater part of which until very recently has supported the president. As I write, a *Newsweek* poll shows that about half of the American public approve of torture.[6] But whatever the reasons for the media's reluctance to use the word "torture," at what point do denial, fear, and caution shade into complicity?

To the media's credit, it has brought news of torture to the attention of U.S. citizens and to the world. Who is ultimately responsible, the major media or individuals, for determining the moral weight of tossing the body of a murdered man into his sister's cell, as reported by the *Los Angeles Times*? Is it torture when a man is nearly drowned by having his head forced into a toilet, as we learn happened at Guantánamo Bay from an article in the

*Washington Post?* Is a broken jaw less painful if it is noted on page 10 than on page 1?

The United States may not have as monumental a literature of war as Russia, or as desolating a one as Germany, but in any good public library one can find vivid descriptions of Americans at war, read about the ordeals and boredom and camaraderie of soldiers, gain some sense of the appeals and horrors of combat, and learn about its aftermath. We also have literature about the home front, about the women and children, the parents waiting for the knock on the door—typically with neighbors determinedly oblivious of what is happening.

But torture plays only the most minor role in our literature. *The Pit and the Pendulum,* if it can be said to describe torture at all, reads like an overheated fantasy. In Faulkner's *Sanctuary* an impotent gangster named Popeye rapes a girl with a corncob. A mob mutilates and murders Joe Christmas in *Light in August.* In Robert Stone's *Dog Soldiers* two drug dealers use a heated clothes iron to terrorize a man into surrendering heroin that he has smuggled into California. In *A Flag for Sunrise* an American nun is tortured in a fictitious Central American country. But such passages only underscore a near absence in our literature. Our literature does not fathom torture. Torture by Americans has spread in a vacuum of language.

Painting and filmmaking have prepared us slightly better. Leon Golub devoted much of his career to painting torturers and their victims. During the Vietnam War Peter Saul painted terrifying, cartoonlike fantasies that map a peculiarly American approach to torture. And *Reservoir Dogs* brought unaestheticized images and sounds of torture to a mass audience. In small ways, perhaps, our visual culture has helped educate us to see the photographs from Abu Ghraib.

Susan Sontag observed that the grins on the faces of U.S. soldiers in photographs from Abu Ghraib resemble those on white faces in photographs of lynchings.[7] Schoolyard bullies have the same smile. The truth that the bully and the torturer share is the truth of unrestrained power, but the bully only glimpses it, while the lyncher and the torturer realize it.

Jean Améry, who was tortured by the Gestapo in Fort Breendonk in Belgium in 1943, remembered the faces of his torturers as "not 'Gestapo faces' with twisted noses, hypertrophied chins, pock-marks and knife scars, as they might appear in a book, but rather faces like anyone else's. Plain, ordinary faces." During torture, these plain, ordinary faces became "concentrated in murderous self-realization. With heart and soul they went about their business, and the name of it was power, domination over spirit and flesh, an orgy of unchecked self-expansion."[8]

Hannah Arendt's insight into the banality of evil applies to bureaucrats and ordinary citizens far removed from the suffering that they cause, but according to Améry does not apply to the men and women who do the actual work of destruction. Améry claims an authority in this regard that exceeds Arendt's, since Arendt was never tortured. The act of torture, he writes, destroys ordinary social bonds and relationships, and propels the torturer far beyond the realm of daily life. The torturer engages in what Elaine Scarry calls "the unmaking of civilization ... [and the] uncreating of the created world."[9]

"An orgy of unchecked self-expansion": Améry's phrase, with its Sadean* grandiosity, is consistent with the smiles on American faces at Abu Ghraib. The reward of torture, according to Améry, is "murderous self-realization." Self-realization in this context suggests a return, however brief, to infantile omnipotence. The smile of the torturer is latent within everyone.

The torturer and his or her superiors mimic God. They and they alone determine who is guilty, what is right, and what is wrong. It comes as no surprise, then, that according to the International Committee of the Red Cross, between 70 and 90 percent of the thousands detained at Abu Ghraib had been arrested "by mistake."[10] Reportedly these were among the victims of torture. At least one hundred prisoners were children. We have less information about the prisoners at Guantánamo Bay, but we know that among them are children and demented old men. Destruction of the innocent is the most incontrovertible proof of power.

Unchecked self-expansion is also consistent with what we know about the Bush administration's efforts to legitimize torture. Many military and intelligence experts claim that torture does not yield reliable information, endangers U.S. prisoners of war, and can serve enemies as a recruitment tool. Other intelligence experts disagree, claiming that torture can yield useful

---

*Sadean: Like the Marquis de Sade, who wrote of sexual torture in eighteenth-century France.

information, and may terrorize opponents, but comes at too high a price: loss of American prestige internationally and corruption of the military. Pragmatic objections to torture are convincing only if national honor and the well-being of our troops and citizens are primary concerns. The administration has had a very different, overriding concern: that the president not be restrained by the Geneva Conventions or the Constitution as traditionally interpreted. We do not need to psychoanalyze George W. Bush or understand the inner life of Dick Cheney to recognize broad patterns in their behavior. Their primary concern is and has been power, irrespective of traditional morality or law.

As every dreamer learns sooner or later, and as the framers of the Constitution, who were hardly sentimental about humankind, knew very well, something in us would sculpt the universe. In itself this is neither good nor bad; it is simply a psychological phenomenon. It informs everything from law to art to child rearing to exploration of the solar system. But it also produces tyranny.

Améry considered torture an essential feature of totalitarian rule. Under German fascism, torture became "the total inversion of the social world ... in the world of torture man exists only by ruining the other person who stands before him."[11] Améry's insights are relevant to us because although the United States is profoundly unlike Nazi Germany, our society accommodates not only democratic practices but undemocratic ones, including outright totalitarian rule as at Abu Ghraib and Guantánamo Bay. For several decades torture has been a feature of U.S. proxy wars, clandestine campaigns, CIA actions, and partnerships with military regimes and death squads. From the 1970s to the 1990s American involvement in torture, especially in Latin America, surfaced from time to time in the media. Numerous reports focused on the School of the Americas (renamed the Western Hemisphere Institute for Security Cooperation in 2001). In 1996 the Pentagon was forced to release school training manuals that taught torture. However, the mainstream media usually characterized the role of the School of the Americas in torture as indirect, and downplayed instances of direct involvement as aberrations.[12]

Until photographs from Abu Ghraib were aired on national television, most Americans probably did not know that their government sometimes encouraged torture. Or, if they did know, they could tell themselves that it was quite rare—this was what

I believed. I believed that torture by Americans existed, but involved very few people and played a very small role in American foreign policy. Relative to other extremely serious problems, such as mass extinctions, global warming, the spread of nuclear weapons, and the population explosion, torture was distinctly less important. I still think that in a very general way this is true, but my failure to comprehend what was happening arose from not wanting to think about torture, from a sense of having no personal connection with torture or the tortured, and from the reports themselves. Arriving intermittently from distant places, the words seemed ghostly and insubstantial in their horror. They needed a catalyst to gain psychological substance. Photographs from Abu Ghraib provided the catalyst.

Writing these notes, I held on to the belief that I had no personal connection to the tortured. I had almost completed my notes (or so I thought) when I began to think about the long-term effects of torture. I began to think about friends who had lost family in the Holocaust—was torture involved? How does torture affect the second and third generations? How does not knowing whether a close relative had been tortured affect a family? I thought about a boy I played with when I was in junior high school. His family was from Armenia. I recalled his mother telling me that the family had arrived in the United States in 1920, but I never learned more. Then there was the doctor from El Salvador who for a short time cleaned house for my mother. What was his story? What was his family's story? I realized that I did not know my degrees of separation from the tortured, or from torturers.

But this too was a trick that I played on myself. Years ago, at a conference in São Paulo, I became acquainted with an amateur scholar of Paracas culture. He was Brazilian, perhaps fifteen years my senior, tall and distinguished-looking, and one evening at dinner he told me in excellent, German-inflected English about his many visits to Nasca to see the ancient earthworks there. The Nasca Lines, which were scraped into the earth some eighteen hundred years ago and stretch for miles across the desert floor, are some of the largest artworks in the world. What they meant to their creators no one knows, but because weaving played a central role in Paracas culture, some authorities believe that the lines diagram the loom of the stars.

I asked him if he had ever seen the lines at night.

"Once," he said. "It was as I imagine the beginning of the universe, and the end." For me that was the beginning of our friendship.

Over the next twelve years we corresponded, mostly about Paracas art but also about ourselves. His father, I learned, had been involved in the 1944 attempt to assassinate Hitler. But we did not discuss this. He made it clear that he did not want me to ask questions. "I never think about it," he wrote. I could only begin to imagine his situation. I had read that the plotters were tortured to death after they were captured. His father had sent him to boarding school in Switzerland, which probably saved his life. From there his mother took him to Brazil.

Several years ago, in declining health, he shot himself. He bungled the attempt and took two months to die.

Writing these notes, I turned to novels for relief, a safe haven from the subject of torture, or so I assumed, typically American. The title character in J. M. Coetzee's *Elizabeth Costello* is a distinguished novelist, navigating the mildly hazardous waters of literary fame. She uses her renown to speak out for animals suffering under industrialism, comparing them with the victims of the Holocaust. Strongly criticized for making this comparison, she reads Paul West's *The Very Rich Hours of Count von Stauffenberg*, a history of the 1944 plot to assassinate Hitler. West recounts in detail how the plotters were tortured to death, and their agonies were filmed so that the Führer could replay them at his leisure. Elizabeth Costello is so wounded by horror that she publicly attacks the author and tells him that he should never have written his book. There is such a thing as too much knowledge.

I found myself arguing with her. The written word, except for a few works of poetry, never provides more than incomplete knowledge. Reading cannot provide too much knowledge, but timing is everything. The art of reading involves intuiting when to read and when not. As readers, we do not enlarge ourselves by taking no risks, but even a masterpiece read at the wrong time is a waste of time, or worse.

If I knew then what I know today, I could have been a better friend. Right now I do not have the heart to read more about what happened to my dead friend's father. But when the time is right I will do the reading.

The outbreak of torture today is different from previous torture by Americans in three significant ways. First, the Bush administration carefully laid the groundwork for torture. In previous wars torture did not result directly from White House planning, even if commanding officers and their civilian superiors were willing to avert their eyes when it occurred. Second, the administration and the Pentagon, for all of their formidable skills in managing imagery, did not take digital cameras and the Internet into account. Third, more information about torture by Americans is available today than ever before.

The election of 2004 was an indirect referendum on torture. Neither George Bush nor John Kerry made torture an election issue, but reports about what had happened at Abu Ghraib and what was happening at Guantánamo Bay and elsewhere appeared intermittently in the major media throughout the campaign. The election confirmed what both candidates apparently knew from the beginning, that torture would bear no political price.

As I write, all that is necessary to practice torture outside the country on noncitizens, and on citizens such as John Lindh, is to maintain a measure of secrecy abroad, and appearances domestically. President Bush has attempted to accomplish the latter by condemning torture as not reflecting American values. "Freedom from torture," he said in a typically hypocritical speech, "is an inalienable right."[13]

On November 4, 2004, the greater part of the electorate became implicated in torture. Nothing like this had happened in any previous American war. The closest parallel to the present situation is, of course, not a previous war but the heyday of lynching. During the half century from the 1880s to the 1930s, most of the American public, along with much of the press and Congress, ignored or downplayed atrocities, and by doing so tacitly endorsed them.

Consider the contrast with the French in the early 1960s, when evidence of torture in Algeria became public. Half the nation rose up in protest. That largely put a stop to torture.

Will new categories of victims emerge, such as foreign nationals living within the boundaries of the United States or citizens suspected of supporting terrorism, ever more broadly defined? Only time will tell, but this much is certain: torture, and the imperial project that favors it, has a price. One part of the price is loss of American innocence.

Improbable as it may seem today, at one time the United States had a genuine claim to innocence. Although the republic was conceived amid genocide and slavery, the sheer daring of the experiment in representative government allowed informed men and women of good faith to believe that even the worst crimes were vestiges of an older order in the process of being outgrown. Balzac* considered the virgin to be the most terrifying of all figures. This is because we are fallen but she is pure. Her inexperience and spiritual invincibility do not predispose her to be merciful to us for our failings. Throughout the nineteenth century America's virginity made the nation invincible, to itself first of all, as it projected itself onto the world. But such innocence cannot indefinitely survive empire. The rhetoric of the Bush administration mimics the old moral invincibility, but today American innocence, except for those elements that have changed to disillusionment or that we share with all other peoples, has completed its transformation into kitsch.

Kitsch has its own powers, and great ones too—the powers of ignorance and public relations. Kitsch innocence is cartoonlike and amplified, all smiles and snarls and formulaic sincerity, rapt with faith one minute, boundlessly cynical the next, but always tuned to public desires. None of this is new, of course. Europe knows all about it. European history cautions against any leader who talks like a cartoon. And Europe is littered with the remains of empires. Many of our leaders, to widespread domestic applause, scorned Old Europe, but amid the cheers America had become like the Europe we read about in books, the Europe of the unromantic past, the genuine Old Europe. The spectacles and orgies of self-expansion, the murderous hypocrisy, the denial and religious fanaticism and systemic corruption of language, and above all the tragic waste began to look familiar. They began to look like what centuries of immigrants crossing oceans to begin again dreamed that they had left behind forever.

According to Jean Améry, the source of torture is our innate drive for unchecked self-expansion. If this is true, the possibility of torture will always be with us. How are we to deal with this today?

Machiavelli summarized the relationship of ordinary people to power as a shadow play of deceptions brought by the people on themselves. A prince "should seem to be all mercy, all loyalty, all sincerity, all humanity, all religion. And nothing is more necessary to seem to have than [religion] … Everybody sees what you appear to be, few feel what you are, and those few will not dare to oppose

---

*Balzac: Honoré de Balzac, a nineteenth-century French novelist and playwright.

themselves to the opinion of the many, who have the majesty of the state to defend them ... Let a prince therefore conquer and maintain his state: his means will always be judged honourable and praised by everyone, for ordinary people will always be taken by appearances and by the outcome of action."[14] To put this into contemporary language, presidents are encouraged in evil by the people, who are eager to be deceived.

Machiavelli wrote about the nature of power after his political career had ended in disaster. He had been accused of plotting against the Medici, and tortured. The experience of torture may have convinced him that human beings are fundamentally evil. His insights into power are brilliant, but his assessment of human nature is as reductive as the belief that human beings are fundamentally good. Such formulations are alluring. They voice our hopes and fears, but they bring only factitious clarity to experience by ignoring evidence that does not fit. The overwhelming lesson of history and of daily life is that human beings are capable of beautiful behavior and terrible behavior, individually and collectively. What this implies is that although taboos, information, empathy, moral intelligence, uncorrupted law, and democratic practices are crucial lines of defense against torture, the single most important defense is the separation of powers. The more concentrated power becomes, the fewer the obstacles to extremity, including torture. The deeper our society descends into militarism, one-party rule, and rule by a single branch of government, the more embedded the practice of torture will become in American life.

## Notes

1   Jennifer K. Harbury, *Truth, Torture, and the American Way* (Boston: Beacon Press, 2005), pp. 2–4.

2   Ibid., pp. 4–5.

3   The memo of August 1, 2002, defines torture as applying only to acts that produce "physical pain ... equivalent in intensity to the pain accompanying ... organ failure ... or even death." The memorandum goes on to say that "even if the defendant knows that severe pain will result from his actions, if causing such pain is not his objective, he lacks the requisite specific intent." What this means is that if extracting information is a torturer's objective, he or she is not legally responsible for causing pain, no matter how intense and no matter how lasting the damage.

    For about two years the memo guided the administration and provided legal protection for torturers and their superiors. After the publication of photographs from Abu Ghraib, the administration revised the guidelines, but in a footnote protected the August 1 memo's extremely limited definition of torture.

4   Human Rights Watch, *Leadership Failure: Firsthand Accounts of Torture of Iraqi Detainees by the U. S. Army's 82nd Airborne Division: Summary.*

5   In February 2006, while this manuscript was being prepared for press, hundreds of additional images were released by the Australian news show *Dateline.*

6   "44 percent of the public thinks that torture is often or sometimes justified to obtain important information ... a clear majority—58 percent—would support torture to thwart a terrorist attack." Evan Thomas and Michael Hirsch, "The Debate over Torture," *Newsweek,* November 21, 2005, p. 29.

7   Susan Sontag, "Regarding the Torture of Others," *New York Times Magazine,* May 23, 2004.

8   Jean Améry, *At the Mind's Limit,* trans. Sidney Rosenfeld and Stella R Rosenfeld (Bloomington and Indianapolis: Indiana University Press, 1980), p. 25.

9   Elaine Scarry, *The Body in Pain* (New York: Oxford University Press, 1985), p. 45.

10  *Report of the International Committee of the Red Cross (ICRC) on the Treatment by the Coalition Forces of Prisoners of War and Other Protected Persons by the Geneva Conventions in Iraq During Arrest, Internment, and Interrogation,* Section 1.7, February 2004. Brigadier General Janice Karpinski, who oversaw Abu Ghraib at the time that the photographs were taken, provides a slightly different but substantially similar assessment: "The vast majority of them [prisoners] were [arrested for] minor crimes. They were missing curfew. They were subjected to a random inspection and a weapon was found in their trunks ... they were minor crimes, nonviolent crimes." Interview with Marjorie Cohn, *Truthout,* August 24, 2005.

11  Jean Améry in ICRC report, p. 35.

12  The School of the Americas' involvement in torture may not always have been indirect. At the school's interrogation classes in Panama, street people may have been used to demonstrate torture techniques. In Uruguay, four homeless people were reportedly used as guinea pigs in an "anatomy class" and tortured to death. Jennifer Harbury in ibid., pp. 95–96.

13  George W. Bush, Reuters, June 26, 2005.

14  Niccolò Machiavelli, *The Prince,* trans. Wayne Rebhorn (New York: Barnes and Noble, 2003), pp. 76–77.

## Reflections and Responses

1. Why does Gessert introduce autobiographical elements into an essay about torture, a subject with which he admits he has very little privileged experience? What are the advantages (and

disadvantages) of an approach to torture told with a strong personal voice as opposed to a detached, analytical one? How does the opening paragraph fit into the essay as a whole? What about Gessert's story of his friend's suicide?

2. Gessert argues that Americans had trouble believing its government tortured prisoners until they saw the photos from Abu Ghraib. "They needed a catalyst to gain psychological substance," he writes. Why are photographs especially powerful in this instance? Do you agree with Gessert's contention that movies have made ours into a "visual culture" in which we must see to understand? Or is the power of photography universal?

3. Gessert concludes with a warning: "The deeper our society descends into militarism, one-party rule, and rule by a single branch of government, the more embedded the practice of torture will become in American life." Gessert was writing in 2006, during the Bush administration. Is his essay obsolete? With future administrations, do you think torture will be less of a concern? What elements of the essay do you think will still resonate?

GARRET KEIZER

# Loaded

*The debate over guns in America has traditionally taken place on established lines: In general, liberals argue for tighter gun control laws in the name of safety, while conservatives argue that the Second Amendment to the Constitution protects ownership of guns, and that they're necessary to maintain a free society. In this essay, Garret Keizer, a self-proclaimed progressive, challenges the liberal orthodoxy, asserting that the ownership of guns should be a right liberals defend as ardently as they do civil rights. Only an armed population—and more broadly a population willing to fight back physically against oppression—can withstand tyranny, Keizer argues. And to the pragmatism of his fellow progressives, who contend that gun ownership is no longer compatible with modern life, Keizer offers a stunning rebuke: "If the Second Amendment is a dispensable anachronism in the era of school shootings, might not the First, Fourth, and Fifth amendments be dispensable anachronisms during a 'war on terror'?"*

*Garret Keizer is a writer in northeastern Vermont, but he has also spent time as an Episcopal priest and a teacher. His books include* No Place But Here: A Teacher's Vocation in a Rural Community *(1996),* A Dresser of Sycamore Trees: The Finding of a Ministry *(2001),* The Enigma of Anger: Essays on a Sometimes Deadly Sin *(2004), and* Help: The Original Human Dilemma *(2005). His most recent books are* The Unwanted Sound of Everything We Want: A Book about Noise *(2010) and* Privacy *(2012). He is a frequent contributor to* Harper's, *where "Loaded" first appeared; it was selected by David Foster Wallace for* The Best American Essays 2007.

"That rifle hanging on the wall of the working-class flat or labourer's cottage is the symbol of democracy. It is our job to see that it stays there."

—George Orwell

*Source:* Garret Keizer, Loaded. First published in *Harper's Magazine* December 2006. Copyright © 2006 by Garret Keizer. Reprinted by permission of the author.

England was not engaged in a war against Islamo-fascists* when Orwell penned the words above, only a war against Nazi fascists— or, as one now feels obliged to say, *fascist* fascists—and the rifle he referred to was in use by the British Home Guard. Still, his reasons for wanting the rifle to stay on the wall obviously had to do with a different sort of homeland security than the War Office had in mind. Otherwise, why specify the gun owner's *class?*

In fact, Orwell was anticipating a time when the rifle might have a revolutionary purpose. His hopes were not altogether in vain, though supporting examples tend to be about as well known as the quotation itself, and for much the same reason.

Here is one from 1947, three years before Orwell's death. In Monroe, North Carolina, a motorcade of Ku Klux Klansmen pulled up to a funeral home to "claim" the body of Bennie Montgomery, a black sharecropper recently tried and executed for killing his white boss. With the help of a skilled mediator and a regimen of trust-building exercises, the night riders might have been persuaded to settle for a limb or a chunk of Bennie's torso, but instead they were met by forty African Americans armed with rifles and shotguns. Among them was a former Army private named Robert Williams (1925–96), whose career as a rogue civil rights activist and NAACP officer, a story he tells in his 1962 book, *Negroes with Guns,* seems to have begun with that (ultimately blood-less) incident.

Although the rifle club he formed in his community had an NRA charter, there is as far as I'm aware no "Rob Williams Armed Citizen Award" offered by that organization, no essay con-test bearing his name sponsored in the public schools. Nor does Williams appear in the official narrative of the civil rights move-ment, where Negroes with guns are seldom permitted to upstage folk singers with guitars.

To talk about guns in America is inevitably to talk about race. Both sides of the so-called gun debate have strange fruit† in their family trees. The Second Amendment speaks of the importance of "a well regulated militia," and although framers like James Madison saw the local militia and the right "to keep and bear arms" as a check to the tyranny of standing armies, some histor-ians have noted that one probable function of a well regulated militia was to keep slaves in their place.

---

*Islamo-fascists: A controversial term for Islamic fundamentalists.

†Strange fruit: A reference to a poem about southern lynchings made popular by a musical version sung by Billie Holiday.

Likewise one of the regulatory questions of Colonial times was what, if any, access slaves ought to have to guns; what, if any, role free blacks ought to have in the militias. Neither slavery nor the militias lasted as long as that dilemma. When Robert Williams aimed his gun at a racist mob during a campaign to integrate a public swimming pool, an old white man burst into tears and cried, "What is this God damn country coming to that the niggers have got guns?" From the beginning, gun control in America has had much to do with that question.

With antecedents like these, one might suppose that adversaries in the ongoing gun debate would have a harder time maintaining their stridency. I happen not to suppose anything of the kind, but then, my suppositions in regard to the limits of human reasonableness are one reason I own a gun.

As with its sister issue abortion, the debate over guns amounts to a clash of absolutes: the right of bodily self-determination versus the right to be born, the right of self-defense versus the right to walk down the street without being shot. In both cases the debate is frequently conducted by pretending that the opponent's concerns hardly deserve mention and by an inevitable transference of opprobrium from the adversary's position to his or her cultural "type." I wonder, for instance, as I read the various pro- and

*John Brown (1800–59) captured by Marines at Harper's Ferry, 1859.*

anti-gun polemics, who the actual enemy is supposed to be: the marauding outlaws who might be deterred by an "armed citizen," or the execrable Clintons, who, according to an editorial in the *American Rifleman,* attacked the Second Amendment *every day.* Are we supposed to be more incensed by the shady dealer who sells guns to Murder Incorporated or by the straight-arrow collector who thinks Charlton Heston* could act? Issue-driven politics in red-and-blue America are like a man whose appetite for a steak is greatly enhanced by his contempt for vegetarians.

The gun issue is further complicated by a good deal of silliness, and in this it differs noticeably from the politics of the womb. Guns are either objects of superstition (they will just about *make* you commit suicide, according to some accounts) or pieces of pornographic paraphernalia, the things that get whipped out at the climax of a thousand socially smutty plots, on TV, in our heads, and then, insanely, in an actual event in which real people die. We all know what the Terminator said and the Taxi Driver said, but who recalls, much less ponders, what Thoreau said in his *Plea for Captain John Brown* (1853): "I speak for the slave when I say that I prefer the philanthropy of Captain John Brown to that philanthropy which neither shoots me nor liberates me.... I do not wish to kill nor to be killed, but I can foresee circumstances in which both these things would be by me unavoidable."

Unfortunately, a progressive, as someone with my politics has come to be called, does not like to ponder such mortal circumstances. Notice the telling grammatical shift by which the adjective "progressive" becomes a titular noun—comparable to a godly person who begins to speak of himself as a god. As the living embodiment of progress itself, a progressive is beyond rage, beyond "the politics of yesterday," and certainly beyond anything as retro as a gun. More than I fear fundamentalists who wish to teach religious myths in place of evolution I fear progressives who wish to teach evolution in place of political science. Or, rather, who forget a central principle of evolutionary thought: that no species completely outgrows its origins.

Like democracy, for example. What is that creature, if not the offspring of literacy and ballistics? Once a peasant can shoot down a knight, the writing is on the wall, including the writing that says, "We hold these truths to be self-evident." Self-evident because Sir Galahad doesn't appear to be moving. *Guns, Germs, and Steel* is a

---

*\*Charlton Heston:* The classic American film actor who later became president of the National Rifle Association.

good title for a book about European imperialism; *Guns, Fonts, and Ballots* would serve for a book about the rise of the European democratic state.

There are those who will insist, and many do, that what might have been true in the days of James Madison and Henry David Thoreau—and even in the days of Robert Williams—is no longer true in the days of neo-Nazis and Guantánamo Bay. But that questionable premise gives rise to an even more interesting question: If the Second Amendment is a dispensable anachronism in the era of school shootings, might not the First, Fourth, and Fifth amendments be dispensable anachronisms during a "war on terror"? Small wonder if some of those who readily make the first concession were equally ready to queue up behind the Republican right in ratifying the second.

Historians of weaponry tell us that one effect of the gun was to change the ideal of courage on the battlefield from a willingness to engage in hand-to-hand combat to an ability to stand firm under fire. At this point in our history, I'll take any form of courage I can get, but had Congress the smallest measure of the gunner's kind, the Patriot Act* might still be a doodle on Dick Cheney's cocktail napkin.

I grew up with guns and I live in a region where many people have them. They have guns because they hunt for meat, and they have guns for the same reason that many of them also have ponds dug close to their barns and houses. In a community with no fire hydrants, you want water for the fire engine. And in an area where a handful of state police and part-time sheriffs patrol a vast web of back roads spread across three counties, you might want the means to defend yourself. I own a fire extinguisher, a first-aid kit, and a shotgun. Not to own any of these would strike me as an affectation.

I hope that I shall never have to confront anyone with my gun, but owning a gun has forced me to confront myself. Anyone who owns firearms for reasons other than hunting and sport shooting (neither of which I do) has admitted that he or she is willing to kill another human being—as opposed to the more civilized course of allowing human beings to be killed by paid functionaries on his or her behalf. Owning a gun does not

---

*Patriot Act: A 2002 law that the Bush administration lobbied heavily for, and that many liberals accused of curtailing civil liberties.

enhance my sense of power; it enhances my sense of compromise and contingency—a feeling curiously like that of holding down a job. In other words, it is one more glaring proof that I am not Mahatma Gandhi or even Che Guevara, just another soft-bellied schlimazel trying to keep the lawn mowed and the psychopaths off the lawn.

If the authorities attempted to confiscate my gun in a house-to-house search, I believe I would offer resistance. What I would not offer is a justifying argument; the argument is implicit in the ramifications of a house-to-house search. But all of this is so much fantasy, another example of the disingenuousness that tends to color our discussion of guns. The Day When All the Guns Are Gathered Up—what the paranoids regard as the end of the world and the Pollyannas as the Rapture—it's never going to happen. There are nearly 1.4 million active troops in the US armed forces; there are an estimated 200 million guns in private hands. The war over the proper interpretation of the Second Amendment is effectively over. The most reasonable and decent thing that gun groups could do at this point is to declare victory and negotiate terms with the generosity that is so becoming in a victor. *Five-day waiting periods? Agreed, but our sense of honor compels us to insist on ten.* (Oh, to have been born in a time of so many guns and so little gallantry! Perhaps we ought not to have shot Sir Galahad after all.) *No assault rifles owned by civilians—also agreed, so long as no assault rifles are used on civilians.*

Of course, none of this is going to happen either. It would require a confidence that scarcely exists. One need only peruse the ads and articles in gun magazines to see the evidence of its rarity—to see that poignant, ironic, and insatiable obsession with overwhelming force. That cry of impotence. The *American Rifleman* I recall from my boyhood was closer to *Field & Stream* than to *Soldier of Fortune,* more like *Popular Mechanics* than *National Review.* My father and my uncles were do-it-yourself guys; their guns were just something else to lube. When I was a kid, I thought a liberal was a person who couldn't fix a car. But the cars aren't so easy to take apart anymore; the "check engine" light comes on and only the dealership has all the codes. As in Detroit, so in Washington: the engineering works the same. I am not the first to point out the sleight of hand that bedevils us: the illusion of power and choice perpetuated to disguise a diminishing sphere of action. A person dry-fires his Ruger in the same reverie of preparedness as another aims her cursor at her favorite blog. What precision, what access, what an array of options! Something's going to happen one of these days, and when it does, man, I'm going to be ready. In the meantime, just listen to that awesome sterile click.

Recreational purposes aside, the problem with guns is that their only conscionable private use is defensive. Even Robert Williams was insistent on this point. Hannah Arendt says as much when, in her book *On Violence,* she writes that "Rage and violence turn irrational only when they are directed against substitutes." Who are you likely to shoot in a modern uprising if not a substitute?

The other trouble with guns is their reductive effect on the question of violent versus nonviolent resistance. They predispose us to think of violence exclusively as gun violence. Arendt herself seems close to this assumption when she defines violence as the forceful use of "implements." Her definition makes sense to me only if the human body also counts as an implement.

In that regard it may be instructive to look at the political history of violent confrontations in America. None has been pretty; perhaps a few led to reform. But of the latter, not all or even many have involved guns. Shootouts always follow a predictable script. They are like bullfights: the matador may get gored but the bull always dies. Red flags wave and perhaps a white flag after that, but with a few exceptions, like Harpers Ferry and Matewan, one finds very little to salute.

The prospect changes when we consider certain mostly unarmed, often spontaneous engagements. They include the worst instances of mass behavior and, if not also the best, at least some of the most defining for their times. One thinks of the Boston Massacre, Haymarket Square, Kent State, Stonewall, Watts.* Some of the participants carried signs and some did not, but in retrospect they all seem to be massing under the same banner: "If you are so afraid of 'the mob' that you would deny us our place at the table, then we will remind you what a real mob looks like." Aeschylus put the Furies under the hill of the Areopagus; that is, under the taming influence of rational persuasion. Under the pretext of taming them further, overweening governments only manage to let them loose.

This is the lesson our leaders seem to have forgotten and that the more comfortable among us would just as soon forget: that

---

*Boston Massacre, Haymarket Square, Kent State, Stonewall, Watts:** All riots in which civilians and law enforcement clashed at various points in American history.

when the rules of participatory government are broken, the governed have a tendency, a right, and an obligation to become unruly.

Saul Alinsky* liked to say that a liberal is someone who leaves the room when an argument is about to turn into a fight. We are currently in need of a liberalism that goes back into the room and starts the fight. We are possibly in need of some civil unrest. This is not a conclusion I come to lightly. I have always believed in the superiority of nonviolent non-cooperation. The Hindu sage Sri Ramakrishna is supposed to have said that if a person could weep for a single day because he had not seen God, he would behold his heart's desire; I continue to believe that if the mass of Americans refused to earn or spend a dollar for a single day following a fishy election—no matter whose guy won—by the dawn's early light we would behold our country. But the likelihood of achieving that kind of solidarity brings us back to the subject of weeping.

The harvest is great but the laborers are few. Still, if asked to choose between an urban guerrilla armed with an AK-47 and a protester armed with a song sheet and a map showing how to get to the designated "free speech zone,"† I would decline on the grounds of insufficient faith and negligible inspiration. Rather, give me some people with very fanatical ideas about the sanctity of habeas corpus and the length of time an African American or any other American ought to have to wait on line to vote. Give me some people who are not so evolved that they have forgotten what it is to stand firm under fire or even to squat near the fire in a cave. Give me an accountant who can still throw a rock.

## Reflections and Responses

1. Although this essay is no doubt an entry into a political argument, it has a personal element as well. Keizer analyzes his own gun ownership and describes his life in Vermont, for instance, as an antidote to the inner-city setting in which liberals often place the gun debate. How does personalizing the argument make it

*Saul Alinsky: An American political activist known as the founder of local organizing.

†Free speech zone: Areas designated for protest, notably set up during political conventions.

more or less effective for you? In your opinion, should writers making a political case use the first person singular as often as Keizer?

2. Keizer offers, or quotes, several tongue-in-cheek definitions of a liberal: "a person who couldn't fix a car," for instance, or "someone who leaves the room when an argument turns into a fight." How does Keizer ultimately define liberalism in the essay? What is his ideal of liberalism, and what does he think the reality is? Do you agree with his definitions? How do they fit with the specific principles he believes liberals should be defending?

3. Characterize the prevailing tone of the essay. Is it collected and methodical overall? Or does it have a more forceful thrust? Identify points at which Keizer's tone becomes aggressive, angry, or even sardonic. How do these advance the essay? Why is it important to sound especially firm in an essay like this?

JAMAICA KINCAID

# On Seeing England
# for the First Time

*One of the most sinister sides of imperialism is the way it promotes the ruling nation's culture and rejects the colony's. The effect of this on an impressionable young person is vividly described in Jamaica Kincaid's sensitive and angry autobiographical essay about growing up in Antigua with the dark shadow of England continually looming over her. England and a reverence for things English invaded every aspect of her daily life and education. Yet it was not until adulthood that she finally journeyed to England and really saw it for the first time. "The space between the idea of something and its reality," Kincaid writes, "is always wide and deep and dark." The real England she finally sees is far different from the other England, whose maps and history she was made to memorize as a schoolgirl in Antigua.*

*Born in Antigua, Kincaid is the author of* At the Bottom of the River *(1983),* Annie John *(1985),* A Small Place *(1988),* Lucy *(1990),* The Autobiography of My Mother *(1996),* My Brother *(1997),* My Garden Book *(1999),* Mr. Potter: A Novel *(2002), and* Among Flowers: A Walk in the Himalaya *(2005). A staff writer for* The New Yorker, *Kincaid has had stories and essays published in* Rolling Stone, Paris Review, *and other literary periodicals. She was the editor of* The Best American Essays 1995, *a visiting professor of creative writing at Harvard University, and currently teaches at Claremont McKenna College in California. Her most recent book is a novel,* See Now Then *(2013). "On Seeing England for the First Time" originally appeared in* Transition *(1991) and was selected by Susan Sontag for* The Best American Essays 1992.

When I saw England for the first time, I was a child in school sitting at a desk. The England I was looking at was laid out on

a map gently, beautifully, delicately, a very special jewel; it lay
on a bed of sky blue—the background of the map—its yellow
form mysterious, because though it looked like a leg of mutton,
it could not really look like anything so familiar as a leg of
mutton because it was England—with shadings of pink and
green, unlike any shadings of pink and green I had seen before,
squiggly veins of red running in every direction. England was a
special jewel all right, and only special people got to wear it.
The people who got to wear England were English people.
They wore it well and they wore it everywhere: in jungles, in
deserts, on plains, on top of the highest mountains, on all the
oceans, on all the seas, in places where they were not welcome,
in places they should not have been. When my teacher had
pinned this map up on the blackboard, she said, "This is
England"—and she said it with authority, seriousness, and
adoration, and we all sat up. It was as if she had said, "This is
Jerusalem, the place you will go to when you die but only if you
have been good." We understood then—we were meant to
understand then—that England was to be our source of myth
and the source from which we got our sense of reality,
our sense of what was meaningful, our sense of what was
meaningless—and much about our own lives and much about
the very idea of us headed that last list.

At the time I was a child sitting at my desk seeing England for
the first time, I was already very familiar with the greatness of it.
Each morning before I left for school, I ate a breakfast of half
a grapefruit, an egg, bread and butter and a slice of cheese, and
a cup of cocoa; or half a grapefruit, a bowl of oat porridge,
bread and butter and a slice of cheese, and a cup of cocoa.
The can of cocoa was often left on the table in front of me.
It had written on it the name of the company, the year the
company was established, and the words "Made in England."
Those words, "Made in England," were written on the box the
oats came in too. They would also have been written on the box
the shoes I was wearing came in; a bolt of gray linen cloth lying
on the shelf of a store from which my mother had bought three
yards to make the uniform that I was wearing had written along
its edge those three words. The shoes I wore were made in
England; so were my socks and cotton undergarments and the
satin ribbons I wore tied at the end of two plaits of my hair.
My father, who might have sat next to me at breakfast, was a
carpenter and cabinet maker. The shoes he wore to work
would have been made in England, as were his khaki shirt and
trousers, his underpants and undershirt, his socks and brown
felt hat. Felt was not the proper material from which a hat

that was expected to provide shade from the hot sun should be made, but my father must have seen and admired a picture of an Englishman wearing such a hat in England, and this picture that he saw must have been so compelling that it caused him to wear the wrong hat for a hot climate most of his long life. And this hat—a brown felt hat—became so central to his character that it was the first thing he put on in the morning as he stepped out of bed and the last thing he took off before he stepped back into bed at night. As we sat at breakfast a car might go by. The car, a Hillman or a Zephyr, was made in England. The very idea of the meal itself, breakfast, and its substantial quality and quantity was an idea from England; we somehow knew that in England they began the day with this meal called breakfast and a proper breakfast was a big breakfast. No one I knew liked eating so much food so early in the day; it made us feel sleepy, tired. But this breakfast business was Made in England like almost everything else that surrounded us, the exceptions being the sea, the sky, and the air we breathed.

At the time I saw this map—seeing England for the first time—I did not say to myself, "Ah, so that's what it looks like," because there was no longing in me to put a shape to those three words that ran through every part of my life, no matter how small; for me to have had such a longing would have meant that I lived in a certain atmosphere, an atmosphere in which those three words were felt as a burden. But I did not live in such an atmosphere. My father's brown felt hat would develop a hole in its crown, the lining would separate from the hat itself, and six weeks before he thought that he could not be seen wearing it—he was a very vain man—he would order another hat from England. And my mother taught me to eat my food in the English way: the knife in the right hand, the fork in the left, my elbows held still close to my side, the food carefully balanced on my fork and then brought up to my mouth. When I had finally mastered it, I overheard her saying to a friend, "Did you see how nicely she can eat?" But I knew then that I enjoyed my food more when I ate it with my bare hands, and I continued to do so when she wasn't looking. And when my teacher showed us the map, she asked us to study it carefully, because no test we would ever take would be complete without this statement: "Draw a map of England."

I did not know then that the statement "Draw a map of England" was something far worse than a declaration of war, for in fact a flat-out declaration of war would have put me on alert, and again in fact, there was no need for war—I had long ago been conquered. I did not know then that this statement was part of a process that would result in my erasure, not my physical erasure, but my erasure all the same. I did not know then that this statement was meant to make me feel in awe and small whenever I heard the word "England": awe at its existence, small because I was not from it. I did not know very much of anything then—certainly not what a blessing it was that I was unable to draw a map of England correctly.

After that there were many times of seeing England for the first time. I saw England in history. I knew the names of all the kings of England. I knew the names of their children, their wives, their disappointments, their triumphs, the names of people who betrayed them, I knew the dates on which they were born and the dates they died. I knew their conquests and was made to feel glad if I figured in them; I knew their defeats. I knew the details of the year 1066 (the Battle of Hastings, the end of the reign of the Anglo-Saxon kings) before I knew the details of the year 1832 (the year slavery was abolished). It wasn't as bad as I make it sound now; it was worse. I did like so much hearing again and again how Alfred the Great, traveling in disguise, had been left to watch cakes, and because he wasn't used to this the cakes got burned, and Alfred burned his hands pulling them out of the fire, and the woman who had left him to watch the cakes screamed at him. I loved King Alfred. My grandfather was named after him; his son, my uncle, was named after King Alfred; my brother is named after King Alfred. And so there are three people in my family named after a man they have never met, a man who died over ten centuries ago. The first view I got of England then was not unlike the first view received by the person who named my grandfather.

This view, though—the naming of the kings, their deeds, their disappointments—was the vivid view, the forceful view. There were other views, subtler ones, softer, almost not there—but these were the ones that made the most lasting impression on me, these were the ones that made me really feel like nothing. "When morning touched the sky" was one phrase, for no morning touched the sky where I lived. The mornings where I lived came on abruptly, with a shock of heat and loud noises. "Evening approaches" was another, but the evenings where I lived did not approach; in fact, I had no evening—I had night and I had day and they came and went in a mechanical way: on, off; on, off. And then there were gentle mountains and low blue skies and moors over which people took walks for nothing but pleasure, when where I lived a walk was an act of labor, a burden, something only death or the automobile could relieve. And there were things that a small turn of a head could convey—entire worlds, whole lives would depend on this thing, a certain turn of a head. Everyday life could be quite tiring, more tiring than anything I was told not to do. I was told not to gossip, but they did that all the time. And they ate so much food, violating another of those rules they taught me: do not indulge in gluttony. And the foods they ate actually: if only sometime I could eat cold cuts after theater, cold cuts of lamb and mint sauce, and Yorkshire pudding and scones, and clotted cream, and sausages that came from upcountry (imagine, "up-country"). And having troubling thoughts at twilight, a good time to have troubling thoughts, apparently; and servants who stole and left in the middle of a crisis, who were born with a limp or some other kind of deformity, not nourished properly in their mother's womb (that last part I figured out for myself; the point was, oh to have an untrustworthy servant); and wonderful cobbled streets onto which solid front doors opened; and people whose eyes were blue and who had fair skins and who smelled only of lavender, or sometimes sweet pea or primrose. And those flowers with those names: delphiniums, foxgloves, tulips, daffodils, floribunda, peonies; in bloom, a striking display, being cut and placed in large glass bowls, crystal, decorating rooms so large twenty families the size of mine could fit in comfortably but used only for passing through. And the weather was so remarkable because the rain fell gently always, only occasionally in deep gusts, and it colored the air various shades of gray, each an appealing shade for a dress to be worn when a portrait was being painted; and when it rained at twilight, wonderful things happened: people bumped into each other unexpectedly and that would lead to all sorts of turns of events—a plot, the mere weather caused plots. I saw that people rushed: they rushed to catch trains, they rushed toward each other and away from each other; they rushed and rushed and rushed. That word: rushed! I did not know what it was to do that. It was too hot to do that, and so I came to envy people who would rush, even though it had no meaning to me to do such a thing. But there they are again. They loved their children; their children were sent to their own rooms as a punishment, rooms larger than my entire house. They were special, everything about them said so, even their clothes; their clothes rustled, swished, soothed. The world was theirs, not mine; everything told me so.

If now as I speak of all this I give the impression of someone on the outside looking in, nose pressed up against a glass window, that is wrong. My nose was pressed up against a glass window all right, but there was an iron vise at the back of my neck forcing my head to stay in place. To avert my gaze was to fall back into something from which I had been rescued, a hole filled with nothing, and that was the word for everything about me, nothing. The reality of my life was conquests, subjugation, humiliation, enforced amnesia. I was forced to forget. Just for instance, this: I lived in a part of St. John's, Antigua, called Ovals. Ovals was made up of five streets, each of them named after a famous English seaman—to be quite frank, an officially sanctioned criminal: Rodney Street (after George Rodney), Nelson Street (after Horatio Nelson), Drake Street (after Francis Drake), Hood Street, and Hawkins Street (after John Hawkins). But John Hawkins was knighted after a trip he made to Africa, opening up a new trade, the slave trade. He was then entitled to wear as his crest a Negro bound with a cord. Every single person living on Hawkins Street was descended from a slave. John Hawkins's ship, the one in which he transported the people he had bought and kidnapped, was called *The Jesus*. He later became the treasurer of the Royal Navy and rear admiral.

Again, the reality of my life, the life I led at the time I was being shown these views of England for the first time, for the second time, for the one-hundred-millionth time, was this: the sun shone with what sometimes seemed to be a deliberate cruelty; we must have done something to deserve that. My dresses did not rustle in the evening air as I strolled to the theater (I had no evening, I had no theater; my dresses were made of a cheap cotton, the weave of which would give way after not too many washings). I got up in the morning, I did my chores (fetched water from the public pipe for my mother, swept the yard), I washed myself, I went to a woman to have my hair combed freshly every day (because before we were allowed into our classroom our teachers would inspect us, and children who had not bathed that day, or had dirt under their fingernails, or whose hair had not been combed anew that day, might not be allowed to attend class). I ate that breakfast. I walked to school. At school we gathered in an auditorium and sang a hymn, "All Things Bright and Beautiful," and looking down on us as we sang were portraits of the Queen of England and her husband; they wore jewels and medals and they smiled. I was a Brownie. At each meeting we would form a little group around a flagpole, and after raising the Union Jack, we would say, "I promise to do my best, to do my duty to God and the Queen, to help other people every day and obey the scouts' law."

Who were these people and why had I never seen them, I mean really seen them, in the place where they lived? I had never been to England. No one I knew had ever been to England, or I should say, no one I knew had ever been and returned to tell me about it. All the people I knew who had gone to England had stayed there. Sometimes they left behind them their small children, never to see them again. England! I had seen England's representatives. I had seen the governor general at the public grounds at a ceremony celebrating the Queen's birthday. I had seen an old princess and I had seen a young princess. They had both been extremely not beautiful, but who of us would have told them that? I had never seen England, really seen it, I had only met a representative, seen a picture, read books, memorized its history. I had never set foot, my own foot, in it.

The space between the idea of something and its reality is always wide and deep and dark. The longer they are kept apart—idea of thing, reality of thing—the wider the width, the deeper the depth, the thicker and darker the darkness. This space starts out empty, there is nothing in it, but it rapidly becomes filled up with obsession or desire or hatred or love—sometimes all of these things, sometimes some of these things, sometimes only one of these things. The existence of the world as I came to know it was a result of this: idea of thing over here, reality of thing way, way over there. There was Christopher Columbus, an unlikable man, an unpleasant man, a liar (and so, of course, a thief) surrounded by maps and schemes and plans, and there was the reality on the other side of that width, that depth, that darkness. He became obsessed, he became filled with desire, the hatred came later, love was never a part of it. Eventually, his idea met the longed-for reality. That the idea of something and its reality are often two completely different things is something no one ever remembers; and so when they meet and find that they are not compatible, the weaker of the two, idea or reality, dies. That idea Christopher Columbus had was more powerful than the reality he met, and so the reality he met died.

And so finally, when I was a grown-up woman, the mother of two children, the wife of someone, a person who resides in a powerful country that takes up more than its fair share of a continent, the owner of a house with many rooms in it and of two automobiles, with the desire and will (which I very much act upon) to take from the world more than I give back to it, more than I deserve, more than I need, finally then, I saw England, the real England, not a picture, not a painting, not through a story in a book, but

England, for the first time. In me, the space between the idea of it
and its reality had become filled with hatred, and so when at last
I saw it I wanted to take it into my hands and tear it into little pieces
and then crumble it up as if it were clay, child's clay. That was
impossible, and so I could only indulge in not-favorable opinions.

There were monuments everywhere; they commemorated victo-
ries, battles fought between them and the people who lived across
the sea from them, all vile people, fought over which of them
would have dominion over the people who looked like me. The
monuments were useless to them now, people sat on them and
ate their lunch. They were like markers on an old useless trail,
like a piece of old string tied to a finger to jog the memory, like
old decoration in an old house, dirty, useless, in the way. Their
skins were so pale, it made them look so fragile, so weak, so ugly.
What if I had the power to simply banish them from their land,
send boat after boatload of them on a voyage that in fact had no
destination, force them to live in a place where the sun's presence
was a constant? This would rid them of their pale complexion and
make them look more like me, make them look more like the people I love and treasure and hold dear, and more like the people
who occupy the near and far reaches of my imagination, my history,
my geography, and reduce them and everything they have ever
known to figurines as evidence that I was in divine favor, what if
all this was in my power? Could I resist it? No one ever has.

And they were rude, they were rude to each other. They didn't
like each other very much. They didn't like each other in the way
they didn't like me, and it occurred to me that their dislike for me
was one of the few things they agreed on.

I was on a train in England with a friend, an English woman.
Before we were in England she liked me very much. In England
she didn't like me at all. She didn't like the claim I said I had on
England, she didn't like the views I had of England. I didn't like
England, she didn't like England, but she didn't like me not liking
it too. She said, "I want to show you my England, I want to show
you the England that I know and love." I had told her many times
before that I knew England and I didn't want to love it anyway.
She no longer lived in England; it was her own country, but it
had not been kind to her, so she left. On the train, the conductor
was rude to her; she asked something, and he responded in a rude
way. She became ashamed. She was ashamed at the way he treated
her; she was ashamed at the way he behaved. "This is the new
England," she said. But I liked the conductor being rude; his behavior seemed quite appropriate. Earlier this had happened: we had

gone to a store to buy a shirt for my husband; it was meant to be a special present, a special shirt to wear on special occasions. This was a store where the Prince of Wales has his shirts made, but the shirts sold in this store are beautiful all the same. I found a shirt I thought my husband would like and I wanted to buy him a tie to go with it. When I couldn't decide which one to choose, the salesman showed me a new set. He was very pleased with these, he said, because they bore the crest of the Prince of Wales, and the Prince of Wales had never allowed his crest to decorate an article of clothing before. There was something in the way he said it; his tone was slavish, reverential, awed. It made me feel angry; I wanted to hit him. I didn't do that. I said, my husband and I hate princes, my husband would never wear anything that had a prince's anything on it. My friend stiffened. The salesman stiffened. They both drew themselves in, away from me. My friend told me that the prince was a symbol of her Englishness, and I could see that I had caused offense. I looked at her. She was an English person, the sort of English person I used to know at home, the sort who was nobody in England but somebody when they came to live among the people like me. There were many people I could have seen England with; that I was seeing it with this particular person, a person who reminded me of the people who showed me England long ago as I sat in church or at my desk, made me feel silent and afraid, for I wondered if, all these years of our friendship, I had had a friend or had been in the thrall of a racial memory.

I went to Bath—we, my friend and I, did this, but though we were together, I was no longer with her. The landscape was almost as familiar as my own hand, but I had never been in this place before, so how could that be again? And the streets of Bath were familiar, too, but I had never walked on them before. It was all those years of reading, starting with Roman Britain. Why did I have to know about Roman Britain? It was of no real use to me, a person living on a hot, drought-ridden island, and it is of no use to me now, and yet my head is filled with this nonsense, Roman Britain. In Bath, I drank tea in a room I had read about in a novel written in the eighteenth century. In this very same room, young women wearing those dresses that rustled and so on danced and flirted and sometimes disgraced themselves with young men, soldiers, sailors, who were on their way to Bristol or someplace like that, so many places like that where so many adventures, the outcome of which was not good for me, began. Bristol, England. A sentence that began "That night the ship sailed from Bristol, England" would end not so good for me. And then I was driving through the countryside in an English motorcar, on narrow winding roads, and they were so familiar, though I had never been on them before; and through little villages the names of which I somehow knew so well though I had never been there before. And the countryside did have all those hedges and hedges, fields hedged in. I was marveling at all the toil of it, the planting of the hedges to begin with and then the care of it, all that clipping, year after year of clipping, and I wondered at the lives of the people who would have to do this, because wherever I see and feel the hands that hold up the world, I see and feel myself and all the people who look like me. And I said, "Those hedges" and my friend said that someone, a woman named Mrs. Rothchild, worried that the hedges weren't being taken care of properly; the farmers couldn't afford or find the help to keep up the hedges, and often they replaced them with wire fencing. I might have said to that, well if Mrs. Rothchild doesn't like the wire fencing, why doesn't she take care of the hedges herself, but I didn't. And then in those fields that were now hemmed in by wire fencing that a privileged woman didn't like was planted a vile yellow flowering bush that produced an oil, and my friend said that Mrs. Rothchild didn't like this either; it ruined the English countryside, it ruined the traditional look of the English countryside.

It was not at that moment that I wished every sentence, everything I knew, that began with England would end with "and then it all died; we don't know how, it just all died." At that moment, I was thinking, who are these people who forced me to think of them all the time, who forced me to think that the world I knew was incomplete, or without substance, or did not measure up because it was not England; that I was incomplete, or without substance, and did not measure up because I was not English. Who were these people? The person sitting next to me couldn't give me a clue; no one person could. In any case, if I had said to her, I find England ugly, I hate England; the weather is like a jail sentence, the English are a very ugly people, the food in England is like a jail sentence, the hair of English people is so straight, so dead looking, the English have an unbearable smell so different from the smell of people I know, real people of course, she would have said that I was a person full of prejudice. Apart from the fact that it is I—that is, the people who look like me—who made her aware of the unpleasantness of such a thing, the idea of such a thing, prejudice, she would have been only partly right, sort of right: I may be capable of prejudice, but my prejudices have no weight to them, my prejudices have no force behind them, my prejudices remain opinions, my prejudices remain my personal opinion. And a great feeling of rage and disappointment came over me as I looked at England, my head full of personal opinions that could not have public, my public, approval. The people I come from are powerless to do evil on a grand scale.

The moment I wished every sentence, everything I knew, that began with England would end with "and then it all died, we don't know how, it just all died" was when I saw the white cliffs of Dover. I had sung hymns and recited poems that were about a longing to see the white cliffs of Dover again. At the time I sang the hymns and recited the poems, I could really long to see them again because I had never seen them at all, nor had anyone around me at the time. But there we were, groups of people longing for something we had never seen. And so there they were, the white cliffs, but they were not that pearly majestic thing I used to sing about, that thing that created such a feeling in these people that when they died in the place where I lived they had themselves buried facing a direction that would allow them to see the white cliffs of Dover when they were resurrected, as surely they would be. The white cliffs of Dover, when finally I saw them, were cliffs, but they were not white; you would only call them that if the word "white" meant something special to you; they were dirty and they were steep; they were so steep, the correct height from which all my views of England, starting with the map before me in my classroom and ending with the trip I had just taken, should jump and die and disappear forever.

## Reflections and Responses

1. Note that Kincaid opens her essay with various images of England. What do these images have in common? How do they reflect colonialism? How do they reflect literature? Why do you think Kincaid begins by placing the images in the context of a classroom?

2. Consider Kincaid's account of her father's hat. In what ways does the "brown felt hat" represent England? How does Kincaid view the hat?

3. When Kincaid finally visits England, what aspects of the country does she dislike the most? What does she mean when she says toward the end of her essay, "I may be capable of prejudice, but my prejudices have no weight to them"? Do you find her opinions prejudiced? In your opinion, has she or has she not "prejudged" England?

MICHAEL LEWIS

# The Mansion: A Subprime Parable

"A man is rich," Henry David Thoreau wrote in Walden, "in proportion to the number of things which he can afford to let alone." Thoreau attempted to reject the material comforts of the world and live as austerely as possible in the woods near his hometown of Concord, Massachusetts. In today's world, in which wealth is exhibited in conspicuous ostentation and often comes at the price of massive debt, journalist Michael Lewis attempts the reverse experiment: He moves into a house he cannot afford. In the context of the housing collapse of 2008, which cost millions of Americans their homes, Lewis wonders if our obsession with big houses has led us into financial ruin. Of the crisis he writes: "The money-lending business didn't create the American desire for unaffordable housing. It simply facilitated it." Moreover, though, he discovers the effects that living in an outsize house has on him and his family; like one of the house's previous tenants, Lewis finds that he was never in control of the mansion—in fact, that "the mansion owned him."

  Michael Lewis initially went to work as a bond trader in London, an experience he documented in his first book, Liar's Poker (1989). He has since written extensively for a wide range of publications on subjects including politics, finance, and baseball. His books include Trail Fever (1997), The New New Thing (2000), Next: The Future Just Happened (2001), Coach: Lessons on the Game of Life (2005), and Panic: The Story of Modern Financial Insanity (2008). Two of his nonfiction books were turned into highly successful movies on American sports: Moneyball (2003) and The Blind Side (2006). Recent books include The Big Short: Inside the Doomsday Machine (2010) and Boomerang: Travels in the New Third World (2011). After the stint in New Orleans described in "The Mansion," Lewis moved back to California *with his wife, former MTV VJ Tabitha Soren, and their children. "The Mansion: A Subprime Parable" originally appeared in* Portfolio *and was selected by Mary Oliver for* The Best American Essays 2009.

I was looking to return to New Orleans, where I'd grown up, to write a book. The move would uproot my wife and three children from California, and I felt a little bad about that. They needed a place to live, but places to live in New Orleans are hard to find. Ever since Hurricane Katrina, the real estate market there has been in turmoil. Owners want to sell, buyers want to rent, and the result is a forest of for sale signs and an army of workers commuting from great distances.

At the bottom of every real estate ad I saw was the name of the same agent. One woman ruled the market, it seemed, and her name was Eleanor Farnsworth. I called her and threw myself on her mercy. She thought my problem over and then said, "I only know of one place that would work for you." She'd suggested it to Brad Pitt and Angelina Jolie, she said, before selling them their more modest place in the French Quarter.

That shouldn't have been a selling point; it should have been a warning. I should have asked the price. Instead, I asked the address.

As soon as I saw it, I knew it—the mansion. The most conspicuously grand house in New Orleans. As a child, I'd ridden my bike past it 2,000 times and always felt a tiny bit unnerved. It wasn't just a mansion; it seemed like the biggest mansion on the street with all the mansions, St. Charles Avenue, an object of fascination for the tourists on the clanging streetcars. But it was hard to imagine a human being standing beside it, much less living inside it, and as far as I could tell, none ever did. There was never any sign of life around it; it was just this awesome, silent pile of pale stone. The Frick Museum,* but closed.

Inside, it was even more awesome than outside. It was as if the architect had set out to show just how much space he could persuade a rich man to waste. The entryway was a kind of ballroom, which gave way to a curved staircase, a replica of one in the Palace of Versailles.† The living room wasn't a kind of ballroom; it *was* a ballroom, with $80,000 worth of gold on the ceiling. The bedrooms were the size of giant living rooms. The changing rooms

---

*The Frick Museum: A museum in Manhattan, located in the former residence of steel magnate Henry Clay Frick.

†Palace of Versailles: Louis XIV's splendidly opulent palace outside of Paris.

*Hisham Ibrahim/Photographer's Choice/Getty Images*

*An example of the type of oversize house (pejoratively referred to as a McMansion) that many Americans have desired since the 1980s*

and closets and bathrooms were the size of bedrooms. There were two of everything that the rest of the world has one of: two dining rooms, two full kitchens, two half kitchens. Ten bathrooms and seven bedrooms.

I didn't ask the price—I was renting—so I didn't know that the last time it changed hands it had sold for close to $7 million, and was now valued at $10 million. I imagined how it would feel to live in such a place. What it wouldn't feel like, clearly, was anything close to being in the other houses in which I'd lived.

Upper middle class: That's how I've always thought of myself. Upper middle class is the class into which I was born, the class to which I was always told I belonged, and the class with which, until this moment, I'd never had a problem. Upper middle class is a sneaky designation, however. It's a way of saying "I'm well-off" without having to say "I'm rich," even if, by most standards, you are. Upper-middle-classness has allowed me to feel like I'm not only competing in the same financial league as most Americans—I'm winning! Playing in the middle class, I have enjoyed huge success.

In this house, I now glimpsed the problem with upper-middle-classness: It isn't really a class. It's a space between classes. The space may once have been bridgeable, but lately it's become a chasm. Middle-class people fantasize about travel upgrades; upper-class people can't imagine life without a jet. Middle-class people help their children with their homework so they'll have a chance of getting into Princeton; upper-class people buy Princeton a new building. Middle-class people have homes; upper-class people have monuments. A man struggling to hold on to the illusion that he is upper middle class has become like a character in a cartoon earthquake: He looks down and sees his feet being dragged ever farther apart by a quickly widening fissure. His legs stretch, then splay, and finally he plunges into the abyss.

This house, and everything it represents, stands on the more appealing side of the chasm. "It's perfect," I said.

Every few days, I googled the house and stared at it. Then a funny thing happened: It began to shrink. Sure it's big, I told myself, but houses come bigger. The White House, for instance. I told my wife and children only that I'd found a house with a swimming pool and enough bathrooms for everyone to have his or her own. Which is to say, they really had no idea what they were getting into. How could they? It didn't occur to them that not only would they have their own bathrooms, they'd need to decide before dinner which of the two dining rooms to eat in—and afterward, which of the three dishwashers to not put their dishes in. To believe it, and to grasp its full upper-class implications, they'd need to see it.

On the day we move in, we're all stuffed together, Beverly Hillbillies-style, in a rented, dirty, gold Hyundai Sonata. For fun, as I drive up and down St. Charles Avenue, I ask them to guess which of these improbably large houses is ours.

"That one?"

"No."

"That one!"

The exercise turns giddy. Each house is bigger than the last. The girls squeal in the backseat and press their noses against the windows, while their mother, in the front, does her best to remain calm. We pass in front of the mansion and they look right past it.

The thing takes up an entire city block, and somehow they can't see it. It's too implausible. It's not a home. It's a mint.

We circle around the block and approach from the rear, the Sonata rolling up the long driveway and coming to a stop beneath the grand stone porte cochere. "This is our new house?" asks Quinn, age eight.

"This is our new house," I say.

She begins to hyperventilate.

"Omigodomigodomigod!"

My small children plunge from the rental car into the driveway. They leap up and down as if they've just won an N.B.A. championship. By the time we get inside, they're gasping. They sprint off to inspect their new home.

"There's another floor!"

"Daddy! There's an elevator!"

My children love me. They have a house with an elevator.

In all the public finger-pointing about the American real estate bust, surprisingly little attention has been paid to its origin. There's obviously a long list of people and ideas that can share in the blame: ratings agencies, mortgage brokers, big Wall Street firms, small Wall Street firms, Angelo Mozilo, Alan Greenspan. Every few weeks, the *New York Times* runs a piece exposing some new way in which a big Wall Street firm has exploited some poor or middle-class family. The rich people on Wall Street blame their bosses. The brokers at Merrill Lynch blame Stan O'Neal; the traders at Bear Stearns blame Jimmy Cayne. Everyone blames Countrywide. But all of this misses the point: However terrible the sins of the financial markets, they're merely a reflection of a cultural predisposition. To blame the people who lent the money for the real estate boom is like blaming the crack dealers for creating addicts.

Americans feel a deep urge to live in houses that are bigger than they can afford. This desire cuts so cleanly through the population that it touches just about everyone. It's the acceptable lust.

Consider, for example, the Garcias. On May 30, the *New York Times* ran a story about a couple, Lilia and Jesus Garcia, who were behind on their mortgage payments and in danger of losing their homes. The Garcias had a perfectly nice house near Stockton, California, that they bought in 2003 for 160 grand. Given their joint income of $65,000, they could afford to borrow about $160,000 against a home. But then, in 2006, they stumbled upon their dream house. The new property was in Linden, California, and, judging from its picture, had distinctly mansionlike qualities. Its price, $535,000, was a stretch.

Then, of course, the market turned. The Garcias failed to make their mortgage payments and couldn't sell their original house. They owed the bank about $700,000 and were facing eviction. The mistake supposedly illustrated by the Garcias' predicament was that they held on to their former home in Stockton as an investment. The moral: Americans are in their current bind because too many of them saw houses as moneymaking opportunities.

But the real moral is that when a middle-class couple buys a house they can't afford, defaults on their mortgage, and then sits down to explain it to a reporter from the *New York Times,* they can be confident that he will overlook the reason for their financial distress: the peculiar willingness of Americans to risk it all for a house above their station. People who buy something they cannot afford usually hear a little voice warning them away or prodding them to feel guilty. But when the item in question is a house, all the signals in American life conspire to drown out the little voice. The tax code tells people like the Garcias that while their interest payments are now gargantuan relative to their income, they're deductible. Their friends tell them how impressed they are—and they mean it. Their family tells them that while theirs is indeed a big house, they have worked hard, and Americans who work hard deserve to own a dream house. Their kids love them for it.

Across America, some version of this drama has become a social norm. As of this spring, one in 11 mortgages was either past due—like Ed McMahon's* $4.8 million jumbo loan on his property—or in foreclosure, like Evander Holyfield's† $10 million Georgia estate. It's no good pretending that Americans didn't know they couldn't afford such properties, or that they were seduced into believing they could afford them by mendacious mortgage brokers or Wall Street traders. If they hadn't lusted after the bigger house, they never would have met the mortgage brokers in the first place. The money-lending business didn't create the American desire for unaffordable housing. It simply facilitated it.

It's this desire we must understand. More than any other possession, houses are what people use to say, "Look how well I'm

---

*Ed McMahon:** For years, Johnnie Carson's sidekick on NBC's *The Tonight Show.*

†Evander Holyfield:** A former heavyweight boxing champion.

doing!" Given the financial anxieties and indignities suffered by the American middle class, it's hardly surprising that a lower-middle-class child who grows up in a small house feels a burning need to acquire a bigger one. The wonder is how an upper-middle-class child who grew up in a big and perfectly enviable house is inexorably drawn to a mansion.

When you move into a house you cannot afford, the first thing you notice is everything that you suddenly need—things that, before you arrived, you didn't even want. The dressing room was a microcosm of our mansion's ability to instruct. It wasn't a closet, but a room as big as the master bedroom we'd left behind in California. Even after my wife had stored her countless pairs of shoes, there was more than enough space for all of my stuff. Three weeks later, I noticed a door near the master-bedroom suite that I hadn't seen before; it was like a magical door that someone had carved into the wall while I slept. What could it be? I opened it to find ... another huge dressing room! Inside, I could have fit every stitch of clothing I owned, three times over. It seemed weird to just leave it empty, but I didn't have anything left to put in it, so I closed the door and pretended the room wasn't there. But the thought occurred: Maybe I need more clothes.

The pool was another example. Because we moved in during the winter, we didn't pay that much attention to it at first. Had we bothered to dip our fingers in, we'd have discovered that it was not merely heated but was saltwater. It was a full six weeks before we really even noticed the pool house. Full bathroom, full kitchen, shiny new Viking range, and a fridge stuffed with 24 bottles of champagne. For a few weeks I felt that all of this was excessive. Then one day I became aware of the inconvenience of having to walk, dripping wet, from the pool back into the main house. This is what you need a pool house for—so you can make the transition from water to dry land without the trouble of walking the whole 15 yards back into the house and climbing a long flight of stairs to the giant dressing room. From that moment on, it seemed to me terribly inconvenient to not have a pool house. How on earth did people with pools, but no special house adjacent to them, cope?

The problems posed by the mansion were different from the problems posed by most other houses. How to locate loved ones, for instance. There's been no room inside any home I'd ever lived in from which, if I yelled at the top of my lungs, I couldn't be heard in every other room. The mansion required a new approach to human communications. Standing inside the mansion and screaming at the top of your lungs, you knew for certain that your voice wasn't reaching at least half the house. If you wanted to find someone, you could run around the house, but that took ages and presupposed that the other person was not similarly wandering in the void. A trek up the Himalayan staircases quickly became the subject of an elaborate cost-benefit analysis. How badly do I really want to find my six-year-old daughter? How much does my one-year-old son's diaper really need to be changed? After a while, it seemed only natural to my wife to begin with the assumption that her husband could not be found. Even when she knew for a fact that I was somewhere in the house, she'd begin her search with a phone call. She'd call my cell when I was two flights up and she'd call my cell when I was a room away. One afternoon she called my cell 20 minutes after I had come home with our three children and had gone looking for her to take them off my hands.

"Where are you?" she asked.

"I'm in the house taking care of the kids," I said, a little indignantly.

"Well, you can't be watching them very closely," she said, "because I'm in the house taking care of the kids."

Even though you couldn't find anybody, all sorts of people could find you. People stumbled into other people's spaces and terrified them. The house was so vast that the sound waves that normally precede the arrival of a living creature got lost. And so while there was, in theory, a great deal of privacy, there was, in practice, none. The mansion came with a gardener, a pool man, a caretaker, and a housekeeper. Any one of these people might turn up anyplace, anytime. The housekeeper, a sweet woman, came twice a week. She developed a habit of turning up over my right shoulder without warning and, as I stared helplessly at my computer screen, booming, "How's that book of yours coming along??!!!"

"Ah!" I'd yell, and leap out of my chair.

"Always writing, writing, writing!" she'd say with a laugh. (Writing in the mansion never ceased to be inherently comical.)

Money was another problem. It was suddenly going out faster than it was coming in. When I'd finally gotten around to asking the real estate agent what the mansion cost to rent, she'd said— in the most offhand tone, as if it were the least important thing about the house—"I'll have to see, but I think it's around 13."

Thirteen. The extra digits are just assumed. One reason is that no one can bring themselves to actually utter the sentence: "Your rent will be $13,000 a month."

Thirteen thousand dollars a month is not the rent I was raised to pay. When I let it slip to my mother what I'd be paying, she just said, "Oh, Michael," in exactly the same tone she'd have used if I'd informed her that I'd just run over the neighbor with a truck or been diagnosed with pancreatic cancer. Thirteen thousand dollars a month might be a record rent in New Orleans, but it was really just the ante.

We'd been there only three weeks when the first bills arrived. Utilities were $2,700. That turned out not to include water, which was another $1,000. Think of it: $1,000 a month for water you don't drink. (The drinking water came in truckloads from a spring-water company.) How did we use so much water? you might reasonably ask. The answer is, we didn't. The mansion did. The pool, the fountains, the sprinklers that came on in the wee hours to keep the great lawn lush and green—all were suddenly necessary. So, it turned out, was cable, at $800 a month. Who was I to argue? I wasn't even entirely sure how many televisions we had. Nine, at least. I thought I'd found the last of them when, two months after we'd arrived, I opened a cabinet and found another.

Walking into the mansion after school one day, my younger daughter, Dixie, asked, "Daddy, what's a Daddy Warbucks?" She'd caught a ride with a new friend's babysitter, who didn't know where we lived. Instead of giving the babysitter directions, the friend's mother had just said, "They live in the Daddy Warbucks house."

The first request for money came exactly 11 days after we arrived. A former schoolmate was calling on behalf of our high school; its fundraising department had somehow learned that I'd not only moved back to town but had moved into the mansion. My old school friend had a number in mind, somewhere between $25,000 and $100,000. Two days later, we had another old friend to dinner and—in hopes that she'd spread the word—I spoke of my amazement that anyone thought we could fork over 100 grand on a whim. "It's funny you should say that," she said. She'd just spoken with the director of a New Orleans museum, who had also heard we'd moved into the mansion. "He's trying to figure out the best way to approach you," she said.

We'd become an engineering problem.

Late one night the doorbell rings. There on our great stone porch is a man, obviously down on his luck, doing his best to appear subservient.

"I was just wondering if you have anything," he asks.

"Have anything?" I ask back.

"Some work that might be done, you know."

It's a feudal exchange right out of the 11th century. Vassal calling on lord with the mutual understanding that lord owes vassal employment. The only thing missing is the offer of a freshly slaughtered rabbit.

A couple of months into our stay, we all sit in the formal dining room, under the gilded ceiling and the crystal chandelier, eating packaged tortellini off paper plates. We are Cuban peasants in late 1959 who have just moved into a Havana mansion on the heels of the rich owner, who has fled in terror from the revolution. Dixie, then five, blurts out, "I hate it when people say, 'Oh, I love your house,' because then I have to say, 'It's not my house.'" To which Quinn adds, "Yeah, I hate it when people say, 'You must be rich.'"

This was new. My children had taken to their new splendor like ducks to water. They'd see the St. Charles streetcar rolling past, and the tourists gawking and pointing at their new house, and their first reaction was not to cringe but to perform. They'd throw on their most princesslike dresses and run out front and dance around the malfunctioning marble fountain, pissing water in all the wrong directions, and wave to the commoners. One morning, as Quinn descended the staircases, overdressed for school, she announced, "I need to look good. I'm the girl who lives in the mansion."

But after a few months, the charm of pretending to be something they know they are not is wearing off.

There's a moment in the life of every American child when it dawns on him or her that the divvying up of material spoils is neither arbitrary nor a matter of personal choice, that money is a tool used by grownups to order and rank themselves, and that the easiest way to establish those rankings is through their houses. At first, everyone's house appears more or less the same; at any rate, you don't spend much time dwelling on the differences. But then, one day, someone's house is either so much humbler or so much grander than anything you've ever seen that you realize: A house is not just a house. It's one of the tools people use to rank me.

Children are basically communists. Seeing other children's material prosperity, they follow their first instinct, which isn't to understand it or stew about it. It's to ask for some of it—to get invited to the mansion. As far as I knew, my children had never given much thought to what their house said about them and their place in the world. They'd been friends with rich kids and poor kids, without dwelling on the differences. That had just changed.

I resist the urge to explain how their misery might be good training for grown-up American life; how we are, quite obviously, a nation of financial imposters, poised to seize the first opportunity to live in houses we cannot afford; and how, if they want to fit in, they'll need to learn to handle the stress. They will have to learn these important lessons for themselves.

Instead, I turn my attention to survival. The mansion was not satisfied with making us uneasy. It wanted us out. It preferred us to leave quietly, without a fuss. But if we didn't, it was prepared to get violent.

The first inkling of this came one lazy Sunday afternoon. I was fathering my one-year-old son by teaching him how best to watch an N.B.A. game—which is to say, in high-def with surround sound. Our bliss was disrupted by the cry of a small child. It was muted, as if someone were calling out from inside the walls. It was from inside the walls. Our girls, with their 10-year-old cousin, were trapped inside the elevator, which had mysteriously jolted to a stop. I tried to yank the metal gate off its hinges to get into the shaft, but failed. It wouldn't have mattered anyway, as they were between floors. For a good 20 minutes, I grunted and groaned and sweated and pretended that this wasn't anything I couldn't handle. Then I called the caretaker, who gave me the number of the man who had made the elevator work in the first place. By some miracle, he was around and willing to drive the 20 miles from his home to ours on a Sunday. Two hours later, the girls, sobbing melodramatically, were sprung. The elevator man turned to me and said, "I'm surprised you let them in there."

"Why?"

"She didn't tell you about the cat?"

No one told me about the cat that had been riding up in the elevator with its billionaire owner. As they ascended, the cat had jumped out of the owner's arms and stuck its head out of the metal gate. Its head had been chopped off.

I shut down the elevator.

A few days later, the phone rang. "We want to let you know that we received a message from the equipment-supervision device on your control panel," said the voice on the other end of the line. The what on the what? The mansion, I learned, was equipped with tiny cameras that enabled it, in effect, to watch its inhabitants. One of these, apparently, had malfunctioned. I went into the basement, found the video-control panel, and yanked out as many plugs as I could find.

The next afternoon, the house felt chilly. I hunted down the many thermostats and turned them back up, from the 68 degrees to which they'd somehow plummeted, to 72. The house ignored the request; no matter what I did, it remained at exactly 68 degrees. My skin became the world's most sensitive thermometer, an expert on the state of being 69 degrees, because the moment the house would reach that temperature, all hell would break loose—one, then another, and then a third of the massive air-conditioning units that sat outside would begin to purr. Every now and again, I'd feel a brief tingle of warmth, a premonition of climate change, but that moment was always followed by the roar of engines and a correction.

The day after I tried to change the mansion's temperature, early in the morning, the alarm went off. Then the phone rang: It was the alarm company, wanting to know our password. I gave it to them.

"I'm sorry, we don't have that as a password," said the lady on the other end of the phone, and then, as I begged and pleaded ("No, please, no! Let me try again!"), she quickly hung up.

Moments later, two squad cars with lights flashing sped into our driveway. Four police officers leapt out and banged on the front door. The mansion had phoned the cops at exactly the moment I appeared most shockingly arrestable: wearing only underpants and a T-shirt, hair sticking up in six different directions, and without a trace of evidence that I belonged there. I grabbed Dixie ("Daddy, I don't want to go! What if they arrest me too?") and pulled her close to me, as a kind of human shield.

"Sir, we're responding to an alarm signal."

"It was obviously a mistake. Sorry to trouble you."

Silence.

"We're just renting the place."

The police drove away, more slowly than they'd arrived. But obviously they weren't the problem. The house had a mind of its own, like one of those old horses you find at dude ranches. You begin with the assumption that you are in control of the beast.

Then you try to guide it as much as two feet off the assigned path, and it resists and takes control of the steering. You are left feeling ashamed of whatever cowboy pretense you had to begin with.

I investigated the history of our property. It was built in 1912 by an entrepreneur named E.V. Benjamin, whose son, raised in the mansion, became eccentric enough for a small group of interested residents of New Orleans to create a gathering called the Benjamin Club, whose sole purpose was to swap stories about him. The house then moved into the hands of another very rich man, J. Edgar Monroe, who had made the bulk of his fortune from taking over the Canal Bank. When the bank was closed by the federal government during the Great Depression, he had himself appointed the bank's liquidator, repaid its shareholders, and then bought up a huge chunk of the leftover shares for pennies.

Monroe went on to buy not only this house but also Rosecliffe, the Newport mansion used in the filming of *The Great Gatsby*. He was famous for telling anyone who would listen how much money he had given away to charity. After he donated a music building to Loyola University New Orleans, he insisted that the school mount a plaque on one of its walls with an inscription he wrote:

J. Edgar Monroe has donated to construction of this building $1,000,000.00 (one million) in cash. my secretary has strongly urged me to make a plaque of this donation so that the students of the music school and the public will know of this gift. father carter, president of loyola university, acknowledged receipt of four $250,000.00 checks, or $1,000,000.00. mr. monroe has given over one hundred million dollars ($100,000,000.00) to organized charity of which the largest share was given to loyola university.

When Monroe's wife, Louise, died in 1989, the old man wrote her obituary. It opened with a paragraph or two about the deceased, but then quickly moved on to detail her husband's incredible generosity. "Mr. Monroe is still living and is 92 years of age," he wrote. "He has been very generous and has given over one hundred million dollars to organized charity ..." and so on. He too died in the house a few years later.

Until the mid-1990s, the house had been owned by men who could comfortably afford it. They didn't need the house to prove how rich they were; everyone knew how rich they were. The moment the house became troubled was the moment someone who couldn't afford it moved in—a man who was using it to slake his own thirst for status. He was a lawyer.

Lawyers are upper middle class. But this lawyer grabbed the saddle horn of magnificence and hung on for dear life—until the day in 2004 when he was bucked off. There in the dust he lay, exposed—in the New Orleans *Times-Picayune*—for defrauding his law partners. His firm defended big companies from class-action suits. To make the kind of money he needed to live in this house, the poor guy had resorted to allegedly cutting secret deals with plaintiffs' lawyers. He reportedly gave up his law license to avoid being formally charged.

The mansion made him do it: That's what I thought when I heard the story. As sordid as his behavior was, I'm incapable of feeling toward him anything but sympathy. He wanted this mansion, he bought this mansion, and then he discovered that the mansion owned him.

The next owner was a woman. She'd grown up middle class in New Orleans, and in her youth had driven past the mansion and fantasized about owning it. Then she'd married an oil-and-gas billionaire who gave her the house as a surprise for her birthday.

The billionaire's wife proceeded to spare no expense in redoing it exactly as she wanted. She spent $250,000 on gold to touch up the gilt fringe of the moldings and the ceiling medallions. I spoke with the interior decorator she hired. It was this man who grasped the inappropriateness of a mere lawyer owning this house. "They tried to shrink it," he said to me one day. "They painted the walls taupe; they had canopies over the beds to make a room within the room. They tried to make it homey." The billionaire's wife succeeded in undoing that. The taupe returned to white, the canopies fell, and the gilding on the ceiling soon gleamed like new. Several million dollars later, she had the mansion looking as she wanted it to look, which was more or less like Versailles. Luckily for her, birthday presents are not community property, because by the time she was finished touching up the house, her husband was divesting himself of her. No matter what the settlement came to, the property belonged to her outright. But she was not happy.

And neither was her mansion. When we moved in, she'd been trying to sell it for the $10 million or so she had put into it. Characteristically, the house was refusing to give her the money back. It resented people trying to sell it, just as it was beginning to resent people who can't afford it.

Now it was expressing that resentment. It committed an act which, for a New Orleans house in summer, is tantamount to eviction. All by itself, with the temperature outside rising into the low 90s, it shut down its air-conditioning. I do not mean that any of its 11 air-conditioning units broke. A broken unit can be repaired. The repairmen came and went, shaking their heads. There was nothing they could see that was wrong with even one of the mansion's massive air compressors. The problem was deep inside the walls, perhaps in the wiring. The ballroom, interestingly, was still 68 degrees, but the bedrooms were now 83. The house not only had microclimates, but also a unifying theme. The grand public spaces continued to be pleasant and comfortable, as if the mansion, in chasing us out, had no interest in sullying its public reputation. Only its putatively private spaces—bedrooms, bathrooms—were uninhabitable. Amazingly, it could be 83 degrees and humid in one room and 68 and dry in another—on the same floor. For the first time inside a house, it occurred to me that it might rain.

And so we fled, back to where we'd come from: the upper middle class. Obviously this presents new problems. Even as my children grew weary of pretending they were richer than they are, they became accustomed to living as the rich do. On the way back to California, my wife drove Quinn, who'd just turned nine, across the Southwest and then up the coast. They came to Hearst Castle* and stopped to take the guided tour. A few minutes into it, as they stood in one of William Randolph Hearst's many bedrooms, the guide asked if anyone had a question. My child raised her hand. The guide smiled indulgently and called on her.

"Why," Quinn asked, "is it so small?"

## Reflections and Responses

1. Lewis never explicitly delineates why he wanted to live in the mansion—why his childhood queasiness cycling past it subsided into a desire to own it. Do you detect an answer to this question in the essay's first few paragraphs? Is he chastising himself for his decision later when he describes the impact the house has on him? What is he suggesting about his motives?

2. Lewis characterizes America as a "nation of financial impostors." Do you agree? How does the desire to appear better off than one really is figure into the crises—personal and macroeconomic—Lewis is discussing?

---

*Hearst Castle: The sprawling, opulent estate of newspaper publisher William Randolph Hearst near San Simeon, California.

3. How does Lewis *personify* the house in his essay, and to what effect? When he writes "The house had a mind of its own, like one of those old horses you find at dude ranches," how is he characterizing the mansion, and why? When he writes of its former felonious tenant that "the mansion made him do it," is he really suggesting that the house has a supernatural effect on its owners? Or that the pretense of wealth it requires does? What is the purpose of this personification?

JILL McCORKLE

# Cuss Time

*The word "profanity" still encapsulates one of the most difficult controversies in our society: Should certain words and phrases be kept out of public conversation because they are notionally obscene? On the one hand, advocates for censorship point to the inherent ugliness of the kinds of words that are banned on TV and radio (you know the ones), and claim discourse is more civil without them. On the other, advocates of free speech argue, like Henry Drummond in the play* Inherit the Wind, *that "we've got to use all the words we've got." In this compelling essay, Jill McCorkle advocates for more freedom in language on two levels: On the larger, political side, she suggests stifling notionally profane language is an unacceptable form of capricious censorship. It is in an examination of her own experience as a child and then as a mother, however, that she fully advances her case that we are only a truly free people when our language is free.*

*Jill McCorkle is the author of eight books of fiction, most recently the short story collection* Going Away Shoes. *Five of her books have been* New York Times *notables, and her work has appeared in the* Best American Short Stories *as well as in the* Essays. *She is the recipient of the New England Book Award, the John Dos Passos Prize for Excellence in Literature, and the North Carolina Award for Literature, among other accolades. "Cuss Time" originally appeared in* The American Scholar *and was selected by Mary Oliver for* The Best American Essays *2009.*

My dad often told a story from his days as a mail carrier when he confronted a little boy no more than five perched up in a tree in a yard severely marked by poverty and neglect. The kid looked down with dirty face and clothes and said, "Whatcha want, you old son of a bitch?" We laughed at his aggressive assertion, but there was something sad and tender in it, too. There was the recognition of his own reality and the hope that his anger and toughness might in time lead him to a better place.

*Source:* Best American Essays, 2011, Jill McCorkle, Cuss Time.

One day when my son was eight, he came into the kitchen while I was cooking and said: "You put bad words in your books, don't you?" No doubt he had overheard my mother, who often tells people who ask about my work: "Well, you'll never find her books in the Christian bookstore."

I said that sometimes—when character and situation called for it—I did use *strong* language, that I couldn't imagine a realistic portrait of human nature, particularly in our contemporary society, without it.

"So can I do that?" he asked, and of course I told him absolutely—that when he writes a short story or novel, he will have all the freedom in the world to do so.

He pulled a ripped sheet of notebook paper from behind his back. "Would you like to hear the first of my book?"

This was when I stopped what I was doing and gave him my full attention, boy in Red Sox shirt and baggy jeans—his uniform of many years. "Now," he said. "Keep in mind that this is a fourteen-year-old girl who is being made to marry a guy she's never even met and she's mad." I could only assume he had read or heard something in school to inspire this—stories of another culture used to enlighten and remind us of our basic rights and freedoms and how important they are. He paused, giving a very serious look before clearing his throat, shaking the paper, and beginning.

*"Goddamnit why would I want to marry that piece of shit boy? I'm damn mad as hell."*

He stopped and looked at me, waiting for my response. It was one of those important parental moments, recognized as it is happening, so I took a few seconds. "Well," I said. "You certainly have captured her anger and frustration." He nodded, a look of great satisfaction on his face, and wandered back to where he was playing video games. Needless to say I confiscated that piece of paper and carefully placed it in the box of treasured writings I have saved. It is right in there with a letter he wrote his sister claiming he had "Shitey conselars" at a camp he was unhappily attending.

A year or so before this took place, I had given him permission to have what we called "cuss time." It began when I realized that he was silently mouthing a lot of new vocabulary while riding in the car or drawing. He saw me see him one day, and he was embarrassed, so I told him I knew that urge to test a word and how important it is to do so. Thus the origin of cuss time. Every day for five minutes, usually right after school, he could say anything he wanted. He liked to bounce on the already beaten-up leather sofa while saying the words, sounds emitted as his feet left the cushion. It was a kind of Trampoline Tourette's*—"hell," "bitch," "doo-doo"—and I'll confess I was always happy that we were never interrupted by UPS or a friend stopping by. What I found particularly endearing is that in his world, all words that were considered inappropriate for public voice weighed exactly the same. "Fart" and "fuck" and "fanny" were equals. "Shit" and "ass." When the kitchen timer rang, all cussing ended until the next day.

I found it liberating to watch his liberation. I was a kid who had gotten my mouth washed out with soap regularly, and all that ever did—other than leave me foaming and gagging—was to make me furious and determined to say everything even more. It's one of the most basic laws of human nature, isn't it? The more we are denied something, the more we want it? The more silence given to this or that topic, the more power. All you need do is look to the binge-drinking or eating-disorder cases that surround us, the multitudes of church sex scandals, to show that the demand for abstinence or any kind of total denial of thought or expression or action can often lead to dangerous consequences. When we know we *can* choose to do this or that, we don't feel as frantic to do so, to make a sudden move or decision that might be the worst thing for us.

When our words and actions are filled with possibilities and potential, we are more likely to weigh out the options. I am convinced that the anticipation of cuss time—the *freedom* of cuss time—kept my son from being overheard by some person in authority who might have had no choice but to reprimand him and assign punishment.

"Potential" is a powerful word. I remember feeling so sad when my children turned a year old and I knew, from reading about human development, that they had forever lost the potential they were born with to emulate the languages of other cultures, clicks and hums and throat sounds foreign to me. For that short period of time, a mere twelve months, they could have been dropped any-where in the world and fully adapted accordingly. But beyond this linguistic loss, we are at risk of losing something far greater each and every time we're confronted with censorship and denial. Per-fectly good words are taken from our vocabulary, limiting the

---

*Tourette's** is a neuropsychiatric disorder characterized by verbal tics. In some patients these manifest themselves in the uncontrollable exclamation of obscene words in public.

expression of a thought or an opinion. I recently read about high schoolers who are not allowed to use the word "vagina." And what should they say instead? When you read about something like this (just one recent example of many), you really have to stop and wonder. Is this restriction because someone in charge thinks vaginas are *bad?* I once had a story editor ask me not to use the word "placenta." I wanted to say: "Now tell me again how you got here?" *Oh, right, an angel of God placed you into the bill of the stork.*

Word by single word, our history will be rewritten if we don't guard and protect it, truth lost to some individual's idea about what is right or wrong. These speech monitors—the Word Gestapo* (speaking of words some would have us deny and forget)—attempt to define and dictate what is acceptable and what is not.

Lenny Bruce,[†] while pushing the First Amendment as far as it can go, famously said, "Take away the right to say 'fuck' and you take away the right to say 'fuck the government.'" And maybe that's *really* what all the rules are about—power and control—someone else's over you. Though I felt the impulse to tell my son cuss time was a secret of sorts, "our own little game," I stifled the urge, knowing what a dangerous and manipulative thing the use of a "secret" can be. Besides, any suggestion of denial of the act would have worked against everything I was trying to give him. Of course, it wasn't any time at all before several little boys started asking to ride the bus home with him. "Can I do cuss time?" they pleaded. I sadly had to tell them the truth: they were not of legal age and so cuss time was something only their own parents could give them.

I have often thought what a better, more confident person I would have been if only I had grown up with cuss time instead of soap licking.

My first public reading from my work was when I was twenty-five years old. At the end, as I stood at the podium speaking to people, I noticed an elderly woman slowly making her way down the aisle. I waited for her to reach me only to have her shake a finger in my face and say, "And you look like such a nice girl!" Unfortunately,

---

*The **Gestapo** was a secret police force in Nazi-occupied Europe most famous for brutally routing out dissenters and political opposition.

[†]**Lenny Bruce** was a comedian famous in the 1950s and 1960s for his bitterly satirical act, which often employed and celebrated so-called "profane" language and ideas.

I was still conditioned to want her to believe that I *was* a nice girl, conditioned to care more about what other people thought of me than what I thought of myself. It was only after the fact that I felt angry, that I wanted to go back and ask if she was even paying attention to what I was reading about—a situation of hurt humans expressing their feelings. I wanted to say "You have every right to your opinions and thoughts, but that doesn't make you *right.*" I wanted to say "Fuck you," and even knowing it would have been completely out of character for me to do so, I like knowing that I *could* have.

By limiting or denying freedom of speech and expression, we take away a lot of potential. We take away thoughts and ideas before they even have the opportunity to hatch. We build a world around negatives—you can't say, think, or do this or that. We teach that if you are safely camouflaged in what is acceptable and walk that narrow road—benign or neutral words, membership in institutions where we are told what to think and believe—then you can get away with a lot of things. You can deny who you are and all that came before you and still be thought of as a *good* person. And what can be positive in that? In fact, what is more positive than a child with an individual mind full of thoughts and sounds and the need to express them who has the freedom to discover under safe and accommodating conditions the best way to communicate something? In other words, you old son of a bitch, I say *Let freedom ring!*

## Reflections and Responses

1. McCorkle's argument in some way rests on her contention that "one of the most basic laws of human nature" is that stifling certain behavior makes people want even more to engage in it: The "demand for abstinence or any kind of total denial of thought or expression or action can often lead to dangerous consequences." Do you agree with this contention in the context of freedom to curse? In other contexts? What do you think of this law of human nature in general? What are its limitations?

2. Explain McCorkle's sarcastic rhetorical question, "Now tell me again how you got here?" in paragraph 8 of her essay. What connection is McCorkle forming between censored speech and

ignorance? How does this relate to the theme of "potential" with which she opens her paragraph?

3. What do you think of "cuss time"? Do you imagine it's an effective child-rearing tool? Would you give your children a similar outlet for behavior deemed inappropriate outside the home? Why or why not? Do you agree that it could expand a child's imagination and versatility, or would it instead give a child an opportunity to act out?

DANIELLE OFRI

# Living Will

*"Living Will" is a fine example of the type of essay that follows a narrative arc as the author describes the process of moving from one state of mind to another, usually from a moral or intellectual dilemma to resolution and insight. Such essays often involve an* epiphany. *The Irish novelist James Joyce first used this ancient religious term in a modern literary sense to describe the sudden flash of recognition or the unexpected illumination that can transform our understanding. "Living Will" takes us inside today's medical profession—with its awesome technological capability— and confronts one of medicine's major issues: Why are severely ill and depressed patients who have lost the will to live kept alive at such an enormous cost of time, expense, and professional effort?*

*Danielle Ofri, MD, PhD, is the author of* Singular Intimacies: Becoming a Doctor at Bellevue (2003), Incidental Findings: Lessons from My Patients in the Art of Medicine (2005), Medicine in Translation: Journeys with My Patients (2010), *and* What Doctors Feel: How Emotions Affect the Practice of Medicine (2013). *Ofri is editor in chief and cofounder of the* Bellevue Literary Review *and associate chief editor of an award-winning medical textbook,* The Bellevue Guide to Outpatient Medicine. *Her stories have appeared in both literary and medical journals as well as in several anthologies. A frequent contributor to* The New York Times, *she is an attending physician at Bellevue Hospital and on the faculty of New York University School of Medicine. "Living Will" originally appeared in* The Missouri Review *and was selected by Susan Orlean for* The Best American Essays 2005.

Wilbur Reston was already in the intensive care unit of the tiny Florida hospital when I arrived at two-thirty A.M. I had been doing a series of temp jobs after having completed my medical residency at New York City's Bellevue Hospital and now found myself in a small town on the Gulf Coast. The breathing tube in Mr. Reston's throat and his heavy sedation precluded formal introductions. But there was a typewritten summary of his medical history that his wife had left with the nurses: a two-page, single-spaced account that chronicled the rebellion and demise of each organ in this sixty-one-year-old white man. He had survived three heart attacks and seven strokes. One kidney had been removed. He suffered from diabetes, high blood pressure, and congestive heart failure. He had emphysema, glaucoma, severe migraines, and arthritis. His medical history included pancreatitis, diverticulitis, pyelonephritis, sinusitis, cholelithiasis, tinnitus, and ankylosing spondylitis. The typed paper also mentioned gastroesophageal reflux, vertigo, and depression. I quickly glanced over to the man hooked up to the ventilator to verify that he was indeed alive.

His wife had told the ER physicians that he'd stopped taking his water pills several days ago. Eventually he could no longer breathe. He possessed a living will stating that he did not want any life-sustaining procedures. In the ER, however, he had apparently agreed to be intubated. It had taken an enormous amount of sedation to get the breathing tube in, and then his blood pressure bottomed out. He was now unconscious in the ICU, on multiple pressor medications to support his blood pressure and augment his weak heart. In Bellevue terminology, he was a "train wreck."

Mr. Reston had been admitted to East General Hospital at two A.M. My colleagues in the small private practice where I was working had instructed me *never* to go to the hospital in the middle of the night. "Give your orders over the phone and see the patient in the morning," they advised. But I was still too new at this kind of medicine to be that confident; I had to at least lay eyes on the patient before I could decide on any medical orders.

I couldn't take a history from Mr. Reston, since he was at present unarousable because of all the sedation. My physical exam was brief. Mainly I plowed through the typed medical summary, converting it into a concise admission note. I handed my admitting orders to the nurse, and then there was nothing for me to do. In this small community hospital, the nurses were used to, and entirely comfortable with, working without any doctors around. How unlike Bellevue, where interns and residents roamed the halls twenty-four hours a day, deeply and intricately involved in the minutiae of medical care. Here the nurses took most of the doctors' orders over the phone and did everything themselves: drew blood, inserted IVs, did EKGs, obtained blood and urine cultures, sent patients for X-rays, followed up on test results, and so on. The doctors, with their busy private practices, usually visited once a day, either very early in the morning or late, after their office hours. The emphasis was on remembering to sign verbal orders within twenty-four hours. Not surprisingly, the head nurse was taken aback and almost alarmed when I showed up in the middle of the night for Mr. Reston's admission.

It was now nearly four A.M. as I drove back to the hotel in my rental car. The main roads of the town were deserted. I rolled down the windows and was quickly enveloped in humid, orange-scented fog. Stretches of flat, boring landscape were broken up periodically by strip malls. Neighborhoods of low-slung, white stucco houses were dotted with pickup trucks and palm trees. The smell of blossoms had not been fully eradicated by the burgeoning construction industry.

Southwest Florida was nothing like West Palm Beach, which I had assumed represented all of Florida. This area was rural, with acres of fields farmed by itinerant workers, mostly from Central America. I had just returned from Guatemala, so I was eager to practice my Spanish, but in the private practice where I worked, I rarely had the opportunity, except for the time when I was called upon to explain to a Honduran fruit picker that we couldn't treat his high blood pressure because he didn't have medical insurance. The hospital emergency room had called me when he'd shown up there needing prescriptions, and I'd said sure, send him over right now. When he arrived at the office, however, the practice manager informed me that we could not treat patients without insurance except for medical emergencies. Since I was the only one in the office who spoke passable Spanish, the duty of telling him fell to me. My verb-conjugating ability floundered, and my pronouns disagreed with their antecedents. My vocabulary in Spanish—and in English for that matter—had never included such phrases as "We cannot take care of you. You must go to a different doctor." I suddenly longed for Bellevue, for the chaos of the emergency room there, with its bubbling tumult of languages, ethnicities, colors, and socioeconomic classes, and its assumption that everybody received medical care regardless of ability to pay.

But aside from that one incident, the office was a pleasant place to work. Three doctors had started this practice several years ago, and they were now extremely successful. They had built an impressive clientele of devoted patients, mainly older but many middle-aged. They had equipped their office with a tiny pharmacy and a stress-test machine, and had arranged for weekly visits from an ultrasound technician, who performed all their sonograms. They'd even opened a small gym next door, in which they sponsored exercise classes for the elderly and rehab classes for their patients with emphysema. The doctors were in their forties, looking for ways to cut down on hours and enter semi-retirement. They were more than happy to hand over a third of the office patients and one hundred percent of the inpatient hospital duties. They gladly acceded to my request for paid prep time so that I could read patients' charts in advance of their appointments, all in a comfortable office with an experienced, full-time nurse to assist me. It was the lap of luxury. Within a week they offered me a permanent, full-time position with a salary that was four times what I'd earned as a resident for half the working hours, plus a share in the practice.

The patients were pleasant and apparently particularly happy to have a woman doctor, something new to that practice. And for the first time in *my* life, medicine was not a struggle: I could practice the best medicine I wanted without having to fight for anything. Coming from the trenches of Bellevue, where medicine felt almost like warfare, I found the ease of practicing good medicine almost disconcerting. I couldn't deny that the job offer was tempting.

But I could never leave Manhattan—certainly not to live in such a tiny town.

The town was a speck on the map in southwest Florida that no one I knew had ever heard of. The pace was unhurried, and the locals were unceasingly friendly and helpful, traits that were sometimes unsettling to a native New Yorker. Overly polite strangers made me suspicious, though everyone assured me that this was the normal style in the South. There was no place to get sushi, but the two-room library across the street from my office did stock Spanish-lesson tapes, and I was able to study a semester's worth of grammar on my way to work each day. Much to my dismay and disbelief, the library did not subscribe to the *New York Times*. A very weak consolation was the *Wall Street Journal*—only available, however, the following day.

The private practice was affiliated with East General, an eighty-eight-bed community hospital. I'd never seen a hospital that small. Eighty-eight beds was one floor at Bellevue, and Bellevue sported twenty-one floors. East General Hospital reminded me of my elementary school—spread out over two wings, each only two stories high. The elevator seemed redundant. Some of the services that I was used to from Bellevue, like twenty-four-hour-a-day access to cardiac catheterization and hemodialysis, were not available, but there were other advantages. With a maximum census of eighty-eight patients, there was never any waiting time for anything I ordered. Stress tests, sonograms, CT scans, pulmonary consults, social-work requests—I had only to jot a request in the chart and it would be completed by the end of the day. The staff was small, but everyone seemed competent and extremely friendly. Within a week even the housekeepers were greeting me by name, and the phone operators recognized my voice when I called.

The following morning Mr. Reston was awake but extremely uncomfortable. He had tried to pull out his breathing tube several times, so the nurses had tied his arms down. I apologized to him for the wrist restraints and explained that I would try to get the tube out as soon as possible. I was self-conscious about my words because Wilbur Reston's body was sentient. He heard and understood everything I said, but the tube and the restraints prevented him from speaking or even gesturing; my awkward reassurances met with no response. I spent the morning in the ICU weaning Mr. Reston off the ventilator and draining fluid from his lungs. When the nurses were rolling him over to change the sheets, he managed to dislodge his own breathing tube and set himself free.

There is an entire scientific literature on the most appropriate time to extubate a patient, based on pulmonary function tests, blood gas values, and chest X-ray findings. But the Bellevue ICU's wisdom was that a patient was ready to be extubated when he or she reached over and yanked the damn tube out. Mr. Reston proved this to be true, since enough fluid had been removed from his lungs that he was able to breathe, if a bit huskily, without the tube. His condition was still tenuous, though, and he was too exhausted from his ordeal to talk much; I waited a while for his wife to arrive, but she never showed up.

Thirty-six hours after his admission I was finally able to actually "meet" Mr. Reston. He was a burly fellow who looked surprisingly robust for a patient with such a thick medical record. I would have expected a shriveled old man, but he had beefy arms and a hefty belly. There was a tattoo of an alligator on his left biceps. The ICU bed sagged slightly under his weight whenever he shifted or turned.

Mr. Reston's face was pulled low on his neck by meaty jowls, and dark bags weighed his eyes down. He had lived his entire life in this small town on the west coast of Florida. He was a veteran of the Korean War, with a specialty in artillery. After the war he'd worked as a police officer and spent some time training guard dogs.

His voice was surprisingly soft and somewhat morose. In slow, deliberate phrases he described a lifetime of progressively declining health. His arthritic pains and severe headaches seemed to have taken a greater toll on him than his many strokes and heart attacks. He was confined to his house, unable even to walk down the driveway to retrieve his mail.

Did he have any hobbies? He heaved a melancholic sigh. "I fancied myself a carpenter. I built miniature furniture for dollhouses. Always used the best wood."

I imagined this bearlike man hunched over delicate divans and bedroom sets.

"Can't do it anymore. My hands." He threw up his gnarled, arthritic paws for inspection.

"I also collect Civil War memorabilia. Once found a belt buckle from the second battle of Bull Run," he said with a puff of pride. "They had it in the museum for a while." But his recollection of his former glory was brief. "My wife thinks it's a stupid hobby," he said.

What about depression? "I've never *not* been depressed," he sighed ruefully. "Ever since college, I suppose." His records showed that he'd been treated at the VA psychiatric clinic with both psychotherapy and antidepressant medications for more than twenty years. His only daughter had died of a brain tumor the year before. His mother and sister had both died in the past five years. So had his dog.

Had he ever attempted suicide? "I'm handy with guns, you know. I have at least five in the house," he said dryly. "Different models. Always keep a loaded one at my bedside."

Did he ever use it? "Well, I stuck the barrel in my mouth. Didn't pull the trigger, though. Too messy. Just stopped taking my pills."

I had an image of Mr. Reston sitting on the side of his bed, shoulders sagging, cradling the gun in his hand. Perhaps he'd raised the gun to his head several times, each time not able to bring it close enough. But then he'd take a quick, dry swallow and, squinting, slide the gun into his mouth. I imagined that he might be startled at how comforting the gun felt in his mouth. But then that very comfort would make him shudder, and he'd rip the gun out, stuff it back into the nightstand drawer, and slam the drawer shut.

Then he'd be left staring at the pill bottles lined up on that nightstand, loaded with promises of good health. He'd finger them, recalling what ill each was meant to cure. And cure they did. And then what?

I envisioned him opening that drawer again and, with the crook of his clublike arm, sweeping the bottles in, their hard plastic clattering against the gun as they came to rest at the bottom. He'd sink his head into his hands, forgetting to shut the nightstand drawer.

What about his wife, I asked. "She's busy with that volunteer work. She don't have time for me and all my pills," he said sadly. An uneasy silence settled in. I could see moisture accumulating at the edges of his soulful eyes, "We haven't shared a bed in fifteen years," he whispered.

His voice was plaintive but resigned. "Why should I live this life? I can't walk, my wife don't speak to me, I can't do nothing. What's the point?" He fixed his mournful gaze upon me. "*You* tell *me*."

It was both a plea and a demand. His simple statement had caused the space between us to evaporate, and I suddenly felt naked. Without my clinical armor to shield me, I was just one human facing another, squinting before the raw question. What *was* the point? What were the reasons for him to go on living?

I struggled to come up with one. Mr. Reston's body had withered sufficiently to keep him in perpetual pain but not enough to let him die. He had no friends; his wife was estranged. His daughter, mother, and sister had died and abandoned him. He was too weak to walk out of his house. He could no longer do any of the things that brought him pleasure. Why should he want to live? I could see why he had stopped taking his pills.

I didn't have an answer for him, but the law dictated what I had to do: actively suicidal patients must be prevented from harming themselves.

Like all good emergencies, this one occurred late on a Friday afternoon. Unlike Bellevue, there was no residency program in psychiatry to supply immediate consultations. There were several psychiatrists in the community, but they were busy with their private practices during the day and rarely made after-hours calls. But the staff of this tiny hospital was resourceful and helpful. They got me in touch with the local mental health agency, which was able to dispatch a psychiatric nurse practitioner. She agreed with my concerns and helped the nursing staff arrange a round-the-clock "suicide watch" over Mr. Reston. I could have Mr. Reston transferred to a psychiatric hospital once his medical condition stabilized if I felt he was still in danger of hurting himself. The nurse practitioner explained the procedures to invoke the Baker Act, the state legislation that allowed involuntary psychiatric commitment in such circumstances.

Over that weekend Mr. Reston's medical condition slowly improved, but his mood did not. Why should it? I thought. What did he have to look forward to? As much as I tried, I could not bring myself to utter flimsy platitudes about the value of life and how things would be better tomorrow. They weren't going to get better—he knew it and I knew it. Although he was clearly depressed, Mr. Reston was perfectly lucid. Despite his many strokes, his mind seemed to be working just fine. He could do all the tasks in the mental status exam: spell "world" backward, count down from one hundred by sevens, name the president, interpret the proverb "A rolling stone gathers no moss."

Although Mr. Reston seemed to have a reasonably realistic grasp on his situation, I wasn't so sure I had a grasp on mine. Doctors aren't supposed to agree with their patients who say they want to kill themselves, but I found myself overwhelmed by the utterly dismal facts of Mr. Reston's situation. Whom did Mr. Reston have left to live for? Even his dog had died.

I tried to imagine pacing the blank landscape of an empty life. How could I survive if every source of pleasure was denied? How could I live if the flavors, colors, and textures that made life palatable were flattened into a monochrome gray? If I were Mr. Reston, I might have pulled that trigger.

To complicate matters, he was in a rather unique medical situation. Although he had multitudes of medical problems, he was not yet terminally ill. He had a long list of diseases, but none was close to killing him. He was sick enough to be miserable but not sick enough to die. He was still able to eat, care for himself, and communicate with others. There were plenty of services and options for people on the verge of death, but Mr. Reston was not sick enough to qualify. His body, honed from years in the military and police force, was holding on too tenaciously. It left him stranded, strung too far from the shores of either health or death. Mr. Reston had severe physical pain, apparently unresponsive to various treatments, but more important, he was being eaten away by psychic pain.

The medico-legal issues were clear: a suicidal patient is prevented from committing suicide, even against his will, period. But the shades of gray needled me. My patient didn't want his life, and I wasn't sure it was ethical to force him to continue living it.

These issues plagued me for the remainder of the week. Ashamed to reveal my heresies to anyone, I secretly toyed with my doubts, picking at them as one does a loose tooth, perversely finding pleasure in its pain. What if I let him go home to his household of loaded guns? What if I discharged him, knowing full well that he'd stop taking his life-saving medicines? What if I turned my head and let him kill himself, as he so desperately wanted to do? There are those who say that all suicidal thoughts are products of depression, but Mr. Reston had been assiduously treated with medications and psychotherapy for decades. Perhaps he was being entirely rational. Who was I to stand in his way?

Then the toothache would burrow down to the raw nerve: What kind of evil doctor was I to even *consider* not protecting my patient from his violent tendencies? How could I be so negligent?

As I drove back and forth to work each day, this dilemma nagged at me. Lulled by the bland landscape, my mind would wander from the Spanish vocabulary coming from the car's tape deck to Mr. Reston languishing in his bare hospital room. Could there ever be any happiness for him? What if I found him a new hobby, one that he could manage with his disabilities? Stamp collecting— that wouldn't require much mobility. But probably his fingers couldn't manipulate the fragile paper stamps. Maybe he could take up painting. Large, easy brushes with hefty tubs of paint— he could manage that. Perhaps there was an artist waiting inside his weary body.

Traffic was stopped as a cumbersome tractor-trailer backed out of a construction site, attempting to turn around. A grove of orange trees had just been plowed, probably for a new strip mall. The trailer was open on top, and I could see the stacks of shimmering steel girders. The driver backed up a few feet, and then the trailer swung in the opposite direction, blocking his turn. The workers on the road waved their hands, shouting contradictory instructions: "Pull back a bit." "Swing to the right." "Turn your wheels on a sharp left." The driver edged forward and back, craning his neck out the window, then up toward his rearview mirror, as he tried to extricate himself from the tight spot. The steel girders flashed in the sunlight each time he changed angles. The smell of fresh, damp earth blended with the intoxicating sweetness of the orange blossoms, something I'd never smelled in New York City.

The metallic clanking and the competing shouts, along with the glare of the sunlight and the overpowering fragrance, made me feel heady and somewhat faint. I leaned my head into the steering wheel, and suddenly I saw the hole in Mr. Reston's armor: he had let himself be intubated. This man, who possessed a living will explicitly refusing all life-sustaining procedures, had *voluntarily* allowed a breathing tube to thrust air into his drowning lungs. He had reached for a life preserver.

I picked my head back up, feeling the murkiness begin to clear. Despite all of Wilbur Reston's misgivings and doubts, a desire to live had somehow percolated through.

As I leaned back in my seat, I wondered how that had come to pass. Was it simply the life-grabbing instinct that springs forward in such moments of near doom? Or was it truly evidence of Mr. Reston's ambivalence, of a desire to be saved and cared for?

Clearly, I had no way to know—I doubted if he himself would even know—but it seemed to me that Mr. Reston had given himself permission for a second chance. Now that he had done so, I had the opportunity, perhaps even the obligation, to allow that chance to flourish. If this second chance wasn't nourished, there probably wouldn't be a third. As if to confirm my realization, the tractor-trailer veered to the left and finally pulled itself out of its trap. The traffic snarl cleared, and I jammed on the accelerator, flying down the road with the breath of orange blossoms sweeping against my face.

When his medical condition stabilized, Mr. Reston was involuntarily committed to a VA psychiatric facility. He didn't protest when I informed him. He just nodded his head, his baggy jowls bobbing. During his entire stay, I'd never once met his wife; her occasional visits never seemed to coincide with mine.

The VA doctors assumed care of Mr. Reston, and I had no more contact. The private practice was busy, and I saw many patients every day. My mind was filled with Shana Elron's brittle diabetes and Henry Shaw's uncontrolled hypertension. There was the couple who lived in Pennsylvania during the summer but spent winters down south, and I was helping them coordinate his prostate cancer treatment between the two locations. I had recommitted myself to Spanish and spent my evenings conjugating verbs. I planned to leave for Mexico as soon as this stint in Florida was over, and I wanted to have the conditional tense under my belt. I had to decide if I wanted to start my trip in Guadalajara and end it in Chiapas, or vice versa. Or maybe just fly straight to Oaxaca and enroll in the Spanish school there. And then there was that shell-beach peninsula set against a tangle of mangroves twenty minutes from my hotel which beckoned me every night after work. I soon forgot about Mr. Reston.

Several weeks later, as my assignment in Florida was drawing to a close, some paperwork concerning Mr. Reston's original hospital admission turned up in my office needing a signature. Wilbur Reston's morose face flickered in my mind, and I thought about his miniature doll furniture. I wished I were still his doctor.

Besides giving himself a second chance, Mr. Reston had granted me the opportunity to tease out some of the more subtle aspects of medicine. He forced me to see beyond his imposing résumé of disease to his simple, hurting human self. The patient is not simply the sum of his illnesses, Wilbur Reston taught me. It is far more—blessedly far more—intricate than that.

After a labyrinth of phone calls through the VA bureaucracy, I finally tracked down his psychiatrist. Mr. Reston had just been discharged a few days ago. The psychiatrist described the long weeks and the laborious effort it had required to get Mr. Reston to take responsibility for simple things like brushing his teeth. By the end, though, he was showing up at the group meetings, even if he rarely spoke. Once in a while he even went to arts and crafts. Mr. Reston did not beome an effusive, energetic person, but according to the psychiatrist he no longer actively expressed the wish to die. That was considered a major success. And once he was no longer suicidal, there was no justification for keeping him involuntarily hospitalized. He could go home to his wife and continue with his regular outpatient therapy.

The psychiatrist commiserated with me over the many painful but immutable realities of Mr. Reston's life. A social worker was trying to help Mr. Reston get a new dog—that was about the only thing they could remedy.

I flew to Mexico the following week. In the end I'd decided to fly directly to Oaxaca for a month of Spanish lessons. Afterward I'd trek to Chiapas to see the Mayan ruins. I plunged into my classes, determined not to speak a word of English for six weeks, if that was possible. I rented a room from a family that spoke no English; I purchased Spanish editions of *Jonathan Livingston Seagull* and *The Little Prince* as my reading material; I tried to minimize my social contacts with the other foreigners in my classes and instead hang out at local cafés.

But I still thought about Wilbur Reston and wondered how he was doing. Those thoughts could only be in English. I imagined that he was sitting alone in his house, his wife at yet another volunteer function, his bones still aching, his weak heart preventing him from even getting the mail. But maybe there was now a puppy yapping at his feet, freely dispensing and demanding love. When the headaches and joint pains became overwhelming, maybe Mr. Reston would again consider ending his life. But then he might stop and think: Who would feed the puppy?

## *Reflections and Responses*

1. Consider Danielle Ofri's title for her essay. What two meanings does it possess simultaneously? How are these two meanings in opposition to each other? How are both of these meanings relevant to the essay as a whole?

2. What dilemma prompts Ofri's "epiphany"—the realization that her patient actually has the will to live? How and where does this sudden realization occur? In what ways is the specific context in which the epiphany occurs appropriate? How does it help to trigger the sudden insight?

3. Note the number of times that Ofri imagines her patient's life and activities. Why do you think she does this? Reexamine the final paragraph, for example. How would you evaluate this conclusion? How would a reader know whether it's at all accurate? Do you find the conclusion satisfying from a narrative point of view? Explain why or why not. How else might the essay have ended?

BRIDGET POTTER

# *Lucky Girl*

*The abortion debate remains one of the most critical rifts in our civilized discourse. Many in both the pro-life and pro-choice camps see their cause as critical to protecting American society from a great encroaching evil. One of the arguments often advanced on the pro-choice side is that, absent legal abortion, women will be forced into the "back alleys" to undergo dangerous and physically brutal procedures. In this essay, Beatrice Potter adds a healthy dose of personal experience to this argument. In 1962, Potter flew to Puerto Rico to terminate a pregnancy that she wasn't nearly ready to see to term. During the long and taxing ordeal, she felt decidedly unfortunate; only after reflecting on the experience of women at the time did she realize how lucky she was.*

*After a long career in television that included fifteen years as senior vice president of original programming at HBO, English-born Bridget Potter returned to college, receiving her BA from Columbia in cultural anthropology in 2007. An instructor in Columbia's University Writing Program, she is working on her first book, a memoir/social history of the 1960s. "Lucky Girl," which will be part of that memoir, originally appeared in* Guernica *and was selected by Edwidge Danticat for* The Best American Essays 2011.

In 1962, I was nineteen, working in my first job, living in my first apartment, having sex with my first real boyfriend. Michael was a tall, thick-haired Italian from the Bronx. For birth control, I was using fluffy pink foam from an aerosol can. I had heard about it from dark-banged, bespectacled Emily Perl in the television production office where I had my first job. I was the floater, filling in when a secretary went to lunch or the switchboard operator needed to go to the bathroom. Emily was a researcher and married. She used the foam as backup to her diaphragm. At the time it was illegal for a gynecologist to prescribe a diaphragm for a

*Source:* Best American Essays, 2011, Bridget Potter, Lucky Girl (2011).

single woman, and I didn't have the nerve to lie. As for condoms, what little I knew of them was that they were disgusting, unreliable, and boys didn't like to use them anyway.

Emily Perl knew a single girl who had been buying the pink foam illicitly from a pharmacy on Madison Avenue and using it—no diaphragm—without a problem. It was a spermicide. When the white-coated pharmacist handed me the plain white box of contraband from beneath the counter I tried to ignore his knowing leer. Sperm killer sounded safe and safe is what I wanted to be.

I used the pink foam.

My period was late.

Historian Rickie Solinger in her book *Wake Up Little Susie* describes what it was like to have an unwanted pregnancy in 1962. The woman might be "futilely appealing to a hospital abortion committee; being diagnosed as neurotic, even psychotic by a mental health professional; expelled from school (by law until 1972); unemployed; in a Salvation Army or some other maternity home; poor, alone, ashamed, threatened by the law." There was also an acute social stigma attached to an unwed mother with an illegitimate child; maternity homes were frequently frightening and far away. All counseled adoption. The only alternatives were a shotgun wedding or an illegal abortion.

According to a 1958 Kinsey* study, illegal abortion was the option chosen by 80 percent of single women with unwanted pregnancies. Statistics on illegal abortion are notoriously unreliable, but the Guttmacher Institute, a respected international organization dedicated to sexual and reproductive health, estimates that during the pre–*Roe v. Wade* years there were up to one million illegal abortions performed in the United States each year. Illegal and often unsafe. In 1965, they count almost two hundred known deaths from illegal abortions, but the actual number was, they estimate, much higher, since the majority went unreported.

Michael and I checked around for remedies. First we had a lot of energetic sex, even though we were hardly in the mood. That didn't work. One night I sat in an extremely hot bath in my walk-up on Waverly Place while Michael fed me a whole quart of gin, jelly jar glass by jelly jar glass. In between my gulps, he refreshed

---

*Alfred Kinsey** was a biologist who founded the Institute for Sex Research in Indiana, an organization that examined human sexuality and issues like abortion more frankly than ever before.

the bath with boiling water from a saucepan on the crusty old gas stove. I got beet-red and nauseous. We waited. I threw up. Nothing more. Another night I ran up and down the apartment building's six flights of stairs, Michael waiting at the top to urge me to go back down and do it again.

On a Friday evening, I drank an overdose of castor oil. By midnight I had horrible cramps of the wrong kind in the wrong place.

When my period was a month late I gave up hoping for a false alarm and went to visit Emily Perl's gynecologist. His ground-floor office in a brownstone on a side street on the Upper East Side was genteel but faded. So was he, a short, stern old man with glasses perched on the top of his head and dandruff flakes on his gray suit jacket. As I explained my problem, he shook his head from side to side in obvious disapproval of the loose behavior that was the cause of my visit. He instructed me to pee in a jar. The test results, he said, would take two weeks.

At that time pregnancy testing involved injecting a lab rabbit with human urine and watching for its effects. I waited to hear if the rabbit died. I learned much later that all lab rabbits used for pregnancy tests died, autopsied to see the results. It was code.

My rabbit died.

Michael was Roman Catholic and at twenty-two was willing to get married but unenthusiastic. We could, he supposed, live with his parents in the Bronx. I didn't know what I wanted to do. My upper-class English parents would have been appalled and, I was sure, unsupportive. Confused, ashamed, scared, and sad, I decided to try to get an abortion.

*Try* was the operative word. I asked the gynecologist for advice. He told me that the law prohibited him from helping me in any way, but he offered to check me later for infection. The idea of infection alarmed me but I thought his gesture was nice.

I'd heard that after twelve weeks the procedure became extremely dangerous. So I had four weeks left to borrow money, find a way to do it, and get it done.

Emily Perl knew someone who knew someone who knew someone who had been taken care of by a woman in an apartment on West Eighty-sixth Street. When Michael and I arrived, she put the chain on the inside of the door and peeped through the crack. She let me in but demanded that Michael wait in the lobby. The room was dark, overheated, and smelled of boiled cabbage. I glimpsed a big Victorian wood-framed red velvet couch and a round oak pedestal table through the dinge. In her fifties, the woman had an Eastern

European accent, suspiciously black hair, and smeary scarlet lipstick. She was curt.

She would "pack" my uterus and send me home, where I must
rest. For a day or two. When I started to bleed I must return, and
she would take care of it. What would she put inside me? I asked
clumsily. "Stoff," she replied. Where would she "take care" of it?
I asked. She pointed to a door. "In ze udder room." I must "svear"
not go to a doctor or a hospital. I understood the chilling threat. "It's
nowting," she said. "If you wanna now is fine. Five hunnerd dollars.
Cash."

My rent was $60 a month. I earned $60 a week, $47 after taxes. I
could barely make it Friday to Friday. I thanked her and fled.
There had to be a cheaper, safer way.

There was. Within a couple of days Emily Perl, born researcher,
came up with the Angel of Ashland, Pennsylvania. Dr. Robert
Spencer was a legend, a general practitioner inspired by compassion to perform, it is said, somewhere between 40,000 and
100,000 illegal abortions over his sporadic career. His price was
$50. He worked in a sterile environment with an anesthetist and
used an orthodox medical procedure called dilation and curet-
tage. What did that mean? I asked Emily. Opening and scraping,
she told me. I was sorry I had asked. His clinic had been closed
down by the law, but she gave me a contact number at a motel
somewhere in Pennsylvania. I should say I wanted an appointment, saying simply that I needed a D & C. It was affordable,
sane, and safe.

I called. The woman who answered told me Dr. Spencer was
unreachable, he would be unreachable for about five months. I
pressed. I might even have cried. The woman in the motel somewhere in Pennsylvania finally told me that he was in jail.

Emily's last suggestion was based on a rumor. There might be a
place in the Santurce district of San Juan, Puerto Rico, called the
Women's Hospital that would give an abortion. It might cost $250.
She knew nothing more. I was becoming frantic. Michael was
unable to do much more than hold my hand. I had two weeks
left. I was on my own.

Sneaking into an empty office at work and locking the door,
I picked up the phone. The overseas operator found the number
and placed the call. The connection was crackly, and the man who
answered neither confirmed nor denied that they would help.
I asked if I would need more than $250. That might be okay, he
said vaguely. I should come down if I wanted to know more. Not
on a weekend, he warned.

I would go. I would need money for the airfare, money for a place to stay for a couple of nights, and money for the abortion. It would add up, I speculated, to about $500.

Michael offered to ask his father, a shoemaker with a repair store on Canal Street, but he couldn't tell him what he needed the money for, and he wasn't sure if his father would have it to lend. I had never asked my parents for money, and they had never offered it. If I did now, they would assume, rightly, that their prediction that I would get into some kind of dreadful trouble had come true. I couldn't face them.

Emily Perl's husband was a book editor. They lived in an apartment with real draperies. They gave dinner parties at which they served wine in long-stemmed glasses. Maybe she had an extra $500. Borrow it from the office, she suggested. Bosses like their employees to feel obligated. They'll get it back by deducting it from your paycheck.

So I sucked in my breath and asked the young partner in the television production company. He didn't ask what it was for. I had been obvious, sniffling and red-eyed around the office. "I'll talk to the accountant," he said. The accountant gave me a check the next day.

It wasn't such a rare occurrence, I learned later.

I had money to fly to Puerto Rico, stay a couple of nights in a motel, and have the procedure taken care of by a doctor in a hospital. I bought a ticket on Pan Am for a Sunday evening flight there and a Tuesday night flight back. The airfare was $100. I picked a place to stay a short distance from the hospital, the White Castle Hotel. There was a White Castle on the corner of Seventh Avenue and Eleventh Street, a block from my apartment, which served a quarter-inch-thin gray burger, pellucid squares of chopped onion on top, on a saccharine sweet bun that dissolved in your mouth without a chew.

I climbed down the stairs from the Pam Am flight at San Juan airport, and as I stepped onto the tarmac, my white patent-leather kitten-heeled shoes sank in, ruined. I had a change of clothes, a nightgown, a toothbrush and toothpaste, a copy of *Henderson the Rain King*,* $350 in American Express traveler's checks, and $150 in cash.

I checked into the White Castle Hotel after dark and gave the clerk $100 in traveler's checks. The rest were for the procedure. The cash was for taxis and food. The room smelled of disinfectant

---

*Henderson the Rain King* was a 1959 novel by Saul Bellow famous for its juxtaposition of comic colloquialism and philosophical complexity.

and stale cigarettes, but it was air-conditioned. Lucky. I hadn't thought to ask. It was one hundred and three degrees that dark night in San Juan.

In the morning, the clerk gave me directions. I didn't want him to know my destination, but I couldn't risk spending money on a taxi. The hospital, I gleaned from the map, was a long walk away. It looked like a friendly suburban institution, built of clean white brick with a sweeping U-shaped driveway. As I walked up the steps under the white-columned portico to the entrance, I allowed myself to believe for the first time that this would work.

The lobby was quiet. Behind a desk stood an official-looking young man in a white coat. I approached tentatively, standing in front of him, praying that he spoke English. He looked up and asked, "Jes?" I had practiced this speech a million times. On the plane. As I tried to sleep. When I woke that morning. On the walk over. Out loud, I said that I had been told on the telephone from New York that I could get a D & C. I want to make an appointment. For today. Please. He nodded and slid me a form to fill out. This was going to work.

He asked me my age.

Nineteen.

He shook his head.

"Oh, no no no. Too young. Only after twenty-one."

I begged, pleaded, told him I had borrowed money to get there, that I didn't have any more, that I was desperate. He told me to leave.

As I walked toward the door, the rain began to fall, splashing back up a foot or two, a few people on the road outside caught in the downpour, running to escape but instantly drenched. I stepped outside, but it was useless. Already dripping, I ducked back in and asked meekly if I might wait until the storm passed. I sat on a brown couch, the backs of my thighs sticking to the plastic surface.

I would be returning pregnant. I wept silently, hoping that anyone who saw me would mistake the tears sliding down my face for rain from the deluge outside. My paperback copy of *Henderson the Rain King* was sodden. Outside, it rained on. I would go back to the White Castle, call Michael, tell him the news, get a plane back to New York that day. I would be able to save a few dollars. But I would have to keep this baby.

I sat and waited. And waited. As I started to pull myself together to leave, a tiny brown man in the green uniform of an orderly approached me, skittish, surreptitious. He held a crumpled piece of lined paper in his hand torn from a notebook. "Go dere," he said in a stage whisper. He offered me the scrap, then disappeared.

Written in pencil was a name and an address. My dress was wet, my tarmacked shoes stuck to the ground as I walked. I had proud long hair then that I ironed straight. It frizzed in the humidity. I handed a cabdriver the paper. He spoke no English, but I could tell that he thought I was mistaken, that I didn't want to go there. That it was far. Yes, yes. I nodded emphatically at the paper, taking it back from him and pointing with my finger at the address. Finally I understood his words: *twenty dollars*. I handed him money and off we went, out of San Juan, on dirt roads for what seemed like hours, to a small village built around a grassy square. The square was still, empty save for a few mangy-looking dogs, a couple of chickens, and two old men sitting on a bench playing a board game, He dropped me in front of an open building, which appeared to be someone's house.

A small man glanced at me from inside, and pointed to the whitewashed stairs that rose along the wall. At the top stood a second man, dressed in white pants and an undershirt. His massive shoulders and arms were those of a wrestler. He must be a bodyguard, I thought. But he immediately started talking about the money in fluent, barely accented English. He could take care of me, but traveler's checks were no good to him. I didn't have enough money for the cab fare to the hotel and back again on top of the $250 that he was demanding. Are you alone, he asked? Yes, I said. We agreed on $200. He would wait. I returned in the twilight with the cash.

A wooden table, no anesthesia, a scraping sound, and a newspaper-lined metal bucket. I moaned. Be quiet, he demanded. Or did I want him to stop? No, no. Go on. Please. Go on.

When it was over he warned me not to fly for two days, gave me two sanitary pads, and called a taxi. By now it was night. The roads seemed ruttier in the dark, every bump jarring my sore body. It was still Monday. I had to change my flight to Wednesday. At the hotel I slept on and off, not knowing day from night. Tuesday, in the dark, I went out to the little bodega across the street and bought some cheese and peanut butter snacks in little rectangular cellophane packages. Peanut butter sticks to the roof of my mouth, so I grabbed a bottle of Coca-Cola. That didn't seem healthy, so I added an orange. I had nothing to cut it with in the hotel room, and the peel didn't want to come off, so I bit off the top, sucked the juice out of it, and threw it empty but whole into the garbage.

Michael met me on Wednesday night at Idlewild. We rode the bus in to the Port Authority. I was tired and craving red meat. We took the IRT downtown to our favorite place for a cheap-enough steak dinner. It was owned by Mickey Ruskin, who became famous later as the proprietor of Max's Kansas City. I had a filet steak, a baked potato, a salad with blue cheese dressing, all for $9.99. The vodka was extra. So was the carafe of house red. Michael paid for dinner, and I felt full and satisfied and safe. The name of the place was the Ninth Circle, the lowest region of Dante's Hell, below which lies only Lethe, the river of forgetfulness.

In the morning I called Emily's gynecologist. He saw me the same day. He examined me and wrote a prescription for penicillin just to be sure. He told me to call if the bleeding got worse. It didn't. I was one of the lucky ones. According to the Guttmacher Institute, in 1962—the year I made my trip to Puerto Rico—nearly sixteen hundred women were admitted to just one New York City hospital for incomplete abortions.

In the *New York Times* in June 2008, Waldo Fielding, a retired gynecologist, described his experience with incomplete abortion complications.

"The familiar symbol of illegal abortion is the infamous 'coat hanger'—which may be the symbol, but is in no way a myth. In my years in New York, several women arrived with a hanger still in place. Whoever put it in—perhaps the patient herself—found it trapped in the cervix and could not remove it ... Almost any implement you can imagine had been and was used to start an abortion—darning needles, crochet hooks, cut-glass salt shakers, soda bottles, sometimes intact, sometimes with the top broken off."

Three years after my trip to San Juan, illegal abortion officially accounted for 17 percent of all deaths attributed to pregnancy and childbirth in the U.S. It is speculated that the actual number was likely much higher.

## Reflections and Responses

1. How is Potter a "lucky girl"? Examine the contrast between the narrative of her abortion and the final three-and-a-half paragraphs, detailing the statistics on illegal abortions during the era. What is the tone of these final paragraphs? How does it clash with

the tone of the rest of the piece? How do the two complement each other? How does the contrast help advance the point Potter is making in her title?

2. Is the essay at all an argument for legal abortion? Why or why not? What moments in the piece, if any, give away an agenda? How do you think an opponent of legal abortion might react to Potter's story? What might he or she argue it proves?

3. What is the purpose of the character of Emily Perl, the knowledgeable coworker in the story? What does the fact that Potter must consult her every step of the way tell you about the conditions in which the essay's narrative takes place? How does Perl add to the atmosphere Potter creates in her account?

PETER SINGER

# The Singer Solution
# to World Poverty

*Philosophy can sometimes be quite practical. The following essay, which argues for our moral responsibility to behave altruistically, even contains two toll-free telephone numbers the reader can use to make a $200 contribution. Peter Singer, the famous and controversial ethical philosopher, sincerely hopes that his argument will convince you to contribute. He reinforces his argument with several intriguing hypothetical situations that put readers in the driver's seat of a moral dilemma. How will you respond? Would you agree not to buy another hooded Gap sweatshirt or that new Jay-Z CD that you don't really need and instead give the money to UNICEF?*

*Peter Singer was born in Melbourne, Australia, and studied philosophy there and at the University of Oxford. One of the leading thinkers of the animal-rights movement, Singer has written influential books on ethical issues, including* Animal Liberation *(1975),* Practical Ethics *(1979), and* Rethinking Life and Death *(1995). Among his recent publications are* Writings on an Ethical Life *and* A Darwinian Left: Politics, Evolution, and Cooperation, *both of which appeared in 2000;* One World: Ethics and Globalization *(2002);* The President of Good and Evil *(2004);* The Way We Eat *(with Jim Mason, 2006), and* The Life You Can Save: Acting Now to End World Poverty *(2009). He is currently DeCamp Professor of Bioethics in the Center for Human Values, Princeton University. "The Singer Solution to World Poverty" originally appeared in* The New York Times Magazine *and was selected by Alan Lightman for* The Best American Essays 2000.

In the Brazilian film *Central Station*, Dora is a retired schoolteacher who makes ends meet by sitting at the station writing

*Source:* "The Singer Solution to World Poverty" by Peter Singer. Reprinted by permission of the author from *The New York Times Sunday Magazine*, September 5, 1999. Copyright © 1999 by Peter Singer.

letters for illiterate people. Suddenly she has an opportunity to pocket a thousand dollars. All she has to do is persuade a homeless nine-year-old boy to follow her to an address she has been given. (She is told he will be adopted by wealthy foreigners.) She delivers the boy, gets the money, spends some of it on a television set, and settles down to enjoy her new acquisition. Her neighbor spoils the fun, however, by telling her that the boy was too old to be adopted—he will be killed and his organs sold for transplantation. Perhaps Dora knew this all along, but after her neighbor's plain speaking, she spends a troubled night. In the morning Dora resolves to take the boy back.

Suppose Dora had told her neighbor that it is a tough world, other people have nice new TVs too, and if selling the kid is the only way she can get one, well, he was only a street kid. She would then have become, in the eyes of the audience, a monster. She redeems herself only by being prepared to bear considerable risks to save the boy.

At the end of the movie, in cinemas in the affluent nations of the world, people who would have been quick to condemn Dora if she had not rescued the boy go home to places far more comfortable than her apartment. In fact, the average family in the United States spends almost one third of its income on things that are no more necessary to them than Dora's new TV was to her. Going out to nice restaurants, buying new clothes because the old ones are

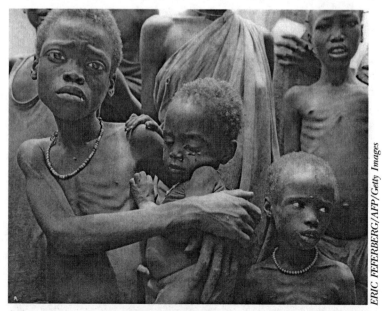

*Sudanese famine victims at a local health care center.*

ERIC FEFERBERG/AFP/Getty Images

no longer stylish, vacationing at beach resorts—so much of our income is spent on things not essential to the preservation of our lives and health. Donated to one of a number of charitable agencies, that money could mean the difference between life and death for children in need.

All of which raises a question: in the end, what is the ethical distinction between a Brazilian who sells a homeless child to organ peddlers and an American who already has a TV and upgrades to a better one, knowing that the money could be donated to an organization that would use it to save the lives of kids in need?

Of course, there are several differences between the two situations that could support different moral judgments about them. For one thing, to be able to consign a child to death when he is standing right in front of you takes a chilling kind of heartlessness; it is much easier to ignore an appeal for money to help children you will never meet. Yet for a utilitarian philosopher like myself— that is, one who judges whether acts are right or wrong by their consequences—if the upshot of the American's failure to donate the money is that one more kid dies on the streets of a Brazilian city, then it is in some sense just as bad as selling the kid to the organ peddlers. But one doesn't need to embrace my utilitarian ethic to see that at the very least, there is a troubling incongruity in being so quick to condemn Dora for taking the child to the organ peddlers while at the same time not regarding the American consumer's behavior as raising a serious moral issue.

In his 1996 book, *Living High and Letting Die*, the New York University philosopher Peter Unger presented an ingenious series of imaginary examples designed to probe our intuitions about whether it is wrong to live well without giving substantial amounts of money to help people who are hungry, malnourished, or dying from easily treatable illnesses like diarrhea. Here's my paraphrase of one of these examples:

Bob is close to retirement. He has invested most of his savings in a very rare and valuable old car, a Bugatti, which he has not been able to insure. The Bugatti is his pride and joy. In addition to the pleasure he gets from driving and caring for his car, Bob knows that its rising market value means that he will always be able to sell it and live comfortably after retirement. One day when Bob is out for a drive, he parks the Bugatti near the end of a railway siding and goes for a walk up the track. As he does so, he sees that a runaway train, with no one aboard, is running down the railway track. Looking farther down the track, he sees the small figure of a child very likely to be killed by the runaway train. He can't stop the train and the child is too far away to warn of the danger, but he can throw a switch that will divert the train down the siding where his Bugatti is parked. Then nobody will be killed—but the train will destroy his Bugatti. Thinking of his joy in owning the car and the financial security it represents, Bob decides not to throw the switch. The child is killed. For many years to come, Bob enjoys owning his Bugatti and the financial security it represents.

Bob's conduct, most of us will immediately respond, was gravely wrong. Unger agrees. But then he reminds us that we too have opportunities to save the lives of children. We can give to organizations like UNICEF or Oxfam America. How much would we have to give one of these organizations to have a high probability of saving the life of a child threatened by easily preventable diseases? (I do not believe that children are more worth saving than adults, but since no one can argue that children have brought their poverty on themselves, focusing on them simplifies the issues.) Unger called up some experts and used the information they provided to offer some plausible estimates that include the cost of raising money, administrative expenses, and the cost of delivering aid where it is most needed. By his calculation, $200 in donations would help a sickly two-year-old transform into a healthy six-year-old—offering safe passage through childhood's most dangerous years. To show how practical philosophical argument can be, Unger even tells his readers that they can easily donate funds by using their credit card and calling one of these toll-free numbers: (800) 367-5437 for UNICEF; (800) 693-2687 for Oxfam America.

Now you too have the information you need to save a child's life. How should you judge yourself if you don't do it? Think again about Bob and his Bugatti. Unlike Dora, Bob did not have to look into the eyes of the child he was sacrificing for his own material comfort. The child was a complete stranger to him and too far away to relate to in an intimate, personal way. Unlike Dora too, he did not mislead the child or initiate the chain of events imperiling him. In all these respects, Bob's situation resembles that of people able but unwilling to donate to overseas aid and differs from Dora's situation.

If you still think that it was very wrong of Bob not to throw the switch that would have diverted the train and saved the child's life, then it is hard to see how you could deny that it is also very wrong not to send money to one of the organizations listed above. Unless, that is, there is some morally important difference between the two situations that I have overlooked.

Is it the practical uncertainties about whether aid will really reach the people who need it? Nobody who knows the world of overseas aid can doubt that such uncertainties exist. But Unger's figure of $200 to save a child's life was reached after he had made conservative assumptions about the proportion of the money donated that will actually reach its target.

One genuine difference between Bob and those who can afford to donate to overseas aid organizations but don't is that only Bob can save the child on the tracks, whereas there are hundreds of millions of people who can give $200 to overseas aid organizations. The problem is that most of them aren't doing it. Does this mean that it is all right for you not to do it?

Suppose that there were more owners of priceless vintage cars—Carol, Dave, Emma, Fred, and so on, down to Ziggy—all in exactly the same situation as Bob, with their own siding and their own switch, all sacrificing the child in order to preserve their own cherished car. Would that make it all right for Bob to do the same? To answer this question affirmatively is to endorse follow-the-crowd ethics—the kind of ethics that led many Germans to look away when the Nazi atrocities were being committed. We do not excuse them because others were behaving no better.

We seem to lack a sound basis for drawing a clear moral line between Bob's situation and that of any reader of this article with $200 to spare who does not donate it to an overseas aid agency. These readers seem to be acting at least as badly as Bob was acting when he chose to let the runaway train hurtle toward the unsuspecting child. In the light of this conclusion, I trust that many readers will reach for the phone and donate that $200. Perhaps you should do it before reading further.

Now that you have distinguished yourself morally from people who put their vintage cars ahead of a child's life, how about treating yourself and your partner to dinner at your favorite restaurant? But wait. The money you will spend at the restaurant could also help save the lives of children overseas! True, you weren't planning to blow $200 tonight, but if you were to give up dining out just for one month, you would easily save that amount. And what is one month's dining out compared to a child's life? There's the rub. Since there are a lot of desperately needy children in the world, there will always be another child whose life you could save for another $200. Are you therefore obliged to keep giving until you have nothing left? At what point can you stop?

Hypothetical examples can easily become farcical. Consider Bob. How far past losing the Bugatti should he go? Imagine that Bob had got his foot stuck in the track of the siding, and if he diverted the train, then before it rammed the car it would also amputate his big toe. Should he still throw the switch? What if it would amputate his foot? His entire leg?

As absurd as the Bugatti scenario gets when pushed to extremes, the point it raises is a serious one: only when the sacrifices become very significant indeed would most people be prepared to say that Bob does nothing wrong when he decides not to throw the switch. Of course, most people could be wrong; we can't decide moral issues by taking opinion polls. But consider for yourself the level of sacrifice that you would demand of Bob, and then think about how much money you would have to give away in order to make a sacrifice that is roughly equal to that. It's almost certainly much, much more than $200. For most middle-class Americans, it could easily be more like $200,000.

Isn't it counterproductive to ask people to do so much? Don't we run the risk that many will shrug their shoulders and say that morality, so conceived, is fine for saints but not for them? I accept that we are unlikely to see, in the near or even medium-term future, a world in which it is normal for wealthy Americans to give the bulk of their wealth to strangers. When it comes to praising or blaming people for what they do, we tend to use a standard that is relative to some conception of normal behavior. Comfortably off Americans who give, say, 10 percent of their income to overseas aid organizations are so far ahead of most of their equally comfortable fellow citizens that I wouldn't go out of my way to chastise them for not doing more. Nevertheless, they should be doing much more, and they are in no position to criticize Bob for failing to make the much greater sacrifice of his Bugatti.

At this point various objections may crop up. Someone may say, "If every citizen living in the affluent nations contributed his or her share, I wouldn't have to make such a drastic sacrifice, because long before such levels were reached the resources would have been there to save the lives of all those children dying from lack of food or medical care. So why should I give more than my fair share?" Another, related objection is that the government ought to increase its overseas aid allocations, since that would spread the burden more equitably across all taxpayers.

Yet the question of how much we ought to give is a matter to be decided in the real world—and that, sadly, is a world in which we know that most people do not, and in the immediate future will not, give substantial amounts to overseas aid agencies. We know too that at least in the next year, the United States government is not going to meet even the very modest United Nations–recommended target of 0.7 percent of gross national product; at the moment it lags far below that, at 0.09 percent, not even half of Japan's 0.22 percent or a tenth of Denmark's 0.97 percent. Thus, we know that the money we can give beyond that theoretical "fair share" is still going to save lives that would otherwise be lost. While the idea that no one need do more than his or her fair share is a powerful one, should it prevail if we know that others are not doing their fair share and that children will die preventable deaths unless we do more than our fair share? That would be taking fairness too far.

Thus, this ground for limiting how much we ought to give also fails. In the world as it is now, I can see no escape from the conclusion that each one of us with wealth surplus to his or her essential needs should be giving most of it to help people suffering from poverty so dire as to be life-threatening. That's right: I'm saying that you shouldn't buy that new car, take that cruise, redecorate the house, or get that pricy new suit. After all, a thousand-dollar suit could save five children's lives.

So how does my philosophy break down in dollars and cents? An American household with an income of $50,000 spends around $30,000 annually on necessities, according to the Conference Board, a nonprofit economic research organization. Therefore, for a household bringing in $50,000 a year, donations to help the world's poor should be as close as possible to $20,000. The $30,000 required for necessities holds for higher incomes as well. So a household making $100,000 could cut a yearly check for $70,000. Again, the formula is simple: whatever money you're spending on luxuries, not necessities, should be given away.

Now, evolutionary psychologists tell us that human nature just isn't sufficiently altruistic to make it plausible that many people will sacrifice so much for strangers. On the facts of human nature, they might be right, but they would be wrong to draw a moral conclusion from those facts. If it is the case that we ought to do things that, predictably, most of us won't do, then let's face that fact head-on. Then, if we value the life of a child more than going to fancy restaurants, the next time we dine out we will know that we could have done something better with our money. If that makes living a morally decent life extremely arduous, well, then that is the way things are. If we don't do it, then we should at least know that we are failing to live a morally decent life—not because it is good to wallow in guilt but because knowing where we should be going is the first step toward heading in that direction.

When Bob first grasped the dilemma that faced him as he stood by that railway switch, he must have thought how extraordinarily unlucky he was to be placed in a situation in which he must choose between the life of an innocent child and the sacrifice of most of his savings. But he was not unlucky at all. We are all in that situation.

## *Reflections and Responses*

1. Do you find Singer's hypothetical examples convincing? If you place yourself in the situations he describes, do you reach the same conclusions he does? Can you refute his hypothetical situations?

2. At one point, Singer identifies himself as a "utilitarian philosopher," that is, "one who judges whether acts are right or wrong by their consequences." Do you find any limitations with this manner of evaluating right and wrong? Can you rewrite Singer's hypothetical examples in such a way that the "right" decision would perhaps lead to a bad consequence? Suppose, for example, that Bob pulled the switch and saved the boy's life, but another child hiding in the runaway train was killed in the collision with Bob's fancy automobile. Would that child's death be a direct consequence of Bob's apparently generous act? Would criminal charges be filed against Bob? Consider other variations.

3. Note that throughout the essay Singer argues for just one cause—child poverty. Why do you think he chose this and not a different sort of cause? What if he had selected AIDS research or Amnesty International as likely ways to help human suffering? Would these be just as effective? Why or why not? And if you did give your money to relieve child poverty, would you be making a conscious decision NOT to assist the causes of AIDS or cancer research or the Red Cross or any other legitimate charitable organization?

JOHN H. SUMMERS

# Gettysburg Regress

*The Battle of Gettysburg, in southern Pennsylvania, is often considered the turning point in the American Civil War. The bloody battle provoked— and later its field was the site of—Abraham Lincoln's short speech famously known as the Gettysburg Address. Ever since, the battleground has remained a hallowed symbol of the struggle for equality and justice. Today, Gettysburg has sparked a new battle among historians: How should the battlefield be preserved in order best to honor and remember the people who died there? In this essay, historian and public intellectual John H. Summers considers the implications of one specific act of "rehabilitation" by the National Park Service: cutting down trees planted in memory of fallen soldiers, in order to make the battlefield appear as it did in 1863. In considering the competing imperatives of precise accuracy and memorial, Summers prompts us to ask the larger questions of what we demand from our history, and how we best serve it.*

*John H. Summers is a historian, the editor of the journal* The Baffler, *and the author and editor of several books, including* Every Fury on Earth, *an essay collection. His family has roots in rural Pennsylvania dating back to the nineteenth century, and he often writes about his connection to that country, a hotbed of the Civil War. "Gettysburg Regress" originally appeared in* The New Republic *and was selected by the late Christopher Hitchens for* The Best American Essays 2010.

Last winter, I was walking with my wife along Seminary Ridge on the Gettysburg battlefield when an odd detail drew into sight: piles of felled trees, stacked alongside a road. The cuts smelled as fresh as the trees looked strong. What happened to them? we wondered. I grew up in Gettysburg, and my mother still lives in the shadow of Lutheran Theological Seminary, low in the lap of the ridge it

*Source:* Best American Essays, 2010, John Summers, Gettysburg Regress (2010). John Summers is the editor-in-chief of *The Baffler.* This essay is reprinted with his permission.

names. Seminary Ridge is one of a string of ridges surrounding the town; General Robert E. Lee* stood there on July 2 and 3, 1863. The woods atop the ridge had made it a sublime place to stroll for as long as I could remember—until that winter walk, which ended with a logging truck lumbering by.

Asking around, I learned that parts of the battlefield were in "rehabilitation." In the hope of providing visitors with an authentic historical experience, the National Park Service was seeking to restore some of Gettysburg's landscapes to their condition when the Union and Confederate armies clashed on them. And so the trees that once crowned Devil's Den—from whose crevices Confederate sharpshooters picked off Union soldiers—were missing also. Hundreds of acres of woodland, actually, were gone or going. (In July 1863, the battlefield contained 898 acres of woodland; since that time, the number has grown to roughly 2,000.) The "rehabilitation," many and varied in its activities, has also rebuilt fences, replanted orchards, and demolished large buildings, including a car dealership. The goal, as NPS regional director Don Barger told the *Christian Science Monitor* in April 2008, is to make visitors "almost feel the bullets ... That is what you want to have happen in a battlefield."

The project likely delights the reenactors who troop to Gettysburg every year in pursuit of authenticity, as well as those tourists who expect less to encounter history during their battlefield trip than to experience it. Academic historians also appear to approve. University of Virginia professor Gary Gallagher, who advised a recent project at the battlefield, cheers in the current issue of *Civil War Times* that "there has never been a better time to visit Gettysburg." Those who might object to the removal of the trees, he says, are "people who don't understand the difference between a historic park and Yosemite." Rehabilitation has something for everyone: it flatters the left's suspicion of cultural authority, its invitation to ordinary Americans to participate in their history, even as it honors conservatism's fetish for an unchanged, historically correct past. Indeed, Gettysburg, the jewel of America's battlefields, is one of several currently targeted for rehabilitation, including Vicksburg and Antietam.

As a historian, I can appreciate the impulse to restore. But my wife, Anna, felt foul about my explanation of salvation-through-improvement, and together we ruminated on her instinctual reaction at Seminary Ridge: Did those trees really have to go?

---

*General Robert E. Lee** was the most famous commander of the Confederate forces during the Civil War.

The more we thought about this question, the more the whole project troubled us. Those trees weighed in our concern, to be sure. But we began to believe we saw something larger, a distinctive pattern of thought sweeping across the battlefield, working in sympathy with the changing expectations Americans apply to their history.

In the Gettysburg Address—delivered just over four months after the battle's conclusion—President Lincoln cautioned that "we cannot dedicate, we cannot consecrate, we cannot hallow this ground. The brave men, living and dead, who struggled here, have consecrated it, far above our poor power to add or detract." In this season of Lincoln, it seems worth asking whether rehabilitating Gettysburg to its original state is really a process of adding or detracting—and whether the managers of our battlefields are, in their quest for maximum authenticity, cheating visitors out of something more important.

In high school in the late 1980s, I worked at the Gettysburg battlefield, imparting names, dates, and locations that were, by and large, irrelevant to the moral history of the war. Which was fine with me. I loaded the customers onto the fleet of blue and gray double-decker buses, climbed to the top, and took my seat at the rear, where I sunned myself avidly. The problem I grappled with most earnestly on these pleasure grounds was how to pry visiting adolescent girls from their fathers. As for the matter of North versus South, I felt, perhaps along with the sunglass-sporting tourists, that I might have gone either way.

The main destinations then were no more inspired than my tours. A few family attractions conveyed some slight educational matter—the Electric Map, National Civil War Wax Museum, Lincoln Train Museum, Hall of Presidents—and, lying beyond town, there were diversions such as the Land of Little Horses. The entertainments were neither authentic nor inauthentic. They were kitsch, lacking any clear point of view; and, as they were pointless, so they were also harmless.

Today's drive to refurbish Gettysburg, more ambitious in every respect, has not stinted on inspiration—or controversy. A $135 million Museum and Visitor Center, which opened in the spring of 2008, has lately grabbed headlines thanks to allegations of ethical impropriety. (Questions are swirling about why two firms—one run by the head of the Gettysburg Foundation, the Park Service's partner in building the new center; the other run by his son—were selected to do work at the battlefield.) Less attention, however, has been trained on the ongoing effort to rehabilitate parts of the battlefield to their July 1863 states. This effort marks the latest chapter in a contest between dueling conceptions of Gettysburg—the battlefield as unchanging relic and the battlefield as living memorial.

In April 1864, the Pennsylvania legislature chartered the Gettysburg Battlefield Memorial Association (GBMA). It had taken burial gangs until March of that year to complete the bulk of their work and inter most of the Union dead in Soldiers' National Cemetery. And not until 1873 were the Confederate dead removed from mass graves and reburied in Richmond and Raleigh, Charleston and Savannah. The GBMA made some efforts in the direction of restoration—repositioning cannons, for example—and its founder argued for maintaining the July 1863 appearance of some key aspects of the battlefield. At the same time, he urged the construction of monuments, while his organization's charter called for it to commemorate the carnage with "works of art and taste." In 1866, the legislature empowered the GBMA to plant trees at the site. By 1895, when the Department of War assumed jurisdiction and created the Gettysburg National Military Park, the GBMA held title to 600 acres of land from which it had carved 17 miles of roads. In its first decade of administration, the War Department added more than 800 acres of land, planted nearly 17,000 additional trees, and improved roads. The commemorative work of boosters and government officials utterly transformed the battlefield.

Administrative control over the land migrated from the War Department to the Department of the Interior and the National Park Service in 1933; and developments surrounding the battlefield continued to reflect tension between the two conceptions of Gettysburg. On the one hand, New Deal officials issued a six-year general plan that identified a desire to return the land to its July 1863 appearance. Barns were restored, fences and walls rebuilt. Using workers from the Civilian Conservation Corps, the Park Service pared away overgrowth for the sake of an authentic view at Little Round Top. Yet in other respects the site continued to migrate away from its 1863 appearance. In 1938, at the battle's seventy-fifth anniversary, President Roosevelt came to dedicate the Eternal Light Peace Memorial, whose torch—situated above a granite and limestone monument—was meant to symbolize domestic unity while Europe rearmed. Fewer than two thousand Gettysburg veterans attended the ceremony, and their average

age was over ninety. Perhaps they exercised something of a check on the drive for authenticity: one can see how wishing for an authentic battle experience in the presence of these survivors—who did not have the experience of the battle so much as they were had by it—might have been considered tasteless.

Eventually, however, the veterans died off, and, as told in Jim Weeks's *Gettysburg: Memory, Market, and an American Shrine* and Harlan Unrau's *Administrative History: Gettysburg National Military Park and Gettysburg National Cemetery, Pennsylvania,* the idea of rehabilitation continued to inform new plans for the park. In the late 1950s, President Eisenhower—whose farm was near the battlefield—egged on the campaign to restore Gettysburg. "I think it is a pity this one piece of terrain is not kept so that youngsters can see it nearly like it was in 1863," the president told *Parade* magazine.

Rehabilitation was a major initiative in the National Park Service's 1999 General Management Plan, thanks to John Latschar, the park's current superintendent. Last summer, Latschar explained to the *Gettysburg Magazine* how he could tell, soon after arriving in 1994, that a comprehensive program was needed to rescue the battlefield from the encroachments of time. "I'd been here a couple of weeks maybe and they scheduled my tour and I went out with a retired Marine colonel who's one of our best guides," he said. "He carried with him a stack of historic photographs that was probably three-quarters of an inch thick. I thought, what's he need all these for? But what he needed them for was to explain the course of the battle. Because so much of what the commanders could see in 1863 was obscured by vegetation that had grown up. And it was at that moment, I can remember thinking to myself, something's got to be done about this."

Is it possible to return vast tracts of land to their appearance in 1863? On the Park Service's website, Latschar explains that he is drawing on maps, participant reports of the battle, diaries, and newspaper accounts for a description of the battlefield's original condition. If that sounds straightforward, consider how little anyone knows for certain about the site's prewar appearance. Very few photographs of the Gettysburg outdoors from before the battle exist. William Frassanito's *Early Photography at Gettysburg,* published in 1995, identified M. S. Converse's map as the lone relatively detailed one available in July 1863, and the Converse map did not portray woods, hills, ridges, and other topographical features. General G. K. Warren and his team of military engineers made a sweeping survey of the battlefield in 1868 and 1869, then revised the map in 1873. But even the Warren map, the most authoritative made after the battle, has gaps and errors. "It is my cumulative observation," writes Frassanito, "that the finished product of 1873 more accurately reflects the appearance of the battlefield in 1869 than in 1863."

The scale and complexity of the carnage at Gettysburg has made it difficult to understand much about it. The approximately 1,328 markers and monuments scattered about the grounds are a stellar collection of public sculpture, but, individually and as a whole, they reflect "a constructed view of a certain version of the past, rather than a factual description of some historical truth," according to Thomas Desjardin's *These Honored Dead: How the Story of Gettysburg Shaped American Memory.* Many of these iron, bronze, and stone structures were placed in the 1880s, and most excluded the Confederates. Apocrypha that still surrounds Little Round Top and other areas originated not in the infallible testimony of eyewitnesses but in remembrances blurred, biased, or invented. Desjardin argues convincingly that "there is no 'what really happened' at Gettysburg; only a mountain of varying, often contradictory accounts that are seldom in accord, all tainted in some way or other by memory, bias, politics, ego, or a host of other factors."

Nobody learned the practical limits of such research faster than the battle's first historian, John Bachelder, who received $50,000 from Congress in 1880 to write a history of the event. In spite of the numerous interviews Bachelder conducted with eyewitnesses and participants soon after the battle and in subsequent years, he never produced the history for which he was paid. Flaws found in his maps, plus the intractable conflicts he found in the collective memory, defeated his attempt to make the story cohere. Soldiers and commanders alike said they found their experience incomprehensible, their vision clouded by fields curtained in smoke. General Abner Doubleday wrote to Bachelder in this chastened spirit five years after the congressional appropriation: "It is difficult in the excitement of battle to see every thing going on around us for each has his own part to play and that absorbs his attention to the exclusion of every thing else. People are very much mistaken when they suppose because a man is in a battle, he knows all about it."

Much of what we think we know about Gettysburg is knowledge gained at a remove beyond the experience of the battle. Paul Philippoteaux and his team painted the Gettysburg Cyclorama in

1884 from ten photographs by William Tipton, photos that depicted the battlefield as it was in 1882, not 1863. Photographers like Mathew Brady, Alexander Gardner, and the Tyson brothers, Charles and Isaac, circulated the earliest images of the battlefield. At Antietam, Gardner had supplied many urban newspaper readers with their first glimpses of dead soldiers. At Gettysburg, he captured images before the burials finished. How easy it is to forget, in light of his achievement, that neither Gardner nor anyone else photographed the battle itself.

But suppose the evidence was overwhelming. Suppose an abundance of available pictures, eyewitness accounts both reliable and comprehensive, and maps could guide history's eye with flawless accuracy. The question would still remain: Why should battlefield visitors want to "almost feel the bullets"?

Earlier generations of tourists brought more modest expectations. In 1869, the Katalysine Springs Hotel opened in Gettysburg on the heels of news that a medicinal spring had been discovered west of town. The hotel offered three hundred guests use of a billiard room and bowling alley, as well as a cupola that provided a panoramic view of the battlefield. This vantage point, high above the grounds, became very popular. In 1878, a private developer constructed an observatory on East Cemetery Hill, which also offered a panoramic view. The War Department raised five steel observation towers overlooking the battlefield. In 1974, a developer erected a tower more than three hundred feet high over the strenuous objections of preservationists.

Latschar demolished this structure (the National Tower, as it was called by its owner) in 2000—a key symbolic moment in his drive for rehabilitation. The towers enforce a moral distance between the seer and the scene. Accordingly, the early ones sprung up when memory of the suffering at Gettysburg was still raw. But towers also impede the ability of visitors to experience the battle; and experience is what today's battlefield managers aim to provide.

To truly experience what it was like to be at Gettysburg, we would need to lie with soldiers as they bled to death, groaning in pain; rotting corpses with missing limbs; streams running red; winds swarming with flies; air smelling of burning horseflesh. As we cannot know the precise cartography of the battlefield, or the movements of every soldier, or the location of every tree, so we should not try to leap backward into authenticity, or expect to become an eyewitness to history simply by showing up. The arrogance laid up around this expectation is astonishing. At

Gettysburg, as elsewhere, the parties of preservation, restoration, and rehabilitation seek to transport us forward into the past by scrubbing off the blemishes of time. But, in offering the illusion of authentic experience, inviting us to "almost feel the bullets," they promise both too much and too little: they forget that historical suffering must be regarded from a distance if tragedy is to make us humble—or even be understood at all.

If a battlefield is not a locus of authentic experience, then what is it? A shrine? A classroom? The trees may teach us something yet. As flesh decayed at Gettysburg, it fertilized the earth for new vegetation. What the Park Service calls "non-historic trees"— that is, trees that grew after 1863—once were seedlings. Since then, in the changefulness of the seasons, they have formed a palimpsest, offering the closest we may come to communing with the lost souls of the battle. "As he gazed around him the youth felt a flash of astonishment at the blue, pure sky and the sun gleaming on the trees and fields," Stephen Crane* wrote in *The Red Badge of Courage.* "It was surprising that Nature had gone tranquilly on with her golden processes in the midst of so much devilment."

Most of us, like my wife Anna on Seminary Ridge, intuit the connective tissues of trees and grief. That humans plant trees on gravesites is a spiritual fact of great and ancient significance. Homer[†] signals a transition from war to peace by telling how Odysseus, returning home, found his father tending a young fruit tree. Ovid, in *Metamorphoses,* tells of Cyparissus "begging the gods to ... let him grieve forever" after he accidentally kills a stag: "As his lifeblood drained away with never-ending tears, his limbs began to take a greenish cast; and the soft hair that used to cluster on his snow-white brow became a bristling crest. The boy was now a rigid tree with frail and spiring crown that gazes on the heavens and the stars." The trees on Seminary Ridge were a standing reminder of the pity and terror of tragedy. Those who run Gettysburg would grasp this—if only they were less obsessed with authenticity and more inclined toward history.

---

*Stephen Crane** was a novelist who, despite any battlefield experience himself, wrote some of the most vivid battle scenes in American literature.

[†]**Homer** and **Ovid** are ancient Greek and Roman poets, respectively.

## Reflections and Responses

1. Summers summarizes the central issue of his essay as the conflict between a "battlefield as unchanging relic and the battlefield as living memorial." Explain in your own words what he means by both of these phrases. What are the arguments on both sides? Which do you ultimately find more convincing, and why? Is there a middle ground between these two ideas of preservation?

2. How does Summers characterize the idea of "rehabilitation" of the battlefield by deforestation? What does he lead us to believe about those who would have every tree and shrub look exactly as it did in 1863? Point to specific moments in the essay in which he (subtly or not) advances that characterization? How does he add to the argument with the contention that really "feeling" Gettysburg would mean experiencing the incredible and vicious carnage of the scene? What argument against the cutting down of trees does he leave out of his case, and why?

3. Summers makes an offhand reference to his own teenage years in Gettysburg when he writes that the problem he "grappled with most earnestly on these pleasure grounds was how to pry visiting adolescent girls from their fathers." How does this comic aside actually lend authority to Summers' overall argument? Why is it important to his view of "living" history that Summers grew up and had apparently ordinary childhood escapades on the site?

JOHN EDGAR WIDEMAN

# *Fatheralong**

*The case of Emmett Till, a fourteen-year-old black boy from Chicago who was tortured, shot through the head, and then tossed into the Tallahatchie River in Mississippi in 1955, shocked America at the time. The acquittal of his two white murderers became a rallying cry in the Civil Rights Era, and remains one of the milestones in the history of the American conversation on race. In the following essay, John Edgar Wideman explores two aspects of the case that are usually ignored: the story of Till's father, a World War II GI executed for murder and rape, and the way the Till story may call into question the very existence or meaning of race itself. In particular, the narrative of absentee African American fathers enters the story and interacts with it in surprising ways.*

*John Edgar Wideman was the second African American to win a Rhodes scholarship; in addition to Oxford and the University of Pennsylvania, he studied at the Iowa Writers' Workshop. He is often considered one of the major black voices in American cultural and social criticism today. He is the author of several novels, including* Philadelphia Fire *(1990),* The Cattle Killing *(1996),* Two Cities *(1998), and* Fanon *(2008), as well as the memoirs* Fatheralong *(1994) and* Hoop Roots *(2001). In 2010 he published a collection of microstories,* Briefs. *"Fatheralong" originally appeared in* Harper's *magazine and was selected by the late Christopher Hitchens for* The Best American Essays 2010.

Louis till, the father of Emmett Till, the fourteen-year-old Chicago boy murdered in Mississippi in 1955, one year after the Supreme Court's school desegregation decision, is the first father I think

---

*The word I heard as a child when the church sang "Farther Along."

about when I am asked to comment on the alleged failure of black males to assume properly the responsibilities of fatherhood. I also think about Freud, about the global crisis demanding a metamorphosis of family that's not new, not black. President Barack Obama, who addressed such issues earlier and eloquently in his *Dreams from My Father* (1995), is clearly the catalyst of the present discussions as he works to apply his personal insights and experiences to a national dilemma. I'm moved by his honest explorations of fatherhood, his witness. The world is a troubled, dangerous place, at best. Unfairly dangerous for young Americans in free fall, growing up too fast or not growing at all, deprived of the love, guidance, positive example, the material, intellectual, and moral support of fathers negotiating the perils with them.

Louis Till's Non-Battle Casualty Report lists his rank as PVT, his serial number as 36392273, lists the Date of Casualty as July 2, his Reporting Theatre as MTO, the Mediterranean Theatre of Operations, lists his Arm or Service as TC, the Transportation Command, a noncombat unit to which nearly every colored soldier in the segregated U.S. Army was assigned, lists the Place of Casualty as Italy, and leaves blank, except for an asterisk, the space in which Type of Casualty should be listed. Mrs. Mamie Till's name (misspelled "Mammie") appears on the Battle Casualty Report, but it does not mention Till's son, Emmett.

The first time Mamie Till knew her husband had been hanged in Italy by the United States Army was in the fall of 1955, not long after their son Emmett was murdered, about a dozen years after she'd seen Louis Till last in Chicago. The telegram she had received from the army on July 13, 1945, composed of selected facts from the Non-Battle Casualty Report, informed her that her husband, Private Louis Till, had died of willful misconduct, but omitted "sol died in non-battle status" and "judicial asphixiation," words typed into a confidential footnote below the official report. Although Mrs. Till was assisted by a lawyer, her attempt to investigate the circumstances surrounding the death of her husband and the father of her only child had been stymied by the government's terminal unresponsiveness, the very same government that ordered its colored soldiers to serve in what amounted to a separate, second-class army of conscripted laborers.

The government that at its highest levels chose to break its own rules and violate the rights of Private Louis Till by sending his confidential service record, which included a transcript of his court-martial (CM288642), to lawyers defending the kidnappers and killers of his son Emmett. Driven by their desire to repair the public image of a state that was being drubbed nationwide by press coverage of Emmett Till's murder, the Mississippi arch-segregationist senators James Eastland and John Stennis are likely the ones who obtained and leaked Louis Till's papers, as only officials with their rank and clout could demand and receive, from the army's adjutant general, a soldier's classified service record. A Colonel Ralph K. Johnson, TJAG (the judge advocate general), on October 14, 1955, did the dirty work of signing off on the release and penciling out the word CONFIDENTIAL stamped on the cover and pages of the Record of Trial by General Courts Martial, dated February 17, 1945.

In November 1955, approximately six weeks after a trial that found two World War II veterans—J. W. Milam and his brother-in-law Roy Bryant—not guilty of murdering Emmett Till, a trial that the Cleveland *Post and Call* derided ("Mississippi Jungle Law Frees Slayers of Child") and the Greenwood, Mississippi, *Morning Star* complimented ("Fair Trial Was Credit to Mississippi"), the state of Mississippi, compelled by the testimony of a sheriff during the trial that Milam and Bryant admitted to him they had taken Emmett Till from his great-uncle Moses Wright's home, sought indictments against the two men for kidnapping. Parties unknown leaked to the press that Emmett Till's father, Mamie Till's husband, Louis, far from being the martyred war hero portrayed in northern papers during the trial, had been hanged by the U.S. Army for committing rape and murder.

This revelation of the crimes of the father doomed any chance that jurors in Sumner, Mississippi, would indict the killers of Louis Till's son for any wrongdoing whatever. Instead of what measure of comfort she might have felt if the court had punished her son's murderers, Mamie Bradley Till found herself watching in dismay as Emmett Till's already dead and brutalized body was tarred, feathered, and lynched again for the father's sins, her fourteen-year-old boy stigmatized, scorned as rotten fruit from a rotten tree.

The novelist Chester Himes, expressing the despair shared by many of his fellow citizens, published a letter in the *New York Post* on September 25, 1955, in which he wrote, "The real horror comes when your dead brain must face the fact that we as a nation don't want it to stop. If we wanted to, we would. So let us all share the guilt, those in New York as well as those in Sumner, Mississippi."

As a father, Louis Till didn't have much time to spend with his son. Emmett Till was born in July of 1941 (a month after I was born), and Louis Till (like my father) went off to war in a segregated army in 1942, returning to Chicago only once, one AWOL night before the army came and knocked on Mamie's door in the morning and hauled him back. A ring Louis Till purchased in Casablanca and had engraved with his initials and the date May 25, 1943, was included among the personal effects Mamie Till received from the army after she was notified of his death. This silver ring, cached in Emmett Till's jewelry box or occasionally worn on his finger, padded by tape until his finger grew thick enough the last year of his life to keep it in place, may have been the most intimate link between father and son, an irony, since the ring also served to identify Emmett Till's battered, bloated, disfigured body when it was pulled from the Tallahatchie River.

What kind of father did Emmett Till imagine when he wore the silver ring? Looking down at the ring encircling his own dark finger, did Louis Till ever think about a son bearing his name, Till, wearing the ring one day?

While his sentence of death by hanging was receiving its mandatory review by the Judge Advocate General's Division, Louis Till was confined in the Disciplinary Training Center, a United States military prison in Metato, near Pisa. The poet Ezra Pound,* facing a capital sentence himself, on charges of treasonous radio broadcasts, was Till's fellow prisoner, the only civilian in a population of 3,600 mostly colored inmates. The Pisan Cantos, written during Pound's internment in the DTC, imagine Louis Till as Outis, Greek for "no one," "nobody," the wanderer of the *Odyssey,* as Zeus the lusty ram, Till's sign, the Chinese ideogram "M4," "a man upon whom the sun has gone down" (Canto LXXIV: 170–178, edited by Richard Sieburth).

If Louis Till had been around to school Emmett about the perils of the South, about how white men treat black boys down south and up north, would Emmett have returned to Chicago safely on the City of New Orleans train from his trip to visit relatives in Money, Mississippi, started up public school in the fall, earned good grades, maybe even have become successful and rich, eluding the fate of his father? Or does his father's fate draw Emmett

---

*American poet **Ezra Pound**'s *The Cantos* is a series of poems often considered one of the most important and difficult in modern literature; The *Odyssey* is the *epic* poem attributed to the ancient Greek poet Homer, to which Pound's book-length poem often refers.

like a fluttering moth to its flame, Emmett flying backward and forward at once, like the African sankofa* bird flies, because part of the father's fate is not to be around to advise and supervise and support the son, the fate of father and son to be divided always? A cycle of predictable missings and absence eternally renewed. A flicker of wings igniting, quickly extinguished, then darkness.

Race is myth. When we stop talking about race, stop believing in race, it will disappear. Except for its career historically and in people's memories as the antithesis of human freedom, the embodiment of inequality and injustice that remained far too long a toxic, unresolved paradox in nations proclaiming themselves free. In a raceless society color wouldn't disappear. Difference wouldn't disappear. Africa wouldn't disappear. In post-race America "white" people would disappear. That is, no group could assume as birth-right and identity a privileged, supernaturally ordained superiority at the top of a hierarchy of other groups, a supremacy that bestows upon their particular kind the right perpetually to rule and regulate the lives of all other kinds. This idea, this belief in "whiteness," whether the belief is expressed in terms of color, ethnicity, nationality, gender, tribe, etc., constitutes the founding principle of race, its appeal and its discontents.

To dismiss race as myth is not to underestimate its power. Race, like religion, is immune to critiques of science and logic because it rests on belief. And people need beliefs. Although science has discredited the biological underpinnings of the notion of race, faith rushes in to seal the cracks, paper over glaring omissions in arrested explanations of human difference offered by racial ideology. Louis Till's color, the color of his son Emmett, the color of Richard Wright's[†] fictional character Bigger Thomas, Colin Powell's color, are not problems until the myth of race and the racialized perspective it authorizes turn color into an indictment, into instant proof of innocence or guilty-as-charged. We should

---

*The **sankofa** bird is a symbol in the Akan culture of Ghana, representing a bird flying forward but pointing its head backwards to retrieve an egg it has forgotten.

[†]**Richard Wright** was an American novelist whose 1940 novel *Native Son* deals with issues of identity in the African American community; **Colin Powell** was Secretary of State under George W. Bush and the only African American in history to serve on the Joint Chiefs of Staff.

understand by now that race can mean anything, everything, or nothing, depending upon whom we ask.

The continuing existence of race in the United States indicates conspiracy and cover-up. An attempt to make more palatable to ourselves, and anyone watching, the not-so-secret dirty secret shared by all Americans that our country, in spite of public professions to the contrary, entertains a deeply internalized segregated vision of itself. We look at ourselves and believe we see White Americans or Black Americans. We perceive our problems as Black or White problems. The urgent task of redressing the shameful neglect of American children gets postponed by hand-wringing and finger-pointing at feckless black fathers and the damage they're inflicting upon their black offspring. Or sidetracked just as effectively by blaming society and exempting blacks because race tells us blacks are permanent victims, not agents of change. The truth of too many black boys in prison, too many black babies dying, too many hungry black youngsters being raised in dire poverty, too many terrible black schools—these truths misrepresented by discourses perpetuating the myth of separate races don't spur us to action but become an occasion for shedding crocodile tears, washing our hands of personal as well as collective responsibility. More than half a century ago James Baldwin* outed this kind of hiding from the consequences of racialized thinking as *willed innocence*. At this late date, displays of surprise or ignorance about how bad things are for our children suggest dishonesty, signify complicity, conscious or unconscious, with the cover-up.

Louis Till was born fatherless in Madrid, Missouri. One could argue that the concept of race abiding today in America is a profound orphaning of all black children. Argue that any attempt to understand black fathers and to interpret their responsibilities, successes, and failures should begin right there, with a consideration of the fact that myths of race isolate children, place them at risk, disinherit and repudiate. Start by listening a moment to the roaring silence in which Louis Till is buried, the silence neither his voice nor his son's voice can break, the dark, impervious silence in which words—*good, bad, responsible, black, white*—vanish.

---

*James Baldwin was a major American novelist, essayist, poet, and playwright whose work focuses on the African American, as well as the gay, experience in mid-century America.

## Reflections and Responses

1. What is the significance of the title "Fatheralong"? (Pay careful attention to the footnote on the title.) How does this misunderstanding of a church hymn represent Wideman's complex point about African American fathers, as well as about fatherhood in general?

2. Wideman's essay can be said to have two themes: first, the false idea of negligent black fathers; and second, the construct of race in our society. How do these two themes come together in the essay? What is the connection between them that the story of Louis Till helps to forge? How does Till's story bear on the current situation Wideman describes in America, and particularly in the African American community?

3. Do you agree with Wideman's contention that "Race is myth"? Why or why not? How does Wideman appear to reach this conclusion, and what flaws—if any—do you see in his process of reasoning or in his perception of the racial situation in America and beyond? Do you agree that many people today are guilty of "hiding from the consequences of racialized thinking," and that this act qualifies as a kind of complicity with racism? Why or why not?

EDWARD O. WILSON

# *Apocalypse Now*

*The rift between science and religion has been at the fore of many of the ethical debates of the recent past: from evolution to stem cells. In this brief, epistolary essay, the renowned scientist Edward O. Wilson frames another crucial debate, over the duty we have to protect the natural environment, in terms of this rift. Wilson, a secular humanist, writes to an imaginary Christian pastor, accusing the evangelical Christian movement of not doing as much as secularists to promote an awareness of environmental concerns—in fact, in some cases Wilson claims evangelicals interpret scripture as an "excuse to trash the planet." But Wilson argues believers and nonbelievers should take the issue up in common. After all, he says, Christianity has a long tradition of teaching that we are stewards of our increasingly endangered world. He writes: "Earth is a laboratory wherein nature—God, if you prefer, pastor—has laid before us the results of countless experiments. We damage her at our own peril."*

*Edward O. Wilson is a biologist and author. Among countless accolades, he was named one of America's 25 most influential people by* Time *magazine in 1995 and has won the National Medal of Science (in 1976) and two Pulitzer Prizes (in 1979 and 1991). Wilson, a native of Alabama, was the Pellegrino University Professor at Harvard and is now a member of the National Academy of Science. His many books include* The Insect Societies *(1971),* Sociobiology: The New Synthesis *(1975),* The Diversity of Life *(1992),* In Search of Nature *(1996),* Consilience: The Utility of Knowledge *(1998),* The Creation: An Appeal to Save Life on Earth *(2006) and* Nature Revealed: Selected Writings, 1949–2006. *In 2010 he won the Heartland Award for his first novel,* Anthill; *his most recent book is* The Social Conquest of the Earth *(2012). "Apocalypse Now" originally appeared in* The New Republic *and was selected by David Foster Wallace for* The Best American Essays 2007.

Dear Pastor,

We have not met, yet I feel I know you well enough to call you a friend. First of all, we grew up in the same faith. As a boy, I, too, answered the altar call; I went under the water. Although I no longer belong to that faith, I am confident that, if we met and spoke privately of our deepest beliefs, it would be in a spirit of mutual respect and goodwill. I know we share many precepts of moral behavior. Perhaps it also matters that we are both Americans and, insofar as it might still affect civility and good manners, we are both Southerners.

I write to you now for your counsel and help. Of course, in doing so, I see no way to avoid the fundamental differences in our worldviews. You are a strict interpreter of Christian Holy Scripture; I am a secular humanist. You believe that each person's soul is immortal, making this planet a waystation to a second, eternal life; I think heaven and hell are what we create for ourselves, on this planet. For you, the belief in God made flesh to save mankind; for me, the belief in Promethean fire seized to set men free. You have found your final truth; I am still searching. You may be wrong; I may be wrong. We both may be partly right.

Do these differences in worldview separate us in all things? They do not. You and I and every other human being strive for the same imperatives of security, freedom of choice, personal dignity, and a cause to believe in that is larger than ourselves. Let us see, then, if we can meet on the near side of metaphysics in order to deal with the real world we share. You have the power to help solve a great problem about which I care deeply. I hope you have the same concern. I suggest that we set aside our differences in order to save the Creation. The defense of living nature is a universal value. It doesn't rise from, nor does it promote, any religious or ideological dogma. Rather, it serves without discrimination the interests of all humanity. Pastor, we need your help. The Creation—living nature—is in deep trouble.

Scientists estimate that, if habitat-conversion and other destructive human activities continue at their present rates, half the species of plants and animals on earth could be either gone or at least fated for early extinction by the end of the century. The ongoing extinction rate is calculated in the most conservative estimates to be about 100 times above that prevailing before humans appeared on earth, and it is expected to rise to at least 1,000 times greater (or more) in the next few decades. If this rise continues unabated, the cost to humanity—in wealth, environmental security, and quality of life—will be catastrophic.

Surely we can agree that each species, however inconspicuous and humble it may seem to us at this moment, is a masterpiece of biology and well worth saving. Each species possesses a unique combination of genetic traits that fits it more or less precisely to a particular part of the environment. Prudence alone dictates that we act quickly to prevent the extinction of species and, with it, the pauperization of earth's ecosystems.

With all the troubles that humanity faces, why should we care about the condition of living nature? *Homo sapiens* is a species confined to an extremely small niche. True, our minds soar out to the edges of the universe and contract inward to subatomic particles— the two extremes encompassing 30 powers of ten in space. In this respect, our intellects are godlike. But, let's face it, our bodies stay trapped inside a proportionately microscopic envelope of physical constraints. Earth provides a self-regulating bubble that sustains us indefinitely without any thought or contrivance of our own. This protective shield is the biosphere, the totality of life, creator of all air, cleanser of all water, manager of all soil—but is itself a fragile membrane that barely clings to the face of the planet. We depend upon its razor-thin health for every moment of our lives. We belong in the biosphere, we were born here as species, we are closely suited to its exacting conditions—and not all conditions, either, but just those in a few of the climatic regimes that exist upon some of the land. Environmental damage can be defined as any change that alters our surroundings in a direction contrary to humanity's inborn physical and emotional needs. We must be careful with the environment upon which our lives ultimately depend.

In destroying the biosphere, we are destroying unimaginably vast sources of scientific information and biological wealth. Opportunity costs, which will be better understood by our descendants than by ourselves, will be staggering. Gone forever will be undiscovered medicines, crops, timber, fibers, soil-restoring vegetation, petroleum substitutes, and other products and amenities. Critics of environmentalism forget, if they ever knew, how the rosy periwinkle of Madagascar provided the alkaloids that cure most cases of Hodgkin's disease and acute childhood leukemia; how a substance from an obscure Norwegian fungus made possible the organ transplant industry; how a chemical from the saliva of leeches yielded a solvent that prevents blood clots during and after surgery; and so on through the pharmacopoeia that has stretched from the herbal medicines of Stone Age shamans to the magic-bullet cures of present-day biomedical science.

These are just a few examples of what could be lost if *Homo sapiens* pursue our current course of environmental destruction. Earth is a laboratory wherein nature—God, if you prefer, pastor— has laid before us the results of countless experiments. We damage her at our own peril.

You may well ask at this point, *Why me?* Simply because religion and science are the two most powerful forces in the world today, and especially in the United States. If religion and science could be united on the common ground of biological conservation, the problem might soon be solved.

It may seem far-fetched for a secular scientist to propose an alliance between science and religion. But the fact is that environmental activists cannot succeed without you and your followers as allies. The political process in American democracy, with rare exceptions, does not start at the top and work its way down to the voting masses. It proceeds in the opposite direction. Political leaders are compelled to calculate as precisely as they can what it will take to win the next election. The United States is an intensely religious nation. It is overwhelmingly Judeo-Christian, with a powerful undercurrent of evangelism. We secularists must face reality. The National Association of Evangelicals has 30 million members; the three leading American humanist organizations combined have, at best, a few thousand. Those who, for religious reasons, believe in saving the Creation, have the strength to do so through the political process; acting alone, secular environmentalists do not. An alliance between science and religion, forged in an atmosphere of mutual respect, may be the only way to protect life on earth, including, in the end, our own.

Yes, the gulf separating our worldviews is wide. The Abrahamic religions—Judaism, Christianity, and Islam—believe that the universe was constructed to be relevant to humanity. The discoveries of science, in unintended opposition, have reduced earth to an infinitesimal speck within an immensity of space unrelated to human destiny. The Abrahamic religions envisage a supreme ruler who, while existing outside the material universe, nevertheless oversees an agenda for each and every one of our immortal souls. Science can find no evidence of an agenda other than that fashioned by the complex interaction of genes and environment within parallel evolving cultures. Religious creation stories have a divinely engineered beginning and a divinely ordained ending. According to science, in contrast, humans descended from apish ancestors; our origin was basically no different from that of other animals, played out over geological time through a tortuous route of mutation and environmentally driven natural selection. In addition, all mainstream religious belief, whether fundamentalist or liberal, is predicated upon the assumption that humanity is not alone, and we are here for a life and purpose beyond our earthly existence. Science says that, as far as verifiable evidence tells, we are alone, and what significance we have is therefore of our own making. This is the heart of the agonizing conflict between science and religion that has persisted for the past 500 years.

I do not see how the difference in worldview between these two great productions of human striving can be closed. But, for the purposes of saving the Creation, I am not sure that it needs to be. To make the point in good gospel manner, let me tell the story of a young man, newly trained for the ministry and so fixed in his Christian faith that he referred all questions of morality to readings from the Bible. When he visited the Atlantic rainforest of Brazil, he saw the manifest hand of God, and in his notebook he wrote, "It is not possible to give an adequate idea of the higher feelings of wonder, admiration, and devotion which fill and elevate the mind." That was Charles Darwin in 1832, early into the voyage of the HMS *Beagle*, before he had given any thought to evolution. And here is Darwin, concluding *On the Origin of Species* in 1859, having first abandoned Christian dogma and then, with his newfound intellectual freedom, formulated the theory of evolution by natural selection: "There is grandeur in this view of life, with its several powers, having been originally breathed into a few forms or into one; and that, whilst this planet has gone cycling on according to the fixed law of gravity, from so simple a beginning endless forms most beautiful and most wonderful have been, and are being, evolved." Darwin's reverence for life remained the same as he crossed the seismic divide that separated his religious phase and his scientific one. And so it can be for the divide that, today, separates mainstream religion and scientific humanism. And that separates you and me.

Indeed, despite all that divides science from religion, there is good reason to hope that an alliance on environmental issues is possible. The spiritual reach of evangelical Christianity is nowadays increasingly extended to the environment. While the Old Testament God commands humanity to take dominion over the earth, the decree is not (as one evangelical leader recently affirmed) an excuse to trash the planet. The dominant theme in scripture as interpreted by many evangelicals is instead stewardship. Organizations like the Green Cross and the Evangelical Environmental Network (the latter a coalition of evangelical Christian agencies and institutions) are expanding their magisterium to include conservation—in religious terms, protection of the living Creation.

This evangelical interest in the environment is part of a worldwide trend among religions. In the United States, the umbrella National Religious Partnership for the Environment works with evangelical groups and other prominent organizations, including the U.S. Conference of Catholic Bishops, the National Council of Churches of Christ, and the Coalition on the Environment and Jewish Life. In 2001, the Archbishop of Canterbury urged that "it may not be time to build an Ark like Noah, but it is high time to take better care of God's creation." Three years earlier, Bartholomew I, Patriarch of the Greek Orthodox Church, had gone further: "For humans to cause species to become extinct and to destroy the biological diversity of God's creation ... these are sins." He and Pope John Paul II later issued a "Common Declaration" that "God has not abandoned the world. It is His will that His Design and our hope for it will be realized through our cooperation in restoring its original harmony. In our own time we are witnessing a growth of an ecological awareness which needs to be encouraged, so that it will lead to practical programs and initiatives." Unfortunately, a corresponding magnitude of engagement has not yet occurred in Islam or the Eastern religions.

Every great religion offers mercy and charity to the poor. The poor of the world, of whom nearly a billion exist in the "poverty trap" of absolute destitution, are concentrated in the developing countries—the home of 80 percent of the world's population and most of Earth's biodiversity. The solution to the problems of both depends on the recognition that each depends on the other. The desperately poor have little chance to improve their lives in a devastated environment. Conversely, natural environments, where most of the Creation hangs on, cannot survive the press of land-hungry people who have nowhere else to go.

To be sure, some leaders of the religious right are reluctant to support biological conservation, an opposition sufficient to create a wedge within the evangelical movement. They may be partly afraid of paganism, by which worship of nature supplants worship of God. More realistically and importantly, opposition rises from the perceived association of environmental activism with the political left. For decades, conservatives have defined environmentalism as a movement bent on strangling the United States with regulations and bureaucratic power. This canard has dogged the U.S. environmental movement and helped keep it off the agenda of the past two presidential campaigns.

Finally, however, opinion may be changing. The mostly evangelical religious right, which, along with big business, has been the decisive source of power in the Republican Party, has begun to move care of the Creation back into the mainstream of conservative discourse. The opportunity exists to make the environment a universal concern and to render it politically nonpartisan.

Still, for all the positive signs, I remain puzzled that so many religious leaders have hesitated to make protection of the Creation an important part of their magisterium. Pastor, help me understand: Do they believe that human-centered ethics and preparation for the afterlife are the only things that matter? Do they believe that the Second Coming* is imminent and that, therefore, the condition of the planet is of little consequence? These and other similar doctrines are not gospels of hope and compassion. They are gospels of cruelty and despair.

You and I are both humanists in the broadest sense: Human welfare is at the center of our thought. So forget our disagreements, I say, and let us meet on common ground. That might not be as difficult as it first seems. When you think about it, our metaphysical differences have remarkably little effect on the conduct of our separate lives. My guess is that you and I are about equally ethical, patriotic, and altruistic. We are products of a civilization that rose from both religion and the science-based Enlightenment. We would gladly serve on the same jury, fight the same wars, and sanctify human life with the same intensity. Surely we also share a love of the Creation—and an understanding that, however the tensions play out between our opposing worldviews, however science and religion wax and wane in the minds of men, there remains the earthborn yet transcendental obligation we are both morally bound to share.

## Reflections and Responses

1. The title of Wilson's essay alludes to Francis Ford Coppola's 1979 film about the horrors of the Vietnam War. But it also plays on the Christian notion of the end of the world by an act of God (as described in the New Testament book of Revelation; in Greek, *Apokalypsis*) and a secular concept of the end of the world by

---

*The Second Coming:** Many evangelical Christians believe that Jesus Christ will return to earth, ending the world as we know it.

natural deterioration. Find other points in the essay where Wilson deliberately conflates notions from evangelical Christianity with non-Christian ideas. What purpose does this conflation serve?

2. Wilson strikes an ostensibly conciliatory tone throughout the essay, notionally refusing to attack the religious worldview as such. But in advancing the environmentalist argument, is Wilson subtly putting forward an argument for secular humanism? Locate a few points in the essay in which Wilson doesn't quite follow his own injunction to "set aside our differences in order to save the Creation." What is the effect of these moments?

3. What is the effect of framing this essay as a letter to an "imaginary" Christian pastor? Why didn't Wilson just write a neutral, third-person essay in defense of his environmentalism?

# INTERVIEW

## THE MIND AT WORK: AN INTERVIEW WITH ROBERT ATWAN BY KYLE GIACOMOZZI AND MATTHEW KEOGH

**Robert Atwan** *is the series editor of the prestigious annual anthology* The Best American Essays, *which he founded in 1985. His essays, reviews, and critical articles have appeared in the* New York Times, *the* Los Angeles Times, *the* Atlantic Monthly, *the* Iowa Review, *the* Denver Quarterly, *the* Kenyon Review, Creative Nonfiction, River Teeth, *and many other publications. His edited books include* The Writer's Presence; Popular Writing in America; America Now; Ten on Ten: Major Essayists on Recurring Themes; Our Times; Convergences; *and* Left, Right, and Center: Voices from Across the Political Spectrum. *He served as director of The Blue Hills Writing Institute at Curry College from 2002 to 2008. In January 2009, Mr. Atwan invited* The Bridge *editors to his home in Milton, Massachusetts (he has since moved to New York City), to gather around a roaring fire to discuss the art and craft of the essay. Editors Kyle Giacomozzi and Matthew Keogh were in charge of the questions; other editors participating in the interview included Laura Bowen, Rachael Dunphy, Jillian Moore, Lauren Rheaume, Shannon Rosenblat, and Tara Sullivan. All of the editors helped maintain the fire.*

*The Bridge* is a journal of literature and fine arts produced and managed entirely by students at Bridgewater State University (BSU) in Bridgewater, Massachusetts. The journal has received multiple Crown Awards from the Columbia Scholastic Press Association (CSPA) and a Gold Medal in the CSPA's Annual Critiques (The CSPA is operated by Columbia University and its Graduate School of Journalism). The Bridge has also received the coveted Pacemaker Award—widely regarded as the "Pulitzer Prize" of student publications—from the Associated Collegiate Press for both its third and fifth volumes, among many other honors. The interview below appeared in the 2009 issue of The Bridge.*

*At the time of the interview, Kyle Giacomozzi was a senior at Bridgewater State University majoring in English with a concentration in writing. He is currently pursuing his MFA in Nonfiction at George Mason University.*

*Matthew Keogh was a double major in math and English at BSU and is currently a graduate student in math at Clemson University.*

**The Bridge:** Could you tell us about what your job as series editor entails?

**Atwan:** There's a guest editor every year and that guest editor is required to read approximately one hundred essays, and then choose about twenty from that pool for the book. So my job is basically to go through all the national periodicals and screen the hundred that I consider best and submit these to that person. To do that, I probably go through about three hundred, three hundred fifty essays, and pick the ones that I think will have the best chance of being selected. The fact is that there aren't a lot of essays published in a given year that are of really high literary quality. So I actually find, say, perhaps sixty really first-rate essays—but we do one hundred because that's sort of a generous sampling and gives the guest editor a chance to look at a variety of topics and forms. But essentially in any given year I think I see only about fifty to sixty really, really solid literary essays.

**The Bridge:** So why do you think it's so difficult to be published if the quality isn't very high? And does that mean that these periodicals are publishing primarily works that are average or less?

**Atwan:** *The New Yorker* isn't. It depends on the periodicals that you're looking at. Many periodicals, such as the *Nation,* the *New Republic,* and *Commentary,* are dealing with the political world and not publishing essays, most likely. They're publishing articles, political commentary. When I'm talking about essays I'm referring mainly to the essay as a work of literature. That's what the series is devoted to. The kinds of things that Emerson wrote, Montaigne wrote, Robert Louis Stevenson, E. B. White, Virginia Woolf, James Baldwin. That's a different animal from the general prose you find in most of the magazines, even *The New Yorker.* I want the series to showcase the kind of literary, reflective, personal essay that is a work of literature. There aren't many periodicals that publish these, nor, I should add, even want to publish these. Most periodicals are interested in journalism, up-to-date reporting—not literary essays.

**The Bridge:** Why do you think that is?

**Atwan:** First of all, it's not their bread and butter and especially not in this economy. *Atlantic,* for example, a terrific magazine, is really interested in informative articles or articles that have some sort of newsy quality. And it's not looking for what magazine editors once called "navel gazing" or "thumb sucking" pieces. They generally, with a few exceptions, want hard news or information or interview material as opposed to a work that demonstrates a literary effort, a clear literary intention. And I'm going to complicate this by saying that so many people are writing memoirs now and many of these memoiristic essays do not qualify for *Best American*. They often seem to be pieces from a longer work or something in progress. I'm finding that a lot of my guest editors would rather have reflective essays, essays *about* something, than the now common "I-I-I-I-I-I." I don't know how many guest editors have said the equivalent of "Bob, please don't send me any more essays in which I see the word 'I' fifteen times on the first page."

**The Bridge:** Should young writers avoid writing essays about themselves?

**Atwan:** No, I wouldn't go that far, and the liberal usage of "I" doesn't mean the piece is bad. Henry David Thoreau used "I" throughout all of his works, but when experiences are entirely mundane and so particularized to an individual, readers will think: "Well you know, why should I care about your experiences unless they translate into something larger that offers me some substance for thought and reflection and experiences that more people can identify with?" I think a big problem with memoirs today is that the writers seem to take a reader's "identification" for granted. Good writing never does that—it earns the reader's identification. When I select the candidates for the volume, I like to see essays contending with a subject. Virginia Woolf, a great essayist, was referring to the essay when she said that "The art of writing has for backbone some fierce attachment to an idea." I'm always looking for essays with "backbone."

**The Bridge:** Was starting *Best American Essays* as easy? How did you get that off the ground?

**Atwan:** I was reviewing books then for the *New York Times Book Review* and they sent me *The O'Henry Stories* to review in 1984, I believe it was. It made me wonder why there wasn't a similar book like that for essays. And so I wrote a proposal and after a few rejections a publisher accepted it. But one day the editor said, "Bob, I've got to bring up a sensitive subject. No one likes to use the word 'essay.' Can we call it something else?" I went back and rethought it. God, what else are you going to call it?

*Best American Articles* doesn't sound right. *Best American Nonfiction* doesn't sound right. So I told the editor that we were just going to have to take the plunge and use the word "essay." And the publishers said, "Okay, we'll take a chance. We'll give you a contract for two years. If at the end of two years, we don't sell anything, we'll kill the series." So I had two years and I made sure the anthology was literary, one that would attract literary people. The first guest editor was Elizabeth Hardwick, a very talented novelist and essayist herself and very prominent in the New York literary world, and the second year I went to Gay Talese, who was considered a founder of New Journalism. It worked. After that, about five, six years later I noticed magazines had begun using the word "essay" in their tables of contents. They'd been avoiding the "E-word" because it reminded people of what they had to write in school. The term was used as a pejorative.

**The Bridge:** In your 2005 foreword, you disclosed your initial uncertainty about the series' longevity. When exactly did you realize that it was here to stay?

**Atwan:** I guess after about the fifth year I knew it was going to stick around. But the first year was very sketchy. No one knew about it. It didn't get promoted very well. It was a good idea to get Gay Talese to do the second year because that got more attention due to the popularity of literary journalism. And we got some reviews. Anthologies are not often reviewed.

**The Bridge:** In the same foreword, 2005, you mentioned that going into the second edition you felt like you had boosted the spirit of the essayists. Do you think that was key in getting the material so that you could continue the series?

**Atwan:** I believe, and many people have told me this, that the series definitely helped re-establish the essay as a literary form. Back in the eighties, very few people considered it to be such, even though there were plenty of talented essayists at work. You would probably be hard pressed if you went into academia, even in the mid-nineties, to find any dissertations, PhD dissertations, on the essay. Very, very few. And yet, in the twentieth century you had incredible essayists. James Baldwin, one of the greatest American essayists, received at first little attention for his nonfiction. Now, however, he's read primarily as an essayist. The essay was, through almost all the twentieth century, the form in which you wrote criticism about fiction, poetry, drama. You didn't write about other essays. Let's put it this way, the essay had no critical stature. In a literature course, you studied twentieth-century American poetry, or you studied the nineteenth-century Victorian novel, or you studied the history of drama or Shakespeare or Milton. You did not have a course called The History of the Essay.

In my graduate school you read Ralph Waldo Emerson, but you did not read him as an essayist. Nobody even talked about him as an essayist. They talked about him as a great American writer or thinker, as a great influence. They talked about his prose. But they never discussed his genre or his craft. And this neglect of criticism kept the essay in the dark for a long time because it was considered a fourth genre. E. B. White once said that because he wrote essays he was a second-class citizen in the republic of letters. There could be no Nobel Prize for him, since he wasn't a dramatist, a poet, or a novelist. Those are the three genres. In the 1950s, one of the most important books of criticism at the time, *The Theory of Literature,* opened with a statement that implicitly defined literature as poems, plays, and novels. It seems that around that time the essay was no longer being taken seriously as literature.

Yet when Fielding wrote *Tom Jones,* one of the great novels of the eighteenth century, he inserted essays between chapters every now and then throughout the book. And you know why he did that? He did it to prove he was a writer. Because he thought that anybody could write a novel. "I'm going to show you how I can *really* write by including these essays," he seemed to be saying. In the eighteenth century, the essay was considered a serious literary endeavor by many.

**The Bridge:** Now *The Best American Essays* is regarded as the most important anthology of its kind. But lately, a few others have sprouted up, such as Lee Gutkind's *Best Creative Nonfiction.* What do you think sets BAE apart from all the others?

**Atwan:** It's really more dedicated to the essay as a work of literature than to nonfiction prose in general. And so the essay—its structures, its various types, the way that the author's mind works inside the essay—these literary matters are all very important to the series. Whereas in creative nonfiction anthologies there are often lots of narrative memoirs, personal narratives, expository narratives, and so on, which years ago would not have been considered essays. So I think the series is distinguished by its dedication to looking at the essay as a craft and as a serious aesthetic form. Still, I try to concentrate on three types of essays: the personal essay, which overlaps with autobiography and memoir;

the informative essay, in which you're reading something that's really well written and well done but you're gaining information at the same time; and the polemical essay, which is your argumentative piece, but done in a way that you can still see, in a sense, the mind at work. Each volume of *The Best American Essays* usually consists of a mix of these three types of essays.

**The Bridge:** Can you elaborate on "the mind at work"?

**Atwan:** The essayist takes a topic and looks at it the way, say, a cubist painter looks at objects, from all different kinds of angles and perspectives. Good essayists are able to do this, to make you see the mind in process. One of the biggest problems I've found when you teach freshman composition is that students have very little sense of process, so they think that they have to begin a paper with their conclusion, then in the middle part support the conclusion, and then, well... conclude. Writing essays isn't necessarily about coming to a conclusion. Few students know how to show a mind reflecting on something and evaluating it as it's in process. Students are rarely taught this nor exposed to appropriate models of writing to gain appreciation for the process. But that's what Montaigne did as an essayist, it's what so many great essayists have done, and so the models are out there, but the models students follow these days are driven by news and commentary. There's one thing you can never say to a talented essayist, and it's "What's your point?" Because a good essayist is going to say: "Wait, there isn't necessarily a single point here. I'm looking at a whole bunch of things." But in freshman composition, the worst way writing can be taught in my opinion is by asking students to write five paragraphs that add up to a single point. Perhaps it has its functional use—writing as utility, so to speak. But the results won't duplicate the literary essay or the way the essayist's mind operates.

**The Bridge:** How do you define the essay?

**Atwan:** I've been trying to define it for a long time. The attempt now strikes me as an unsatisfying enterprise. It's like defining anything. If you try to define the novel your definition leaves out seven different kinds of novels. Just try defining poetry. Basically, briefly, the essay to me is a literary form that's marked by a mind in the process of its own unfolding.

**The Bridge:** How do you define creative nonfiction?

**Atwan:** I never was sure what that was. It's a term of convenience, I think. The term I first used was "literary journalism." That was the term that everybody used back in the sixties and early seventies. It's an umbrella term that also includes "literary nonfiction," but it isn't necessarily essayistic. Literary journalism or nonfiction could be a long book by Tracy Kidder on how people build houses. John McPhee has written probably twenty-five to thirty books of nonfiction, but he has published only a handful of essays in his entire career, and he would acknowledge that. Literary nonfiction and creative nonfiction are very topic driven. They—and I'll use the terms interchangeably—consist of interviews, profiles, information-gathering. They involve a lot of skillful reporting techniques. But these are done in a much more literary fashion than standard journalism, which is trying hard not to be too literary. John McPhee, for example, might choose salmon as a topic, perhaps seeking to discover why salmon is now a major part of American cuisine, which it didn't used to be. And then he would go research the history of salmon, visit rivers and fishermen, and conduct interviews, and then he'd craft all of the information he's gathered into a prose narrative. He called his course at Princeton The Literature of Fact and that's not an essayistic method. He's collecting facts and then orchestrating and choreographing them into prose in the best possible way, but his own mind in action isn't a significant part of his writing process as he's doing it. The subjective mental process is largely eliminated. He's giving you this factual, objective treatment of a subject. Still, he truly cares about the *form* in in*form*ation.

**The Bridge:** And so the essay and creative nonfiction are not synonymous?

**Atwan:** Not really. Creative nonfiction could refer to a three hundred page book. That's not an essay. *Walden* is not an essay. *Walden* is a nonfiction book, although you probably could make a case that the basic structures behind it are essays. Creative nonfiction just became a popular term to encompass the literary nonfiction that was coming from the New Journalism. Quite a few really good writers back in the sixties and seventies—Tom Wolfe, Gay Talese, Lillian Ross, Hunter Thompson—began developing this form of reporting that was very personalized and impressionistic. It got them in a lot of trouble because the older and more traditional journalists couldn't stand it. And there were some knotty legal problems because most people assume nonfiction is true.

**The Bridge:** Isn't it?

**Atwan:** One of the biggest issues when you're writing nonfiction is that you have to think about what it is that we can't know. The New Journalists were doing things that seemed overly impressionistic and subjective, and Tom Wolfe was at the forefront of that. There was steady criticism, but that work really took off because it was so much more entertaining and more fun to read than the standard fare. But people lost jobs along the way, especially newspaper columnists, when they began making things up. By the eighties and nineties, there was a lack of tolerance for these kinds of columns as opposed to what had been the case in the past. The essay has been damaged by this, in my opinion, because essayists no longer feel comfortable inventing characters and situations.

**The Bridge:** Was there a time when they were comfortable doing this?

**Atwan:** In the eighteenth century, when the essay was considered a solid literary form, Addison and Steele, Samuel Johnson, and Oliver Goldsmith were among the chief practitioners, and they had enormous influence on America's first major literary essayist, Washington Irving. None of these writers had problems with making up stuff, even though they were writing for newspapers. No one said, "You can't say that without documentation or without two witnesses, etc." The audience was sophisticated enough to know there may be made-up characters and situations. We've reached this real problem, I think, with writing essays, and now with memoirs, always demanding to know if something is true or not. If you're writing something that's verifiable, you better be careful. But if it isn't, you have some creative room.

**The Bridge:** In the wake of the whole James Frey debacle.

**Atwan:** These liberties with factuality were going on long before he was born. But because Oprah went overboard with that book it created so much more publicity. Now there's a new memoir scandal. Did you see the news about the Holocaust story [*Angel at the Fence*, by Herman Rosenblat]?

**The Bridge:** It's about the little girl with the apples. She would bring him apples and then they met in America and they got married.

**Atwan:** Now, what they said in the *Times* the other day is that they're now not going to publish it as a memoir. It's going to be published as a novel. And you think, "Wait a minute, someone

writes a memoir, some parts are discovered untrue and then suddenly the same work can be called a novel?" What happened to art
forms? Can you simply say, "I wrote a work of nonfiction but it had
some fictional details, so now it's a novel"? What talented writer
would imagine that you could do that? The novel is an art form.
It's a literary form that is a complex and extremely difficult thing
to do. You don't just write a nonfiction narrative and say, "Oops,
it's not all true, so now I'll just call it a novel." These stories just
show us how little critical judgment the public possesses. It's too
bad Americans as a whole aren't better readers.

**The Bridge:** But if you write a nonfiction piece and it's not one
hundred percent true, what would you call it? Does nonfiction
equal "not true," and, if it's not true, doesn't "not true" equal
fiction?

**Atwan:** Ah, now you're getting at the heart of the problem, the
heart of darkness, actually. It's really tough to get into that.
I think we need to return to a notion of the essay that allows for
fictive, or say semi-fictive characters, situations, and events.
Humorous essays do this frequently. I find David Sedaris's autobiographical humor hilariously funny but does anyone think he's not
exaggerating and bending facts and situations for comic purposes?
One of the greatest essays in American literature is Hawthorne's
preface to *The Scarlet Letter,* in which he writes about finding an
actual scarlet letter used by Puritan officials in his office drawer,
and that's how the famous novel comes into being. Well, that
never happened. Now, does that automatically make his essay a
short story?

**The Bridge:** If you are about to go to press with *Best American
Essays* and someone called you and said, "I confess, everything in
my essay is made up," what would you do?

**Atwan:** Well, that of course would depend on what's at stake—
libel? Hurtful lies? But generally I would encourage my publisher
to go with it if I thought it could still be regarded as an essay. To
me it's an issue of form and genre, not truthfulness. Why couldn't
someone write an essay about intelligent life on Mars even if we
don't have proof there is such life on Mars—couldn't there be a
speculative essay? Logical inconsistency can also be considered
untruthful, but if you found such inconsistency in a political
essay would you then conclude it's therefore not an essay but a
fiction? That would be nutty, no? But anyway my publisher would
most likely get nervous and say no. When I was working with

Joseph Epstein on *Best American Essays 1993* I came across an unlabeled piece and I couldn't tell whether it was fiction or nonfiction. I assumed it was fiction, because the author was a prominent short-story writer, but it turned out to be nonfiction. And I remember Joe said something to the effect: "Well, if it were a story it would have been a real good one, but as an essay it stinks." I thought that his remark underscored the importance of artistic criteria. A piece can't just interchangeably move between the two genres.

As I mentioned, Addison and Steele represent the origins of the modern essay. They wrote for a newspaper and they used fictional characters and fictional events. There are responses to fictional letters that would come in from so-called readers who were also fictional. Now, what do we call what they wrote? They have never been known as short story writers. There wasn't even a genre called the "short story" then. When the modern essay began its course in the eighteenth century with the great English periodical essayists and then was carried on into the nineteenth century by some American essayists—there was no short story. The short story evolved long after the essay. Writers like Washington Irving and Nathaniel Hawthorne developed the short story as they experimented with various kinds of essays. Writers at the time often called what they were doing tales and sketches. Hawthorne and Irving referred to their collections as "Tales" and "Sketches."

**The Bridge:** I want to follow up on something you said a short while ago, that most readers assume that nonfiction is true. What should writers of nonfiction assume when they start writing in the genre? Should they assume that they are obligated to tell the truth? Or should they understand that maybe truth isn't relevant in nonfiction?

**Atwan:** Truth is a big, troublesome word. I think if you're looking at what the truth is that you need to think more along the lines of literature than contemporary journalism. But literary truth isn't veracity and accuracy and all the things you're told in J-school or a court of law. What Hawthorne would consider the truth would be the truth of the human heart. If he were writing an essay, he wouldn't be bothered by inventing a character or a composite character he might meet during a leisurely walk. I imagine very few readers at the time were going to say, well, Mr. Hawthorne Liar, you never met that person, you're just making that person up. Unless he was referring to a specified and named individual, readers would understand the literary or compositional purpose of the made-up character. Today, we live in a much different literary world. Anyway, I will just come back to this point: I think you can do anything you want to do in nonfiction as long as you don't cross the line and present information as fact that somebody can challenge and establish as false. Then you get into trouble.

**The Bridge:** So would you say the truth is a lie you can get away with?

**Atwan:** I'm not saying that's the truth. I'm saying that in writing you can get away with things because who's going to say you aren't telling the exact truth? You may know you aren't, but who else knows? And what does it matter? Virginia Woolf's "Death of the Moth" is a wonderful essay, one of her classics. Did she really watch a moth dying on her windowsill that lovely September afternoon? Virginia was there with a moth and that moth was dying all the time? And did it look just like that and was she really watching out this window, or was she thinking that morning, you know, "I'd like to write an essay about a moth that sort of dies because I saw one yesterday and now I'm going to set it in my window and...." Who can tell? Who knows? So, are we supposed to then say, "No, that's not an essay because we didn't know it happened, we can't prove it happened"? If her husband wrote in his journal, "I was home with Virginia that afternoon, and now and then I peeked into her study and she was writing away. But let me go on record to say that it was a rainy day, not a sunny day, and, second, there was no moth." So if a scholar discovered this testimony tomorrow in a newly found journal of her husband's, would a classic English essay suddenly be eliminated from the history of the essay because the event as she describes it apparently didn't happen? What can we say other than that we don't know whether some of the things we read happened or not.

**The Bridge:** So a writer of nonfiction should not be constrained by fact?

**Atwan:** I think a writer of nonfiction is constrained by fact. But verifiable facts. It may be that if no one can verify something it doesn't qualify as a fact. These are muddy waters.

**The Bridge:** So, if it's not verifiable, then you can get away with lying and no one can say you're lying? But is there any kind of moral obligation to tell the truth, just for your own sake, with your own writing?

**Atwan:** I'm not someone to dictate moral obligations. Those should be for an individual writer to decide. Yet remember one thing—in a very real sense, just transcribing actual physical events into words entails some degree of falsification—of time sequence, specific details, perspective, and so on. Writers of memoirs seem often to recall what others said to them when they were six years old—do you believe this dialogue is accurate?

**The Bridge:** Should we say that putting things in nonfiction that did not happen is the equivalent of leaving things out that did?

**Atwan:** I've got to think that through. That's a very good question. I suppose the answer would involve the old sins of commission as opposed to the sins of omission. But yes, memoirs very often commit sins of omission. My favorite examples have to do with celebrity memoirs where there is so much left out because the celebrity is trying to write a success story. And every celebrity—no matter what field they're in—wants their fans to believe that their success is self-made. They didn't become a success because they had a parental connection that got them into Yale and then that connection helped them get their first job and then one day help them get elected president. Those connections are not going to be a main feature of the autobiography. They're going to be either eliminated or glossed over. The message is: "I made it on my own." That's just one example of omission that I find frequently.

**The Bridge:** Hopefully we'll get an in-depth answer out of a very simple and our next to last question: What should we write about?

**Atwan:** Don't always write about what you know. In the first issue of *Best American Essays 1986,* there is a great essay, one of the best in the whole series, and I was so happy to have it, by Donald Barthelme—a great short-story writer. He died years ago. His essay is called "Not-Knowing," and it's about the importance of seeking rather than having knowledge. Some of the best writing is by people who are struggling with understanding something. That's what the essay is really all about.

Many of us operate under two very questionable principles: (1) We should write about what we know best, and (2) since we know ourselves best we would write best if we write about ourselves. Both of these seem bogus to me.

**The Bridge:** Final question: Do you have anything else you'd like to share with our readers?

**Atwan:** Oh, no, ... we covered so much! It was invigorating intellectually. A lot of things I hadn't thought of. Thanks for the opportunity and thanks for keeping the fire going.

**The Bridge:** Thank you for inviting us.

# CREDITS

CPSIA information can be obtained
at www.ICGtesting.com
Printed in the USA
FFOW02n2324240817
39205FF